OXFORD READINGS IN PHILOSOPHY

VIRTUE E

Published in this series

The Problem of Evil, edited by Marilyn McCord Adams and Robert Merrihew Adams
The Philosophy of Artificial Intelligence, edited by Margaret A. Boden
The Philosophy of Artificial Life, edited by Margaret A. Boden
Self-Knowledge, edited by Quassim Cassam
Perceptual Knowledge, edited by Jonathan Dancy
The Philosophy of Law, edited by R. M. Dworkin
Environmental Ethics, edited by Robert Elliot
Theories of Ethics, edited by Philippa Foot
The Philosophy of History, edited by Patrick Gardiner
The Philosophy of Mind, edited by Jonathan Glover
Scientific Revolutions, edited by Ian Hacking
The Philosophy of Mathematics, edited by W. D. Hart
Conditionals, edited by Frank Jackson
The Philosophy of Time, edited by Robin Le Poidevin and Murray MacBeath
The Philosophy of Action, edited by Alfred R. Mele
The Philosophy of Religion, edited by Basil Mitchell
Meaning and Reference, edited by A. W. Moore
A Priori Knowledge, edited by Paul K. Moser
The Philosophy of Science, edited by David Papineau
Political Philosophy, edited by Anthony Quinton
Explanation, edited by David-Hillel Ruben
The Philosophy of Social Explanation, edited by Alan Ryan
Propositions and Attitudes, edited by Nathan Salmon and Scott Soames
Consequentialism and its Critics, edited by Samuel Scheffler
Applied Ethics, edited by Peter Singer
Causation, edited by Ernest Sosa and Michael Tooley
Theories of Rights, edited by Jeremy Waldron
Free Will, edited by Gary Watson
Demonstratives, edited by Palle Yourgrau

Other volumes are in preparation

VIRTUE ETHICS

Edited by
ROGER CRISP
and
MICHAEL SLOTE

OXFORD UNIVERSITY PRESS

Oxford University Press, Great Clarendon Street, Oxford OX2 6DP
Oxford New York
Athens Auckland Bangkok Bogota Buenos Aires Calcutta
Cape Town Chennai Dar es Salaam Delhi Florence Hong Kong Istanbul
Karachi Kuala Lumpur Madrid Melbourne Mexico City Mumbai
Nairobi Paris São Paolo Singapore Taipei Tokyo Toronto Warsaw

and associated companies in
Berlin Ibadan

Oxford is a registered trade mark of Oxford University Press

Published in the United States by
Oxford University Press Inc., New York

First published in hardback and paperback 1997
Reprinted in paperback 1998

British Library Cataloguing in Publication Data
Data available

Library of Congress Cataloging in Publication Data
Data available
ISBN 0-19-875189-3
ISBN 0-19-875188-5 (Pbk.)

Printed in Great Britain
on acid-free paper by
Biddles Ltd., Guildford and King's Lynn

CONTENTS

INTRODUCTION

ROGER CRISP AND MICHAEL SLOTE

I

This book amounts to a detailed map of some highly significant changes which have been taking place in the landscape of moral philosophy in the second half of the twentieth century.

Before these changes, discussion of practical or normative ethics had centred around two traditions. These were Kantianism, or 'deontology', which has its roots in the work of the eighteenth-century German philosopher Immanuel Kant, and utilitarianism, or 'consequentialism', which found its main expression in the writings from the eighteenth century onwards of the British philosophers Jeremy Bentham, J. S. Mill, and Henry Sidgwick.

According to the Kantian tradition, morality is based on a universal and impartial law of rationality, captured in Kant's famous Categorical Imperative. Why should I not make a false promise to get what I want from you? Because I cannot will that it be a law of nature that everyone who wants something from someone else lies. Why can I not will this? Because the very notion makes no sense: promising could not survive in such a world. Rationality consists in adherence to the laws of rationality, and making false promises cannot possibly be in accordance with such a law.

Utilitarianism, which represents a tendency in ethics to which Kant was implacably opposed, sees value only in the well-being of human beings. Action aims at the good, and if the only good is human well-being, then that is what rational action must aim at. Why should I not aim solely at my own well-being? Because there is no difference between a 'unit' of my own pleasure and that of someone else's. Morality is again seen as impartial, this time obliging me to produce as much overall well-being as possible.

In 1958 Elizabeth Anscombe launched a scathing attack on both of these traditions simultaneously. Both of them, she argued, sought a foundation for morality grounded in legalistic notions such as 'obligation', and these notions make no sense when no lawgiver is assumed. Now that many of us no longer believe in God, our only route to providing a foundation for ethics is in the notion of virtue, understood independently from obligation as part of human flourishing. And to approach the notion of virtue, we must stop doing philosophy until we get our psychology straight. It is worth pointing out, perhaps, that some of the main lines of Anscombe's critique were foreshadowed in Arthur Schopenhauer's *On the Basis of Morality* (1841).

In speaking of human flourishing, Anscombe was referring back to the ancient Greek philosopher Aristotle, of the fourth century BC, who has been the main source of inspiration for modern virtue ethicists. Aristotle, in his *Nicomachean Ethics*, argued that the best life for a human being—*eudaimonia*—consists in the exercise of the virtues (or the 'excellences'). Indeed his is perhaps one of the most radical virtue ethics ever, since he can be understood to be saying that there is *nothing* worth having in life except the exercise of the virtues. This is the view which was taken up and developed by the Stoics.

Anscombe's article had a huge effect, though it did not on the whole turn philosophers in the direction of doing psychology. Some writers, represented by the three chapters that follow hers in this volume, continued her critique of modern ethical theory. Others sought to develop an ethics of virtue from within philosophy. Some of the most important of these attempts can be found in Chapters 5–8, discussed in Section II of this introduction. Of course, such positive thinking met with its own objections, and some of these can be found powerfully stated in Chapters 9–10, discussed in Section III. In the very recent past, virtue ethics has begun both to respond to these new objections and to develop in some new directions. Illustration of this can be found in the final three chapters in the volume, which we cover in Section IV.

One of the questions discussed in several of the chapters in this book is fundamental: what is virtue ethics? It is tempting to say that it is a moral theory according to which we should live the virtuous life, or act virtuously. But this is not enough. J. S. Mill, for example, a paradigm utilitarian, would probably have agreed with these recommendations. His reasons for doing so, however, would be utilitarian ones: one should be virtuous because that will give one the best chance of maximizing overall well-being. Similarly, a Kantian may suggest that one should be virtuous because that is the way to obey the moral law.

How, then, is a virtue ethicist to carve out his or her own niche? It must be by providing an account of ultimate moral reasons which not only is neither utilitarian nor Kantian, but makes essential reference to the rationality of virtue itself. Thus, for example, the real reason why I should not lie to you is not that it is against the moral law, nor that it is likely not to maximize well-being, but because it is *dishonest*. The notions of virtue, then, are more basic than the notions at the heart of utilitarian and Kantian theory. They may even replace some of these notions, including perhaps 'obligation' itself. The virtue ethicist at least does not *need* such language. Certainly, it is characteristic of modern virtue ethics that it puts primary emphasis on aretaic or virtue-centred concepts rather than deontic or obligation-centred concepts.

Another striking feature of virtue ethics is its focus on moral agents and their lives, rather than on discrete actions (telling a lie, having an abortion, giving to a beggar) construed in isolation from the notion of character, and the rules governing these actions. One deep question which remains unresolved in modern ethics, and on which many of the papers in this volume provide some illumination, is whether this is a difference between types of *theory*, or between types of *theorist*. There is no doubt that modern ethics has indeed concentrated, in a legalistic fashion, upon rules concerning particular actions. But is it possible for utilitarians and Kantians to enlarge the focus of their own theories to incorporate agents' lives as a whole, their characters as well as or even instead of their actions? Must utilitarianism, for example, be a theory about actions? Or could it not also be a theory about character? This raises a question related to the discussion above concerning the language of obligation: is it needed by utilitarians? One might even wonder whether a moral view at least heavily influenced by Kant might not do without it.

II

As we mentioned above, Elizabeth Anscombe's 'Modern Moral Philosophy', which appeared in 1958, is widely regarded as having inaugurated the present revival of virtue ethics. This recognition occurs with considerable benefit of hindsight. For one thing, the article contains significant discussions of a number of topics that are only loosely related to the idea of (a revived) virtue ethics; but, more importantly, the article originally attracted notice principally because of its strongly worded criticisms of modern and recent moral philosophy and philosophers and, in particular, of the idea that no kind of action is morally out of bounds as long as its expected consequences are good enough. But the rejection of this idea does not univocally point toward virtue ethics—Kantians and religious believers would also reject it. The movement towards virtue ethics generated by Anscombe's article also depends on two further factors in Anscombe's thinking: her claim that notions like moral obligation require a legislative model of morality in order to make sense and her claim that Kantian 'self-legislation' is not a sensible notion.

Under this combination of assumptions, Anscombe can argue that secular moral philosophy that has no use for the idea of divine lawgiving cannot make meaningful use of the idea of moral obligation and of moral rightness and wrongness to the extent these notions are seen as tied to moral obligation. But how, then, can we do ethics? Anscombe's answer is that ethics can be based, instead, on the idea of a virtue and of human flourishing and that this leads us back to Plato and Aristotle as models of how to do ethics. But Anscombe also insists that we do not really understand the idea of a virtue, that Plato and Aristotle do not fully clarify that notion, and that we have to get a better grip on terms like 'intention', 'wanting', 'pleasure', and 'action' before we can say what (a) virtue is. Hence Anscombe's conclusion that we should *stop doing* moral philosophy until we gain some clarity about philosophical psychology.

We saw earlier that virtue ethics differs from other forms of moral philosophy through its insistence that aretaic notions like virtue, admirability, and excellence are more basic than—or even replace—deontic notions like moral obligation and rightness. Clearly, what Anscombe says about the emptiness of attributions of moral obligation favours virtue ethics, so understood, over other approaches that have been taken in the recent history of ethics. What also argues in favour of virtue ethics, however, is the fact that, unlike moral philosophers 'since Sidgwick', Plato and Aristotle appear to consider certain actions out of bounds independently of considerations of consequences. Given the 'corruption' of the opposite view, this should encourage us (once we have done our homework in philosophical psychology) to pursue an ethics more like Plato's or Aristotle's and in particular, then, an ethics with a distinctly virtue-ethical commitment to making virtuous character or character traits central to ethical concern.

Anscombe's article anticipates much of the recent development of virtue ethics in large part through having *influenced* that development. But many present-day ethicists—including both defenders and opponents of virtue ethics—would question some of Anscombe's main assumptions in 'Modern Moral Philosophy'. Many contemporary Kantians believe we can make more sense of self-legislation than Anscombe supposes, and some virtue ethicists think that deontic notions of right and wrong need not be tied to typical, familiar assumptions about moral obligation, but, rather, naturally emerge from aretaic notions like excellence and badness (if an act is said to be bad, are we not implicitly committed to viewing it as wrong?).

However, the three chapters that follow Anscombe's in this volume take up various important themes of her article and seek, in effect, to push them further or in a somewhat different direction. All three in some sense point away from familiar modern or contemporary ethical views and, at least to some extent, in the direction of virtue ethics.

Bernard Williams's 'Morality, the Peculiar Institution' criticizes our ordinary and Kantian ideas about moral obligation in ways that differ from, but also are reminiscent of, what Anscombe says against the notion. His discussion presupposes and frequently alludes to a distinction between the moral and the more generally ethical that is introduced early in his book *Ethics and the Limits of Philosophy*, but is most fully elaborated in chapter 10 of that book, the selection reprinted here. Williams begins by characterizing what he calls 'the morality system'—our ordinary thought and feeling about morality as captured (largely) by Immanuel Kant—and contrasting it with forms of ethics that are not similarly constrained. He argues that the notion of moral obligation is a dominant concept of morality and tends to drive out or replace all other kinds of ethical consideration.

Moral obligation, in turn, is characterized by its strong connection with blame and blameworthiness, and this notion is then connected by Williams to the idea that someone who is blameworthy for having acted immorally was *free* to act otherwise than she did and had *reason* to do so. Williams thinks the latter assumption constitutes a (perhaps socially useful) illusion. We may properly say of some immoral or amoral person that *there is* reason for him to behave differently, but to say that *he has* reason to act differently presupposes that the person has desires and inclinations (including moral inclinations) similar to our own, and that is simply not true of many of the people we want to blame for failing to fulfil important or even minimal obligations.

However, the argument for illusoriness here depends on assuming that blaming involves the ascription to the agent of a reason to act otherwise and that someone with no moral compunctions and no concern for anyone else has no reason to be moral. Both assumptions can be questioned. So-called 'externalists' hold that a person might have reason to be concerned with things (like health or happiness) that *he or she* is in fact utterly unconcerned about, and the arguments for and against this view have not come to any definite resolution in the literature on this topic. More significantly, perhaps, one may ask why Williams thinks that blaming involves the assumption that the agent *had* reason to act otherwise rather than merely that there *was* (moral) reason for the agent to act otherwise. One may be tempted to answer this question by claiming that, if an agent has no desire to be moral (and no respect for morality), she is not *free* to act morally, but most people who believe free will and determinism are compatible would reject such a response. As Hume put it, the fact that a hangman is in every way intent upon executing a condemned criminal may not entail that what he does to the criminal is involuntary or unfree.

Williams, however, is sceptical about the notions of voluntariness and free agency that attach to blaming. He thinks it a mistake to distinguish the accidental consequences and circumstances of action from an essential core (perhaps of willing or choosing) that lies entirely within the sphere of the agent's freedom and responsibility. If such notions are themselves essential to the defence of human freedom, then such freedom may indeed be doubted or denied. But the idea of paring responsible action down to an essential core connects with another idea that Williams attributes to the morality system, namely, that morality and moral attributions should not be subject to luck—that one cannot fairly or, therefore, correctly be blamed or, for that matter, praised for the unforeseen and uncontrollable consequences of an action that lie beyond its essential core.

But for Williams the moral system's own idea that morality cannot be subject to luck connects with and is motivated by a deeper concern that life, or at least what is most important in life, should not be subject to luck, but rather should be *fair* or *just*. Since success, enjoyment, long life, and so on can depend on luck, the idea that life should be just translates into the assumption that none of these worldly goods ultimately matters in anything like the way it matters whether one is moral. The idea, then, is that, if one is moral, one has what is most important in life, and that, because one's being moral is not subject to luck, life itself is not subject to luck in any important way.

Williams points out the similarity of such a view to the consolations of religion, but also notes some significant differences. The consolations of religion can to a great extent be understood from outside and independently of the religious perspective, but the fact that only morality is ultimately important in life represents a consolation it is difficult to detach from morality's own point of view. In addition, most forms of Christianity allow luck to enter into personal salvation (God's decisions are beyond our control and knowledge), but the morality system precludes even this degree or kind of luck with regard to what it considers to be ultimately important in life. Williams's view that the morality system is ultimately based on a desire to avoid (the anxieties engendered by) luck in life is offered without argument, and many contemporary defenders of morality might balk at this assumption. Others might even insist that life is *not* subject to luck in its most important aspects and subscribe, therefore, to the Kantian view that it is better to be worthy of happiness than actually to be happy. The so-called morality system can *fight back* and claim that it is Williams, not the system, who is under an illusion about the character of moral truth(s).

Williams sketchily depicts what ethics could or should be like once freed from the illusions of the morality system. Shame will have a central role along with a host of other emotions that the morality system downgrades in favour of a select and narrow group of emotions. The individual's connections with other people and with society will enter into the ethical evaluation of what she does rather than, as at present, lying beyond the essential moral core of thought and action. The notion of importance will replace the idea of moral obligation, but this will still leave room for ethical ideals of social justice. In modern times social justice has been considered a matter of social *morality*—but Plato and Aristotle spoke of justice without having recourse to the morality system and on a virtue-ethical basis, and so Williams's expressed hopes at the very least point somewhat in the direction of virtue ethics.

But it is also worth noting that the notion of importance that Williams so greatly emphasizes is not an aretaic one. There may be a connection between importance and what is admirable or excellent, but, unless that connection treats the idea of excellence as fundamental to understanding what is personally or generally important, the ethics arrived at will not be a typical kind of virtue ethics and perhaps will merit some other classification. In any event, some of Williams's arguments are grist for the virtue ethicist's mill.

Michael Stocker's 'The Schizophrenia of Modern Ethical Theories' picks up and develops another theme in Anscombe's earlier paper. Anscombe had claimed that ethics needs to be based in ideas about human flourishing or the good life, and Stocker wishes to criticize modern ethical theories in terms of their implications for the good life, for *eudaimonia*. He argues that the moral justifications modern views offer can be embodied as motives in our actual lives only on pain of depriving us of the possibility of a good life. What justifies an act as right according to utilitarianism, for example, is its production of a greater balance of pleasure over pain than any alternative action, but, if we are always motivated to produce such a greater balance, it will be impossible for us to care for, love, or value particular individuals, and the important goods of love and friendship will be denied us.

On the other hand, if we act from love and friendship rather than from the considerations that morally justify an action, there is a disharmony or 'schizophrenia' between our reasons/justifications and our motives/feelings. So, if harmony is a great human good, modern moral theories, if true, make it impossible to achieve *eudaimonia*: if we are schizophrenic, our lives lack harmony, but if we are not, we are unable to experience the goods of love and friendship.

Stocker takes this to be a reason for rejecting modern theories like utilitarianism and, presumably, Kantianism—but this assumption is far from obvious. It constitutes, in effect, a form of the *eudaimonism* that was prevalent in ancient virtue ethics but has been notably absent in most modern theories. *Eudaimonism* in the sense intended holds that genuine virtue must be in the interest of the virtuous individual, and Stocker's views represent a variation on this rather controversial idea.

Stocker also criticizes modern views for talking about actions and almost never about what morally justifies motives. But even where motives are considered, Stocker argues that modern theories evaluate them wrongly. Conscientiousness, acting from a sense of duty, is said to be the morally best of motives, but Stocker claims, to the contrary, that someone who visits a friend in hospital out of a sense of duty is a less good friend and to that extent morally inferior to the person who visits out of (feelings of) friendship.

It is worth asking ourselves, however, whether the lesser merit of the less good friend is really a *moral* deficiency rather than a deficiency in ethical admirability or excellence more widely understood. Finally, it should also be pointed out that some of Stocker's own values may lead to the kind of disharmony he deplores. If it is (morally) better to act from friendship than from a sense of duty, it is presumably also (morally) better to act from friendship than from a sense that it is (morally) better to act from friendship rather than from duty, and the person who acts from such a sense on all relevant occasions shows herself to be no (good) friend and perhaps even incapable of friendship. Thus, if one embodies Stocker's claim fully in one's life, one precludes the good of friendship in the ways Stocker describes, and, if one does not, one's life is disharmonious and schizophrenic. One may start wondering whether schizophrenia is inevitable and whether it is, in the end, such a very bad thing.

Susan Wolf's 'Moral Saints' criticizes modern moral theories in a somewhat different fashion from what we find in Anscombe, Williams, or Stocker. She argues that the perspective of individual perfection should be set against, though it overlaps with, the perspective of (common-sense, utilitarian, or Kantian) morality. A morally perfect individual according to any one of these views is not as perfect, or perfectly wonderful, as it is possible for someone to be; and moral theories go wrong to the extent they (metamorally) assume that one does best always to strive after (the goals of) moral perfection.

For Wolf, this indicates the need to consider and discuss perfectionistic individual ideals that purely *moral* theories either ignore or fail to do justice to. She rejects the alternative of adjusting the *content* of morality so that it includes everything relevant to individual perfection, because she assumes that an individual should not always be guided by such an enlarged moral view, just as he should not always be guided by any narrower kind of morality. It is logically impossible, for example, to act lovingly or passionately *out of* a consideration that these things make one, in a broad sense, morally better—and love and passion are necessary to broad moral perfection.

By the same token, she says, if we retain a narrower ideal of morality and try to develop a comprehensive perfectionist theory of how moral admirability is to be balanced against non-moral admirability, we still end up with a doctrine that cannot be practically action-guiding with regard to many of the actions and activities it praises. Once again, Wolf assumes that this undercuts any such comprehensive doctrine, but it would also be open to her to reject the idea that ideals should always be action-guiding. Certainly, this leads us back to the 'schizophrenia' Stocker deplores, but just how bad it is to have a gap between motive and justification is still a matter of considerable controversy.

III

Iris Murdoch, while continuing and extending Anscombe's critique of modern philosophy, attempts to move beyond it in the direction of a broad account of the virtues against a Platonic background. The main strut she wants to dislodge from the philosophical framework of modernity is the Kantian ideal of the Rational Person—the result, as she sees it, of the decline of religion and the advance of science. Such a person, believing that the universe lacks any purpose, construes herself as a purely free will, able bravely to choose in whichever way she wishes, quite unconstrained by any external demands.

Against this conception of the self as alienated from the world, Murdoch paints a picture of a self that recognizes external authority. Murdoch believes that the concepts central to ethics can best be understood if they are first considered in non-ethical contexts, and one of her mundane examples here is that of learning a language. I cannot choose how to speak Russian: the language itself consists in an authoritative structure which I must treat with respect if I am to succeed. And, Murdoch suggests, such respect can also be found in the ethical sphere, primarily in the exercise of love and justice, where again it exemplifies a response to demands which are not themselves chosen. Indeed, Murdoch would claim that the ethical sphere is not separate from the rest of life; morality is not to be understood as, say, a set of contractual arrangements, but as a matter of our whole mode of life. As Socrates said, our primary question in moral philosophy is, 'How should one live?'

The practice of learning a language, and many other human practices, Murdoch believes, require the exercise of the virtues. The language-learner must exemplify both honesty and the paradigmatic Murdochian virtue of humility, being ready to admit what she does not know. The artist—the good artist, that is—must be brave and patient as well. Like Plato, Murdoch brings together the aesthetic and the moral, and what she says about art illustrates one of the deep tensions in her work. On the one hand, she wishes to reject the Kantian ideal of the Rational Person; on the other hand, however, she herself thinks that human life has no purpose or *telos*.

This attempt to combine aspects of ancient virtue ethics with a certain scepticism about objective accounts of the good is characteristic of much contemporary work on the virtues, and the problems in such a project are clear. Murdoch, in trying to bring out the connections between art and virtue, suggests that the arts demonstrate the pointlessness of virtue *and* its supreme importance. She appears to argue both that our world is one of Death and Chance, empty of purpose, and that virtue really matters. This raises not only the question which plagued the Stoics—how virtue can matter if nothing else does—but the issue of how any good can find its home in a purposeless world, unless it arises from the free choice of its inhabitants.

One of the main faults Murdoch finds in the Kantian ideal is that it will not dislodge us from our selfishness, and her own account is presumably to be seen as at least partly intended to move us in what she sees as the right direction. What she calls 'unselfing'—that is, the shifting of perspective from concerns of the self to those outside it—can be seen in response to the beauty in nature and art. Virtue, for Murdoch, seems partly to consist in this movement beyond the self, not only requiring virtues such as humility and honesty, but also developing a capacity for love itself, and ultimately love of what she calls 'the Good'.

Murdoch is surely right to say that virtue, as we conceive of it now, requires one not to focus too readily on oneself and one's own concerns. But one might doubt the idea that aesthetes are more likely to be moral. It could indeed be argued that in some cases the development and exercise of aesthetic sensibilities can actually distract one from attention to moral demands: so keen is he to see the Modigliani at the Met that he does not even notice the hungry child begging by the subway exit.

One of the links between art and morality drawn out by Murdoch owes as much to Aristotle as it does to Plato, and this is the idea of moral sensitivity. For Murdoch, the self is a source of falsity and deception, and moving beyond it is to make contact with the world as it is. 'The authority of morals', she says, 'is the authority of truth, that is of reality.' And coming to understand reality is a matter not just of abstract intellect, but of looking and seeing. This view of moral perception has its roots in Aristotle's account of the practical wisdom (*phronēsis*) of the virtuous man, who sees matters as they are and responds appropriately. The Good, Murdoch believes, brings unity into a world of chaos, and that is partly through the understanding we can have of the relationships between and hierarchy in the virtues. But this understanding has to be complemented by an awareness of the richness and complexity of detail in everyday situations, an awareness itself grounded in love of the Good.

Several of these themes in Murdoch can be found running through the work of Alasdair MacIntyre. Again, MacIntyre is pessimistic about the resources modern life offers for a well-grounded moral philosophy. MacIntyre's book *After Virtue*, from which we reprint a central chapter, begins with the claim that much contemporary ethical discussion is literally nonsense. Followers of various moral theories are using concepts which are mere fragments from past traditions, and which have no content when wrenched out of context. We are reminded here of Anscombe's suggestion that the notion of 'ought' is no longer well grounded. MacIntyre's book is a survey of modernity and past traditions in the hope of deliverance from the malaise of modernity.

MacIntyre eventually advocates a form of Thomistic virtue ethics, but before that he provides a broad account of virtue itself. He begins the chapter reprinted here by noting that previous chapters in *After Virtue*, in discussing the virtues as described in Homer, Sophocles, and many other writers, have uncovered huge diversity in conceptions of the virtues. There is much disagreement about which items should be entered onto any list of the virtues, about the hierarchy of these items, and about the relationship between the virtues and social order. Do virtues enable one to fulfil one's social role (Homer), fulfil one's purpose or *telos* (Aristotle), or achieve earthly and heavenly success (Franklin)? Is there really anything common to the different accounts of the virtues?

MacIntyre's interpretations of various writers have been doubted, but he is, of course, correct that disagreements in this area are profound. He attempts to provide an account of the virtues which brings out what is common to them in any conception. This has three stages: (i) an account of the notion of a practice (reprinted here); (ii) an account of the narrative order of a human life (in which MacIntyre continues the critique of the alienated self of modernity); (iii) an account of what constitutes a moral tradition.

Like Murdoch, MacIntyre extends his focus to consider not only the territory occupied by morality, as understood in contemporary ethics, but the whole area of human excellence. MacIntyre claims that the virtues are grounded in human practices, and, again, one of his central examples is aesthetic, that of portrait-painting. Portrait-painting is a complex and co-operative human activity which allows its practitioners to develop goods internal to the practice. They do this by seeking to attain those objective standards of excellence appropriate to the activity itself (recall Murdoch on language-learning). Such goods are internal in that they can be gained in no other way than by painting portraits, whereas other goods to be attained from the practice, such as money or reputation, could be gained in many other ways, and so are external to the practice itself.

One central question here concerns the individuation of practices. Bricklaying is not a practice, according to MacIntyre, whereas architecture is. But bricklaying does seem to meet MacIntyre's criteria for being a practice, and there is no doubt that certain standards of excellence are appropriate to it.

But we should move on to consider the relation of virtues to practices and internal goods. According to MacIntyre, again developing a Murdochian theme, practices require the virtues. For portrait-painting to exist there must be a certain number of its practitioners who are just, courageous, and honest, and those virtues are also required when being introduced to the practice itself. The virtues, then, MacIntyre tentatively defines as those qualities that enable us to achieve internal goods.

At this point, one might fear that MacIntyre is instrumentalizing the virtues, seeing them as mere means to external goods (the internal goods of practices). But what MacIntyre has in mind is that exercising the virtues is partly constitutive of excellent practice. Nor does he insist that all practices must be good. He allows that there may be evil practices, and that evil can flow from the exercise of virtues such as courage in sustaining such practices. Two related questions, however, do remain. First, if ethical discussion has really broken down, as MacIntyre claims, how can he expect to persuade us of his own views, which do seem to take much from various earlier traditions? Secondly, how are we to decide between competing practices which are worth pursuing? In later chapters of *After Virtue* and in later writing, MacIntyre seeks to answer both of these questions. But it is at least arguable that in so doing he is returning to engage with opponents whom he earlier castigated as shouting incomprehensibly at one another across unbridgeable conceptual voids.

John McDowell also seeks to distance himself from much of contemporary ethical theory, and similar questions arise about whether he succeeds in so doing. McDowell suggests that the reason virtue is offered only a secondary role in certain ethical views is that these views concern themselves primarily with right conduct and the principles governing it. He advocates turning this priority around, and approaching right conduct 'from the inside out'—that is, by beginning with the notion of the virtuous person. The issue raised in our first section remains, however: is it really only virtue theorists who can expand the focus of ethics, and begin with the question, 'How should one live?'

McDowell follows Socrates in claiming that virtue is knowledge, and he develops his views, like Murdoch, in an Aristotelian direction. Virtue requires 'getting it right', in some sense, and McDowell understands virtue as a sensitivity to the requirements placed on one by the salient features of the situations in which one finds oneself. Like MacIntyre, McDowell believes that the ascription of virtues can explain behaviour (hence he would agree with MacIntyre about the failure of any 'value-free' social science), and, he suggests, the sensitivity he postulates can also explain. Thus we can postulate that the virtue just is the sensitivity. Further, because virtue requires getting it right, McDowell commits himself to the implication of the Socratic view of the 'unity of virtue'—that all the virtues are in fact one. There is no such thing, say, as a courageous villain.

There is an obvious problem for such a Socratic view of virtue: incontinence, or *akrasia*. Can a person not have the same view of a situation as the virtuous person, and yet fail to act virtuously? If so, the virtue cannot be identified with the sensitivity alone.

McDowell develops an Aristotelian solution to this problem, suggesting that the views taken of the same situation by the virtuous, on the one hand, and the continent and the incontinent, on the other, are different. On the battlefield, for example, in a situation calling for courage, the continent person, though he stands his ground, will be tempted to run. That, McDowell suggests, is because he sees the avoidance of wounds as a reason for running, whereas for the virtuous person this consideration is 'silenced'.

What McDowell wants to avoid here is the idea that the virtuous person's judgement is a matter of balancing reasons for and against. But it might seem that his claim brings the perspective of the virtuous person closer to blindness than sensitivity, for the fact that one will avoid wounds by running is surely a reason for so doing. We might follow Aristotle in another way, admitting that virtue does require a certain amount of non-rational habituation of the passions. The sensitivities of the virtuous and the continent are equally discerning; it is their characters that differ, the virtuous person finding it no struggle to act on his view of the requirements of the situation. And, because there is no struggle, there may in fact be no actual 'balancing': he may just see what is called for, and do it.

What kind of knowledge does the virtuous person have? Again, McDowell follows Aristotle in claiming that morality cannot fully be codified. The virtuous person has a conception of how to live that cannot be captured in a set of universal principles that could then be taken and applied by a non-virtuous person to deliver the right action in each case. Again, the spectre of irrationalism appears: rationality requires consistency, and that can be assured only if one can follow a universal principle. This view of McDowell's, recently elaborated by Jonathan Dancy, might seem to amount to the denial of the widely accepted view that moral reasons are 'universalizable'—that is, the view that any moral reason in one situation applies also in any relevantly similar situation.

One obvious solution here would be to allow that the virtuous person does follow a principle: the principle that one should be virtuous (see Rosalind Hursthouse's chapter in this volume for elucidation of this idea). But McDowell interprets Aristotle as holding, and himself holds, that there are *no* true generalizations in ethics. So his response is to appeal to the so-called 'rule-following considerations' in the work of Ludwig Wittgenstein. On McDowell's view, Wittgenstein is correctly suggesting that the rules of any form of rationality can be grounded only in human practice. There is, as Murdoch and MacIntyre both argue about virtue, no external guarantee. Moral education consists in enabling the person to see correctly, rather than to apply principles, and, like Murdoch, McDowell sees being fully virtuous as a difficult achievement.

If we cannot adduce universal principles, how are we to explain the virtuous person's behaviour? This is important for McDowell, since his case for identifying virtue with sensitivity rested on the possibility of such explanations. Again, McDowell follows Aristotle, and uses the idea of the 'practical syllogism'. We shall explain a virtuous action by postulating a major premiss (the conception of how to live), and a minor premiss (an immediate awareness of certain salient features of the present situation). Because of the uncodifiability of the conception, this means that an attempt to construe that conception as a mere non-cognitive state (some form of desire) will fail, since we cannot say what that desire is for independently of our grasp of that conception itself.

There is serious doubt about whether such a non-cognitive view can account for the phenomenology of virtue or of value in general. It is not clear, however, why the non-cognitivist could not accept uncodifiability and yet claim that the major premiss here is a mere desire. The 'seeing' required will be that of understanding the content of the desire itself. The virtuous person just desires to live like *this*, while the vicious person just desires to live like *that*. Unlike in mathematics, there is no right and wrong here, just tastes for different forms of life. In other words, not only is there no external standpoint of assessment; there is no internal standard either. And, if we deny McDowell's views about silencing, it may be that a non-virtuous person could see her way into understanding the virtuous person's conception of how she wishes to live, but just differ from her in her own desires.

In the end, however, McDowell's cognitivism has greater explanatory power than its non-cognitive rival. It can explain, for example, why ethical disagreements are not seen by their participants as matters of taste. And his description of the virtuous person as sensitive to reason-giving considerations which are independent of her desires not only offers a better account of moral phenomenology but allows us to retain the very notion of reasons for action which is put in jeopardy by non-cognitivism.

The final chapter we discuss in this section is by Philippa Foot, who says in the introduction to the collection of papers from which this selection is taken that she believes that 'a sound moral philosophy should start from a theory of the virtues and vices'.

Foot again follows the ancient route of attempting to establish the connection between human well-being and the virtues. It is often tempting to generalize in this area (to ask 'Why should I be moral?' rather than 'Why should I be generous?' or 'Why should I be just?'), but Foot avoids this temptation admirably. She notes that certain virtues—wisdom and the so-called 'executive' virtues of courage and temperance—can be beneficial to the agent herself, enabling her to advance her own well-being. Other virtues, however, such as charity, are other-regarding.

Foot's view is another example of the combination of virtue ethics with a non-Aristotelian and indeed non-objective account of the good. According to Foot, both our well-being and our reasons for action depend on our desires (she is what is called an 'internalist'). So a person with no desire for justice has no reason to be just. Such an account, however, has to rely upon a certain amount of bootstrapping. If the fact that an action open to me is just does not in itself give me a reason to do it, then it is not clear why it is the sort of thing I should want to desire. In other words, if I do have a reason to desire to be just (independent of my present desires), it is not clear why this cannot ground a reason to *act* justly. And if I have no reason to desire it, then why people do desire to be just becomes hard to explain (is it a mere taste?). We can, perhaps, agree with Foot, however, in her modest claims about the connection between virtue and well-being. Virtue cannot, despite the views of the ancients, guarantee happiness; but it can often be an important aid in attaining it.

Foot then asks what marks virtue out from other beneficial qualities, such as health. Her answer is that virtue is connected to the will. We shall not criticize a man who just falls sick, whereas we shall judge him by his intentions and his willed dispositions. Even the intellectual virtue of practical wisdom is related to the will. Instrumental rationality consists not just in knowing the means, but also in willing them, and wisdom concerning the ends worth pursuing is to do with a person's attachments (there is, of course, a question about how internalists can make room for the notion of wisdom concerning ends).

Foot's view about the relation between virtue and the will seems at least largely correct. But one wonders whether it can account for the whole domain of moral judgement. Foot herself later in the chapter raises the question of whether the moral saint, who does not have to struggle to be virtuous, is superior to the moral hero, who does have to struggle. Foot appears to give priority to the saint. Now the moral saint may act virtuously without effort, perhaps just because she is that sort of person by nature and by nurture. But we shall, as Foot suggests, admire her nevertheless. When it comes to the power of *will*, however, it is the hero who displays this most clearly. Perhaps we do not fully understand the ground of our own judgements here, and admiring the moral saint is in fact almost aesthetic, analogous to admiring someone's excellent health.

Foot notes the importance of an account of human nature for a theory of the virtues, and she puts forward the interesting hypothesis that the virtues are correctives to certain aspects of human nature as it is. If we were not by nature, for example, more attached to our own interests than to those of others, there would be no need for the virtue of benevolence. This insight of Foot's explains, for example, why the virtue of self-love either does not exist or is spoken of only rarely. But we might want to add two things, influenced by Aristotle and Hume respectively. First, the temptations, passions, and so on that require correction can go wrong in two directions. One can feel not only too much fear, but not enough, and the virtuous person is the one who gets it right on each occasion. Secondly, there is, as

Foot says, a need here for a convincing account of human nature. We might put a constraint on any account of what is reasonable (and virtue ethics is just such an account) that it be consonant with, and appealing in the light of, the true account of human nature. Foot writes as if benevolent sympathy is somehow unnatural to human beings, and that is something that Hume would deny. For Hume, benevolence is not a corrective to human nature, but the flowering of it. Other thinkers, such as William Godwin and perhaps Plato, have thought that self-love is not only not natural, but an aberration from the purely rational nature of man.

Foot ends her chapter by entering the debate about the unity of virtue. Recall that McDowell accepted this view in its strict Socratic form: virtue is knowledge. Virtue always issues in right conduct, so that courageous villains are out of the question. Foot goes along with McDowell in thinking that the virtues bound one another, and that properly to possess a certain virtue requires one to possess those that bound it: a mere desire to help others, for example, is not benevolence if it can issue in injustice. Like Socrates, however, McDowell fails to explain why it is that we naturally speak of those who are clearly vicious in one sphere as nevertheless possessing certain virtues. Foot offers an interesting suggestion here—namely, that virtues need not always *act as* virtues. Just as a poison need not act as a poison wherever it exists, so the virtue of courage, which *characteristically* issues in good actions and good desires, need not always act as a virtue.

The difference between McDowell and Foot here is related to their disagreement over the nature of reasons. McDowell is not an internalist, in that he believes that there are reasons for action independent of our desires, and the virtuous person is the one who can discern them. Foot looks at reasons from the point of view of desire, so it is not open to her to say that, since courage consists in a response to considerations which speak, independently of desire, in favour of courageous action, the allegedly courageous villain is being irrational. We have already noted how various writers in virtue ethics have called for accounts of psychology, human nature, and the human good. What virtue ethics also needs is a full account of the notion of a reason for action.

IV

Just as much of the writing by those sympathetic towards the virtues has been critical of the Kantian and utilitarian traditions, so virtue ethics has itself come under attack. Both J. B. Schneewind and Robert Louden agree that it is hard to grasp exactly what virtue ethics is, and begin their chapters with an attempt to define it. The first question a defender of virtue ethics will want to ask, of course, is whether their attempts succeed.

Schneewind and Louden both suggest that what chiefly sets virtue ethics apart is the primary role it attaches to claims about virtue or the virtuous agent, as opposed to claims about acts or rules. Schneewind adds that virtue ethicists will also give epistemological priority to the virtuous person: he or she will be the source of moral knowledge. According to an act-centred theory, it is the theory itself, or the person who understands it, which is the source of understanding in particular cases. And in those particular cases, Louden argues, we should also expect to find differences in views about moral motivation. The Kantian will prefer duty for duty's sake, while the utilitarian will advocate concern for the happiness of all. The virtue ethicist, however, will recommend acting out of a commitment to the value of, say, charity, for its own sake.

As we said earlier, virtue ethics was largely passed over in the moral philosophy of the first half of this century. Schneewind traces the history of this neglect of virtue, arguing that it arose out of serious defects at the heart of virtue ethics itself. The first two blows to virtue ethics, he claims, were Christianity, and the natural-law theory which developed from the work of Grotius in the seventeenth century. Christianity was essentially duty-based, and duty was understood as obedience to divine law. At this point one may begin to wonder whether a hole has appeared in the net woven by Schneewind to capture virtue ethics, for could Christianity not be seen as a duty-based virtue ethics, according to which our duty is to manifest certain virtues, such as love?

Virtue ethics owes much to Aristotle, who was severely criticized by Grotius. His attack concentrated on Aristotle's account of justice as a 'mean' between two vices, but the moral of it applies to all versions of virtue ethics. The motive of the just agent does not matter; what does matter is following the rules of justice, performing certain acts rather than being a certain kind of person. Further, like Grotius, Pufendorf went on to impugn the notion that the virtuous person has any kind of special access to moral truth.

Not all was lost for virtue ethics, however, for the natural lawyers had left some room for virtue in their drawing of a distinction between perfect and imperfect duties. How to make this distinction precise is a perennial problem in moral philosophy, but one plausible way of so doing—adopted by both Grotius and J. S. Mill—is in terms of rights. If I have contracted with you to perform a certain task, then you have a right to my performance, and I have a perfect duty correlative to that right. If you are a beggar in the street, however, you have no right to alms from me. Though I do have an imperfect duty to be generous, I have some discretion when and to whom to distribute my goods. And, the natural lawyers argued, in the case of imperfect duties, the spirit in which they are carried out does matter. In this way, then, room was left for talk of virtue.

This room came to be occupied by David Hume, and Schneewind argues that Hume's distinction between natural virtues, such as benevolence, and artificial virtues, such as justice, can be mapped onto the distinction between perfect and imperfect duties.

Hume wished to naturalize morality, in the sense of showing how it can develop from human nature without the aid of divine intervention. Human beings have a natural sympathy with one another, and this directly grounds the natural virtues. But they do not have any such tendency, say, to respect property, and here conventions must develop 'artificially' to which we become attached through an extension of self-interest to cover the interests of society as a whole. These conventions will constitute the practices of justice—perfect duty—while the natural virtues cover the sphere of imperfect duty.

Schneewind argues that Hume's theory collapses when it is faced with a demand for clear guidance in particular cases, as indeed it was by Adam Smith. If Hume claims that only virtue is sufficient for moral action, then his theory will be redundant. If he attempts to offer guidance, however, his theory will head straight in the direction of Benthamite utilitarianism, since Hume believed that the content of morality can be determined only by what is desired by individuals. Whether this exegesis of Hume is correct can be decided only by close analysis of the text. But even if it were, the modern virtue ethicist could claim at this point that there are in fact goods or reasons which are independent of the value of human well-being.

Kant, in the *Metaphysics of Morals*, also allowed room for the virtues in his account of morality. Schneewind suggests that Kant's view can be seen as a revival of the natural-law view, again based on the perfect/imperfect duty distinction and again amounting to the splitting of morality into an ethic of rules and an ethic of virtue. Schneewind concludes that this is the best that can be hoped for by the friends of virtue. Modern society, constituted as it is by vast populations comprising many subgroups with very different interests and views, is riven by disagreement. This fact was recognized by the natural lawyers, and their stress on rules was an attempt to provide guidance to ensure the survival of society. Aristotle's ethics was developed in the much more confined context of a stable and fairly homogeneous city state. He gives us little help in identifying just *who* the virtuous person is, and no help at all in dealing with conflict. And here,

Schneewind argues, the thesis of epistemological priority is likely to lead to sheer disrespect: rather than argue with you, I am likely to think that you are plain mistaken.

The charge that virtue ethics cannot provide guidance is put in a modern form by Louden, and he links the charge also to the epistemological priority thesis. Moral dilemmas arise over particular courses of action. If what I am to do in any particular case is to be decided by my own virtuous perception, then moral theory can offer little help. But people have always sought such help from philosophy, and act-centred views can deliver it. In the case of abortion, for example, utilitarianism can tell us that it is wrong if it leads to utility's not being maximized, while a Kantian view can tell us that it is permissible if no rights are infringed.

Like Schneewind, Louden also alleges that virtue ethics does not enable us to identify virtuous people. We cannot identify them through their actions, since the relation between action and character is contingent. The person we think is virtuous may just be pretending. Even if neuroscience took us to the point where we could correlate character traits with brain states, this would be of no help, since we still would not know whose brain states correlated with virtues.

There is something disingenuous in this criticism. As Aristotle points out several times in his lectures on ethics, one cannot expect philosophy to do all the work. If you have absolutely *no* idea about virtue, then moral philosophy is probably, for you, going to be a waste of time. But if you have some basic grip on who is virtuous and who is vicious—you have a hunch, perhaps, that your spouse, who has done so much to support you through your long illness, is closer to the Aristotelian ideal than the child-murderer sentenced to life imprisonment last week—then philosophy may well enable you to come to an understanding of virtue such that you can make finer discriminations.

This also raises the question whether the charge of anachronism made by both Schneewind and Louden against virtue ethics is not also an exaggeration. Do we really have no consensus on what counts as a virtue in modern society? Of course, we shall disagree radically about what constitutes certain virtues, such as justice, but that sort of disagreement was as intense within ancient Athens as it is in New York.

Louden has further criticisms of the agent-orientation of virtue ethics. Because of its concentration on long-term assessment of character, it is likely to be blind to the ethical implications of cases, such as those depicted in tragedies, in which a good person performs some morally terrible action. Likewise, it will play down the importance of the consequences of actions, even if these are very bad. And it will be unable to spell out the importance of accepting absolute prohibitions on certain specific acts. This is likely to result in our finding it easier to break such prohibitions, feeling that we are acting 'out of character', and so not to be blamed. Finally, because character can change, we need something more secure on the basis of which to assess action.

What is this more secure basis to be? Louden suggests a pluralistic scheme which gives priority neither to agents nor to acts, and we cannot help but be reminded here of Schneewind's interpretation of the natural lawyers, of Hume, and of Kant. But the question remains whether both Schneewind and Louden really have virtue ethics in their sights, or some much narrower construction of their own devising. Could a virtue ethics construed more generously not allow for Louden's pluralistic insights without being a mere bolt-on addition to one of the two more traditional kinds of moral theory?

V

Rosalind Hursthouse's 'Virtue Theory and Abortion' addresses some of the criticisms of (traditional) virtue ethics raised by Louden and Schneewind. She argues that virtue ethics can focus on particular actions and evaluate them as right and wrong, can formulate moral rules to guide action, and can help us to resolve practical or applied moral issues such as whether (in some particular case) abortion is or was morally permissible. She also shows how it is possible for a virtue theory to claim that right actions are actions a virtuous person would perform in the relevant circumstances, without falling into circularity. It is possible, because the concept of a virtuous person can be unpacked in terms of the notion of particular virtues, and these latter, in turn, can be understood as traits human beings need in order to live well, to achieve *eudaimonia*.

However, Hursthouse also seems to equate right actions with actions that display no vice, and that equivalence does not in fact follow from, indeed seems to run contrary to, the rest of her view. Could not an action that exhibited cowardice or ignorance somehow turn out to be exactly what the wise, courageous person would also have chosen? But even if such a thing is possible, Hursthouse's defence of rules in the context of virtue ethics seems to survive pretty well intact.

The way Hursthouse grounds rightness in the notion of good character traits and the latter, in turn, in the idea of *eudaimonia* or happiness is reminiscent of two-tiered moral theories like rule-utilitarianism. Rule-utilitarianism is open to familiar forms of criticism, and there is a need to consider whether similar difficulties arise for a two-tiered virtue ethics like that of Hursthouse. But perhaps the most distinctive accomplishment of Hursthouse's article lies in its discussion of how virtue theory can be practically relevant to a difficult moral issue like abortion. Her view involves claiming that the permissibility or wrongness of abortions will vary with the circumstances and is, to that extent, then, in agreement with act-utilitarianism. But, unlike the latter, this variation, according to Hursthouse, depends on the differing motives and thinking of women who have abortions, rather than on the different (probable) consequences of abortions in different circumstances.

Many women who believe in a *right* of abortion will disagree that the permissibility of a woman's obtaining an abortion can vary with her *motives*, but if a virtue theory like Hursthouse's were somehow extended into the sphere of law and politics, it might find the resources to claim that, even if some sorts of abortions are morally wrong, *the State has no moral right to prohibit them*. This might be a sufficient concession to feminism and liberalism to make Hursthouse's view seem plausible, despite its denial of ground-floor rights. After all, even if there is a significant right of abortion, a woman who has an abortion solely in order, say, to spite her husband might plausibly be thought to be acting in a morally unacceptable way. Clearly, though, such possibilities need to be explored further.

The form of virtue ethics defended in Michael Slote's 'Agent-Based Virtue Ethics' is more *radical* than Hursthouse's views in at least two ways. Rather than make an act's rightness depend on what a hypothetical virtuous person *would* do, it insists that the rightness of someone's action depends on the *actual* motivation that lies or lay behind it. Moreover, agent-based views treat motives or traits like benevolence as good or virtuous not because of their conduciveness to human happiness, but because of their intrinsic moral character as motives (something we are supposed to be able intuitively to discern). Virtue thus does not have to be based in anything else in order to ground moral evaluations of action, and all this, according to Slote, can be done without falling into circularity.

The absence of circularity, however, depends on the character of the particular motive or motives selected and advocated as fundamentally admirable. An agent-based theory cannot base everything on the moral goodness, say, of the desire to keep one's promises, because the goodness of that desire is clearly parasitic upon moral claims about actions. The desire is good only because it involves a certain conscientiousness with respect to the moral rule that prohibits the breaking of promises except in certain well-defined circumstances. The goodness of the motive, that is, is predicated on the validity of a certain rule and hence on the wrongness of acts that contravene that rule. In that case, the desire to keep promises cannot, without circularity, also ground the wrongness of breaking promises. But agent-basing makes sense in regard to motives like benevolence, caring, and love, because (as Hume pointed out) such motives can develop or arise in a natural fashion without someone's having an eye on moral rules or laws.

Slote does not talk about moral rules, but agent-based views clearly allow of moral rules—e.g. the rule 'never perform (one ought not to perform) actions that reflect a deficiency of benevolence'. Such a rule is consistent with 'ought implies can' because (assuming the compatibility of freedom and determinism) a totally malicious person in a position to help or hurt a fellow human being is least *able* to perform a helping act that would not reflect his bad character (even though we can comfortably predict he will not in fact do what he is thus able to do). The above rule also allows more specific, familiar rules like 'don't steal' to function as valid rules of thumb, since there is a tendency for acts of stealing to reflect bad or deficient motives—e.g. greed or selfishness—that are a far cry from ideal motives like (universal) benevolence.

Having outlined a morality of caring that encompasses good motivation with regard both to strangers and to near and dear, Slote claims that such an agent-based view can probably be extended in the direction of political philosophy: towards an account, for example, of social justice. But he does not indicate how he proposes to do this. By contrast, the preoccupation of Annette Baier's 'What Do Women Want in a Moral Theory?' with both moral *and* political issues is fairly clear throughout. Like Slote, she notes Carol Gilligan's claim that women think morally in terms of caring and interrelatedness, whereas men think in terms of justice and autonomy, but instead of trying to expand the 'feminine' notion of caring towards a conception of political ideals in the way that Slote recommends, but only partially pursues, she thinks it best to look for a moral ideal that combines 'masculine' autonomy and 'feminine' caring (or love). She argues that the idea of trust and trustworthiness is precisely such an ideal, and her chapter sketches some ways in which that ideal might serve to undergird both political and individual moral values. Crucial to motivating her conception is the thought that society cannot exist and be perpetuated without the relation of trust and trustworthiness that occurs between mothers (parents) and their children, and Baier's chapter, like Slote's, moves at one and the same time both in a feminist and in a virtue-ethical direction. In addition, Baier's approach to moral and political issues seems (close to being) agent-based, but it is difficult to be sure, because Baier never explicitly discusses this issue.

Clearly, virtue ethics needs to expand its recent moral horizons so as to take in larger questions of political morality. Otherwise, contemporary virtue ethics will fail to meet Schneewind's criticism that virtue ethics, while acceptable in and for the relatively homogeneous and peaceful societies that typified the ancient world, is unsuitable to the more diverse and conflict-ridden conditions of modern and contemporary life, conditions that require political thought and political principles that can help to reduce tensions and allow us to live with one another.

There is danger for virtue ethics in the attempt to meet this challenge—not merely because it may be unable to produce a political philosophy, but because the political philosophy it manages to produce may be of the wrong kind. The political ideals associated with virtue ethics in the ancient world were by and large anti- or non-democratic. Neither Plato nor Aristotle, for example, thought democracy an ideal form of government, and it is difficult to see how a plausibly democratic social ideal could be developed, say, out of Aristotle's ethical views. However, both Rosalind Hursthouse and Martha Nussbaum have recently defended just such a possibility, and if this work proves fruitful, then virtue ethics will have succeeded in answering Schneewind's challenge.

But we must not assume that the challenge can be met only by relying on Aristotle or other ancient models of virtue ethics such as the Stoics. Both Baier's and Slote's chapters invoke the 'sentimentalist' tradition of Hutcheson and Hume, which emphasized 'natural' motives and attitudes such as benevolence and trust. Moral sentimentalism in many ways resembles utilitarianism (not surprisingly, because it *gave rise* to utilitarianism), and utilitarianism is thought to be *able* to accommodate modern-day democratic and even liberal ideals. So perhaps a political philosophy grounded in ideals like trust, benevolence, or caring would have an easier time defending democracy and showing us how conflict can be *justly* resolved than accounts that depended on ancient models of virtue ethics.

If virtue ethics cannot produce some plausible conception of social justice and of political morality more generally, then its main contemporary rivals, consequentialism and Kantianism, will have a distinct advantage. These approaches clearly can be systematically applied to both individual moral and political questions (contract theory typically does not aspire to cover all questions of individual morality), so, if virtue ethics cannot do the same, and perhaps even has to borrow an acceptable political philosophy from consequentialism or Kantianism, it is bound ultimately to seem inferior to these other approaches.

However, at this very moment a number of virtue ethicists are working on questions of social justice and politics with the hope of arriving at something relevant to contemporary life, and we should be hearing more about such efforts over the next few years. In the Aristotelian corpus, the book on political philosophy that follows the *Ethics* is called the *Politics*; so, if those currently working on political philosophy in a virtue-ethical vein are in any degree successful, the present volume may perhaps in the not-too-distant future have a companion volume called Oxford Readings in Virtue Politics.

1

MODERN MORAL PHILOSOPHY

G. E. M. ANSCOMBE

I will begin by stating three theses which I present in this paper. The first is that it is not profitable for us at present to do moral philosophy; that should be laid aside at any rate until we have an adequate philosophy of psychology, in which we are conspicuously lacking. The second is that the concepts of obligation, and duty—*moral* obligation and *moral* duty, that is to say—and of what is *morally* right and wrong, and of the *moral* sense of 'ought', ought to be jettisoned if this is psychologically possible; because they are survivals, or derivatives from survivals, from an earlier conception of ethics which no longer generally survives, and are only harmful without it. My third thesis is that the differences between the well-known English writers on moral philosophy from Sidgwick to the present day are of little importance.

Anyone who has read Aristotle's *Ethics* and has also read modern moral philosophy must have been struck by the great contrasts between them. The concepts which are prominent among the moderns seem to be lacking, or at any rate buried or far in the background, in Aristotle. Most noticeably, the term 'moral' itself, which we have by direct inheritance from Aristotle, just doesn't seem to fit, in its modern sense, into an account of Aristotelian ethics. Aristotle distinguishes virtues as moral and intellectual. Have some of what he calls 'intellectual' virtues what *we* should call a 'moral' aspect? It would seem so; the criterion is presumably that a failure in an 'intellectual' virtue—like that of having good judgement in calculating how to bring about something useful, say in municipal government—may be *blameworthy*. But—it may reasonably be asked—cannot *any* failure be made a matter of blame or reproach? Any derogatory criticism, say of the workmanship of a product or the design of a machine, can be called blame or reproach. So we want to put in the word 'morally' again: sometimes such a failure may be *morally* blameworthy, sometimes

From *The Collected Philosophical Papers of G. E. M. Anscombe*, iii. *Ethics, Religion and Politics* (Oxford: Basil Blackwell, 1981), 26–42. This paper originally appeared in *Philosophy*, 33 (1958) and is reprinted here by permission.

not. Now has Aristotle got this idea of *moral* blame, as opposed to any other? If he has, why isn't it more central? There are some mistakes, he says, which are causes, not of involuntariness in actions, but of scoundrelism, and for which a man is blamed. Does this mean that there is a *moral* obligation not to make certain intellectual mistakes? Why doesn't he discuss obligation in general, and this obligation in particular? If someone professes to be expounding Aristotle and talks in a modern fashion about 'moral' such-and-such, he must be very imperceptive if he does not constantly feel like someone whose jaws have somehow got out of alignment: the teeth don't come together in a proper bite.

We cannot, then, look to Aristotle for any elucidation of the modern way of talking about 'moral' goodness, obligation, etc. And all the best-known writers on ethics in modern times, from Butler to Mill, appear to me to have faults as thinkers on the subject which make it impossible to hope for any direct light on it from them. I will state these objections with the brevity which their character makes possible.

Butler exalts conscience, but appears ignorant that a man's conscience may tell him to do the vilest things.

Hume defines 'truth' in such a way as to exclude ethical judgements from it, and professes that he has proved that they are so excluded. He also implicitly defines 'passion' in such a way that aiming at anything is having a passion. His objection to passing from 'is' to 'ought' would apply equally to passing from 'is' to 'owes' or from 'is' to 'needs'. (However, because of the historical situation, he has a point here, which I shall return to.)

Kant introduces the idea of 'legislating for oneself', which is as absurd as if in these days, when majority votes command great respect, one were to call each reflective decision a man made a *vote* resulting in a majority, which as a matter of proportion is overwhelming, for it is always 1–0. The concept of legislation requires superior power in the legislator. His own rigoristic convictions on the subject of lying were so intense that it never occurred to him that a lie could be relevantly described as anything but just a lie (e.g. as 'a lie in such-and-such circumstances'). His rule about universalizable maxims is useless without stipulations as to what shall count as a relevant description of an action with a view to constructing a maxim about it.

Bentham and Mill do not notice the difficulty of the concept 'pleasure'. They are often said to have gone wrong through committing the naturalistic fallacy; but this charge does not impress me, because I do not find accounts of it coherent. But the other point—about pleasure—seems to me a fatal objection from the very outset. The ancients found this concept pretty baffling. It reduced Aristotle to sheer babble about 'the bloom on the cheek of youth' because, for good reasons, he wanted to make it out both identical with and different from the pleasurable activity. Generations of modern philosophers found this concept quite unperplexing, and it reappeared in the literature as a problematic one only a year or two ago when Ryle wrote about it. The reason is simple: since Locke, pleasure was taken to be some sort of internal impression. But it was superficial, if that was the right account of it, to make it the point of actions. One might adapt something Wittgenstein said about 'meaning' and say 'Pleasure cannot be an internal impression, for no internal impression could have the consequences of pleasure.'

Mill also, like Kant, fails to realize the necessity for stipulation as to relevant descriptions, if his theory is to have content. It did not occur to him that acts of murder and theft could be otherwise described. He holds that where a proposed action is of such a kind as to fall under some one principle established on grounds of utility, one must go by that; where it falls under none or several, the several suggesting contrary views of the action, the thing to do is to calculate particular consequences. But pretty well any action can be so described as to make it fall under a variety of principles of utility (as I shall say for short) if it falls under any.

I will now return to Hume. The features of Hume's philosophy which I have mentioned, like many other features of it, would incline me to think that Hume was a mere—brilliant—sophist; and his procedures are certainly sophistical. But I am forced, not to reverse, but to add to, this judgement by a peculiarity of Hume's philosophizing: namely that, although he reaches his conclusions—with which he is in love—by sophistical methods, his considerations constantly open up very deep and important problems. It is often the case that in the act of exhibiting the sophistry one finds oneself noticing matters which deserve a lot of exploring: the obvious stands in need of investigation as a result of the points that Hume pretends to have made. In this, he is unlike, say, Butler. It was already well known that conscience could dictate vile actions; for Butler to have written disregarding this does not open up any new topics for us. But with Hume it is otherwise: hence he is a very profound and great philosopher, in spite of his sophistry. For example:

Suppose that I say to my grocer 'Truth consists in *either* relations of ideas, as that 20*s.* = £1, *or* matters of fact, as that I ordered potatoes, you supplied them, and you sent me a bill. So it doesn't apply to such a proposition as that I *owe* you such-and-such a sum.'

Now if one makes this comparison, it comes to light that the relation of the facts mentioned to the description '*X* owes *Y* so much money' is an interesting one, which I will call that of being 'brute relative to' that description. Further, the 'brute' facts mentioned here themselves have descriptions relatively to which *other* facts are 'brute'—as, e.g., *he had potatoes carted to my house* and *they were left there* are brute facts relative to 'he supplied me with potatoes'. And the fact *X owes Y money* is in turn 'brute' relative to other descriptions—e.g. '*X* is solvent.' Now the relation of 'relative bruteness' is a complicated one. To mention a few points: if *xyz* is a set of facts brute relative to a description *A*, then *xyz* is a set out of a range some set among which holds if *A* holds; but the holding of some set among these does not necessarily entail *A*, because exceptional circumstances can always make a difference; and what are exceptional circumstances relatively to *A* can generally only be explained by giving a few diverse examples, and *no* theoretically adequate provision can be made for exceptional circumstances, since a further special context can theoretically always be imagined that would reinterpret any special context. Further, though, in normal circumstances, *xyz* would be a justification for *A*, that is not to say that *A* just comes to the same as '*xyz*'; and also there is apt to be an institutional context which gives its point to the description *A*, of which institution *A* is of course not itself a description. (For example, the statement that I give someone a shilling is not a description of the institution of money or of the currency of this country.) Thus, though it would be ludicrous to pretend that there can be no such thing as a transition from, e.g., 'is' to 'owes', the character of the transition is in fact rather interesting and comes to light as a result of reflecting on Hume's arguments.[1]

That I owe the grocer such-and-such a sum would be one of a set of facts which would be 'brute' in relation to the description 'I am a bilker.' 'Bilking' is, of course, a species of 'dishonesty' or 'injustice'. (Naturally the consideration will not have any effect on my actions unless I want to commit or avoid acts of injustice.)

So far, in spite of their strong associations, I conceive 'bilking', 'injustice', and 'dishonesty' in a merely 'factual' way. That I can do this for 'bilking' is obvious enough; 'justice' I have no idea how to define, except that its sphere is that of actions which relate to someone else, but 'injustice', for its defect, can provisionally be offered as a generic name covering various species, e.g. bilking, theft (which is relative to whatever property institutions exist), slander, adultery, punishment of the innocent.

In present-day philosophy an explanation is required how an unjust man is a bad man, or an unjust action a bad one; to give such an explanation belongs to ethics; but it cannot even be begun until we are equipped with

[1] The above two paragraphs are an abstract of the paper 'On Brute Facts', repr. in *The Collected Philosophical Papers of G. E. M. Anscombe*, iii. *Ethics, Religion and Politics* (Oxford: Basil Blackwell, 1981), ch. 3.

a sound philosophy of psychology. For the proof that an unjust man is a bad man would require a positive account of justice as a 'virtue'. This part of the subject matter of ethics is, however, completely closed to us until we have an account of what *type of characteristic* a virtue is—a problem, not of ethics, but of conceptual analysis—and how it relates to the actions in which it is instanced: a matter which I think Aristotle did not succeed in really making clear. For this we certainly need an account at least of what a human action is at all, and how its description as 'doing such-and-such' is affected by its motive and by the intention or intentions in it; and for this an account of such concepts is required.

The terms 'should' or 'ought' or 'needs' relate to good and bad: e.g. machinery needs oil, or should or ought to be oiled, in that running without oil is bad for it, or it runs badly without oil. According to this conception, of course, 'should' and 'ought' are not used in a special 'moral' sense when one says that a man should not bilk. (In Aristotle's sense of the term 'moral' (ἠθικός), they are being used in connection with a *moral* subject matter: namely that of human passions and (non-technical) actions.) But they have now acquired a special so-called 'moral' sense—i.e. a sense in which they imply some absolute verdict (like one of guilty/not guilty on a man) on what is described in the 'ought' sentences used in certain types of context: not merely the contexts that *Aristotle* would call 'moral'—passions and actions—but also some of the contexts that he would call 'intellectual'.

The ordinary (and quite indispensable) terms 'should', 'needs', 'ought', 'must'—acquired this special sense by being equated in the relevant contexts with 'is obliged', or 'is bound', or 'is required to', in the sense in which one can be obliged or bound by law, or something can be required by law.

How did this come about? The answer is in history: between Aristotle and us came Christianity, with its *law* conception of ethics. For Christianity derived its ethical notions from the Torah. (One might be inclined to think that a law conception of ethics could arise only among people who accepted an allegedly divine positive law; that this is not so is shown by the example of the Stoics, who also thought that whatever was involved in conformity to human virtues was required by divine law.)

In consequence of the dominance of Christianity for many centuries, the concepts of being bound, permitted, or excused became deeply embedded in our language and thought. The Greek word ἁμαρτάνειν, the aptest to be turned to that use, acquired the sense 'sin', from having meant 'mistake', 'missing the mark', 'going wrong'. The Latin *peccatum* which roughly corresponded to ἁμάρτημα was even apter for the sense 'sin', because it was already associated with *culpa*—'guilt'—a juridical term. The blanket term 'illicit', 'unlawful', meaning much the same as our blanket term 'wrong', explains itself. It is interesting that Aristotle did not have such a blanket term. He has blanket terms for wickedness—'villain', 'scoundrel'; but of course a man is not a villain or a scoundrel by the performance of one bad action, or a few bad actions. And he has terms like 'disgraceful', 'impious'; and specific terms signifying defect of the relevant virtue, like 'unjust'; but no term corresponding to 'illicit'. The extension of this term (i.e. the range of its application) could be indicated in his terminology only by a quite lengthy sentence: that is 'illicit', which, whether it is a thought or a consented-to passion or an action or an omission in thought or action, is something contrary to one of the virtues the lack of which shows a man to be bad *qua* man. That formulation would yield a concept co-extensive with the concept 'illicit'.

To have a *law* conception of ethics is to hold that what is needed for conformity with the virtues failure in which is the mark of being bad *qua* man (and not merely, say, *qua* craftsman or logician)—that what is needed for *this*, is required by divine law. Naturally it is not possible to have such a conception unless you believe in God as a law-giver; like Jews, Stoics, and Christians. But if such a conception is dominant for many centuries, and then is given up, it is a natural result that the concepts of 'obligation', of being bound or required as by a law, should remain though they had lost their root; and if the word 'ought' has become invested in certain contexts with the sense of 'obligation', it too will remain to be spoken with a special emphasis and a special feeling in these contexts.

It is as if the notion 'criminal' were to remain when criminal law and criminal courts had been abolished and forgotten. A Hume discovering this situation might conclude that there was a special sentiment, expressed by 'criminal', which alone gave the word its sense. So Hume discovered the situation in which the notion 'obligation' survived, and the word 'ought' was invested with that peculiar force having which it is said to be used in a 'moral' sense, but in which the belief in divine law had long since been abandoned: for it was substantially given up among Protestants at the time of the Reformation.[2] The situation, if I am right, was the interesting one of the survival of a concept outside the framework of thought that made it a really intelligible one.

When Hume produced his famous remarks about the transition from 'is'

[2] They did not deny the existence of divine law; but their most characteristic doctrine was that it was given, not to be obeyed, but to show man's incapacity to obey it, even by grace; and this applied not merely to the ramified prescriptions of the Torah, but to the requirements of 'natural divine law'. Cf. in this connection the decree of Trent against the teaching that Christ was only to be trusted in as mediator, not obeyed as legislator.

to 'ought', he was, then, bringing together several quite different points. One I have tried to bring out by my remarks on the transition from 'is' to 'owes' and on the relative 'bruteness' of facts. It would be possible to bring out a different point by enquiring about the transition from 'is' to 'needs'; from the characteristics of an organism to the environment that it needs, for example. To say that it needs that environment is not to say, e.g., that you want it to have that environment, but that it won't flourish unless it has it. Certainly, it all depends whether you *want* it to flourish! as Hume would say. But what 'all depends' on whether you want it to flourish is whether the fact that it needs that environment, or won't flourish without it, has the slightest influence on your actions. Now *that* such-and-such 'ought' to be or 'is needed' is supposed to have an influence on your actions: from which it seemed natural to infer that to judge that it 'ought to be' was in fact to grant what you judged 'ought to be' influence on your actions. And no amount of truth as to what *is* the case could possibly have a logical claim to have influence on your actions. (It is not judgement as such that sets us in motion; but our judgement on how to get or do something we *want*.) Hence it *must* be impossible to infer 'needs' or 'ought to be' from 'is'. But in the case of a plant, let us say, the inference from 'is' to 'needs' is certainly not in the least dubious. It is interesting and worth examining; but not at all fishy. Its interest is similar to the interest of the relation between brute and less brute facts: these relations have been very little considered. And while you can contrast 'what it needs' with 'what it's got'—like contrasting *de facto* and *de iure*—that does not make its needing this environment less of a 'truth'.

Certainly in the case of what the plant needs, the thought of a need will only affect action if you want the plant to flourish. Here, then, there is no necessary connection between what you can judge the plant 'needs' and what you want. But there is some sort of necessary connection between what you think *you* need, and what you want. The connection is a complicated one; it is possible *not* to want something that you judge you need. But, e.g., it is not possible never to want *anything* that you judge you need. This, however, is a fact not about the meaning of the word 'to need', but about the phenomenon of *wanting*. Hume's reasoning, we might say, in effect, leads one to think it must be about the word 'to need', or 'to be good for'.

Thus we find two problems already wrapped up in the remark about a transition from 'is' to 'ought'; now supposing that we had clarified the 'relative bruteness' of facts, on the one hand, and the notions involved in 'needing', and 'flourishing', on the other—there would *still* remain a third point. For, following Hume, someone might say: Perhaps you have made out your point about a transition from 'is' to 'owes' and from 'is' to 'needs': but only at the cost of showing 'owes' and 'needs' sentences to express a *kind* of truths, a *kind* of facts. And it remains impossible to infer '*morally ought*' from 'is'.

This comment, it seems to me, would be correct. This word 'ought', having become a word of mere mesmeric force, could not, in the character of having that force, be inferred from anything whatever. It may be objected that it could be inferred from other 'morally ought' sentences: but that cannot be true. The appearance that this is so is produced by the fact that we say 'All men are φ' and 'Socrates is a man' implies 'Socrates is φ'. But here 'φ' is a dummy predicate. We mean that if you substitute a real predicate for 'φ' the implication is valid. A real predicate is required; not just a word containing no intelligible thought: a word retaining the suggestion of force, and apt to have a strong psychological effect, but which no longer signifies a real concept at all.

For its suggestion is one of a *verdict* on my action, according as it agrees or disagrees with the description in the 'ought' sentence. And where one does not think there is a judge or a law, the notion of a verdict may retain its psychological effect, but not its meaning. Now imagine that just this word 'verdict' *were* so used—with a characteristically solemn emphasis—as to retain its atmosphere but not its meaning, and someone were to say: 'For a *verdict*, after all, you need a law and a judge.' The reply might be made: 'Not at all, for if there were a law and a judge who gave a verdict, the question for us would be whether accepting that verdict is something that there is a *Verdict* on.' This is an analogue of an argument which is so frequently referred to as decisive: if someone does have a divine law conception of ethics, all the same, he has to agree that he has to have a judgement that he *ought* (morally ought) to obey the divine law; so his ethic is in exactly the same position as any other: he merely has a 'practical major premiss':[3] 'Divine law ought to be obeyed' where someone else has, e.g., 'The greatest happiness principle ought to be employed in all decisions.'

I should judge that Hume and our present-day ethicists had done a considerable service by showing that no content could be found in the notion 'morally ought', if it were not that the latter philosophers try to find an alternative (very fishy) content and to retain the psychological force of the term. It would be most reasonable to drop it. It has no reasonable sense outside a law conception of ethics; they are not going to maintain such a

[3] As it is absurdly called. Since major premiss = premiss containing the term which is predicate in the conclusion, it is a solecism to speak of it in the connection with practical reasoning.

conception; and you can do ethics without it, as is shown by the example of Aristotle. It would be a great improvement if, instead of 'morally wrong', one always named a genus such as 'untruthful', 'unchaste', 'unjust'. We should no longer ask whether doing something was 'wrong', passing directly from some description of an action to this notion; we should ask whether, e.g., it was unjust; and the answer would sometimes be clear at once.

I now come to the epoch in modern English moral philosophy marked by Sidgwick. There is a startling change that seems to have taken place between Mill and Moore. Mill assumes, as we saw, that there is no question of calculating particular consequences of an action such as murder or theft; and we saw too that his position was stupid, because it is not at all clear how an action *can* fall under just one principle of utility. In Moore and in subsequent academic moralists of England we find it taken to be pretty obvious that 'the right action' means the one which produces the best possible consequences (reckoning among consequences the intrinsic values ascribed to certain kinds of act by some 'Objectivists'[4]). Now it follows from this that a man does well, subjectively speaking, if he acts for the best in the particular circumstances according to his judgement of the total consequences of this particular action. I say that this follows, not that any philosopher has said precisely that. For discussion of these questions can of course get extremely complicated: e.g. it can be doubted whether 'such-and-such is the right action' is a satisfactory formulation, on the grounds that things have to exist to have predicates—so perhaps the best formulation is 'I am obliged'; or again, a philosopher may deny that 'right' is a 'descriptive' term, and then take a roundabout route through linguistic analysis to reach a view which comes to the same thing as 'the right action is the one productive of the best consequences' (e.g. the view that you frame your 'principles' to effect the end you choose to pursue, the connection between 'choice' and 'best' being supposedly such that choosing reflectively means that you choose how to act so as to produce the best consequences); further, the roles of what are called 'moral principles' and of the 'motive of duty' have to be described; the differences between 'good' and 'morally good' and 'right' need to be explored, the special characteristics of 'ought' sentences investigated. Such discussions generate an appearance of significant diversity of views where what is really signifi-

[4] Oxford Objectivists, of course, distinguish between 'consequences' and 'intrinsic values' and so produce a misleading appearance of not being consequentialists. But they do not hold—and Ross explicitly denies—that the gravity of, e.g., procuring the condemnation of the innocent is such that it cannot be outweighed by, e.g., national interest. Hence their distinction is of no importance.

cant is an overall similarity. The overall similarity is made clear if you consider that every one of the best known English academic moral philosophers has put out a philosophy according to which, e.g., it is not possible to hold that it cannot be right to kill the innocent as a means to any end whatsoever and that someone who thinks otherwise is in error. (I have to mention both points; because Mr Hare, for example, while teaching a philosophy which would encourage a person to judge that killing the innocent would be what he ought to choose for overriding purposes, would also teach, I think, that, if a man chooses to make avoiding killing the innocent for any purpose his 'supreme practical principle', he cannot be impugned for error: that just is his 'principle'. But with that qualification, I think it can be seen that the point I have mentioned holds good of every single English academic moral philosopher since Sidgwick.) Now this is a significant thing: for it means that all these philosophies are quite incompatible with the Hebrew–Christian ethic. For it has been characteristic of that ethic to teach that there are certain things forbidden whatever *consequences* threaten, such as: choosing to kill the innocent for any purpose, however good; vicarious punishment; treachery (by which I mean obtaining a man's confidence in a grave matter by promises of trustworthy friendship and then betraying him to his enemies); idolatry; sodomy; adultery; making a false profession of faith. The prohibition of certain things simply in virtue of their description as such-and-such identifiable kinds of action, regardless of any further consequences, is certainly not the whole of the Hebrew–Christian ethic; but it is a noteworthy feature of it; and, if every academic philosopher since Sidgwick has written in such a way as to exclude this ethic, it would argue a certain provinciality of mind not to see this incompatibility as the most important fact about these philosophers, and the differences between them as somewhat trifling by comparison.

It is noticeable that none of these philosophers displays any consciousness that there is such an ethic, which he is contradicting: it is pretty well taken for obvious among them all that a prohibition such as that on murder does not operate in face of some consequences. But of course the strictness of the prohibition has as its point *that you are not to be tempted by fear or hope of consequences.*

If you notice the transition from Mill to Moore, you will suspect that it was made somewhere by someone; Sidgwick will come to mind as a likely name; and you will in fact find it going on, almost casually, in him. He is rather a dull author; and the important things in him occur in asides and footnotes and small bits of argument which are not concerned with his grand classification of the 'methods of ethics'. A divine-law theory of ethics is reduced to an insignificant variety by a footnote telling us that 'the best theologians' (God knows whom he meant) tell us that God is to be obeyed in his capacity of a *moral* being. ἦ φορτικός ὁ ἔπαινος; one seems to hear Aristotle saying: 'Isn't the praise vulgar?'[5]—but Sidgwick *is* vulgar in that kind of way: he thinks, for example, that humility consists in underestimating your own merits—i.e. in a species of untruthfulness; and that the ground for having laws against blasphemy was that it was offensive to believers; and that to go accurately into the virtue of purity is to offend against its canons, a thing he reproves 'medieval theologians' for not realizing.

From the point of view of the present enquiry, the most important thing about Sidgwick was his definition of intention. He defines intention in such a way that one must be said to intend any foreseen consequences of one's voluntary action. This definition is obviously incorrect, and I dare say that no one would be found to defend it now. He uses it to put forward an ethical thesis which would now be accepted by many people: the thesis that it does not make any difference to a man's responsibility for something that he foresaw, that he felt no desire for it, either as an end or as a means to an end. Using the language of intention more correctly, and avoiding Sidgwick's faulty conception, we may state the thesis thus: it does not make any difference to a man's responsibility for an effect of his action which he can foresee, that he does not intend it. Now this sounds rather edifying; it is I think quite characteristic of very bad degenerations of thought on such questions that they sound edifying. We can see what it amounts to by considering an example. Let us suppose that a man has a responsibility for the maintenance of some child. Therefore deliberately to withdraw support from it is a bad sort of thing for him to do. It would be bad for him to withdraw its maintenance because he didn't want to maintain it any longer; *and* also bad for him to withdraw it because by doing so he would, let us say, compel someone else to do something. (We may suppose for the sake of argument that compelling that person to do that thing is in itself quite admirable.) But now he has to choose between doing something disgraceful and going to prison; if he goes to prison, it will follow that he withdraws support from the child. By Sidgwick's doctrine, there is no difference in his responsibility for ceasing to maintain the child, between the case where he does it for its own sake or as a means to some other purpose, and when it happens as a foreseen and unavoidable consequence of his going to prison rather than do something disgraceful. It follows that he must weigh up the relative badness of withdrawing support from the child and of doing the

[5] *Nicomachean Ethics* 1178ᵇ 16.

disgraceful thing; and it may easily be that the disgraceful thing is in fact a less vicious action than intentionally withdrawing support from the child would be; if then the fact that withdrawing support from the child is a side-effect of his going to prison does not make any difference to his responsibility, this consideration will incline him to do the disgraceful thing; which can still be pretty bad. And of course, once he has started to look at the matter in this light, the only reasonable thing for him to consider will be the consequences and not the intrinsic badness of this or that action. So that, given that he judges reasonably that no *great* harm will come of it, he can do a much more disgraceful thing than deliberately withdrawing support from the child. And if his calculations turn out in fact wrong, it will appear that he was not responsible for the consequences, because he did not foresee them. For in fact Sidgwick's thesis leads to its being quite impossible to estimate the badness of an action except in the light of *expected* consequences. But if so, then *you* must estimate the badness in the light of the consequences *you* expect; and so it will follow that you can exculpate yourself from the *actual* consequences of the most discraceful actions, so long as you can make out a case for not having foreseen them. Whereas I should contend that a man is responsible for the bad consequences of his bad actions, but gets no credit for the good ones; and contrariwise is not responsible for the bad consequences of good actions.

The denial of *any* distinction between foreseen and intended consequences, as far as responsibility is concerned, was not made by Sidgwick in developing any one 'method of ethics'; he made this important move on behalf of everybody and just on its own account; and I think it plausible to suggest that *this* move on the part of Sidgwick explains the difference between old-fashioned Utilitarianism and that *consequentialism*, as I name it, which marks him and every English academic moral philosopher since him. By it, the kind of consideration which would formerly have been regarded as a temptation, the kind of consideration urged upon men by wives and flattering friends, was given a status by moral philosophers in their theories.

It is a necessary feature of consequentialism that it is a shallow philosophy. For there are always borderline cases in ethics. Now if you are either an Aristotelian, or a believer in divine law, you will deal with a borderline case by considering whether doing such-and-such in such-and-such circumstances is, say, murder, or is an act of injustice; and according as you decide it is or it isn't, you judge it to be a thing to do or not. This would be the method of casuistry; and while it may lead you to stretch a point on the circumference, it will not permit you to destroy the centre. But if you are a consequentialist, the question 'What is it right to do in such-and-such circumstances?' is a stupid one to raise. The casuist raises such a question only to ask 'Would it be *permissible* to do so-and-so?' or 'Would it be permissible *not* to do so-and-so?' Only if it would *not* be permissible *not* to do so-and-so could he say '*This* would be *the* thing to do.'[6] Otherwise, though he may speak *against* some action, he cannot prescribe any—for in an *actual* case, the circumstances (beyond the ones imagined) might suggest all sorts of possibilities, and you can't know in advance what the possibilities are going to be. Now the consequentialist has no footing on which to say 'This would be permissible, this not'; because by his own hypothesis, it is the consequences that are to decide, and he has no business to pretend that he can lay it down what possible twists a man could give doing this or that; the most he can say is: a man must not *bring about* this or that; he has no right to say he will, in an actual case, bring about such-and-such unless he does so-and-so. Further, the consequentialist, in order to be imagining borderline cases at all, has of course to assume some sort of law or standard according to which this is a borderline case. Where then does he get the standard from? In practice the answer invariably is: from the standards current in his society or his circle. And it has in fact been the mark of all these philosophers that they have been extremely conventional; they have nothing in them by which to revolt against the conventional standards of their sort of people; it is impossible that they should be profound. But the chance that a whole range of conventional standards will be decent is small. Finally, the point of considering hypothetical situations, perhaps very improbable ones, *seems* to be to elicit from yourself or someone else a hypothetical decision to do something of a bad kind. I don't doubt this has the effect of predisposing people—who will never get into the situations for which they have made hypothetical choices—to consent to similar bad actions, or to praise and flatter those imagined as doing them, so long as their crowd does so too, when the desperate circumstances imagined don't hold at all.

Those who recognize the origins of the notions of 'obligation' and of the emphatic, 'moral', *ought*, in the divine-law conception of ethics, but who reject the notion of a divine legislator, sometimes look about for the possibility of retaining a law conception without a divine legislator. This search, I think, has some interest in it. Perhaps the first thing that suggests itself is the 'norms' of a society. But just as one cannot be impressed by Butler when one reflects what conscience can tell people to do, so, I think, one cannot be impressed by this idea if one reflects what the 'norms' of a

[6] Necessarily a rare case: for the positive precepts, e.g. 'Honour your parents', hardly ever prescribe, and seldom even necessitate, any particular action.

society can be like. That legislation can be 'for oneself' I reject as absurd; whatever you do 'for yourself' may be admirable; but is not legislating. Once one sees this, one may say: I have to frame my own rules, and these are the best I can frame, and I shall go by them until I know something better: as a man might say, 'I shall go by the customs of my ancestors.' Whether this leads to good or evil will depend on the *content* of the rules or of the customs of one's ancestors. If one is lucky it will lead to good. Such an attitude would be hopeful in this at any rate: it seems to have in it some Socratic doubt where, from having to fall back on such expedients, it should be clear that Socratic doubt is good; in fact rather generally it must be good for anyone to think 'Perhaps in some way I can't see, I may be on a bad path, perhaps I am hopelessly wrong in some essential way.' The search for 'norms' might lead someone to look for laws of nature, as if the universe were a legislator; but in the present day this is not likely to lead to good results: it might lead one to eat the weaker according to the laws of nature, but would hardly lead anyone nowadays to notions of justice; the pre-Socratic feeling about justice as comparable to the balance or harmony which kept things going is very remote to us.

There is another possibility here: 'obligation' may be contractual. Just as we look at the law to find out what a man subject to it is required by it to do, so we look at a contract to find out what the man who has made it is required by it to do. Thinkers, admittedly remote from us, might have the idea of a *foedus rerum*, of the universe not as a legislator but as the embodiment of a contract. Then if you could find out what the contract was, you would learn your obligations under it. Now, you cannot be under a law unless it has been promulgated to you; and the thinkers who believed in 'natural divine law' held that it was promulgated to every grown man in his knowledge of good and evil. Similarly you cannot be in a contract without having contracted, i.e. given signs of entering upon the contract. Just possibly, it might be argued that the use of language which one makes in the ordinary conduct of life amounts in some sense to giving the signs of entering into various contracts. If anyone had this theory, we should want to see it worked out. I suspect that it would be largely formal; it might be possible to construct a system embodying the law (whose status might be compared to that of 'laws' of logic): 'what's sauce for the goose is sauce for the gander,' but hardly one descending to such particularities as the prohibition on murder or sodomy. Also, while it is clear that you can be subject to a law that you do not acknowledge and have not thought of as law, it does not seem reasonable to say that you can enter upon a contract without knowing that you are doing so; such ignorance is usually held to be destructive of the nature of a contract.

It might remain to look for 'norms' in human virtues: just as *man* has so many teeth, which is certainly not the average number of teeth men have, but is the number of teeth for the species, so perhaps the species *man*, regarded not just biologically, but from the point of view of the activity of thought and choice in regard to the various departments of life—powers and faculties and use of things needed—'has' such-and-such virtues: and this 'man' with the complete set of virtues is the 'norm', as 'man' with, e.g., a complete set of teeth is a norm. But in *this* sense 'norm' has ceased to be roughly equivalent to 'law'. In *this* sense the notion of a 'norm' brings us nearer to an Aristotelian than a law conception of ethics. There is, I think, no harm in that; but if someone looked in this direction to give 'norm' a sense, then he ought to recognize what has happened to the term 'norm', which he wanted to mean 'law—without bringing God in': it has ceased to mean 'law' at all; and *so* the expressions 'moral obligation', 'the moral ought', and 'duty' are best put on the Index, if he can manage it.

But meanwhile—is it not clear that there are several concepts that need investigating simply as part of the philosophy of psychology and—as I should recommend—*banishing ethics totally* from our minds? Namely—to begin with: 'action', 'intention', 'pleasure', 'wanting'. More will probably turn up if we start with these. Eventually it might be possible to advance to considering the concept of a virtue; with which, I suppose, we should be beginning some sort of a study of ethics.

I will end by describing the advantages of using the word 'ought' in a non-emphatic fashion, and not in a special 'moral' sense; of discarding the term 'wrong' in a 'moral' sense, and using such notions as 'unjust'.

It is possible, if one is allowed to proceed just by giving examples, to distinguish between the intrinsically unjust, and what is unjust given the circumstances. Seriously to get a man judicially punished for something which it can be clearly seen he has not done is intrinsically unjust. This might be done, of course, and often has been done, in all sorts of ways; by suborning false witnesses, by a rule of law by which something is 'deemed' to be the case which is admittedly not the case as a matter of fact, and by open insolence on the part of the judges and powerful people when they more or less openly say: 'A fig for the fact that you did not do it; we mean to sentence you for it all the same.' What is unjust given, e.g., normal circumstances is to deprive people of their ostensible property without legal procedure, not to pay debts, not to keep contracts, and a host of other things of the kind. Now, the circumstances can clearly make a great deal of difference in estimating the justice or injustice of such procedures as these; and these circumstances may *sometimes* include expected consequences; for example, a man's claim to a bit of property can become a nullity when its seizure and use can avert some obvious disaster: as, e.g., if you could use a machine of his to produce an explosion in which it would be destroyed, but by means of which you could divert a flood or make a gap which a fire could not jump. Now this certainly does not mean that what would ordinarily be an act of injustice, but is not intrinsically unjust, can always be rendered just by a reasonable calculation of better consequences; far from it; but the problems that would be raised in an attempt to draw a boundary line (or boundary area) here are obviously complicated. And while there are certainly some general remarks which ought to be made here, and some boundaries that can be drawn, the decision on particular cases would for the most part be determined κατὰ τὸν ὀρθὸν λόγον—'according to what's reasonable'—e.g. that *such-and-such* a delay of payment of a *such-and-such* debt to a person *so* circumstanced, on the part of a person *so* circumstanced, would or would not be unjust, is really only to be decided 'according to what's reasonable'; and for this there can *in principle* be no canon other than giving a few examples. That is to say, while it is because of a big gap in philosophy that we can give no general account of the concept of virtue and of the concept of justice, but have to proceed, using the concepts, only by giving examples; still there is an area where it is not because of any gap, but is in principle the case, that there is no account except by way of examples: and that is where the canon is 'what's reasonable': which of course is *not* a canon.

That is all I wish to say about what is just in some circumstances, unjust in others; and about the way in which expected consequences can play a part in determining what is just. Returning to my example of the intrinsically unjust: if a procedure *is* one of judicially punishing a man for what he is clearly understood not to have done, there can be absolutely no argument about the description of this as unjust. No circumstances, and no expected consequences, which do *not* modify the description of the procedure as one of judicially punishing a man for what he is known not to have done can modify the description of it as unjust. Someone who attempted to dispute this would only be pretending not to know what 'unjust' means: for this is a paradigm case of injustice.

And here we see the superiority of the term 'unjust' over the terms 'morally right' and 'morally wrong'. For in the context of English moral philosophy since Sidgwick it appears legitimate to discuss whether it *might* be 'morally right' in some circumstances to adopt that procedure; but it cannot be argued that the procedure would in any circumstances be just.

Now I am not able to do the philosophy involved—and I think that no one in the present situation of English philosophy *can* do the philosophy involved—but it is clear that a good man is a just man; and a just man is a man who habitually refuses to commit or participate in any unjust actions for fear of any consequences, or to obtain any advantage, for himself or anyone else. Perhaps no one will disagree. But, it will be said, what *is* unjust is sometimes determined by expected consequences; and certainly that is true. But there are cases where it is not: now if someone says, 'I agree, but all this wants a lot of explaining,' then he is right, and, what is more, the situation at present is that we can't do the explaining; we lack the philosophic equipment. But if someone really thinks, *in advance*,[7] that it is open to question whether such an action as procuring the judicial execution of the innocent should be quite excluded from consideration—I do not want to argue with him; he shows a corrupt mind.

In such cases our moral philosophers seek to impose a dilemma upon us. 'If we have a case where the term "unjust" applies purely in virtue of a factual description, can't one raise the question whether one sometimes conceivably ought to do injustice? If "what is unjust" is determined by consideration of whether it is *right* to do so-and-so in such-and-such circumstances, then the question whether it is "right" to commit injustice can't arise, just because "wrong" has been built into the definition of injustice. But if we have a case where the description "unjust" applies purely in virtue of the facts, without bringing "wrong" in, then the question can arise whether one "ought" perhaps to commit an injustice, whether it might not be "right" to. And of course "ought" and "right" are being used in their *moral* senses here. Now either you must decide what is "morally right" in the light of certain *other* "principles", or you make a "principle" about *this* and decide that an injustice is never "right"; but even if you do the latter you are going beyond the facts; you are making a decision that you will not, or that it is wrong to, commit injustice. But in either case, *if* the term "unjust" is determined simply by the facts, it is not the term "unjust" that determines that the term "wrong" applies, but a decision that injustice is *wrong*, together with the diagnosis of the "factual" description as entailing injustice. But the man who makes an absolute decision that injustice is "wrong" has no footing on which to criticize someone who does *not* make that decision as judging falsely.'

[7] If he thinks it in the concrete situation, he is of course merely a normally tempted human being. In discussion when this paper was read, as was perhaps to be expected, this case was produced: a government is required to have an innocent man tried, sentenced and executed under threat of a 'hydrogen bomb war'. It would seem strange to me to have much hope of so averting a war threatened by such men as made this demand. But the most important thing about the way in which cases like this are invented in discussions, is the assumption that only two courses are open: here, compliance and open defiance. No one can say in advance of such a situation what the possibilities are going to be—e.g. that there is none of stalling by a feigned willingness to comply, accompanied by a skilfully arranged 'escape' of the victim.

In this argument 'wrong' of course is explained as meaning 'morally wrong', and all the atmosphere of the term is retained while its substance is guaranteed quite null. Now let us remember that 'morally wrong' is the term which is the heir of the notion 'illicit', or 'what there is an obligation *not* to do'; which belongs in a divine-law theory of ethics. Here it really does add something to the description 'unjust' to say there is an obligation not to do it; for what obliges is the divine law—as rules oblige in a game. So if the divine law obliges not to commit injustice by forbidding injustice, it really does add something to the description 'unjust' to say there is an obligation not to do it. And it is because 'morally wrong' is the heir of this concept, but an heir that is cut off from the family of concepts from which it sprang, that 'morally wrong' *both* goes beyond the mere factual description 'unjust' *and* seems to have no discernible content except a certain compelling force, which I should call purely psychological. And such is the force of the term that philosophers actually suppose that the divine law notion can be dismissed as making no essential difference even if it is held—*because* they think that a 'practical principle' running 'I *ought* (i.e. am morally obliged) to obey divine laws' is required for the man who believes in divine laws. But actually *this* notion of obligation is a notion which only operates in the context of law. And I should be inclined to congratulate the present-day moral philosophers on depriving 'morally ought' of its now delusive appearance of content, if only they did not manifest a detestable desire to retain the atmosphere of the term.

It may be possible, if we are resolute, to discard the term 'morally ought', and simply return to the ordinary 'ought', which, we ought to notice, is such an extremely frequent term of human language that it is difficult to imagine getting on without it. Now if we do return to it, can't it reasonably be asked whether one might ever need to commit injustice, or whether it won't be the best thing to do? Of course it can. And the answers will be various. One man—a philosopher—may say that since justice is a virtue, and injustice a vice, and virtues and vices are built up by the performance of the actions in which they are instanced, an act of injustice will tend to make a man bad; and essentially the flourishing of a man *qua* man consists in his being good (e.g. in virtues); but for any *X* to which such terms apply, *X* needs what makes it flourish, so a man needs, or ought to perform, only virtuous actions; and even if, as it must be admitted may happen, he flourishes less, or not at all, in inessentials, by avoiding injustice, his life is spoiled in essentials by not avoiding injustice—so he still needs to perform only just actions. That is roughly how Plato and Aristotle talk; but it can be seen that philosophically there is a huge gap, at present unfillable as far as we are concerned, which needs to be filled by an account of human nature, human action, the type of characteristic a virtue is, and above all of human 'flourishing'. And it is the last concept that appears the most doubtful. For it is a bit much to swallow that a man in pain and hunger and poor and friendless is flourishing, as Aristotle himself admitted. Further, someone might say that one at least needed to stay alive to flourish. Another man unimpressed by all that will say in a hard case 'What we need is such-and-such, which we won't get without doing this (which is unjust)—so this is what we ought to do.' Another man, who does not follow the rather elaborate reasoning of the philosophers, simply says 'I know it is in any case a disgraceful thing to say that one had better commit this unjust action.' The man who believes in divine laws will say perhaps 'It is forbidden, and however it looks, it cannot be to anyone's profit to commit injustice'; he like the Greek philosophers can think in terms of flourishing. If he is a Stoic, he is apt to have a decidedly strained notion of what flourishing consists in; if he is a Jew or Christian, he need not have any very distinct notion: the way it will profit him to abstain from injustice is something that he leaves it to God to determine, himself only saying 'It can't do me any good to go against his law.' (He also hopes for a great reward in a new life later on, e.g. at the coming of Messiah; but in this he is relying on special promises.)

It is left to modern moral philosophy—the moral philosophy of all the well-known English ethicists since Sidgwick—to construct systems according to which the man who says 'We need such-and-such, and will only get it this way' *may* be a virtuous character: that is to say, it is left open to debate whether such a procedure as the judicial punishment of the innocent may not in some circumstances be the 'right' one to adopt; and though the present Oxford moral philosophers would accord a man *permission* to 'make it his principle' not to do such a thing, they teach a philosophy according to which the particular consequences of such an action *could* 'morally' be taken into account by a man who was debating what to do; and if they were such as to accord with his ends, it might be a step in his moral education to frame a moral principle under which he 'managed' (to use Mr Nowell-Smith's phrase[8])' to bring the action; or it might be a new 'decision of principle', making which was an advance in the formation of his moral thinking (to adopt Mr Hare's conception), to decide: in such-and-such circumstances one ought to procure the judicial condemnation of the innocent. And that is my complaint.

[8] P. H. Nowell-Smith, *Ethics* (Harmondsworth, 1954), 308.

2

MORALITY, THE PECULIAR INSTITUTION

BERNARD WILLIAMS

Morality is a special system, a particular variety of ethical thought. Let me explain what I take it to be, and why we would be better off without it.

The important thing about morality is its spirit, its underlying aims, and the general picture of ethical life it implies. In order to see them, we shall need to look carefully at a particular concept, *moral obligation*. The mere fact that it uses a notion of obligation is not what makes morality special. There is an everyday notion of obligation, as one consideration among others, and it is ethically useful. Morality is distinguished by the special notion of obligation it uses, and by the significance it gives to it. It is this special notion that I shall call 'moral obligation'. Morality is not one determinate set of ethical thoughts. It embraces a range of ethical outlooks; and morality is so much with us that moral philosophy spends much of its time discussing the differences between those outlooks, rather than the difference between all of them and everything else. They are not all equally typical or instructive examples of the morality system, though they do have in common the idea of moral obligation. The philosopher who has given the purest, deepest, and most thorough representation of morality is Kant. But morality is not an invention of philosophers. It is the outlook, or, incoherently, part of the outlook, of almost all of us.

In the morality system, moral obligation is expressed in one especially important kind of deliberative conclusion—a conclusion that is directed towards what to do, governed by moral reasons, and concerned with a particular situation. (There are also general obligations, and we shall come back to them later.) Not every conclusion of a particular moral deliberation, even within the morality system, expresses an obligation. To go no further, some moral conclusions merely announce that you *may* do something. Those do not express an obligation, but they are in a sense still

From Bernard Williams, *Ethics and the Limits of Philosophy* (London: Fontana, 1985), 174–96. Reprinted by permission.

governed by the idea of obligation: you ask whether you are under an obligation, and decide that you are not.

This description is in terms of the output or conclusion of moral deliberation. The moral considerations that go into a deliberation may themselves take the form of obligations, but one would naturally say that they did not need to do so. I might, for instance, conclude that I was under an obligation to act in a certain way, because it was for the best that a certain outcome should come about and I could bring it about in that way. However, there is a pressure within the morality system to represent every consideration that goes into a deliberation and yields a particular obligation as being itself a general obligation; so if I am now under an obligation to do something that would be for the best, this will be because I have some general obligation, perhaps among others, to do what is for the best. We shall see later how this happens.

The fact that moral obligation is a kind of practical conclusion explains several of its features. An obligation applies to someone with respect to an action—it is an obligation to do something—and the action must be in the agent's power. '*Ought* implies *can*' is a formula famous in this connection. As a general statement about *ought* it is untrue, but it must be correct if it is taken as a condition on what can be a particular obligation, where that is practically concluded. If my deliberation issues in something I cannot do, then I must deliberate again. The question of what counts as in the agent's power is notoriously problematical, not only because of large and unnerving theories claiming that everything (or everything psychological) is determined, but also because it is simply unclear what it means to say that someone can act, or could have acted, in a certain way. To say anything useful about these problems needs a wide-ranging discussion that I shall not attempt here.[1] What I shall have to say, however, will suggest that morality, in this as in other respects, encounters the common problems in a peculiarly acute form.

Another feature of moral obligations in this sense is that they cannot conflict, ultimately, really, or at the end of the line. This will follow directly from the last point, that what I am obliged to do must be in my power, if one grants a further principle (it has been called the 'agglomeration principle'), that if I am obliged to do *X* and obliged to do *Y*, then I am obliged to do *X* and *Y*. This requirement, too, reflects the practical shape of this notion of obligation. In an ordinary sense of 'obligation', not con-

[1] I touch briefly on some points later in this chapter. Most discussions of free will do not pay enough attention to the point that causal explanation may have a different impact on different parts of our thought about action and responsibility. It is worth consideration that deliberation requires only *can*, while blame requires *could have*.

trolled by these special requirements, obligations obviously can conflict. One of the most common occasions of mentioning them at all is when they do.[2]

The philosopher David Ross invented a terminology, still sometimes used, for discussing the conflict of obligations, which distinguished between prima facie and actual obligations. A *prima-facie* obligation is a conclusion, supported by moral considerations, which is a candidate for being one's actual obligation. It will be the proper conclusion of one's moral deliberation if it is not outweighed by another obligation. Ross tried to explain (without much success) why a merely *prima-facie* obligation—one that is eventually outweighed—is more than an apparent obligation. It is to be seen as exerting some force on the place of decision, but not enough, granted the competition, to get into that place. The effect, in more concrete terms, is that the considerations that supported the defeated *prima-facie* obligation can come to support some other, actual, obligation. If I have for good and compelling reasons broken a promise, I may acquire an actual obligation to do something else because of that, such as compensate the person who has been let down.

It is not at all clear why I should be under this further obligation, since it is one's own business, on this view of things, to observe one's obligations, and I shall have done that. No actual obligation has been broken. This has a comforting consequence, that I should not blame myself. I may blame myself for something else, such as getting into the situation, but it is mistaken to blame or reproach myself for not doing the rejected action: self-reproach belongs with broken obligations, and, it has turned out, there was no obligation. It is conceded that I may reasonably feel bad about it, but this feeling is distinguished by the morality system from remorse or self-reproach, for instance under the title 'regret', which is not a moral feeling. This reclassification is important, and very characteristic of what happens when the ethical is contracted to the moral. To say that your feelings about something done involuntarily, or as the lesser of two evils, are to be understood as regret, a non-moral feeling, implies that you should feel towards those actions as you feel towards things that merely happen, or towards the actions of others. The thought *I did it* has no special significance; what is significant is whether I voluntarily did what I ought to have done. This turns our attention away from an important dimension of ethical experience, which lies in the distinction simply between what one

[2] I have discussed the question of conflict in several essays, in both *Problems of the Self* (Cambridge, 1973) and *Moral Luck* (Cambridge, 1981). It is important that, if it were logically impossible for two actual obligations to conflict, I could not get into a situation of their conflicting even through my own fault. What is it supposed that I get into?

has done and what one has not done. That can be as important as the distinction between the voluntary and the non-voluntary.[3]

Moral obligation is inescapable. I may acquire an obligation voluntarily, as when I make a promise: in that case, indeed, it is usually said that it has to be voluntarily made to be a promise at all, though there is a grey area here, as with promises made under constraint. In other cases, I may be under an obligation through no choice of mine. But, either way, once I am under the obligation, there is no escaping it, and the fact that a given agent would prefer not to be in this system or bound by its rules will not excuse him; nor will blaming him be based on a misunderstanding. Blame is the characteristic reaction of the morality system. The remorse or self-reproach or guilt I have already mentioned is the characteristic first-personal reaction within the system, and if an agent never felt such sentiments, he would not belong to the morality system or be a full moral agent in its terms. The system also involves blame between persons, and unless there were such a thing, these first-personal reactions would doubtless not be found, since they are formed by internalization. But it is possible for particular agents who belong to the system never to blame anyone, in the sense of expressing blame and perhaps even of feeling the relevant sentiments. They might, for instance, be scrupulously sceptical about what was in other people's power. The point that self-blame or remorse requires one's action to have been voluntary is only a special application of a general rule, that blame of anyone is directed to the voluntary. The moral law is more exigent than the law of an actual liberal republic, because it allows no emigration, but it is unequivocally just in its ideas of responsibility.

In this respect, utilitarianism is a marginal member of the morality system. It has a strong tradition of thinking that blame and other social reactions should be allocated in a way that will be socially useful, and while this might lead to their being directed to the voluntary, equally it might not. This follows consistently from applying the utilitarian criterion to all actions, including the social actions of expressing blame and so forth. The same principle can be extended to unexpressed blame and critical thoughts; indeed, at another level, a utilitarian might well ask whether the most useful policy might not be to forget that the point of blame, on utilitarian grounds, was usefulness. These manœuvres do seem to receive a check when it comes to self-reproach and the sense of moral obligation. Utilitarians are often immensely conscientious people, who work for hu-

[3] This point is discussed in my essay 'Moral Luck', in the book of that title. It illustrates the general point that the morality system lays particularly heavy weight on the unsure structure of voluntariness.

manity and give up meat for the sake of the animals. They think this is what they morally ought to do and feel guilty if they do not live up to their own standards. They do not, and perhaps could not, ask: How useful is it that I think and feel like this? It is because of such motivations, and not only because of logical features, that utilitarianism in most versions is a kind of morality, if a marginal one.

The sense that moral obligation is inescapable, that what I am obliged to do is what I *must* do, is the first-personal end of the conception already mentioned, that moral obligation applies to people even if they do not want it to. The third-personal aspect is that moral judgement and blame can apply to people even if, at the limit, they want to live outside that system altogether. From the perspective of morality, there is nowhere outside the system, or at least nowhere for a responsible agent. Taking Kant's term, we may join these two aspects in saying that moral obligation is *categorical.*

I shall come back later to people outside the system. There is more that needs to be said first about what a moral obligation is for someone within the system. It is hard to agree that the course of action which, on a given occasion, there is most moral reason to take must necessarily count as a moral obligation. There are actions (also policies, attitudes, and so on) that are either more or less than obligations. They may be heroic or very fine actions, which go beyond what is obligatory or demanded. Or they may be actions that from an ethical point of view it would be agreeable or worthwhile or a good idea to do, without one's being required to do them. The point is obvious in terms of people's reactions. People may be greatly admired, or merely well thought of, for actions they would not be blamed for omitting. How does the morality system deal with the considerations that seemingly do not yield obligations?

One way in which the central, deontological, version of morality deals with them is to try to make as many as possible into obligations. (It has a particular motive for the reductivist enterprise of trying to make all ethical considerations into one type). There are some instructive examples of this in the work of Ross, whose terminology of prima-facie obligations I have already mentioned. He lists several types of what he regards as general obligations or, as he also calls them, duties.[4] The first type includes what everyone calls an obligation, keeping promises and, by a fairly natural extension, telling the truth. The second class involves 'duties of gratitude': to do good to those who have done services for you. But it is not really clear that these are *duties*, unless the benefactor (as the word 'services'

[4] W. D. Ross, *The Right and the Good* (Oxford, 1930), 21 ff.

may imply) has acquired a right to expect a return—in which case, it will follow from some implied promise, and the obligation will belong with the first type. Good deeds I have not asked for may indeed be oppressive, but I should not simply take that oppression for obligation.[5]

What Ross is trying to force into the mould of obligation is surely a different ethical idea, that it is a sign of good character to want to return benefits. This characteristic is not the same thing as a disposition to do what one is morally obliged to do. A different ethical thought, again, is disguised in Ross's third class, which he calls 'duties of justice'. What he says about this is extraordinary:

> [these duties] rest on the fact or possibility of a distribution of pleasure or happiness or the means thereto which is not in accordance with the merits of the persons concerned; in which case there arises a duty to upset or prevent such a distribution.

There are such things as duties or obligations of justice, but this incitement to insurrection against the capitalist economy (or any other, come to that) can hardly be the right account of what they are. The requirements of justice concern, in the first place, *what ought to happen*. The way in which a given requirement of justice relates to what a given person has reason to do, or more specifically is under an obligation to do, is a matter of how that person stands to the requirement. In politics, the question of how far personal action stands from the desirable—the *utopia measure*, as it might be called—is itself one of the first, and one of the first ethical, questions.

It is a mistake of morality to try to make everything into obligations. But the reasons for the mistake go deep. Here we should recall that what is *ordinarily* called an obligation does not necessarily have to win in a conflict of moral considerations. Suppose you are under an everyday obligation—to visit a friend, let us say (a textbook example), because you have promised to. You are then presented with a unique opportunity, at a conflicting time and place, to further significantly some important cause. (To make the example realistic, one should put in more detail; and, as often in moral philosophy, if one puts in the detail the example may begin to dissolve. There is the question of your friend's attitude towards the cause and also towards your support of the cause. If he or she favours both, or merely the second, and would release you from the promise if you could get in touch, only the stickiest moralist would find a difficulty. If the friend would not release you, you may wonder what sort of friend you have . . . But it should not be hard for each person reading this to find some example that will

[5] This is so even when the good deeds are part of a general practice that others hope I will join. The point is admirably pressed by Robert Nozick in *Anarchy, State, and Utopia* (New York, 1974), ch. 5.

make the point.) You may reasonably conclude that you should take the opportunity to further the cause.[6] But obligations have a moral stringency, which means that breaking them attracts blame. The only thing that can be counted on to cancel this, within the economy of morality, is that the rival action should represent another and more stringent obligation. Morality encourages the idea, *only an obligation can beat an obligation.*[7]

Yet how can this action of yours have been an obligation, unless it came from some more general obligation? It will not be easy to say what the general obligation is. You are not under an unqualified obligation to pursue this cause, nor to do everything you possibly can for causes you have adopted. We are left with the limp suggestion that one is under an obligation to assist some important cause on occasions that are specially propitious for assisting it. The pressure of the demand within the morality system to find a general obligation to back a particular one—what may be called the *obligation-out, obligation-in* principle—has a clearer result in those familiar cases where some general ethical consideration is focused onto a particular occasion by an emergency, such as the obligation to try to assist someone in danger. I am not under an obligation to assist all people at risk, or to go round looking for people at risk to assist. Confronted[8] with someone at risk, many feel that they are under an obligation to try to help (though not at excessive danger to themselves, and so on: various sensible qualifications come to mind). In this case, unlike the last, the underlying obligation seems ready-made. The immediate claim on me, 'In this emer-

[6] The example is of a conflict between an obligation and a consideration that is not at first sight an obligation. It may very readily represent another conflict as well, between private and public. For various considerations on this, and particularly on the role of utilitarian considerations in public life, see the essays in Stuart Hampshire (ed.), *Public and Private Morality* (Cambridge, 1978).

[7] Morality encourages the idea, certainly in cases of this kind, but it does not always insist on it, at least in the form that an obligation of mine can be overridden only by another obligation of mine. If some vital interest of mine would have to be sacrificed in order to carry out a promise, particularly if the promise were relatively unimportant, even the severest moralist may agree that I would have the right to break the promise, without requiring that I would be under an obligation to do so (I owe this point to Gilbert Harman). This is correct but, unless the promise is very trivial, the severe moralist will agree, I suspect, only if the interests involved are indeed vital. This suggests an interpretation under which my obligation would indeed be beaten by an obligation, but not one of mine. In insisting that only vital interests count, it is likely that the moralist, when he says that I have the right to safeguard my interest, does not mean simply that I may do that, but that I have what has been called a claim-right to do so: that is to say, others are under an obligation not to impede me in doing so. Then my original obligation will be cancelled by an obligation *of the promissee*, to waive his or her right to performance.

[8] What counts as being confronted is a real question, and a very practical one for doctors in particular. I touch on the question later, in giving an account of immediacy which does not need the *obligation-out, obligation-in* principle. This is notoriously a kind of obligation increasingly unrecognized in modern cities, to the extent that it is not saluted even by people guiltily leaving the scene.

gency, I am under an obligation to help,' is thought to come from, 'One is under this general obligation: to help in an emergency.' If we add the thought that many, perhaps any, moral considerations could overrule some obligation on some occasion, we find that many, perhaps all, such considerations are related to some general obligations, even if they are not the simple and unqualified ones suggested by Ross's reductionism.

Once the journey into more general obligations has started, we may begin to get into trouble—not just philosophical trouble, but conscience trouble—with finding room for morally indifferent actions. I have already mentioned the possible moral conclusion that one *may* take some particular course of action. That means that there is nothing else I am obliged to do. But if we have accepted general and indeterminate obligations to further various moral objectives, as the last set of thoughts encourages us to do, they will be waiting to provide work for idle hands, and the thought can gain a footing (I am not saying that it has to) that I could be better employed than in doing something I am under no obligation to do, and, if I could be, then I ought to be: I am under an obligation not to waste time in doing things I am under no obligation to do. At this stage, certainly, only an obligation can beat an obligation, and in order to do what I wanted to do, I shall need one of those fraudulent items, a duty to myself. If obligation is allowed to structure ethical thought, there are several natural ways in which it can come to dominate life altogether.

In order to see around the intimidating structure that morality has made out of the idea of obligation, we need an account of what obligations are when they are rightly seen as merely one kind of ethical consideration among others. This account will help to lead us away from morality's special notion of moral obligation, and eventually out of the morality system altogether.

We need, first, the notion of *importance*. Obviously enough, various things are important to various people (which does not necessarily mean that those things are important for those people's interests). This involves a relative notion of importance, which we might also express by saying that someone *finds* a given thing important. Beyond this merely relative idea, we have another notion, of something's being, simply, important (important *überhaupt*, as others might put it, or important *period*). It is not at all clear what it is for something to be, simply, important. It does not mean that it is important to the universe: in that sense, nothing is important. Nor does it mean that it is as a matter of fact something that most human beings find important; nor that it is something people ought to find important. I doubt that there can be an incontestable account of this idea; the explanations people give of it are necessarily affected by what they find important.

It does not matter for the present discussion that this notion is poorly understood. I need only three things of it. One is that there is such a notion. Another is that if something is important in the relative sense to somebody, this does not necessarily imply that he or she thinks it is, simply, important. It may be of the greatest importance to Henry that his stamp collection be completed with a certain stamp, but even Henry may see that it is not, simply, important. A significant ideal lies in this: people should find important a number of things that are, simply, important, as well as many things that are not, and they should be able to tell the difference between them.

The third point is that the question of importance, and above all the question of what is, simply, important, needs to be distinguished from questions of *deliberative priority*. A consideration has high deliberative priority for us if we give it heavy weighting against other considerations in our deliberations. (This includes two ideas, that when it occurs in our deliberations, it outweighs most other considerations, and also that it occurs in our deliberations. There are some reasons for treating the second idea separately, and I shall touch on one later, but in general it is simpler to consider them together.)

Importance has some connections with deliberative priority, but they are not straightforward. There are many important things that no one can do much about, and very many that a given person can do nothing about. Again, it may not be that person's business to do anything: there is a deliberative division of labour. Your deliberations are not connected in a simple way even with what is important to you. If you find something important, then that will affect your life in one way or another, and so affect your deliberations, but those effects do not have to be found directly in the content of your deliberations.

A consideration may have high deliberative priority for a particular person, for a group of people, or for everyone. In this way priority is relativized, to people. But it should not be relativized in another way: it should not be marked for subject matter, so that things will have moral or prudential deliberative priority. This would be a misunderstanding. It may be said that moral considerations have a high priority from a moral point of view. If this is so, what it will mean is that someone within the moral system gives those considerations a high priority. It does not define a kind of priority. A major point about deliberative priority is that it can relate considerations of different types.[9] The same thing is true of importance. In a sense, there are kinds of importance, and we naturally say that some things are morally important, others aesthetically important, and so on. But there must be a question at the end, in a particular case or more generally, whether one kind of importance is more important than another kind.

Those who are within the morality system usually think that morality is important. Moreover, morality has by definition something to do with personal conduct, so here importance is likely to have something to do with deliberation. But what it has to do with it depends crucially on the way one understands morality and morality's importance. For utilitarians, what is important is that there should be as much welfare as possible. The connection with deliberation is a subsequent question, and it is entirely open. We saw when we considered indirect utilitarianism how the question is open of what moral considerations should occur in a utilitarian agent's deliberations. More than that, it is open whether any moral considerations at all should occur in them. Some kinds of utilitarian thought have supposed that the best results would follow if people did not think in moral terms at all, and merely (for instance) acted selfishly. With less faith in the invisible hand, others give moral considerations some priority, and some of them, as we have seen, take a highly conscientious line. But for any utilitarian it should always be an empirical question: What are the implications for deliberation of welfare's being important? In this respect, however, there are many utilitarians who belong to the morality system first and are utilitarians second.

At the other extreme, the purest Kantian view locates the importance of morality in the importance of moral motivation itself. What is important is that people should give moral considerations the highest deliberative priority. This view was relentlessly and correctly attacked by Hegel, on the grounds that it gave moral thought no content and also that it was committed to a double-mindedness about the improvement of the world. The content of the moral motivation was the thought of obligation to do certain things, as against mere inclination; the need for that thought implied that individuals were not spontaneously inclined to do those things; its supreme importance implied that it was better so.

Neither view is adequate, and a better view is not going to consist of any simple compromise. Ethical life itself is important, but it can see that things other than itself are important. It contains motivations that indeed serve

[9] The point is related to the discussion of deliberative questions in my *Ethics and the Limits of Philosophy* (London, 1985), ch. 1.

these other ends but at the same time are seen from within that life as part of what make it worth living. On any adequate showing, ethical motivations are going to be important, and this has consequences for how we should deliberate. One consequence is that some kinds of ethical consideration will have high deliberative priority. This is only one way in which ethical motivations may affect people's deliberations. They may equally affect their style and their occasion, among other things.[10]

There is one kind of ethical consideration that directly connects importance and deliberative priority, and this is obligation. It is grounded in the basic issue of what people should be able to rely on. People must rely as far as possible on not being killed or used as a resource, and on having some space and objects and relations with other people they can count as their own. It also serves their interests if, to some extent at least, they can count on not being lied to. One way in which these ends can be served, and perhaps the only way, is by some kind of ethical life; and, certainly, if there is to be ethical life, these ends have to be served by it and within it. *One* way in which ethical life serves them is by encouraging certain motivations, and *one* form of this is to instil a disposition to give the relevant considerations a high deliberative priority—in the most serious of these matters, a virtually absolute priority, so that certain courses of action must come first, while others are ruled out from the beginning. An effective way for actions to be ruled out is that they never come into thought at all, and this is often the best way. One does not feel easy with the man who in the course of a discussion of how to deal with political or business rivals says, 'Of course, we could have them killed, but we should lay that aside right from the beginning.' It should never have come into his hands to be laid aside. It is characteristic of morality that it tends to overlook the possibility that some concerns are best embodied in this way, in deliberative silence.

Considerations that are given deliberative priority in order to secure reliability constitute obligations; corresponding to those obligations are rights, possessed by people who benefit from the obligations. One type of obligations is picked out by the basic and standing importance of the interests they serve. These are all negative in force, concerning what we should not do. Another, and now positive, sort involves the obligations of immediacy. Here, a high deliberative priority is imposed by an emergency, such as the rescue case we considered before. A general ethical recognition of people's vital interests is focused into a deliberative priority by immediacy, and it is immediacy to *me* that generates *my* obligation, one I cannot

[10] It is relevant to recall, as well, a point made in *Ethics and the Limits of Philosophy*, ch. 1: the deliberative considerations that go with a given ethical motivation, such as a virtue, may not be at all simply related to it.

ignore without blame. Two connected things follow from understanding the obligations of emergency in this way. First, we do not after all have to say that the obligation comes from a more general obligation. The point of the negative obligations does lie in their being general; they provide a settled and permanent pattern of deliberative priorities. In the positive kind of case, however, the underlying disposition is a general concern, which is not always expressed in deliberative priority, and what produces an obligation from it is, precisely, the emergency. We need not accept the *obligation-out, obligation-in* principle.

More important, there are ethical consequences of understanding these obligations in this way. Some moralists say that if we regard immediacy or physical nearness as relevant, we must be failing in rationality or imagination; we are irrational if we do not recognize that those starving elsewhere have as big a claim on us as those starving here. These moralists are wrong, at least in trying to base their challenge simply on the structure of obligations. Of course this point does not dispose of the challenge itself. We should be more concerned about the sufferings of people elsewhere. But a correct understanding of what obligation is will make it clearer how we should start thinking about the challenge. We should not banish the category of immediacy, but we must consider what for us, in the modern world, should properly count as immediacy, and what place we have in our lives for such concerns when they are not obligations.

The obligations considered so far involve (negatively) what is fundamentally important and (positively) what is important and immediate. They are both based ultimately on one conception, that each person has a life to lead. People need help but (unless they are very young, very old, or severely handicapped) not all the time. All the time they need not to be killed, assaulted, or arbitrarily interfered with. It is a strength of contractualism to have seen that such positive and negative obligations will follow from these basic interests.[11]

The obligations that are most familiarly so called, those of promises, differ from both of these because what I am obliged to do, considered in itself, may not be important at all. But just because of that, they are an example of the same connection, between obligation and reliability. The institution of promising operates to provide portable reliability, by offering a formula that will confer high deliberative priority on what might otherwise not receive it. This is why it is odd for someone to promise not to kill you—if he does not already give it high priority, why should his promising

[11] The reference to contractualism brings out the point that the account is, in a certain sense, individualist. For some further remarks on this aspect, see the Postscript in *Ethics and the Limits of Philosophy*.

be relied upon to provide it? (There are answers to this question, in special cases, and considering what they might be will help to show how the system works.)

Obligation works to secure reliability, a state of affairs in which people can reasonably expect others to behave in some ways and not in others. It is only one among other ethical ways of doing this. It is one that tries to produce an expectation *that* through an expectation *of*. These kinds of obligation very often command the highest deliberative priority and also present themselves as important—in the case of promises, because they are promises and not simply because of their content. However, we can also see how they need not always command the highest priority, even in ethically well-disposed agents. Reflecting that some end is peculiarly important, and the present action importantly related to it, an agent can reasonably conclude that the obligation may be broken on this occasion, as we noticed before, and indeed this conclusion may be acceptable,[12] in the sense that he can explain within a structure of ethical considerations why he decided as he did. But there is no need for him to call this course another and more stringent obligation. An obligation is a special kind of consideration, with a general relation to importance and immediacy. The case we are considering is simply one in which there is a consideration important enough to outweigh this obligation on this occasion,[13] and it is cleaner just to say so. We should reject morality's other maxim, that only an obligation can beat an obligation.

When a deliberative conclusion embodies a consideration that has the highest deliberative priority and is also of the greatest importance (at least to the agent), it may take a special form and become the conclusion not merely that one should do a certain thing, but that one *must*, and that one cannot do anything else. We may call this a conclusion of practical necessity. Sometimes, of course, 'must' in a practical conclusion is merely relative and means only that some course of action is needed for an end that is not at all a matter of 'must'. 'I must go now' may well be completed '. . . if I am to get to the movies', where there is no suggestion that I have to go to the movies: I merely am going to the movies. We are not concerned with this, but with a 'must' that is unconditional and *goes all the way down*.

It is an interesting question, how a conclusion in terms of what we must

[12] It is a mistake to suppose that it has to be equally acceptable to everyone. Some may have a greater right than others to complain.

[13] This *kind* of occasion? Yes. But particularizing facts, such as that this is the second time (to her, this year), can certainly be relevant.

do, or equally of what we cannot do, differs from a conclusion expressed merely in terms of what we have most reason to do; in particular, how it can be stronger, as it seems to be. (How, in deliberation, can anything stronger be concluded in favour of a course of action than that we have most reason to take it?) I shall not try to discuss this question here.[14] What is immediately relevant is that practical necessity is in no way peculiar to ethics. Someone may conclude that he or she unconditionally must do a certain thing, for reasons of prudence, self-protection, aesthetic or artistic concern, or sheer self-assertion. In some of these cases (basic self-defence, for instance), an ethical outlook may itself license the conclusion. In others, it will disapprove of it. The fundamental point is that a conclusion of practical necessity is the same sort of conclusion whether it is grounded in ethical reasons or not.

Practical necessity, and the experience of reaching a conclusion with that force, is one element that has gone into the idea of moral obligation (this may help to explain the sense, which so many people have, that moral obligation is at once quite special and very familiar). Yet practical necessity, even when it is grounded in ethical reasons, does not necessarily signal an obligation. The course of action the agent 'must' take may not be associated with others' expectations, or with blame for failure. The ethically outstanding or possibly heroic actions I mentioned before, in being more than obligations, are not obligatory, and we cannot usually be asked to do them or be blamed for not doing them. But the agent who does such a thing may feel that he must do it, that there is no alternative for him, while at the same time recognizing that it would not be a demand on others. The thought may come in the form that it is a demand on him, but not on others, because he is different from others; but the difference will then typically turn out to consist in the fact that he is someone who has this very conviction. His feelings, indeed, and his expectations of feelings he will have if he does not act, may well be like those associated with obligations (more like them than morality admits[15]).

I have already mentioned Kant's description of morality as categorical. When he claimed that the fundamental principle of morality was a Categorical Imperative, Kant was not interested in any purely logical distinc-

[14] I have made a suggestion about it in 'Practical Necessity', *Moral Luck*, 124–32.

[15] How alike? This touches on an important question that I cannot pursue here, the distinction between guilt and shame. There is such a distinction, and it is relevant to ethics, but it is much more complex than is usually thought. Above all, it is a mistake to suppose that guilt can be distinguished as a mature and autonomous reaction that has a place in ethical experience, whereas shame is a more primitive reaction that does not. Morality tends to deceive itself about its relations to shame. See my *Shame and Necessity* (Berkeley and Los Angeles, 1993), esp. ch. 4 and n. 1.

tion between forms of what are literally imperatives. He was concerned with the recognition of an *I must* that is unconditional and goes all the way down, but he construed this unconditional practical necessity as being peculiar to morality. He thought it was unconditional in the sense that it did not depend on desire at all: a course of action presented to us with this kind of necessity was one we had reason to take *whatever we might happen to want*, and it was only moral reasons that could transcend desire in that way. As I have introduced it, however, practical necessity need not be independent of desire in so strong a sense. I distinguished a 'must' that is unconditional from one that is conditional on a desire *that the agent merely happens to have*; but a conclusion of practical necessity could itself be the expression of a desire, if the desire were not one that the agent merely happened to have, but was essential to the agent and had to be satisfied. The difference between this conception of practical necessity and Kant's is not of course merely a matter of definition or of logical analysis. Kant's idea of practical necessity is basically this more familiar one, but it is given a particularly radical interpretation, under which the only necessary practical conclusions are those absolutely unconditioned by any desire. For Kant there could be a practical conclusion that was radically unconditioned in this way, because of his picture of the rational self as free from causality, and because there were reasons for action which depended merely on rational agency and not on anything (such as a desire) that the agent might not have had.[16]

Kant also describes the conclusion of practical necessity, understood as peculiar to morality, as a recognition of the demands of moral law, and when he speaks of this in psychological terms, he refers to a special feeling or sentiment, a 'sense of reverence for the law'. Modern moralists are not likely to use those words, but they do not find it hard to recognize what Kant was describing. (Some of them still want to invoke a conception of moral law. Others, reluctant to do so, are using ideas that implicitly involve it.) Kant did not think that the compelling sense of moral necessity, regarded as a feeling, was itself what provided the reason for moral action.

[16] This is connected with the differing conceptions of the self entertained by Kant and by his Hegelian critics: see *Ethics and the Limits of Philosophy*, ch. 1, n. 6. It is important here to distinguish two different ideas. Other people, and indeed I myself, can have an 'external' idea of different ideals and projects that I might have had, for instance if I had been brought up differently: there are few reasons for, and many reasons against, saying that if I had been brought up differently, it would not have been me. This is the area of metaphysical necessity. But there is a different area, of practical necessity, concerned with what are possible lines of action and possible projects for me, granted that I have the ideals and character I indeed have. This is the level at which we must resist the Kantian idea that the truly ethical subject is one for whom nothing is necessary except agency itself. This is also closely related to the matter of real interests, discussed in *Ethics and the Limits of Philosophy*, ch. 3.

As a feeling, it was just a feeling and had no more rational power than any other merely psychological item had. The reason lay not in what that feeling was, but in what it represented, the truth that moral universality was a requirement of practical reason itself.

That truth, as Kant took it to be, meant that morality had an objective foundation, and he took the experience of the moral demand to represent this foundation. However, it must be said that it also significantly misrepresents it. The experience is like being *confronted* with something, a law that is part of the world in which one lives.[17] Yet the power of the moral law, according to Kant, does not lie and could not conceivably lie in anything ouside oneself. Its power lies in its objective foundation, and no experience could adequately represent that kind of objectivity. The objectivity comes from this, that the requirements of practical reason will be met only by leading a life in which moral considerations play a basic and characteristic role; and that role is one they perform only if, unlike other motivations, they present themselves in the form of an objective demand. But then what is it for a consideration to present itself as an objective demand? It cannot consist in its presenting itself as so related to that very argument. It must have some other psychological form, and the form will be, to that extent, misleading.

On Kant's assumptions, however, one can at least come to understand how, and why, such an experience is bound to be misleading, and this will help to make it stable to reflection. If Kant is right, I can come to understand what the 'sense of reverence for the law' is, and not lose my respect for it or for the moral law. This stability is helped by a further thought, that there is one sense in which the law is rightly represented by the experience as being outside me: it is equally in other people. The moral law is the law of the notional republic of moral agents. It is a notional republic, but they are real agents and, because it is rationally self-imposed by each of them, it is a real law.

Once we have ceased to believe in Kant's own foundation or anything like it, we cannot read this experience in this way at all. It is the conclusion of practical necessity, no more and no less, and it seems to come 'from outside' in the way that conclusions of practical necessity always seem to come from outside—from deeply inside. Since ethical considerations are in

[17] The model of a moral law helps to explain why the system should have the difficulties it has with those ethical acts that, as I put it before, are more or less than obligations. It is not surprising that something interpreted as law should leave only the three categories of the required, the forbidden, and the permitted. Kant's own attempts to deal with some problems of these other ethical motives within his framework of duty involve his interpretations (which changed over time) of the traditional distinction between perfect and imperfect duties. On this, see M. J. Gregor, *Laws of Freedom* (New York, 1963), chs. 7–11.

question, the agent's conclusions will not usually be solitary or unsupported, because they are part of an ethical life that is to an important degree shared with others. In this respect, the morality system itself, with its emphasis on the 'purely moral' and personal sentiments of guilt and self-reproach, actually conceals the dimension in which ethical life lies outside the individual.

When we know what the recognition of obligation is, if we still make it the special centre of ethical experience, we are building ethical life around an illusion. Even in Kant's own view, this experience involves a misrepresentation, but it is a necessary and acceptable one, a consequence of transposing objectivity from the transcendental level to the psychological. But if this experience is special only in the psychological mode, then it is worse than a misrepresentation: there is nothing (or nothing special) for it to represent.

Kant's construction also explains how the moral law can unconditionally apply to all people, even if they try to live outside it. Those who do not accept his construction, but still accept the morality system, need to say how moral obligation binds those who refuse it. They need to say how there can be a moral *law* at all.[18] The fact that a law applies to someone always consists in more than a semantic relation; it is not merely that the person falls under some description contained in the law. The law of a state applies to a person because he belongs to a state that can apply power. The law of God applied because God applied it. Kant's moral law applied because as a rational being one had a reason to apply it to oneself. For the moral law to apply now, it can only be that we apply it.

When we say that someone ought to have acted in some required or desirable way in which he has not acted, we sometimes say that *there was a reason* for him to act in that way—he had promised, for instance, or what he actually did violated someone's rights. Although we can say this, it does not seem to be connected in any secure way with the idea that *he had a reason* to act in that way. Perhaps he had no reason at all. In breaking the obligation, he was not necessarily behaving irrationally or unreasonably, but badly. We cannot take for granted that he had a reason to behave well, as opposed to our having various reasons for wishing that he would behave well. How do we treat him? We recognize in fact, very clumsily in the law,

[18] The question of a categorical imperative and its relation to reasons for action has been pursued by Philippa Foot in several papers, collected in *Virtues and Vices* (Oxford, 1978). I am indebted to these, though our conclusions are different. The moral *ought* was one of several targets assaulted by G. E. M. Anscombe in her vigorous 'Modern Moral Philosophy', Chapter 1 in this volume.

less clumsily in informal practice, that there are many different ways in which people can fail to be what we would ethically like them to be. At one extreme there is general deliberative incapacity. At another extreme is the sincere and capable follower of another creed. Yet again there are people with various weaknesses or vices, people who are malicious, selfish, brutal, inconsiderate, self-indulgent, lazy, greedy. All these people can be part of our ethical world. No ethical world has ever been free of those with such vices (though their classification will be a matter of the culture in question); and any individual life is lined by some of them. There are, equally, various negative reactions to them, from hatred and horror in the most extreme cases, to anger, regret, correction, blame. When we are not within the formal circumstances of the state's law, there is the further dimension of who is reacting: not everyone can or should sustain every complaint. It is another consequence of the fiction of the moral law that this truth does not occur to us. It is as if every member of the notional republic were empowered to make a citizen's arrest.

Within all this there is a range, quite a wide one, of particular deviations that we treat with the machinery of everyday blame. They include many violations of obligations, but not all of them: some of the most monstrous proceedings, which lie beyond ordinary blame, involve violations of basic human rights. Nor, on the other hand, is there blame only for broken obligations; particularly in bringing up children, actions that merely manifest imperfect dispositions are blamed. But blame always tends to share the particularized, practical character of moral obligation in the technical sense. Its negative reaction is focused closely on an action or omission, and this is what is blamed. Moreover—though there are many inevitable anomalies in its actual working—the aspiration of blame is that it should apply only to the extent that the undesired outcome is the product of voluntary action on the particular occasion.

This institution, as opposed to other kinds of ethically negative or hostile reaction to people's doings (it is vital to remember how many others there are), seems to have something special to do with the idea that the agent had a reason to act otherwise. As I have already said, this is often not so.[19]

[19] Of course, much depends on what is to count as having a reason. I do not believe that there can be an absolutely 'external' reason for action, one that does not speak to any motivation the agent already has (as I have stressed, Kant did not think so either). There are indeed distinctions between, for instance, simply drawing an agent's attention to a reason he already has and persuading him to act in a certain way. But it is basically important that a spectrum is involved, and such distinctions are less clear than the morality system and other rationalistic conceptions require them to be. See my 'Internal and External Reasons', in *Moral Luck*; 'Internal Reasons and the Obscurity of Blame', repr. in my *Making Sense of Humanity* (Cambridge, 1995); and my discussion on pp. 186–94 of J. E. J. Altharn and R. Harrison (eds.), *World, Mind, and Ethics* (Cambridge, 1995).

The institution of blame is best seen as involving a fiction, by which we treat the agent as one for whom the relevant ethical considerations are reasons. The 'ought to have' of blame can be seen as an extension into the unwilling of the 'ought to have' we may offer, in advice, to those whose ends we share. This fiction has various functions. One is that if we treat the agent as someone who gives weight to ethical reasons, this may help to make him into such a person.

The device is specially important in helping to mediate between two possibilities in people's relations. One is that of shared deliberative practices, where to a considerable extent people have the same dispositions and are helping each other to arrive at practical conclusions. The other is that in which one group applies force or threats to constrain another. The fiction underlying the blame system helps at its best to make a bridge between these possibilities, by a process of continuous recruitment into a deliberative community. At its worst, it can do many bad things, such as encouraging people to misunderstand their own fear and resentment—sentiments they may quite appropriately feel—as the voice of the Law.

The fiction of the deliberative community is one of the positive achievements of the morality system. As with other fictions, it is a real question whether its working could survive a clear understanding of how it works. This is part of the much larger question of what needs to be, and what can be, restructured in the light of a reflective and non-mythical understanding of our ethical practices. It is certain that the practices of blame, and more generally the style of people's negative ethical reactions to others, will change. The morality system, in my view, can no longer help them to do so in a desirable way. One reason is that morality is under too much pressure on the subject of the voluntary.

To the extent that the institution of blame works coherently, it does so because it attempts less than morality would like it to do. When we ask whether someone acted voluntarily, we are asking, roughly, whether he really acted, whether he knew what he was doing, and whether he intended this or that aspect of what happened. This practice takes the agent together with his character, and does not raise questions about his freedom to have chosen some other character. The blame system, most of the time, closely concentrates on the conditions of the particular act; and it is able to do this because it does not operate on its own. It is surrounded by other practices of encouragement and discouragement, acceptance and rejection, which work on desire and character to shape them into the requirements and possibilities of ethical life.

Morality neglects this surrounding and sees only that focused, particularized judgement. There is a pressure within it to require a voluntariness that will be total and will cut through character and psychological or social determination, and allocate blame and responsibility on the ultimately fair basis of the agent's own contribution, no more and no less. It is an illusion to suppose that this demand can be met (as opposed to the less ambitious requirements of voluntariness that take character largely as given). This fact is known to almost everyone, and it is hard to see a long future for a system committed to denying it. But so long as morality itself remains, there is danger in admitting the fact, since the system itself leaves us, as the only contrast to rational blame, forms of persuasion it refuses to distinguish in spirit from force and constraint.

In truth, almost all worthwhile human life lies between the extremes that morality puts before us. It starkly emphasizes a series of contrasts: between force and reason, persuasion and rational conviction, shame and guilt, dislike and disapproval, mere rejection and blame. The attitude that leads it to emphasize all these contrasts can be labelled its *purity*. The purity of morality, its insistence on abstracting the moral consciousness from other kinds of emotional reaction or social influence, conceals not only the means by which it deals with deviant members of its community, but also the virtues of those means. It is not surprising that it should conceal them, since the virtues can be seen as such only from outside the system, from a point of view that can assign value to it, whereas the morality system is closed in on itself and must consider it an indecent misunderstanding to apply to the system any values other than those of morality itself.

The purity of morality itself represents a value. It expresses an ideal, presented by Kant, once again, in a form that is the most unqualified and also one of the most moving: the ideal that human existence can be ultimately just. Most advantages and admired characteristics are distributed in ways that, if not unjust, are at any rate not just, and some people are simply luckier than others. The idea of morality is a value, moral value, that transcends luck. It must therefore lie beyond any empirical determination. It must lie not only in trying rather than succeeding, since success depends partly on luck, but in a kind of trying that lies beyond the level at which the capacity to try can itself be a matter of luck. The value must, further, be supreme. It will be no good if moral value is merely a consolation prize you get if you are not in worldly terms happy or talented or good-humoured or loved. It has to be what ultimately matters.

This is in some ways like a religious conception. But it is also unlike any real religion, and in particular unlike orthodox Christianity. The doctrine of grace in Christianity meant that there was no calculable road from moral effort to salvation; salvation lay beyond merit, and men's efforts, even their moral efforts, were not the measure of God's love.[20] Moreover, when it was said by Christianity that what ultimately mattered was salvation, this was thought to involve a difference that anyone would recognize as a difference, as *the* difference. But the standpoint from which pure moral value has its value is, once more, only that of morality itself. It can hope to transcend luck only by turning in on itself.

The ideals of morality have without doubt, and contrary to a vulgar Marxism that would see them only as an ideology of unworldliness, played a part in producing some actual justice in the world and in mobilizing power and social opportunity to compensate for bad luck in concrete terms. But the idea of a value that lies beyond all luck is an illusion, and political aims cannot continue to draw any conviction from it. Once again, the other conceptions of morality cannot help us. They can only encourage the idea, which always has its greedy friends, that when these illusions have gone there can be no coherent ideas of social justice, but only efficiency, or power, or uncorrected luck.

Many philosophical mistakes are woven into morality. It misunderstands obligations, not seeing how they form just one type of ethical consideration. It misunderstands practical necessity, thinking it peculiar to the ethical. It misunderstands ethical practical necessity, thinking it peculiar to obligations. Beyond all this, morality makes people think that, without its very special obligation, there is only inclination; without its utter voluntariness, there is only force; without its ultimately pure justice, there is no justice. Its philosophical errors are only the most abstract expressions of a deeply rooted and still powerful misconception of life.

[20] This is why I said in *Ethics and the Limits of Philosophy*, ch. 4, that Kant's conception was like that of the Pelagian heresy, which did adjust salvation to merit.

3

THE SCHIZOPHRENIA OF MODERN ETHICAL THEORIES

MICHAEL STOCKER

Modern ethical theories, with perhaps a few honorable exceptions, deal only with reasons, with values, with what justifies. They fail to examine motives and the motivational structures and constraints of ethical life. They not only fail to do this, they fail as ethical theories by not doing this—as I shall argue in this paper. I shall also attempt two correlative tasks: to exhibit some constraints that motivation imposes on ethical theory and life; and to advance our understanding of the relations between reason and motive.

One mark of a good life is a harmony between one's motives and one's reasons, values, justifications. Not to be moved by what one values—what one believes good, nice, right, beautiful, and so on—bespeaks a malady of the spirit. Not to value what moves one also bespeaks a malady of the spirit. Such a malady, or such maladies, can properly be called *moral schizophrenia*—for they are a split between one's motives and one's reasons. (Here and elsewhere, 'reasons' will stand also for 'values' and 'justifications'.)

An extreme form of such schizophrenia is characterized, on the one hand, by being moved to do what one believes bad, harmful, ugly, abasing; on the other, by being disgusted, horrified, dismayed by what one wants to do. Perhaps such cases are rare. But a more modest schizophrenia between reason and motive is not, as can be seen in many examples of weakness of the will, indecisiveness, guilt, shame, self-deception, rationalization, and annoyance with oneself.

At the very least, we should be moved by our major values and we should value what our major motives seek. Should, that is, if we are to lead a good life. To repeat, such harmony is a mark of a good life. Indeed, one

Reprinted from *Journal of Philosophy*, 73 (1976), 453–66, by permission of the *Journal of Philosophy* and the author.

might wonder whether human life—good or bad—is possible without some such integration.

This is not, however, to say that in all cases it is better to have such harmony. It is better for us if self-seeking authoritarians feel fettered by their moral upbringing; better, that is, than if they adopt the reason of their motives. It would have been far better for the world and his victims had Eichmann not wanted to do what he thought he should do.[1]

Nor is this to say that in all areas of endeavour such harmony is necessary or even especially conducive to achieving what is valued. In many cases, it is not. For example, one's motives in fixing a flat tyre are largely irrelevant to getting under way again. (In many such cases, one need not even value the intended outcome.)

Nor is this even to say that in all 'morally significant' areas such harmony is necessary or especially conducive to achieving what is valued. Many morally significant jobs, such as feeding the sick, can be done equally well pretty much irrespective of motive. And, as Ross, at times joined by Mill, argues, for a large part of ethics, there simply is no philosophical question of harmony or disharmony between value and motive: you can do what is right, obligatory, your duty no matter what your motive for so acting. If it is your duty to keep a promise, you fulfil that duty no matter whether you keep the promise out of respect for duty, fear of losing your reputation, or whatever. What motivates is irrelevant so far as rightness, obligatoriness, duty are concerned.

Notwithstanding the very questionable correctness of this view so far as rightness, obligatoriness, duty are concerned,[2] there remain at least two problems. The first is that even here there is still a question of harmony. What sort of life would people have who did their duties but never or rarely wanted to? Second, duty, obligation, and rightness are only one part—indeed, only a small part, a dry and minimal part—of ethics. There is the whole other area of the values of personal and interpersonal relations and activities; and also the area of moral goodness, merit, virtue. In both, motive is an essential part of what is valuable; in both, motive and reason must be in harmony for the values to be realized.

For this reason and for the reason that such harmony is a mark of a good life, any theory that ignores such harmony does so at great peril. Any theory that makes difficult, or precludes, such harmony stands, if not convicted, then in need of much and powerful defence. What I shall now

[1] It might be asked what is better for such people, to have or lack this harmony, given their evil motives or values; in which way they would be morally better. Such questions may not be answerable.

[2] See my 'Act and Agent Evaluations', *Review of Metaphysics*, 27 (Sept. 1973), 42–61.

argue is that modern ethical theories—those theories prominent in the English-speaking philosophical world—make such harmony impossible.

CRITICISM OF MODERN ETHICS

Reflection on the complexity and vastness of our moral life, on what has value, shows that recent ethical theories have by far overconcentrated on duty, rightness, and obligation.[3] This failure—of overconcentrating—could not have been tolerated but for the failure of not dealing with motives or with the relations of motives to values. (So, too, the first failure supports and explains the second.) In this second failure, we find a far more serious defect of modern ethical theories than such overconcentration: they necessitate a schizophrenia between reason and motive in vitally important and pervasive areas of value, or alternatively they allow us the harmony of a morally impoverished life, a life deeply deficient in what is valuable. It is not possible for moral people, that is, people who would achieve what is valuable, to act on these ethical theories, to let them comprise their motives. People who do let them comprise their motives will, for that reason, have a life seriously lacking in what is valuable.

These theories are, thus, doubly defective. As ethical theories, they fail by making it impossible for a person to achieve the good in an integrated way. As theories of the mind, of reasons and motives, of human life and activity, they fail, not only by putting us in a position that is psychologically uncomfortable, difficult, or even untenable, but also by making us and our lives essentially fragmented and incoherent.

The sort of disharmony I have in mind can be brought out by considering a problem for egoists, typified by hedonistic egoists. Love, friendship, affection, fellow feeling, and community are important sources of personal pleasure. But can such egoists get these pleasures? I think not—not so long as they adhere to the motive of pleasure-for-self.

The reason for this is not that egoists cannot get together and decide, as it were, to enter into a love relationship. Surely they can (leaving aside the irrelevant problems about deciding to do such a thing). And they can do the various things calculated to bring about such pleasure: have absorbing talks, make love, eat delicious meals, see interesting films, and so on, and so on.

None the less, there is something necessarily lacking in such a life: love.

[3] See ibid. and my 'Rightness and Goodness: Is There a Difference?', *American Philosophical Quarterly*, 10/2 (Apr. 1973), 87–98.

For it is essential to the very concept of love that one care for the beloved, that one be prepared to act for the sake of the beloved. More strongly, one must care for the beloved and act for that person's sake as a final goal; the beloved, or the beloved's welfare or interest, must be a final goal of one's concern and action.

To the extent that my consideration for you—or even my trying to make you happy—comes from my desire to lead an untroubled life, a life that is personally pleasing for me, I do not act for your sake. In short, to the extent that I act in various ways towards you with the final goal of getting pleasure—or, more generally, good—for myself, I do not act for your sake.

When we think about it this way, we may get some idea of why egoism is often claimed to be essentially lonely. For it is essentially concerned with external relations with others, where, except for their effects on us, one person is no different from, nor more important, valuable, or special than any other person or even any other thing. The individuals as such are not important, only their effects on us are; they are essentially replaceable, anything else with the same effects would do as well. And this, I suggest, is intolerable personally. To think of yourself this way, or to believe that a person you love thinks of you this way, is intolerable. And for conceptual, as well as psychological, reasons it is incompatible with love.

It might be suggested that it is rather unimportant to have love of this sort. But this would be a serious error. The love here is not merely modern-romantic or sexual. It is also the love among members of a family, the love we have for our closest friends, and so on. Just what sort of life would people have who never 'cared' for anyone else, except as a means to their own interests? And what sort of life would people have who took it that no one loved them for their own sake, but only for the way they served the other's interest?

Just as the notion of doing something for the sake of another, or of caring for the person for that person's sake, is essential for love, so too is it essential for friendship and all affectionate relations. Without this, at best we could have good relations, friendly relations. And similarly, such caring and respect is essential for fellow feeling and community.

Before proceeding, let us contrast this criticism of egoism with a more standard one. My criticism runs as follows: Hedonistic egoists take their own pleasure to be the sole justification of acts, activities, ways of life; they should recognize that love, friendship, affection, fellow feeling, and community are among the greatest (sources of) personal pleasures. Thus, they have good reason, on their own grounds, to enter such relations. But they cannot act in the ways required to get those pleasures, those great goods, if they act on their motive of pleasure-for-self. They cannot act for the sake of the intended beloved, friend, and so on; thus, they cannot love, be or have a friend, and so on. To achieve these great personal goods, they have to abandon that egoistical motive. They cannot embody their reason in their motive. Their reasons and motives make their moral lives schizophrenic.

The standard criticism of egoists is that they simply cannot achieve such non-egoistical goods, that their course of action will, as a matter of principle, keep them from involving themselves with others in the relevant ways, and so on. This criticism is not clearly correct. For there may be nothing inconsistent in egoists' adopting a policy that will allow them to forget, as it were, that they are egoists, a policy that will allow and even encourage them to develop such final goals and motives as caring for another for that person's own sake. Indeed, as has often been argued, the wise egoist would do just this.

Several questions should be asked of this response: would the transformed person still be an egoist? Is it important, for the defence of egoism, that the person remain an egoist? Or is it important only that the person live in a way that would be approved of by an egoist? It is, of course, essential to the transformation of the person from egoistical motivation to caring for others that the person-as-egoist lose conscious control of him/herself. This raises the question of whether such people will be able to check up and see how their transformed selves are getting on in achieving egoistically approved goals. Will they have a mental alarm clock which wakes them up from their non-egoistical transforms every once in a while, to allow them to reshape these transforms if they are not getting enough personal pleasure—or, more generally, enough good? I suppose that this would not be impossible. But it hardly seems an ideal, or even a very satisfactory, life. It is bad enough to have a private personality, which you must hide from others; but imagine having a personality that you must hide from (the other parts of) yourself. Still, perhaps this is possible. If it is, then it seems that egoists may be able to meet this second criticism. But this does not touch my criticism: that they will not be able to embody their reason in their motives; that they will have to lead a bifurcated, schizophrenic life to achieve what is good.

This might be thought a defect of only such ethical theories as egoism. But consider those utilitarianisms which hold that an act is right, obligatory, or whatever if and only if it is optimific in regard to pleasure and pain (or weighted expectations of them). Such a view has it that the only good reason for acting is pleasure vs. pain, and thus should highly value love, friendship, affection, fellow feeling, and community. Suppose, now, you embody this utilitarian reason as your motive in your actions and thoughts towards someone. Whatever your relation to that person, it is necessarily not love (nor is it friendship, affection, fellow feeling, or community). The person you supposedly love engages your thought and action not for him/herself, but rather as a source of pleasure.

The problem is not simply that pleasure is taken to be the only good, the only right-making feature. To see this, consider G. E. Moore's formalistic utilitarianism, which tells us to maximize goodness, without claiming to have identified all the goods. If, as I would have it and as Moore agrees, love relations and the like are goods, how could there be any disharmony here? Would it not be possible to embody Moore's justifying reason as a motive and still love? I do not think so.

First, if you try to carry on the relationship for the sake of goodness, there is no essential commitment even to that activity, much less to the persons involved. So far as goodness is involved, you might as well love as ski or write poetry or eat a nice meal or . . . Perhaps it would be replied that there is something special about that good, the good of love—treating it now not *qua* good but *qua* what is good or *qua* this good. In such a case, however, there is again an impersonality so far as the individuals are concerned. Any other person who would elicit as much of this good would be as proper an object of love as the beloved. To this it might be replied that it is that good which is to be sought—with emphasis on the personal and individual features, the features that bind these people together. But now it is not clear in what sense goodness is being sought, nor that the theory is still telling us to maximize goodness.[4] True, the theory tells us to bring about this good, but now we cannot separate what is good, the love, from its goodness. And this simply is not Moore's utilitarianism.

Just as egoism and the above sorts of utilitarianisms necessitate a schizophrenia between reason and motive—and just as they cannot allow for love, friendship, affection, fellow feeling, and community—so do current rule utilitarianisms. And so do current deontologies.

What is lacking in these theories is simply—or not so simply—the person. For, love, friendship, affection, fellow feeling, and community all require that the other person be an essential part of what is valued. The

[4] Taking love and people-in-certain-relations as intrinsically valuable helps show mistaken various views about acting rationally (or well). First, maximization: i.e., if you value 'item' *C* and if state *S* has more *C* than does *S'*, you act rationally only if you choose *S*—unless *S'* has more of other items you value than does *S*, or your cost in getting *S*, as opposed to *S'*, is too high, or you are not well enough informed. Where *C* is love (and indeed where *C* is many, if not most, valuable things), this does not hold—not even if all the values involved are self-regarding. Second, paying attention to value differences, being alive to them and their significance for acting rationally: just consider a person who (often) checks to see whether a love relation with another person would be 'better' than the present love.

person—not merely the person's general values nor even the person-*qua*-producer-or-possessor-of-general-values—must be valued. The defect of these theories in regard to love, to take one case, is not that they do not value love (which, often they do not) but that they do not value the beloved. Indeed, a person who values and aims at simply love, that is, love-in-general or even love-in-general-exemplified-by-this-person, 'misses' the intended beloved as surely as does an adherent of the theories I have criticized.

The problem with these theories is not, however, with *other*-people-as-valuable. It is simply—or not so simply—with *people*-as-valuable. Just as they would do *vis-à-vis* other people, modern ethical theories would prevent each of us from loving, caring for, and valuing ourself—as opposed to loving, caring for, and valuing our general values or ourself-*qua*-producer-or-possessor-of-general-values. In these externality-ridden theories, there is as much a disappearance or non-appearance of the self as of other people. Their externality-ridden universes of what is intrinsically valuable are not solipsistic; rather, they are devoid of all people.[5]

It is a truism that it is difficult to deal with people as such. It is difficult really to care for them for their own sake. It is psychically wearing and exhausting. It puts us in too open, too vulnerable a position. But what must also be looked at is what it does to us—taken individually and in groups as small as a couple and as large as society—to view and treat others externally, as essentially replaceable, as mere instruments or repositories of general and non-specific value; and what it does to us to be treated, or believe we are treated, in these ways.

At the very least, these ways are dehumanizing. To say much more than this would require a full-scale philosophical anthropology showing how such personal relations as love and friendship are possible, how they relate to larger ways and structures of human life, and how they—and perhaps only they—allow for the development of those relations which are constitutive of a human life worth living: how, in short, they work together to produce the fullness of a good life, a life of eudaimonia.

Having said this, it must be acknowledged that there are many unclarities and difficulties in the notion of valuing a person, in the notion of a person-as-valuable. When we think about this—e.g., what and why we value—we seem driven either to omitting the person and ending up with a person-*qua*-producer-or-possessor-of-general-values or with a person's

[5] Moore's taking friendship to be an intrinsic good is an exception to this. But if the previous criticism of Moore holds, his so taking friendship introduces serious strains, verging on inconsistencies, into his theory.

general values, or to omitting them and ending up with a bare particular ego.

In all of this, perhaps we could learn from the egoists. Their instincts, at least, must be to admit themselves, each for self, into their values. At the risk of absurdity—indeed, at the risk of complete loss of appeal of their view—what they find attractive and good about good-for-self must be, not only the good, but also and pre-eminently the for-self.

At this point, it might help to restate some of the things I have tried to do and some I have not. Throughout I have been concerned with what sort of motives people can have if they are to be able to realize the great goods of love, friendship, affection, fellow feeling, and community. And I have argued that, if we take as motives, embody in our motives, those various things which recent ethical theories hold to be ultimately good or right, we will, of necessity, be unable to have those motives. Love, friendship, affection, fellow feeling, and community, like many other states and activities, essentially contain certain motives and essentially preclude certain others; among those precluded we find motives comprising the justifications, the goals, the goods of those ethical theories most prominent today. To embody in one's motives the values of current ethical theories is to treat people externally and to preclude love, friendship, affection, fellow feeling, and community—both with others and with oneself. To get these great goods while holding those current ethical theories requires a schizophrenia between reason and motive.

I have not argued that if you have a successful love relationship, friendship, . . . , then you will be unable to achieve the justifications, goals, goods posited by those theories. You can achieve them, but not by trying to live the theory directly. Or, more exactly, to the extent that you live the theory directly, to that extent you will fail to achieve its goods.

So far I have urged the charge of disharmony, bifurcation, schizophrenia only in regard to the personal relationships of love, friendship, affection, fellow feeling, and community. The importance of these is, I would think, sufficient to carry the day. However, let us look at one further area: enquiry, taken as the search for understanding, wisdom. Although I am less sure here, I also think that many of the same charges apply.

Perhaps the following is only a special case, but it seems worth considering. You have been locked up in a psychiatric hospital, and are naturally most eager to get out. You ask the psychiatrist when you will be released; he replies, 'Pretty soon.' You find out that, instead of telling patients what he really believes, he tells them what he believes is good for them to hear (good for them to believe he believes). Perhaps you could 'crack his code', by discovering his medical theories and his beliefs about you. None the less, your further conversations—if they can be called that—with him are hardly the model of enquiry. I am not so unsure that we would be in a different position when confronted with people who engage in enquiry for their own sake, for God's glory, for the greatest pleasure, or even for the greatest good. Again, we might well be able to crack their codes—e.g., we could find out that someone believes his greatest chance for academic promotion is to find out the truth in a certain area. None the less. . . .

(Is the residual doubt 'But what if he comes to believe that what is most pleasing to the senior professors will gain promotion; and how can we tell what he really believes?' of any import here? And is it essentially different from 'But what if he ceases to value truth as such; and how can we tell what he really values?' Perhaps if understanding, not 'mere knowledge', is the goal, there is a difference.)

It might be expected that, in those areas explicitly concerned with motives and their evaluation, ethical theories would not lead us into this disharmony or the corresponding morally defective life. And to some extent this expectation is met. But even in regard to moral merit and demerit, moral praise- and blameworthiness, the moral virtues and vices, the situation is not wholly dissimilar. Again, the problem of externality and impersonality, and the connected disharmony, arises.

The standard view has it that a morally good intention is an essential constituent of a morally good act. This seems correct enough. On that view, further, a morally good intention is an intention to do an act for the sake of its goodness or rightness. But now, suppose you are in a hospital, recovering from a long illness. You are very bored and restless and at loose ends when Smith comes in once again. You are now convinced more than ever that he is a fine fellow and a real friend—taking so much time to cheer you up, travelling all the way across town, and so on. You are so effusive with your praise and thanks that he protests that he always tries to do what he thinks is his duty, what he thinks will be best. You at first think he is engaging in a polite form of self-deprecation, relieving the moral burden. But the more you two speak, the more clear it becomes that he was telling the literal truth: that it is not essentially because of you that he came to see you, not because you are friends, but because he thought it his duty, perhaps as a fellow Christian or Communist or whatever, or simply because he knows of no one more in need of cheering up and no one easier to cheer up.

Surely there is something lacking here—and lacking in moral merit or value. The lack can be sheeted home to two related points: again, the wrong sort of thing is said to be the proper motive; and, in this case at least, the wrong sort of thing is, again, essentially external.[6]

SOME QUESTIONS AND CONCLUDING REMARKS

I have assumed that the reasons, values, justifications of ethical theories should be such as to allow us to embody them in our motives and still act morally and achieve the good. But why assume this? Perhaps we should take ethical theories as encouraging indirection—getting what we want by seeking something else: e.g., some say the economic well-being of all is realized, not by everyone's seeking it but by everyone's seeking his/her own well-being. Or perhaps we should take ethical theories as giving only indices, not determinants, of what is right and good.

Theories of indirection have their own special problems. There is always a great risk that we will get the something else, not what we really want. There are, also, these two related problems. A theory advocating indirection needs to be augmented by another theory of motivation, telling us which motives are suitable for which acts. Such a theory would also have to explain the connections, the indirect connections, between motive and real goal.

Second, it may not be very troubling to talk about indirection in such large-scale and multi-person matters as the economics of society. But in regard to something of such personal concern, so close to and so internal to a person as ethics, talk of indirection is both implausible and baffling. Implausible in that we do not seem to act by indirection, at least not in such areas as love, friendship, affection, fellow feeling, and community. In these cases, our motive has to do directly with the loved one, the friend, . . . , as does our reason. In doing something for a loved child or parent, there is no need to appeal to, or even think of, the reasons found in contemporary ethical theories. Talk of indirection is baffling, in an action- and understanding-defeating sense, since, once we begin to believe that there is something beyond such activities as love which is necessary to justify them, it is only by something akin to self-deception that we are able to continue them.

One partial defence of these ethical theories would be that they are not intended to supply what can serve as both reasons and motives; that they are intended only to supply indices of goodness and rightness, not determi-

[6] For a way to evade this problem, see my 'Morally Good Intentions', *Monist*, 54/1 (Jan. 1970), 124–41, where it is argued that goodness and rightness need not be the object of a morally good intention, but rather that various goods or right acts can be.

nants. Formally, there may be no problems in taking ethical theories this way. But several questions do arise. Why should we be concerned with such theories, theories that cannot be acted on? Why not simply have a theory that allows for harmony between reason and motive? A theory that gives determinants? And indeed, will we not need to have such a theory? True, our pre-analytic views might be sufficient to judge among index theories; we may not need a determinant theory to pick out a correct index theory. But will we not need a determinant theory to know why the index is correct, why it works, to know what is good about what is so indexed?[7]

Another partial defence of recent theories would be that, first, they are concerned almost entirely with rightness, obligation, and duty, and not with the whole of ethics; and, second, that within this restricted area, they do not suffer from disharmony or schizophrenia. To some extent this defence, especially its second point, has been dealt with earlier. But more should be said. It is perhaps clear enough by now that recent ethicists have ignored large and extremely important areas of morality—e.g., that of personal relations and that of merit. To this extent, the first point of the defence is correct. What is far from clear, however, is whether these theories were advanced only as partial theories, or whether it was believed by their proponents that duty and so on were really the whole, or at least the only important part, of ethics.

We might be advised to forget past motivation and belief, and simply look at these theories and see what use can be made of them. Perhaps they were mistaken about the scope and importance of duty and so on. None the less they could be correct about the concepts involved. In reply, several points should be made. First, they were mistaken about these concepts, as even a brief study of supererogation and self-regarding notions would indicate. Second, these theories are dangerously misleading; for they can all too readily be taken as suggesting that all of ethics can be treated in an external, legislation-model, index way. (On 'legislation-model', see below.) Third, the acceptance of such theories as partial theories would pose

[7] Taking contemporary theories to be index theories would help settle one of the longest-standing disputes in ethical philosophy—a dispute which finds Aristotle and Marx on the winning side and many if not most contemporary ethicists on the other. The dispute concerns the relative explanatory roles of pleasure and good activity and good life. Put crudely, many utilitarians and others have held that an activity is good only because and in so far as it is productive of pleasure; Aristotle and Marx hold of at least many pleasures that if they are good this is because they are produced by good activity. The problem of immoral pleasures has seemed to many the most important test case for this dispute. To the extent that my thesis is correct, we have another way to settle the dispute. For, if I am correct, pleasure cannot be what makes all good activity good, even prescinding from immoral pleasures. It must be activity, such as love and friendship, which makes some pleasures good.

severe difficulties of integration within ethical theory. Since these theories are so different from those concerning, e.g., personal relations, how are they all to be integrated? Of course, this third point may not be a criticism of these theories of duty, but only a recognition of the great diversity and complexity of our moral life.[8]

In conclusion, it might be asked how contemporary ethical theories come to require either a stunted moral life or disharmony, schizophrenia. One cluster of (somewhat speculative) answers surrounds the pre-eminence of duty, rightness, and obligation in these theories. This pre-eminence fits naturally with theories developed in a time of diminishing personal relations; of a time when the ties holding people together and easing the frictions of their various enterprises were less and less affection; of a time when commercial relations superseded family (or family-like) relations; of a time of growing individualism. It also fits naturally with a major concern of those philosophers: legislation. When concerned with legislation, they were concerned with duty, rightness, obligation. (Of course, the question then is, Why were they interested in legislation, especially of this sort? To some small extent this has been answered, but no more will be said on this score.) When viewing morality from such a legislator's point of view, taking such legislation to be the model, motivation too easily becomes irrelevant. The legislator wants various things done or not done; it is not important why they are done or not done; one can count on and know the actions, but not the motives. (This is also tied up with a general devaluing of our emotions and emotional possibilities—taking emotions to be mere feelings or urges, without rational or cognitive content or constraint; and taking us to be pleasure-seekers and pain-avoiders—forgetting or denying that love, friendship, affection, fellow feeling, and desire for virtue are extremely strong movers of people.) Connected with this is the legislative or simply the third-person's eye view, which assures us that others are getting on well if they are happy, if they are doing what gives them pleasure, and the like. The effect guarantees the cause—in the epistemic sense. (One might wonder whether the general empiricist confusion of *ratio cognoscendi* and *ratio essendi* is at work here.)

[8] Part of this complexity can be seen as follows: Duty seems relevant in our relations with our loved ones and friends, only when our love, friendship, and affection lapse. If a family is 'going well', its members 'naturally' help each other; that is, their love, affection, and deep friendship are sufficient for them to care for and help one another (to put it a bit coolly). Such 'feelings' are at times worn thin. At these times, duty may have to be looked to or called upon (by the agent or by others) to get done at least a modicum of those things which love would normally provide. To some rough extent, the frequency with which a family member acts out of duty, instead of love, towards another in the family is a measure of the lack of love the first has for the other. But this is not to deny that there are duties of love, friendship, and the like.

These various factors, then, may help explain this rather remarkable inversion (to use Marx's notion): of taking the 'effect', pleasure and the like, for the 'cause', good activity.

Moore's formalistic utilitarianism and the traditional views of morally good action also suffer from something like an inversion. Here, however, it is not causal, but philosophical. It is as if these philosophers have taken it that, because these various good things can all be classified as good, their goodness consists in this, rather than conversely. The most general classification seems to have been reified and itself taken as the morally relevant goal.

These inversions may help answer a question which afflicts this paper: why have I said that contemporary ethics suffers from schizophrenia, bifurcation, disharmony rather than just that these theories are mistaken in their denomination of what is good and bad, right- and wrong-making? For it is clear enough that, if we aim for the wrong goal, then we are unlikely to achieve what we really want, what is good, and the like. My reason for claiming more than a mere mistake is that the mistake is well reasoned; it is closely related to the truth, it bears many of the features of the truth. To take only two examples (barring bad fortune and bad circumstances), good activity does bring about pleasure; love clearly benefits the lover. There is, thus, great plausibility in taking as good what these theories advance as good. But when we try to act on the theories, try to embody their reasons in our motives—as opposed to simply seeing whether our or others' lives would be approved of by the theories—then in a quite mad way, things start going wrong. The personalities of loved ones get passed over for their effects, moral action becomes self-stultifying and self-defeating. And perhaps the greatest madnesses of all are—and they stand in a vicious interrelation—first, the world is increasingly made such as to make these theories correct; and, second, we take these theories to be correct and thus come to see love, friendship, and the like only as possible, and not very certain, sources of pleasure or whatever. We mistake the effect for the cause and when the cause-seen-as-effect fails to result from the effect-seen-as-cause, we devalue the former, relegating it, at best, to good as a means and embrace the latter, wondering why our chosen goods are so hollow, bitter, and inhumane.[9]

[9] I wish to thank all those who have heard or read various versions of this paper and whose comments have greatly encouraged and helped me.

4

MORAL SAINTS

SUSAN WOLF

I don't know whether there are any moral saints. But if there are, I am glad that neither I nor those about whom I care most are among them. By *moral saint* I mean a person whose every action is as morally good as possible, a person, that is, who is as morally worthy as can be. Though I shall in a moment acknowledge the variety of types of person that might be thought to satisfy this description, it seems to me that none of these types serves as an unequivocally compelling personal ideal. In other words, I believe that moral perfection, in the sense of moral saintliness, does not constitute a model of personal well-being towards which it would be particularly rational or good or desirable for a human being to strive.

Outside the context of moral discussion, this will strike many as an obvious point. But, within that context, the point, if it be granted, will be granted with some discomfort. For within that context it is generally assumed that one ought to be as morally good as possible and that what limits there are to morality's hold on us are set by features of human nature of which we ought not to be proud. If, as I believe, the ideals that are derivable from common sense and philosophically popular moral theories do not support these assumptions, then something has to change. Either we must change our moral theories in ways that will make them yield more palatable ideals, or, as I shall argue, we must change our conception of what is involved in affirming a moral theory.

In this paper, I wish to examine the notion of a moral saint, first, to understand what a moral saint would be like and why such a being would be unattractive, and, second, to raise some questions about the significance of this paradoxical figure for moral philosophy. I shall look first at the model(s) of moral sainthood that might be extrapolated from the morality or moralities of common sense. Then I shall consider what relations these have to conclusions that can be drawn from utilitarian and Kantian moral

Reprinted from *Journal of Philosophy*, 79 (1982), 419–39, by permission of the *Journal of Philosophy* and the author.

theories. Finally, I shall speculate on the implications of these considerations for moral philosophy.

MORAL SAINTS AND COMMON SENSE

Consider first what, pretheoretically, would count for us—contemporary members of Western culture—as a moral saint. A necessary condition of moral sainthood would be that one's life be dominated by a commitment to improving the welfare of others or of society as a whole. As to what role this commitment must play in the individual's motivational system, two contrasting accounts suggest themselves to me which might equally be thought to qualify a person for moral sainthood.

First, a moral saint might be someone whose concern for others plays the role that is played in most of our lives by more selfish, or, at any rate, less morally worthy concerns. For the moral saint, the promotion of the welfare of others might play the role that is played for most of us by the enjoyment of material comforts, the opportunity to engage in the intellectual and physical activities of our choice, and the love, respect, and companionship of people whom we love, respect, and enjoy. The happiness of the moral saint, then, would truly lie in the happiness of others, and so he would devote himself to others gladly, and with a whole and open heart.

On the other hand, a moral saint might be someone for whom the basic ingredients of happiness are not unlike those of most of the rest of us. What makes him a moral saint is rather that he pays little or no attention to his own happiness in light of the overriding importance he gives to the wider concerns of morality. In other words, this person sacrifices his own interests to the interests of others, and feels the sacrifice as such.

Roughly, these two models may be distinguished according to whether one thinks of the moral saint as being a saint out of love or one thinks of the moral saint as being a saint out of duty (or some other intellectual appreciation and recognition of moral principles). We may refer to the first model as the model of the Loving Saint; to the second, as the model of the Rational Saint.

The two models differ considerably with respect to the qualities of the motives of the individuals who conform to them. But this difference would have limited effect on the saints' respective public personalities. The shared content of what these individuals are motivated to be—namely, as morally good as possible—would play the dominant role in the determination of their characters. Of course, just as a variety of large-scale projects, from tending the sick to political campaigning, may be equally and maximally morally worthy, so a variety of characters are compatible with the ideal of moral sainthood. One moral saint may be more or less jovial, more or less garrulous, more or less athletic than another. But, above all, a moral saint must have and cultivate those qualities which are apt to allow him to treat others as justly and kindly as possible. He will have the standard moral virtues to a non-standard degree. He will be patient, considerate, even-tempered, hospitable, charitable in thought as well as in deed. He will be very reluctant to make negative judgements of other people. He will be careful not to favour some people over others on the basis of properties they could not help but have.

Perhaps what I have already said is enough to make some people begin to regard the absence of moral saints in their lives as a blessing. For there comes a point in the listing of virtues that a moral saint is likely to have where one might naturally begin to wonder whether the moral saint isn't, after all, too good—if not too good for his own good, at least too good for his own well-being. For the moral virtues given that they are, by hypothesis, *all* present in the same individual, and to an extreme degree, are apt to crowd out the non-moral virtues, as well as many of the interests and personal characteristics that we generally think contribute to a healthy, well-rounded, richly developed character.

In other words, if the moral saint is devoting all his time to feeding the hungry or healing the sick or raising money for Oxfam, then necessarily he is not reading Victorian novels, playing the oboe, or improving his backhand. Although no one of the interests or tastes in the category containing these latter activities could be claimed to be a necessary element in a life well lived, a life in which *none* of these possible aspects of character is developed may seem to be a life strangely barren.

The reasons why a moral saint cannot, in general, encourage the discovery and development of significant non-moral interests and skills are not logical but practical reasons. There are, in addition, a class of non-moral characteristics that a moral saint cannot encourage in himself for reasons that are not just practical. There is a more substantial tension between having any of these qualities unashamedly and being a moral saint. These qualities might be described as going against the moral grain. For example, a cynical or sarcastic wit, or a sense of humour that appreciates this kind of wit in others, requires that one take an attitude of resignation and pessimism toward the flaws and vices to be found in the world. A moral saint, on the other hand, has reason to take an attitude in opposition to this—he should try to look for the best in people, give them the benefit of the doubt as long as possible, try to improve regrettable situations as long as there is any hope of success. This suggests that, although a moral saint might well enjoy a good episode of *Father Knows Best*, he may not in good conscience be able to laugh at a Marx Brothers movie or enjoy a play by George Bernard Shaw.

An interest in something like gourmet cooking will be, for different reasons, difficult for a moral saint to rest easy with. For it seems to me that no plausible argument can justify the use of human resources involved in producing a *paté de canard en croûte* against possible alternative beneficent ends to which these resources might be put. If there is a justification for the institution of *haute cuisine*, it is one which rests on the decision *not* to justify every activity against morally beneficial alternatives, and this is a decision a moral saint will never make. Presumably, an interest in high fashion or interior design will fare much the same, as will, very possibly, a cultivation of the finer arts as well.

A moral saint will have to be very, very nice. It is important that he not be offensive. The worry is that, as a result, he will have to be dull-witted or humourless or bland.

This worry is confirmed when we consider what sorts of characters, taken and refined both from life and from fiction, typically form our ideals. One would hope they would be figures who are morally good—and by this I mean more than just not morally bad—but one would hope, too, that they are not *just* morally good, but talented or accomplished or attractive in non-moral ways as well. We may make ideals out of athletes, scholars, artists—more frivolously, out of cowboys, private eyes, and rock stars. We may strive for Katharine Hepburn's grace, Paul Newman's 'cool'; we are attracted to the high-spirited passionate nature of Natasha Rostov; we admire the keen perceptiveness of Lambert Strether. Though there is certainly nothing immoral about the ideal characters or traits I have in mind, they cannot be superimposed upon the ideal of a moral saint. For although it is a part of many of these ideals that the characters set high, and not merely acceptable, moral standards for themselves, it is also essential to their power and attractiveness that the moral strengths go, so to speak, alongside specific, independently admirable, non-moral ground projects, and dominant personal traits.

When one does finally turn one's eyes towards lives that are dominated by explicitly moral commitments, moreover, one finds oneself relieved at the discovery of idiosyncrasies or eccentricities not quite in line with the picture of moral perfection. One prefers the blunt, tactless, and opinionated Betsy Trotwood to the unfailingly kind and patient Agnes Copperfield; one prefers the mischievousness and the sense of irony in Chesterton's Father Brown to the innocence and undiscriminating love of St Francis.

It seems that, as we look in our ideals for people who achieve non-moral varieties of personal excellence in conjunction with or coloured by some version of high moral tone, we look in our paragons of moral excellence for people whose moral achievements occur in conjunction with or coloured by some interests or traits that have low moral tone. In other words, there seems to be a limit to how much morality we can stand.

One might suspect that the essence of the problem is simply that there is a limit to how much of *any* single value, or any single type of value, we can stand. Our objection then would not be specific to a life in which one's dominant concern is morality, but would apply to any life that can be so completely characterized by an extraordinarily dominant concern. The objection in that case would reduce to the recognition that such a life is incompatible with well-roundedness. If that were the objection, one could fairly reply that well-roundedness is no more supreme a virtue than the totality of moral virtues embodied by the ideal it is being used to criticize. But I think this misidentifies the objection. For the way in which a concern for morality may dominate a life, or, more to the point, the way in which it may dominate an ideal of life, is not easily imagined by analogy to the dominance an aspiration to become an Olympic swimmer or a concert pianist might have.

A person who is passionately committed to one of these latter concerns might decide that her attachment to it is strong enough to be worth the sacrifice of her ability to maintain and pursue a significant portion of what else life might offer which a proper devotion to her dominant passion would require. But a desire to be as morally good as possible is not likely to take the form of one desire among others which, because of its peculiar psychological strength, requires one to forgo the pursuit of other weaker and separately less demanding desires. Rather, the desire to be as morally good as possible is apt to have the character not just of a stronger, but of a higher desire, which does not merely successfully compete with one's other desires but which rather subsumes or demotes them. The sacrifice of other interests for the interest in morality, then, will have the character, not of a choice, but of an imperative.

Moreover, there is something odd about the idea of morality itself, or moral goodness, serving as the object of a dominant passion in the way that a more concrete and specific vision of a goal (even a concrete *moral* goal) might be imagined to serve. Morality itself does not seem to be a suitable object of passion. Thus, when one reflects, for example, on the Loving Saint easily and gladly giving up his fishing trip or his stereo or his hot fudge sundae at the drop of the moral hat, one is apt to wonder not at how much he loves morality, but at how little he loves these other things. One thinks that, if he can give these up so easily, he does not know what it *is* truly to love them. There seems, in other words, to be a kind of joy which the Loving Saint, either by nature or by practice, is incapable of experiencing. The Rational Saint, on the other hand, might retain strong non-moral and concrete desires—he simply denies himself the opportunity to act on them. But this is no less troubling. The Loving Saint one might suspect of missing a piece of perceptual machinery, of being blind to some of what the world has to offer. The Rational Saint, who sees it but forgoes it, one suspects of having a different problem—a pathological fear of damnation, perhaps, or an extreme form of self-hatred that interferes with his ability to enjoy the enjoyable in life.

In other words, the ideal of a life of moral sainthood disturbs not simply because it is an ideal of a life in which morality unduly dominates. The normal person's direct and specific desires for objects, activities, and events that conflict with the attainment of moral perfection are not simply sacrificed but removed, suppressed, or subsumed. The way in which morality, unlike other possible goals, is apt to dominate is particularly disturbing, for it seems to require either the lack or the denial of the existence of an identifiable, personal self.

This distinctively troubling feature is not, I think, absolutely unique to the ideal of the moral saint, as I have been using that phrase. It is shared by the conception of the pure aesthete, by a certain kind of religious ideal, and, somewhat paradoxically, by the model of the thoroughgoing, self-conscious egoist. It is not a coincidence that the ways of comprehending the world of which these ideals are the extreme embodiments are sometimes described as 'moralities' themselves. At any rate, they compete with what we ordinarily mean by 'morality'. Nor is it a coincidence that these ideals are naturally described as fanatical. But it is easy to see that these other types of perfection cannot serve as satisfactory personal ideals; for the realization of these ideals would be straightforwardly immoral. It may come as a surprise to some that there may in addition be such a thing as a *moral* fanatic.

Some will object that I am being unfair to 'common-sense morality'—that it does not really require a moral saint to be either a disgusting goody-goody or an obsessive ascetic. Admittedly, there is no logical inconsistency between having any of the personal characteristics I have mentioned and being a moral saint. It is not morally wrong to notice the faults and shortcomings of others or to recognize and appreciate non-moral talents and skills. Nor is it immoral to be an avid Celtics fan or to have a passion for caviar or to be an excellent cellist. With enough imagination, we can always contrive a suitable history and set of circumstances that will embrace such characteristics in one or another specific fictional story of a perfect moral saint.

If one turned onto the path of moral sainthood relatively late in life, one may have already developed interests that can be turned to moral purposes. It may be that a good golf game is just what is needed to secure that big donation to Oxfam. Perhaps the cultivation of one's exceptional artistic talent will turn out to be the way one can make one's greatest contribution to society. Furthermore, one might stumble upon joys and skills in the very service of morality. If, because the children are short of a ninth player for the team, one's generous offer to serve reveals a natural fielding arm or if one's part in the campaign against nuclear power requires accepting a lobbyist's invitation to lunch at Le Lion d'Or, there is no moral gain in denying the satisfaction one gets from these activities. The moral saint, then, may, by happy accident, find himself with non-moral virtues on which he can capitalize morally or which make psychological demands to which he has no choice but to attend. The point is that, for a moral saint, the existence of these interests and skills can be given at best the status of happy accidents—they cannot be encouraged for their own sakes as distinct, independent aspects of the realization of human good.

It must be remembered that from the fact that there is a tension between having any of these qualities and being a moral saint it does not follow that having any of these qualities is immoral. For it is not part of common-sense morality that one ought to be a moral saint. Still, if someone just happened to want to be a moral saint, he or she would not have or encourage these qualities, and, on the basis of our common-sense values, this counts as a reason *not* to want to be a moral saint.

One might still wonder what kind of reason this is, and what kind of conclusion this properly allows us to draw. For the fact that the models of moral saints are unattractive does not necessarily mean that they are unsuitable ideals. Perhaps they are unattractive because they make us feel uncomfortable—they highlight our own weaknesses, vices, and flaws. If so, the fault lies not in the characters of the saints, but in those of our unsaintly selves.

To be sure, some of the reasons behind the disaffection we feel for the model of moral sainthood have to do with a reluctance to criticize ourselves and a reluctance to committing ourselves to trying to give up activities and interests that we heartily enjoy. These considerations might provide an *excuse* for the fact that we are not moral saints, but they do not provide a basis for criticizing sainthood as a possible ideal. Since these considerations rely on an appeal to the egoistic, hedonistic side of our natures, to use them as a basis for criticizing the ideal of the moral saint would be at best to beg the question and at worst to glorify features of ourselves that ought to be condemned.

The fact that the moral saint would be without qualities which we have and which, indeed, we like to have does not in itself provide reason to condemn the ideal of the moral saint. The fact that some of these qualities are good qualities, however, and that they are qualities we *ought* to like, does provide reason to discourage this ideal and to offer other ideals in its place. In other words, some of the qualities the moral saint necessarily lacks are virtues, albeit non-moral virtues, in the unsaintly characters who have them. The feats of Groucho Marx, Reggie Jackson, and the head chef at Lutèce are impressive accomplishments that it is not only permissible but positively appropriate to recognize as such. In general, the admiration of and striving towards achieving any of a great variety of forms of personal excellence are character traits it is valuable and desirable for people to have. In advocating the development of these varieties of excellence, we advocate non-moral reasons for acting, and in thinking that it is good for a person to strive for an ideal that gives a substantial role to the interests and values that correspond to these virtues, we implicitly acknowledge the goodness of ideals incompatible with that of the moral saint. Finally, if we think that it is *as* good, or even better for a person to strive for one of these ideals than it is for him or her to strive for and realize the ideal of the moral saint, we express a conviction that it is good not to be a moral saint.

MORAL SAINTS AND MORAL THEORIES

I have tried so far to paint a picture—or, rather, two pictures—of what a moral saint might be like, drawing on what I take to be the attitudes and beliefs about morality prevalent in contemporary, common-sense thought. To my suggestion that common-sense morality generates conceptions of moral saints that are unattractive or otherwise unacceptable, it is open to someone to reply, 'so much the worse for common-sense morality'. After all, it is often claimed that the goal of moral philosophy is to correct and improve upon common-sense morality, and I have as yet given no attention to the question of what conceptions of moral sainthood, if any, are generated from the leading moral theories of our time.

A quick, breezy reading of utilitarian and Kantian writings will suggest the images, respectively, of the Loving Saint and the Rational Saint. A utilitarian, with his emphasis on happiness, will certainly prefer the Loving Saint to the Rational one, since the Loving Saint will himself be a happier person than the Rational Saint. A Kantian, with his emphasis on reason, on the other hand, will find at least as much to praise in the latter as in the former. Still, both models, drawn as they are from common sense, appeal to an impure mixture of utilitarian and Kantian intuitions. A more careful examination of these moral theories raises questions about whether either model of moral sainthood would really be advocated by a believer in the explicit doctrines associated with either of these views.

Certainly, the utilitarian in no way denies the value of self-realization. He in no way disparages the development of interests, talents, and other personally attractive traits that I have claimed the moral saint would be without. Indeed, since just these features enhance the happiness both of the individuals who possess them and of those with whom they associate, the ability to promote these features both in oneself and in others will have considerable positive weight in utilitarian calculations.

This implies that the utilitarian would not support moral sainthood as a universal ideal. A world in which everyone, or even a large number of people, achieved moral sainthood—even a world in which they *strove* to achieve it—would probably contain less happiness than a world in which people realized a diversity of ideals involving a variety of personal and perfectionist values. More pragmatic considerations also suggest that, if the utilitarian wants to influence more people to achieve more good, then he would do better to encourage them to pursue happiness-producing goals that are more attractive and more within a normal person's reach.

These considerations still leave open, however, the question of what kind of an ideal the committed utilitarian should privately aspire to himself. Utilitarianism requires him to want to achieve the greatest general happiness, and this would seem to commit him to the ideal of the moral saint.

One might try to use the claims I made earlier as a basis for an argument that a utilitarian should choose to give up utilitarianism. If, as I have said, a moral saint would be a less happy person both to be and to be around than many other possible ideals, perhaps one could create more total happiness by not trying too hard to promote the total happiness. But this argument is simply unconvincing in light of the empirical circumstances of our world. The gain in happiness that would accrue to oneself and one's neighbours by a more well-rounded, richer life than that of the moral saint would be pathetically small in comparison to the amount by which one could increase the general happiness if one devoted oneself explicitly to the care of the sick, the downtrodden, the starving, and the homeless. Of course, there may be psychological limits to the extent to which a person can devote himself to such things without going crazy. But the utilitarian's individual limitations would not thereby become a positive feature of his personal ideals.

The unattractiveness of the moral saint, then, ought not rationally to convince the utilitarian to abandon his utilitarianism. It may, however, convince him to take efforts not to wear his saintly moral aspirations on his sleeve. If it is not too difficult, the utilitarian will try not to make those around him uncomfortable. He will not want to appear 'holier than thou'; he will not want to inhibit others' ability to enjoy themselves. In practice, this might make the perfect utilitarian a less nauseating companion than the moral saint I earlier portrayed. But in so far as this kind of reasoning produces a more bearable public personality, it is at the cost of giving him a personality that must be evaluated as hypocritical and condescending when his private thoughts and attitudes are taken into account.

Still, the criticisms I have raised against the saint of common-sense morality should make some difference to the utilitarian's conception of an ideal which neither requires him to abandon his utilitarian principles nor forces him to fake an interest he does not have or a judgement he does not make. For it may be that a limited and carefully monitored allotment of time and energy to be devoted to the pursuit of some non-moral interests or to the development of some non-moral talents would make a person a better contributor to the general welfare than he would be if he allowed himself no indulgences of this sort. The enjoyment of such activities in no way compromises a commitment to utilitarian principles as long as the involvement with these activities is conditioned by a willingness to give them up whenever it is recognized that they cease to be in the general interest.

This will go some way in mitigating the picture of the loving saint that an understanding of utilitarianism will on first impression suggest. But I think it will not go very far. For the limitations on time and energy will have to be rather severe, and the need to monitor will restrict not only the extent but also the quality of one's attachment to these interests and traits. They are only weak and somewhat peculiar sorts of passions to which one can consciously remain so conditionally committed. Moreover, the way in which the utilitarian can enjoy these 'extra-curricular' aspects of his life is simply not the way in which these aspects are to be enjoyed in so far as they figure into our less saintly ideals.

The problem is not exactly that the utilitarian values these aspects of his life only as a means to an end, for the enjoyment he and others get from these aspects are not a means to, but a part of, the general happiness. None the less, he values these things only because of and in so far as they *are* a part of the general happiness. He values them, as it were, under the description 'a contribution to the general happiness'. This is to be contrasted with the various ways in which these aspects of life may be valued by non-utilitarians. A person might love literature because of the insights into human nature literature affords. Another might love the cultivation of roses because roses are things of great beauty and delicacy. It may be true that these features of the respective activities also explain why these activities are happiness-producing. But, to the non-utilitarian, this may not be to the point. For if one values these activities in these more direct ways, one may not be willing to exchange them for others that produce an equal, or even a greater amount of happiness. From that point of view, it is not because they produce happiness that these activities are valuable; it is because these activities are valuable in more direct and specific ways that they produce happiness.

To adopt a phrase of Bernard Williams's, the utilitarian's manner of valuing the not explicitly moral aspects of his life 'provides (him) with one thought too many'.[1] The requirement that the utilitarian have this thought—periodically, at least—is indicative of not only a weakness but a shallowness in his appreciation of the aspects in question. Thus, the ideals towards which a utilitarian could acceptably strive would remain too close to the model of the common-sense moral saint to escape the criticisms of that model which I earlier suggested. Whether a Kantian would be similarly committed to so restrictive and unattractive a range of possible ideals is a somewhat more difficult question.

The Kantian believes that being morally worthy consists in always acting from maxims that one could will to be universal law, and doing this not out of any pathological desire but out of reverence for the moral law as such. Or, to take a different formulation of the categorical imperative, the Kantian believes that moral action consists in treating other persons always as ends and never as means only. Presumably, and according to Kant himself, the Kantian thereby commits himself to some degree of benevolence as well as to the rules of fair play. But we surely would not will that *every* person become a moral saint, and treating others as ends hardly requires bending over backwards to protect and promote their interests. On one interpretation of Kantian doctrine, then, moral perfection would be achieved simply by unerring obedience to a limited set of side-constraints. On this interpretation, Kantian theory simply does not yield an ideal conception of a person of any fullness comparable to that of the moral saints I have so far been portraying.

[1] Bernard Williams, 'Persons, Character and Morality', in Amélie O. Rorty (ed.), *The Identities of Persons* (Berkeley and Los Angeles, 1976), 214.

On the other hand, Kant does say explicitly that we have a duty of benevolence, a duty not only to allow others to pursue their ends, but to take up their ends as our own. In addition, we have positive duties to ourselves, duties to increase our natural as well as our moral perfection. These duties are unlimited in the degree to which they *may* dominate a life. If action in accordance with and motivated by the thought of these duties is considered virtuous, it is natural to assume that the more one performs such actions, the more virtuous one is. Moreover, of virtue in general Kant says, 'it is an ideal which is unattainable while yet our duty is constantly to approximate to it'.[2] On this interpretation, then, the Kantian moral saint, like the other moral saints I have been considering, is dominated by the motivation to be moral.

Which of these interpretations of Kant one prefers will depend on the interpretation and the importance one gives to the role of the imperfect duties in Kant's overall system. Rather than choose between them here, I shall consider each briefly in turn.

On the second interpretation of Kant, the Kantian moral saint is, not surprisingly, subject to many of the same objections I have been raising against other versions of moral sainthood. Though the Kantian saint may differ from the utilitarian saint as to *which* actions he is bound to perform and which he is bound to refrain from performing, I suspect that the range of activities acceptable to the Kantian saint will remain objectionably restrictive. Moreover, the manner in which the Kantian saint must think about and justify the activities he pursues and the character traits he develops will strike us, as it did with the utilitarian saint, as containing 'one thought too many'. As the utilitarian could value his activities and character traits only in so far as they fell under the description of 'contributions to the general happiness', the Kantian would have to value his activities and character traits in so far as they were manifestations of respect for the moral law. If the development of our powers to achieve physical, intellectual, or artistic excellence, or the activities directed towards making others happy are to have any moral worth, they must arise from a reverence for the dignity that members of our species have as a result of being endowed with pure practical reason. This is a good and noble motivation, to be sure. But it is hardly what one expects to be dominantly behind a person's aspirations to dance as well as Fred Astaire, to paint as well as Picasso, or to solve some outstanding problem in abstract algebra, and it is hardly what one hopes to find lying dominantly behind a father's action on behalf of his son or a lover's on behalf of her beloved.

[2] Immanuel Kant, *The Doctrine of Virtue*, trans. Mary J. Gregor (New York, 1964), 71.

Since the basic problem with any of the models of moral sainthood we have been considering is that they are dominated by a single, all-important value under which all other possible values must be subsumed, it may seem that the alternative interpretation of Kant, as providing a stringent but finite set of obligations and constraints, might provide a more acceptable morality. According to this interpretation of Kant, one is as morally good as can be so long as one devotes some limited portion of one's energies towards altruism and the maintenance of one's physical and spiritual health, and otherwise pursues one's independently motivated interests and values in such a way as to avoid overstepping certain bounds. Certainly, if it be a requirement of an acceptable moral theory that perfect obedience to its laws and maximal devotion to its interests and concerns be something we can whole-heartedly strive for in ourselves and wish for in those around us, it will count in favour of this brand of Kantianism that its commands can be fulfilled without swallowing up the perfect moral agent's entire personality.

Even this more limited understanding of morality, if its connection to Kant's views is to be taken at all seriously, is not likely to give an unqualified seal of approval to the non-morally directed ideals I have been advocating. For Kant is explicit about what he calls 'duties of apathy and self-mastery'[3]—duties to ensure that our passions are never so strong as to interfere with calm, practical deliberation, or so deep as to wrest control from the more disinterested, rational part of ourselves. The tight and self-conscious rein we are thus obliged to keep on our commitments to specific individuals and causes will doubtless restrict our value in these things, assigning them a necessarily attenuated place.

A more interesting objection to this brand of Kantianism, however, comes when we consider the implications of placing the kind of upper bound on moral worthiness which seemed to count in favour of this conception of morality. For to put such a limit on one's capacity to be moral is effectively to deny, not just the moral necessity, but the moral goodness of a devotion to benevolence and the maintenance of justice that passes beyond a certain, required point. It is to deny the possibility of going morally above and beyond the call of a restricted set of duties. Despite my claim that all-consuming moral saintliness is not a particularly healthy and desirable ideal, it seems perverse to insist that, were moral saints to exist, they would not, in their way, be remarkably noble and admirable figures. Despite my conviction that it is as rational and as good for a person to take Katharine Hepburn or Jane Austen as her role model instead of Mother

[3] Ibid. 69–70.

Theresa, it would be absurd to deny that Mother Theresa is a morally better person.

I can think of two ways of viewing morality as having an upper bound. First, we can think that altruism and impartiality are indeed positive moral interests, but that they are moral only if the degree to which these interests are actively pursued remains within certain fixed limits. Second, we can think that these positive interests are only incidentally related to morality and that the essence of morality lies elsewhere, in, say, an implicit social contract or in the recognition of our own dignified rationality. According to the first conception of morality, there is a cut-off line to the amount of altruism or to the extent of devotion to justice and fairness that is worthy of moral praise. But to draw this line earlier than the line that brings the altruist in question into a worse-off position than all those to whom he devotes himself seems unacceptably artificial and gratuitous. According to the second conception, these positive interests are not essentially related to morality at all. But then we are unable to regard a more affectionate and generous expression of goodwill towards others as a natural and reasonable extension of morality, and we encourage a cold and unduly self-centred approach to the development and evaluation of our motivations and concerns.

A moral theory that does not contain the seeds of an all-consuming ideal of moral sainthood thus seems to place false and unnatural limits on our opportunity to do moral good and our potential to deserve moral praise. Yet the main thrust of the arguments of this paper has been leading to the conclusion that, when such ideals are present, they are not ideals to which it is particularly reasonable or healthy or desirable for human beings to aspire. These claims, taken together, have the appearance of a dilemma from which there is no obvious escape. In a moment, I shall argue that, despite appearances, these claims should not be understood as constituting a dilemma. But, before I do, let me briefly describe another path which those who are convinced by my above remarks may feel inclined to take.

If the above remarks are understood to be implicitly critical of the views on the content of morality which seem most popular today, an alternative that naturally suggests itself is that we revise our views about the content of morality. More specifically, my remarks may be taken to support a more Aristotelian, or even a more Nietzschean, approach to moral philosophy. Such a change in approach involves substantially broadening or replacing our contemporary intuitions about which character traits constitute moral virtues and vices and which interests constitute moral interests. If, for example, we include personal bearing, or creativity, or sense of style, as features that contribute to one's *moral* personality, then we can create moral ideals which are incompatible with and probably more attractive than the Kantian and utilitarian ideals I have discussed. Given such an alteration of our conception of morality, the figures with which I have been concerned above might, far from being considered to be moral saints, be seen as morally inferior to other more appealing or more interesting models of individuals.

This approach seems unlikely to succeed, if for no other reason, because it is doubtful that any single, or even any reasonably small number of substantial personal ideals could capture the full range of possible ways of realizing human potential or achieving human good which deserve encouragement and praise. Even if we could provide a sufficiently broad characterization of the range of positive ways for human beings to live, however, I think there are strong reasons not to want to incorporate such a characterization more centrally into the framework of morality itself. For, in claiming that a character trait or activity is morally good, one claims that there is a certain kind of reason for developing that trait or engaging in that activity. Yet, lying behind our criticism of more conventional conceptions of moral sainthood, there seems to be a recognition that among the immensely valuable traits and activities that a human life might positively embrace are some of which we hope that, if a person does embrace them, he does so *not* for moral reasons. In other words, no matter how flexible we make the guide to conduct which we choose to label 'morality', no matter how rich we make the life in which perfect obedience to this guide would result, we will have reason to hope that a person does not wholly rule and direct his life by the abstract and impersonal consideration that such a life would be morally good.

Once it is recognized that morality itself should not serve as a comprehensive guide to conduct, moreover, we can see reasons to retain the admittedly vague contemporary intuitions about what the classification of moral and non-moral virtues, interests, and the like should be. That is, there seem to be important differences between the aspects of a person's life which are currently considered appropriate objects of moral evaluation and the aspects that might be included under the altered conception of morality we are now considering, which the latter approach would tend wrongly to blur or to neglect. Moral evaluation now is focused primarily on features of a person's life over which that person has control; it is largely restricted to aspects of his life which are likely to have considerable effect on other people. These restrictions seem as they should be. Even if responsible people could reach agreement as to what constituted good taste or a healthy degree of well-roundedness, for example, it seems wrong to insist that everyone try to achieve these things or to blame someone who fails or refuses to conform.

If we are not to respond to the unattractiveness of the moral ideals that contemporary theories yield either by offering alternative theories with more palatable ideals or by understanding these theories in such a way as to prevent them from yielding ideals at all, how, then, are we to respond? Simply, I think, by admitting that moral ideals do not, and need not, make the best personal ideals. Earlier, I mentioned one of the consequences of regarding as a test of an adequate moral theory that perfect obedience to its laws and maximal devotion to its interests be something we can wholeheartedly strive for in ourselves and wish for in those around us. Drawing out the consequences somewhat further should, I think, make us more doubtful of the proposed test than of the theories which, on this test, would fail. Given the empirical circumstances of our world, it seems to be an ethical fact that we have unlimited potential to be morally good, and endless opportunity to promote moral interests. But this is not incompatible with the not-so-ethical fact that we have sound, compelling, and not particularly selfish reasons to choose not to devote ourselves univocally to realizing this potential or to taking up this opportunity.

Thus, in one sense at least, I am not really criticizing either Kantianism or utilitarianism. In so far as the point of view I am offering bears directly on recent work in moral philosophy, in fact, it bears on critics of these theories who, in a spirit not unlike the spirit of most of this paper, point out that the perfect utilitarian would be flawed in this way or the perfect Kantian flawed in that.[4] The assumption lying behind these claims, implicitly or explicitly, has been that the recognition of these flaws shows us something wrong with utilitarianism as opposed to Kantianism, or something wrong with Kantianism as opposed to utilitarianism, or something wrong with both of these theories as opposed to some nameless third alternative. The claims of this paper suggest, however, that this assumption is unwarranted. The flaws of a perfect master of a moral theory need not reflect flaws in the intramoral content of the theory itself.

MORAL SAINTS AND MORAL PHILOSOPHY

In pointing out the regrettable features and the necessary absence of some desirable features in a moral saint, I have not meant to condemn the moral

[4] See, e.g., Williams, 'Persons, Character and Morality', and J. J. C. Smart and Bernard Williams, *Utilitarianism: For and Against* (New York, 1973). Also Michael Stocker, 'The Schizophrenia of Modern Ethical Theories', Chapter 3 in this volume.

saint or the person who aspires to become one. Rather, I have meant to insist that the ideal of moral sainthood should not be held as a standard against which any other ideal must be judged or justified, and that the posture we take in response to the recognition that our lives are not as morally good as they might be need not be defensive.[5] It is misleading to insist that one is *permitted* to live a life in which the goals, relationships, activities, and interests that one pursues are not maximally morally good. For our lives are not so comprehensively subject to the requirement that we apply for permission, and our non-moral reasons for the goals we set ourselves are not excuses, but may rather be positive, good reasons which do not exist *despite* any reasons that might threaten to outweigh them. In other words, a person may be *perfectly wonderful* without being *perfectly moral.*

Recognizing this requires a perspective which contemporary moral philosophy has generally ignored. This perspective yields judgements of a type that is neither moral nor egoistic. Like moral judgements, judgements about what it would be good for a person to be are made from a point of view outside the limits set by the values, interests, and desires that the person might actually have. And, like moral judgements, these judgements claim for themselves a kind of objectivity or a grounding in a perspective which any rational and perceptive being can take up. Unlike moral judgements, however, the good with which these judgements are concerned is not the good of anyone or any group other than the individual himself.

None the less, it would be equally misleading to say that these judgements are made for the sake of the individual himself. For these judgements are not concerned with what kind of life it is in a person's interest to lead, but with what kind of interests it would be good for a person to have, and it need not be in a person's interest that he acquire or maintain objectively good interests. Indeed, the model of the Loving Saint, whose interests are identified with the interests of morality, is a model of a person for whom the dictates of rational self-interest and the dictates of morality coincide. Yet, I have urged that we have reason not to aspire to this ideal and that some of us would have reason to be sorry if our children aspired to and achieved it.

The moral point of view, we might say, is the point of view one takes up

[5] George Orwell makes a similar point in 'Reflections on Gandhi', in *A Collection of Essays by George Orwell* (New York, 1945), 176: 'sainthood is . . . a thing that human beings must avoid . . . It is too readily assumed that . . . the ordinary man only rejects it because it is too difficult; in other words, that the average human being is a failed saint. It is doubtful whether this is true. Many people genuinely do not wish to be saints, and it is probable that some who achieve or aspire to sainthood have never felt much temptation to be human beings.'

in so far as one takes the recognition of the fact that one is just one person among others equally real and deserving of the good things in life as a fact with practical consequences, a fact the recognition of which demands expression in one's actions and in the form of one's practical deliberations. Competing moral theories offer alternative answers to the question of what the most correct or the best way to express this fact is. In doing so, they offer alternative ways to evaluate and to compare the variety of actions, states of affairs, and so on that appear good and bad to agents from other, non-moral points of view. But it seems that alternative interpretations of the moral point of view do not exhaust the ways in which our actions, characters, and their consequences can be comprehensively and objectively evaluated. Let us call the point of view from which we consider what kinds of lives are good lives, and what kinds of persons it would be good for ourselves and others to be, the *point of view of individual perfection.*

Since either point of view provides a way of comprehensively evaluating a person's life, each point of view takes account of, and, in a sense, subsumes the other. From the moral point of view, the perfection of an individual life will have some, but limited, value—for each individual remains, after all, just one person among others. From the perfectionist point of view, the moral worth of an individual's relation to his world will likewise have some, but limited, value—for, as I have argued, the (perfectionist) goodness of an individual's life does not vary proportionally with the degree to which it exemplifies moral goodness.

It may not be the case that the perfectionist point of view is like the moral point of view in being a point of view we are ever *obliged* to take up and express in our actions. None the less, it provides us with reasons that are independent of moral reasons for wanting ourselves and others to develop our characters and live our lives in certain ways. When we take up this point of view and ask how much it would be good for an individual to act from the moral point of view, we do not find an obvious answer.[6]

The considerations of this paper suggest, at any rate, that the answer is not 'as much as possible'. This has implications both for the continued development of moral theories and for the development of metamoral views and for our conception of moral philosophy more generally. From

[6] A similar view, which has strongly influenced mine, is expressed by Thomas Nagel in 'The Fragmentation of Value', in *Mortal Questions* (Cambridge, 1979), 128–41. Nagel focuses on the difficulties such apparently incommensurable points of view create for specific, isolable practical decisions that must be made both by individuals and by societies. In focusing on the way in which these points of view figure into the development of individual personal ideals, the questions with which I am concerned are more likely to lurk in the background of any individual's life.

the moral point of view, we have reasons to want people to live lives that seem good from outside that point of view. If, as I have argued, this means that we have reason to want people to live lives that are not morally perfect, then any plausible moral theory must make use of some conception of supererogation.[7]

If moral philosophers are to address themselves at the most basic level to the question of how people should live, however, they must do more than adjust the content of their moral theories in ways that leave room for the affirmation of non-moral values. They must examine explicitly the range and nature of these non-moral values, and, in light of this examination, they must ask how the acceptance of a moral theory is to be understood and acted upon. For the claims of this paper do not so much conflict with the content of any particular currently popular moral theory as they call into question a metamoral assumption that implicitly surrounds discussions of moral theory more generally. Specifically, they call into question the assumption that it is always better to be morally better.

The role morality plays in the development of our characters and the shape of our practical deliberations need be neither that of a universal medium into which all other values must be translated nor that of an ever-present filter through which all other values must pass. This is not to say that moral value should not be an important, even the most important, kind of value we attend to in evaluating and improving ourselves and our world. It is to say that our values cannot be fully comprehended on the model of a hierarchical system with morality at the top.

The philosophical temperament will naturally incline, at this point, towards asking, 'What, then, *is* at the top—or, if there is no top, how *are* we to decide when and how much to be moral?' In other words, there is a temptation to seek a metamoral—though not, in the standard sense, metaethical—theory that will give us principles, or, at least, informal directives on the basis of which we can develop and evaluate more comprehensive personal ideals. Perhaps a theory that distinguishes among the various

[7] The variety of forms that a conception of supererogation might take, however, has not generally been noticed. Moral theories that make use of this notion typically do so by identifying some specific set of principles as universal moral requirements and supplement this list with a further set of directives which it is morally praiseworthy but not required for an agent to follow. (See, e.g., Charles Fried, *Right and Wrong* (Cambridge, Mass., 1979).) But it is possible that the ability to live a morally blameless life cannot be so easily or definitely secured as this type of theory would suggest. The fact that there are some situations in which an agent is morally required to do something and other situations in which it would be good but not required for an agent to do something does not imply that there are specific principles such that, in any situation, an agent is required to act in accordance with these principles and other specific principles such that, in any situation, it would be good but not required for an agent to act in accordance with those principles.

roles a person is expected to play within a life—as professional, as citizen, as friend, and so on—might give us some rules that would offer us, if nothing else, a better framework in which to think about and discuss these questions. I am pessimistic, however, about the chances of such a theory to yield substantial and satisfying results. For I do not see how a metamoral theory could be constructed which would not be subject to considerations parallel to those which seem inherently to limit the appropriateness of regarding moral theories as ultimate comprehensive guides for action.

This suggests that, at some point, both in our philosophizing and in our lives, we must be willing to raise normative questions from a perspective that is unattached to a commitment to any particular well-ordered system of values. It must be admitted that, in doing so, we run the risk of finding normative answers that diverge from the answers given by whatever moral theory one accepts. This, I take it, is the grain of truth in G. E. Moore's 'open-question' argument. In the background of this paper, then, there lurks a commitment to what seems to me to be a healthy form of intuitionism. It is a form of intuitionism which is not intended to take the place of more rigorous, systematically developed, moral theories—rather, it is intended to put these more rigorous and systematic moral theories in their place.[8]

[8] I have benefited from the comments of many people who have heard or read an earlier draft of this paper. I wish particularly to thank Douglas MacLean, Robert Nozick, Martha Nussbaum, and the Society for Ethics and Legal Philosophy.

5

THE SOVEREIGNTY OF GOOD OVER OTHER CONCEPTS

IRIS MURDOCH

The development of consciousness in human beings is inseparably connected with the use of metaphor. Metaphors are not merely peripheral decorations or even useful models, they are fundamental forms of our awareness of our condition: metaphors of space, metaphors of movement, metaphors of vision. Philosophy in general, and moral philosophy in particular, has in the past often concerned itself with what it took to be our most important images, clarifying existing ones and developing new ones. Philosophical argument which consists of such image-play, I mean the great metaphysical systems, is usually inconclusive, and is regarded by many contemporary thinkers as valueless. The status and merit of this type of argument raises, of course, many problems. However, it seems to me impossible to discuss certain kinds of concepts without resort to metaphor, since the concepts are themselves deeply metaphorical and cannot be analysed into non-metaphorical components without a loss of substance. Modern behaviouristic philosophy attempts such an analysis in the case of certain moral concepts, it seems to me without success. One of the motives of the attempt is a wish to 'neutralize' moral philosophy, to produce a philosophical discussion of morality which does not take sides. Metaphors often carry a moral charge, which analysis in simpler and plainer terms is designed to remove. This too seems to me to be misguided. Moral philosophy cannot avoid taking sides, and would-be neutral philosophers merely take sides surreptitiously. Moral philosophy is the examination of the most important of all human activities, and I think that two things are required of it. The examination should be realistic. Human nature, as opposed to the natures of other hypothetical spiritual beings, has certain discoverable attributes, and these should be suitably considered in any discussion of morality. Secondly, since an ethical system cannot but commend an ideal,

From Iris Murdoch, *The Sovereignty of Good* (London: Ark, 1985), 77–104. Reprinted by permission of Routledge and the author.

it should commend a worthy ideal. Ethics should not be merely an analysis of ordinary mediocre conduct, it should be a hypothesis about good conduct and about how this can be achieved. How can we make ourselves better? is a question moral philosophers should attempt to answer. And if I am right the answer will come partly at least in the form of explanatory and persuasive metaphors. The metaphors which I myself favour and the philosopher under whose banner I am fighting I will make clear shortly.

First, however, I wish to mention very briefly two fundamental assumptions of my argument. If either of these is denied, what follows will be less convincing. I assume that human beings are naturally selfish and that human life has no external point or τέλος. That human beings are naturally selfish seems true on the evidence, whenever and wherever we look at them, in spite of a very small number of apparent exceptions. About the quality of this selfishness modern psychology has had something to tell us. The psyche is a historically determined individual relentlessly looking after itself. In some ways it resembles a machine; in order to operate it needs sources of energy, and it is predisposed to certain patterns of activity. The area of its vaunted freedom of choice is not usually very great. One of its main pastimes is daydreaming. It is reluctant to face unpleasant realities. Its consciousness is not normally a transparent glass through which it views the world, but a cloud of more or less fantastic reverie designed to protect the psyche from pain. It constantly seeks consolation, either through imagined inflation of self or through fictions of a theological nature. Even its loving is more often than not an assertion of self. I think we can probably recognize ourselves in this rather depressing description.

That human life has no external point or τέλος is a view as difficult to argue as its opposite, and I shall simply assert it. I can see no evidence to suggest that human life is not something self-contained. There are properly many patterns and purposes within life, but there is no general and as it were externally guaranteed pattern or purpose of the kind for which philosophers and theologians used to search. We are what we seem to be, transient mortal creatures subject to necessity and chance. This is to say that there is, in my view, no God in the traditional sense of that term; and the traditional sense is perhaps the only sense. When Bonhoeffer says that God wants us to live as if there were no God, I suspect he is misusing words. Equally the various metaphysical substitutes for God—Reason, Science, History—are false deities. Our destiny can be examined but it cannot be justified or totally explained. We are simply here. And if there is any kind of sense or unity in human life, and the dream of this does not cease to haunt us, it is of some other kind and must be sought within a human experience which has nothing outside it.

The idea of life as self-enclosed and purposeless is of course not simply a product of the despair of our own age. It is the natural product of the advance of science and has developed over a long period. It has already in fact occasioned a whole era in the history of philosophy, beginning with Kant and leading on to the existentialism and the analytic philosophy of the present day. The chief characteristic of this phase of philosophy can be briefly stated: Kant abolished God and made man God in His stead. We are still living in the age of the Kantian man, or Kantian man-god. Kant's conclusive exposure of the so-called proofs of the existence of God, his analysis of the limitations of speculative reason, together with his eloquent portrayal of the dignity of rational man, has had results which might possibly dismay him. How recognizable, how familiar to us, is the man so beautifully portrayed in the *Grundlegung*, who confronted even with Christ turns away to consider the judgement of his own conscience and to hear the voice of his own reason. Stripped of the exiguous metaphysical background which Kant was prepared to allow him, this man is with us still, free, independent, lonely, powerful, rational, responsible, brave, the hero of so many novels and books of moral philosophy. The *raison d'être* of this attractive but misleading creature is not far to seek. He is the offspring of the age of science, confidently rational and yet increasingly aware of his alienation from the material universe which his discoveries reveal; and since he is not a Hegelian (Kant, not Hegel, has provided Western ethics with its dominating image), his alienation is without cure. He is the ideal citizen of the liberal state, a warning held up to tyrants. He has the virtue which the age requires and admires, courage. It is not such a very long step from Kant to Nietzsche, and from Nietzsche to existentialism and the Anglo-Saxon ethical doctrines which in some ways closely resemble it. In fact Kant's man had already received a glorious incarnation nearly a century earlier in the work of Milton: his proper name is Lucifer.

The centre of this type of post-Kantian moral philosophy is the notion of the will as the creator of value. Values which were previously in some sense inscribed in the heavens and guaranteed by God collapse into the human will. There is no transcendent reality. The idea of the good remains indefinable and empty so that human choice may fill it. The sovereign moral concept is freedom, or possibly courage in a sense which identifies it with freedom, will, power. This concept inhabits a quite separate top level of human activity, since it is the guarantor of the secondary values created by choice. Act, choice, decision, responsibility, independence are emphasized in this philosophy of puritanical origin and apparent austerity. It must be said in its favour that this image of human nature has been the inspiration of political liberalism. However, as Hume once wisely observed, good political philosophy is not necessarily good moral philosophy.

This impression is indeed an austere one, but there is something still to be added to it. What place, one might ask, is left in this stern picture of solitary all-responsible man for the life of the emotions? In fact the emotions have a rather significant place. They enter through a back door left open by Kant and the whole romantic movement has followed after. Puritanism and romanticism are natural partners and we are still living with their partnership. Kant held a very interesting theory about the relation of the emotions to the reason. He did not officially recognize the emotions as part of the structure of morality. When he speaks of love he tells us to distinguish between practical love, which is a matter of rational actions, and pathological love, which is a mere matter of feeling. He wants to segregate the messy warm empirical psyche from the clean operations of the reason. However, in a footnote in the *Grundlegung* he allows a subordinate place to a particular emotion, that of *Achtung*, or respect for the moral law. This emotion is a kind of suffering pride which accompanies, though it does not motivate, the recognition of duty. It is an actual experience of freedom (akin to the existentialist *Angst*), the realization that although swayed by passions we are also capable of rational conduct. A close relation of this concept is Kant's handsome conception of the Sublime. We experience the Sublime when we confront the awful contingency of nature or of human fate and return into ourselves with a proud shudder of rational power. How abject we are, and yet our consciousness is of an infinite value. Here it is Belial not Satan who speaks.

> For who would lose,
> Though full of pain, this intellectual being,
> Those thoughts that wander through eternity . . .

The emotions are allowed to return to the scene as a kind of allowable, rather painful, thrill which is a by-product of our status as dignified rational beings.

What appears in Kant as a footnote and a side issue takes, however, a central place in the development which his philosophy underwent in the romantic movement. I would sum this up by saying that romanticism tended to transform the idea of death into the idea of suffering. To do this is of course an age-old human temptation. Few ideas invented by humanity have more power to console than the idea of purgatory. To buy back evil by suffering in the embrace of good: what could be more satisfying, or, as a romantic might say, more thrilling? Indeed the central image of Christianity lends itself just this illegitimate transformation. The *Imitatio Christi* in the later work of Kierkegaard is a distinguished instance of romantic self-indulgence on this theme, though it may seem unkind to say this of a great and most endearing writer who really did suffer for telling his society some truths. The idea of a rather exciting suffering freedom soon began to enliven the austerity of the puritan half of the Kantian picture, and with this went a taming and beautifying of the idea of death, a cult of pseudo-death and pseudo-transience. Death becomes *Liebestod*, painful and exhilarating, or at worst charming and sweetly tearful. I speak here of course, not of the great romantic artists and thinkers at their best, but of the general beaten track which leads from Kant to the popular philosophies of the present day. When the neo-Kantian Lucifer gets a glimpse of real death and real chance, he takes refuge in sublime emotions and veils with an image of tortured freedom that which has been rightly said to be the proper study of philosophers.

When Kant wanted to find something clean and pure outside the mess of the selfish empirical psyche, he followed a sound instinct but, in my view, looked in the wrong place. His enquiry led him back again into the self, now pictured as angelic, and inside this angel-self his followers have tended to remain. I want now to return to the beginning and look again at the powerful energy system of the self-defensive psyche in the light of the question, How can we make ourselves better? With such an opponent to deal with, one may doubt whether the idea of the proud, naked will directed towards right action is a realistic and sufficient formula. I think that the ordinary man, with the simple religious conceptions which make sense for him, has usually held a more just view of the matter than the voluntaristic philosopher, and a view incidentally which is in better accord with the findings of modern psychology. Religion normally emphasizes states of mind as well as actions, and regards states of mind as the genetic background of action: pureness of heart, meekness of spirit. Religion provides devices for the purification of states of mind. The believer feels that he needs, and can receive, extra help. 'Not I, but Christ.' The real existence of such help is often used as an argument for the truth of religious doctrines. Of course prayer and sacraments may be 'misused' by the believer as mere instruments of consolation. But, whatever one thinks of its theological context, it does seem that prayer can actually induce a better quality of consciousness and provide an energy for good action which would not otherwise be available. Modern psychology here supports the ordinary person's, or ordinary believer's, instinctive sense of the importance of his states of mind and the availability of supplementary energy. Psychology might indeed prompt contemporary behaviouristic philosophers to re-examine their discarded concepts of 'experience' and 'consciousness'. By opening our eyes we do not necessarily see what confronts us. We are anxiety-ridden animals. Our minds are continually active, fabricating an anxious, usually self-preoccupied, often falsifying *veil* which partially conceals the world. Our states of consciousness differ in quality, our fantasies and reveries are not trivial and unimportant, they are profoundly connected with our energies and our ability to choose and act. And if quality of consciousness matters, then anything which alters consciousness in the direction of unselfishness, objectivity, and realism is to be connected with virtue.

Following a hint in Plato (*Phaedrus* 250), I shall start by speaking of what is perhaps the most obvious thing in our surroundings which is an occasion for 'unselfing', and that is what is popularly called beauty. Recent philosophers tend to avoid this term because they prefer to talk of reasons rather than of experiences. But the implication of experience with beauty seems to me to be something of great importance which should not be bypassed in favour of analysis of critical vocabularies. Beauty is the convenient and traditional name of something which art and nature share, and which gives a fairly clear sense to the idea of quality of experience and change of consciousness. I am looking out of my window in an anxious and resentful state of mind, oblivious of my surroundings, brooding perhaps on some damage done to my prestige. Then suddenly I observe a hovering kestrel. In a moment everything is altered. The brooding self with its hurt vanity has disappeared. There is nothing now but kestrel. And when I return to thinking of the other matter it seems less important. And of course this is something which we may also do deliberately: give attention to nature in order to clear our minds of selfish care. It may seem odd to start the argument against what I have roughly labelled as 'romanticism' by using the case of attention to nature. In fact I do not think that any of the great romantics really believed that we receive but what we give and in our life alone does nature live, although the lesser ones tended to follow Kant's lead and use nature as an occasion for exalted self-feeling. The great romantics, including the one I have just quoted, transcended 'romanticism'. A self-directed enjoyment of nature seems to me to be something forced. More naturally, as well as more properly, we take a self-forgetful pleasure in the sheer alien pointless independent existence of animals, birds, stones, and trees. 'Not how the world is, but that it is, is the mystical.'

I take this starting-point, not because I think it is the most important place of moral change, but because I think it is the most accessible one. It is so patently a good thing to take delight in flowers and animals that people who bring home potted plants and watch kestrels might even be surprised at the notion that these things have anything to do with virtue. The surprise is a product of the fact that, as Plato pointed out, beauty is the only spiritual thing which we love by instinct. When we move from beauty in nature to beauty in art we are already in a more difficult region. The experience of art is more easily degraded than the experience of nature. A great deal of art, perhaps most art, actually is self-consoling fantasy, and even great art cannot guarantee the quality of its consumer's consciousness. However, great art exists and is sometimes properly experienced and even a shallow experience of what is great can have its effect. Art, and by 'art' from now on I mean good art, not fantasy art, affords us a pure delight in the independent existence of what is excellent. Both in its genesis and its enjoyment it is a thing totally opposed to selfish obsession. It invigorates our best faculties and, to use Platonic language, inspires love in the highest part of the soul. It is able to do this partly by virtue of something which it shares with nature: a perfection of form which invites unpossessive contemplation and resists absorption into the selfish dream life of the consciousness.

Art, however, considered as a sacrament or a source of good energy, possesses an extra dimension. Art is less accessible than nature but also more edifying since it is actually a human product, and certain arts are actually 'about' human affairs in a direct sense. Art is a human product, and virtues as well as talents are required of the artist. The good artist, in relation to his art, is brave, truthful, patient, humble; and even in non-representational art we may receive intuitions of these qualities. One may also suggest, more cautiously, that non-representational art does seem to express more positively something which is to do with virtue. The spiritual role of music has often been acknowledged, though theorists have been chary of analysing it. However that may be, the representational arts, which more evidently hold the mirror up to nature, seem to be concerned with morality in a way which is not simply an effect of our intuition of the artist's discipline.

These arts, especially literature and painting, show us the peculiar sense in which the concept of virtue is tied on to the human condition. They show us the absolute pointlessness of virtue while exhibiting its supreme importance; the enjoyment of art is a training in the love of virtue. The pointlessness of art is not the pointlessness of a game; it is the pointlessness of human life itself, and form in art is properly the simulation of the self-contained aimlessness of the universe. Good art reveals what we are usually too selfish and too timid to recognize, the minute and absolutely random detail of the world, and reveals it together with a sense of unity and form. This form often seems to us mysterious because it resists the easy patterns of the fantasy, whereas there is nothing mysterious about the forms of bad art since they are the recognizable and familiar rat-runs of selfish daydream. Good art shows us how difficult it is to be objective by showing us how differently the world looks to an objective vision. We are presented with a truthful image of the human condition in a form which can be steadily contemplated; and indeed this is the only context in which many of us are capable of contemplating it at all. Art transcends selfish and obsessive limitations of personality and can enlarge the sensibility of its consumer. It is a kind of goodness by proxy. Most of all it exhibits to us the connection, in *human* beings, of clear realistic vision with compassion. The realism of a great artist is not a photographic realism, it is essentially both pity and justice.

Herein we find a remarkable redemption of our tendency to conceal death and chance by the invention of forms. Any story which we tell about ourselves consoles us, since it imposes pattern upon something which might otherwise seem intolerably chancy and incomplete. However, human life is chancy and incomplete. It is the role of tragedy, and also of comedy, and of painting to show us suffering without a thrill and death without a consolation. Or if there is any consolation, it is the austere consolation of a beauty which teaches that nothing in life is of any value except the attempt to be virtuous. Masochism is the artist's greatest and most subtle enemy. It is not easy to portray death, real death, not fake prettified death. Even Tolstoy did not really manage it in *Ivan Ilyich*, although he did elsewhere. The great deaths of literature are few, but they show us with an exemplary clarity the way in which art invigorates us by a juxtaposition, almost an identification, of pointlessness and value. The death of Patroclus, the death of Cordelia, the death of Petya Rostov. All is vanity. The only thing which is of real importance is the ability to see it all clearly and respond to it justly which is inseparable from virtue. Perhaps one of the greatest achievements of all is to join this sense of absolute mortality not to the tragic but to the comic. Shallow and Silence. Stefan Trofimovich Verhovensky.

Art then is not a diversion or a side issue, it is the most educational of all human activities and a place in which the nature of morality can be *seen*. Art gives a clear sense to many ideas which seem more puzzling when we meet with them elsewhere, and it is a clue to what happens elsewhere. An understanding of any art involves a recognition of hierarchy and authority. There are very evident degrees of merit, there are heights and distances; even Shakespeare is not perfect. Good art, unlike bad art, unlike 'happenings', is something pre-eminently outside us and resistant to our consciousness. We surrender ourselves to its *authority* with a love which is unpossessive and unselfish. Art shows us the only sense in which the permanent and incorruptible is compatible with the transient; and whether representational or not it reveals to us aspects of our world which our ordinary dull dream-consciousness is unable to see. Art pierces the veil and gives sense to the notion of a reality which lies beyond appearance; it exhibits virtue in its true guise in the context of death and chance.

Plato held that beauty could be a starting-point of the good life, but he came to mistrust art and we can see played out in that great spirit the peculiarly distressing struggle between the artist and the saint. Plato allowed to the beauty of the lovely boy an awakening power which he denied to the beauty of nature or of art. He seems to have come to believe that all art is bad art, a mere fiction and consolation which distorts reality. About nature he seems, in the context of the theory of forms, to have been at least once in doubt. Are there forms of mud, hair, and dirt? If there are then nature is redeemed into the area of truthful vision. (My previous argument assumes of course, in Platonic terms, that there are.) Another starting-point, or road, which Plato speaks of more often, however, is the way of the τέχναι, the sciences, crafts, and intellectual disciplines excluding the arts. I think there is a way of the intellect, a sense in which intellectual disciplines are moral disciplines, and this is not too difficult to discern. There are important bridge ideas between morality and other at first sight different human activities, and these ideas are perhaps most clearly seen in the context of the τέχναι. And as when we use the nature of art as a clue, we may be able to learn more about the central area of morality if we examine what are essentially the same concepts more simply on display elsewhere. I mean such concepts as justice, accuracy, truthfulness, realism, humility, courage as the ability to sustain clear vision, love as attachment or even passion without sentiment or self.

The τέχνη which Plato thought was most important was mathematics, because it was most rigorous and abstract. I shall take an example of a τέχνη more congenial to myself: learning a language. If I am learning, for instance, Russian, I am confronted by an authoritative structure which commands my respect. The task is difficult and the goal is distant and perhaps never entirely attainable. My work is a progressive revelation of something which exists independently of me. Attention is rewarded by a knowledge of reality. Love of Russian leads me away from myself towards something alien to me, something which my consciousness cannot take over, swallow up, deny or make unreal. The honesty and humility required of the student—not to pretend to know what one does not know—is the preparation for the honesty and humility of the scholar who does not even feel tempted to suppress the fact which damns his theory. Of course a τέχνη can be misused; a scientist might feel he ought to give up a certain branch of study if he knew that his discoveries would be used wickedly. But apart from special contexts, studying is normally an exercise of virtue as well as of talent, and shows us a fundamental way in which virtue is related to the real world.

I suggested that we could see most clearly in the case of the τέχναι the nature of concepts very central to morality such as justice, truthfulness, or humility. We can see too the growth and the interconnection of these concepts, as when what looks like mere accuracy at one end looks more like justice or courage, or even love, at the other. Developing a *Sprachgefühl* is developing a judicious respectful sensibility to something which is very like another organism. An intellectual discipline can play the same kind of role as that which I have attributed to art, it can stretch the imagination, enlarge the vision, and strengthen the judgement. When Plato made mathematics the king τέχνη, he was regarding mathematical thought as leading the mind away from the material world and enabling it to perceive a reality of a new kind, very unlike ordinary appearances. And one might regard other disciplines, history, philology, chemistry, as presenting us with a new kind of subject matter and showing us a new reality behind appearance. These studies are not only an exercise in virtue, they might be thought of as introductory images of the spiritual life. But they are not the spiritual life itself and the mind which has ascended no farther has not achieved the whole of virtue.

I want now to make a closer approach to the central subject of my argument, the Good. Beauty and the τέχναι are, to use Plato's image, the text written in large letters. The concept Good itself is the much harder to discern but essentially similar text written in small letters. In intellectual disciplines and in the enjoyment of art and nature we discover value in our ability to forget self, to be realistic, to perceive justly. We use our imagination not to escape the world but to join it, and this exhilarates us because of the distance between our ordinary dulled consciousness and an apprehension of the real. The value concepts are here patently tied onto the world, they are stretched as it were between the truth-seeking mind and the world, they are not moving about on their own as adjuncts of the personal will. The authority of morals is the authority of truth, that is of reality. We can see the length, the extension, of these concepts as patient attention transforms accuracy without interval into just discernment. Here too we can see it as natural to the particular kind of creatures that we are that love should be inseparable from justice, and clear vision from respect for the real.

That virtue operates in exactly the same kind of way in the central area of morality is less easy to perceive. Human beings are far more complicated and enigmatic and ambiguous than languages or mathematical concepts, and selfishness operates in a much more devious and frenzied manner in our relations with them. Ignorance, muddle, fear, wishful thinking, lack of tests often make us feel that moral choice is something arbitrary, a matter for personal will rather than for attentive study. Our attachments tend to be selfish and strong, and the transformation of our loves from selfishness to unselfishness is sometimes hard even to conceive of. Yet is the situation really so different? Should a retarded child be kept at home or sent to an institution? Should an elderly relation who is a trouble-maker be cared for or asked to go away? Should an unhappy marriage be continued for the sake of the children? Should I leave my family in order to do political work? Should I neglect them in order to practise my art? The love which brings the right answer is an exercise of justice and realism and really *looking*. The difficulty is to keep the attention fixed upon the real situation and to prevent it from returning surreptitiously to the self with consolations of self-pity, resentment, fantasy, and despair. The refusal to attend may even induce a fictitious sense of freedom: I may as well toss a coin. Of course virtue is good habit and dutiful action. But the background condition of such habit and such action, in human beings, is a just mode of vision and a good quality of consciousness. It is a *task* to come to see the world as it is. A philosophy which leaves duty without a context and exalts the idea of freedom and power as a separate top level value ignores this task and obscures the relation between virtue and reality. We act rightly 'when the time comes' not out of strength of will but out of the quality of our usual attachments and with the kind of energy and discernment which we have available. And to this the whole activity of our consciousness is relevant.

The central explanatory image which joins together the different aspects of the picture which I have been trying to exhibit is the concept of Good. It is a concept which is not easy to understand partly because it has so many false doubles, jumped-up intermediaries invented by human selfishness to make the difficult task of virtue look easier and more attractive: History, God, Lucifer, Ideas of power, freedom, purpose, reward, even judgement are irrelevant. Mystics of all kinds have usually known this and have attempted by extremities of language to portray the nakedness and aloneness of Good, its absolute for-nothingness. One might say that true morality is a sort of unesoteric mysticism, having its source in an austere and unconsoled love of the Good. When Plato wants to explain Good he uses the image of the sun. The moral pilgrim emerges from the cave and begins to see the real world in the light of the sun, and last of all is able to look at the sun itself. I want now to comment on various aspects of this extremely rich metaphor.

The sun is seen at the end of a long quest which involves a reorientation (the prisoners have to turn round) and an ascent. It is real, it is out there, but very distant. It gives light and energy and enables us to know truth. In its light we see the things of the world in their true relationships. Looking at it itself is supremely difficult and is unlike looking at things in its light. It is a different kind of thing from what it illuminates. Note the metaphor of 'thing' here. Good is a concept about which, and not only in philosophical language, we naturally use a Platonic terminology, when we speak about seeking the Good, or loving the Good. We may also speak seriously of ordinary things, people, works of art, as being good, although we are also well aware of their imperfections. Good lives as it were on both sides of the barrier and we can combine the aspiration to complete goodness with a realistic sense of achievement within our limitations. For all our frailty the command 'be perfect' has sense for us. The concept Good resists collapse into the selfish empirical consciousness. It is not a mere value tag of the choosing will, and functional and casual uses of 'good' (a good knife, a good fellow) are not, as some philosophers have wished to argue, clues to the structure of the concept. The proper and serious use of the term refers us to a perfection which is perhaps never exemplified in the world we know ('There is no good in us') and which carries with it the ideas of hierarchy and transcendence. How do we know that the very great are not the perfect? We see differences, we sense directions, and we know that the Good is still somewhere beyond. The self, the place where we live, is a place of illusion. Goodness is connected with the attempt to see the unself, to see and to respond to the real world in the light of a virtuous consciousness. This is the non-metaphysical meaning of the idea of transcendence to which philosophers have so constantly resorted in their explanations of goodness. 'Good is a transcendent reality' means that virtue is the attempt to pierce the veil of selfish consciousness and join the world as it really is. It is an empirical fact about human nature that this attempt cannot be entirely successful.

Of course we are dealing with a metaphor, but with a very important metaphor and one which is not just a property of philosophy and not just a model. As I said at the beginning, we are creatures who use irreplaceable metaphors in many of our most important activities. And the decent man has probably always, if uncertainly and inexplicably, been able to distinguish between the real Good and its false double. In most ideological contexts virtue can be loved for its own sake. The fundamental metaphors as it were carry this love through and beyond what is false. Metaphors can be a mode of understanding, and so of acting upon, our condition. Philosophers merely do explicitly and systematically and often with art what the ordinary person does by instinct. Plato, who understood this situation better than most of the metaphysical philosophers, referred to many of his theories as 'myths', and tells us that the *Republic* is to be thought of as an allegory of the soul. 'Perhaps it is a pattern laid up in heaven where he who wishes can see it and become its citizen. But it doesn't matter whether it exists or ever will exist; it is the only city in whose politics [the good man] can take part' (*Republic* 592).

I want now to continue to explain the concept of the Good and its peculiar relation to other concepts by speaking first of the unifying power of this idea, and secondly of its indefinability. I said earlier that as far as I could see there was no metaphysical unity in human life: all was subject to mortality and chance. And yet we continue to dream of unity. Art is our most ardent dream. In fact morality does actually display to us a sort of unity, though of a peculiar kind and quite unlike the closed theoretical unity of the ideologies. Plato pictures the journeying soul as ascending through four stages of enlightenment, progressively discovering at each stage that what it was treating as realities were only shadows or images of something more real still. At the end of its quest it reaches a non-hypothetical first principle which is the form or idea of the Good, which enables it then to descend and retrace its path, but moving only through the forms or true conception of that which it previously understood only in part (*Republic* 510–11). This passage in the *Republic* has aroused a great deal of discussion but it seems to me that its general application to morality is fairly clear. The mind which has ascended to the vision of the Good can subsequently see the concepts through which it has ascended (art, work, nature, people, ideas, institutions, situations, etc., etc.) in their true nature and in their proper relationships to each other. The good man knows whether and when art or politics is more important than family. The good man sees the way in which the virtues are related to each other. Plato never in fact anywhere expounds a systematic and unitary view of the world of the forms, though he implies that there is a hierarchy of forms. (Truth and Knowledge, for instance, come fairly closely underneath Good (*Republic* 509a).) What he does suggest is that we work with the idea of such a hierarchy in so far as we introduce order into our conceptions of the world through our apprehension of Good.

This seems to me to be true. Plato's image implies that complete unity is not seen until one has reached the summit, but moral advance carries with it intuitions of unity which are increasingly less misleading. As we deepen our notions of the virtues, we introduce relationship and hierarchy. Courage, which seemed at first to be something on its own, a sort of specialized daring of the spirit, is now seen to be a particular operation of wisdom and love. We come to distinguish a self-assertive ferocity from the kind of courage which would enable a man coolly to choose the labour camp rather than the easy compromise with the tyrant. It would be impossible to have only one virtue unless it were a very trivial one such as thrift. Such transformations as these are cases of seeing the order of the world in the light of the Good and revisiting the true, or more true, conceptions of that which we formerly misconceived. Freedom, we find out, is not an inconsequential chucking of one's weight about, it is the disciplined overcoming of self. Humility is not a peculiar habit of self-effacement, rather like having an inaudible voice, it is selfless respect for reality and one of the most difficult and central of all virtues.

Because of his ambiguous attitude to the sensible world, of which I have already spoken, and because of his confidence in the revolutionary power of mathematics, Plato sometimes seems to imply that the road towards the Good leads away from the world of particularity and detail. However, he speaks of a descending as well as an ascending dialectic and he speaks of a return to the cave. In any case, in so far as goodness is for use in politics and in the market place it must combine its increasing intuitions of unity with an increasing grasp of complexity and detail. False conceptions are often generalized, stereotyped, and unconnected. True conceptions combine just modes of judgement and ability to connect with an increased perception of detail. The case of the mother who has to consider each one of her family carefully as she decides whether or not to throw auntie out. This double revelation of both random detail and intuited unity is what we receive in every sphere of life if we seek for what is best. We can see this, once more, quite clearly in art and intellectual work. The great artists reveal the detail of the world. At the same time their greatness is not something peculiar and personal like a proper name. They are great in ways which are to some extent similar, and increased understanding of an art reveals its unity through its excellence. All serious criticism assumes this, though it might be wary of expressing it in a theoretical manner. Art reveals reality and because there is a way in which things are there is a fellowship of artists. Similarly with scholars. Honesty seems much the same virtue in a chemist as in a historian and the evolution of the two could be similar. And there is another similarity between the honesty required to tear up one's theory and the honesty required to perceive the real state of one's marriage, though doubtless the latter is much more difficult. Plato, who is sometimes accused of overvaluing intellectual disciplines, is quite explicit in giving these, when considered on their own, a high but second place. A serious scholar has great merits. But a serious scholar who is also a good man knows not only his subject but the proper place of his subject in the whole of his life. The understanding which leads the scientist to the right decision about giving up a certain study, or leads the artist to the right decision about his family, is superior to the understanding of art and science as such. (Is this not what καίτοι νοητῶν ὄντων μετὰ ἀρχῆς means? (*Republic* 511d).) We are admittedly specialized creatures where morality is concerned, and merit in one area does not seem to guarantee merit in another. The good artist is not necessarily wise at home, and the concentration-camp guard can be a kindly father. At least this can seem to be so, though I would feel that the artist had at least got a starting-point and that on closer inspection the concentration-camp guard might prove to have his limitations as a family man. The scene remains disparate and complex beyond the hopes of any system, yet at the same time the concept Good stretches through the whole of it and gives it the only kind of shadowy unachieved unity which it can possess. The area of morals, and ergo of moral philosophy, can now be seen, not as a hole-and-corner matter of debts and promises, but as covering the whole of our mode of living and the quality of our relations with the world.

Good has often been said to be indefinable for reasons connected with freedom. Good is an empty space into which human choice may move. I want now to suggest that the indefinability of the good should be conceived of rather differently. On the kind of view which I have been offering, it seems that we do really know a certain amount about Good and about the way in which it is connected with our condition. The ordinary person does not, unless corrupted by philosophy, believe that he creates values by his choices. He thinks that some things really are better than others and that he is capable of getting it wrong. We are not usually in doubt about the direction in which Good lies. Equally we recognize the real existence of evil: cynicism, cruelty, indifference to suffering. However, the concept of Good still remains obscure and mysterious. We see the world in the light of the Good, but what is the Good itself? The source of vision is not in the ordinary sense seen. Plato says of it: 'It is that which every soul pursues and for the sake of which it does all that it does, with some intuition of its nature, and yet also baffled' (*Republic* 505). And he also says that Good is the source of knowledge and truth and yet is something which surpasses them in splendour (*Republic* 508–9).

There is a sort of logical, in the modern sense of the word, answer to the question but I think it is not the whole answer. Asking what Good is is not like asking what Truth is or what Courage is, since in explaining the latter the idea of Good must enter in; it is that in the light of which the explanation must proceed. 'True courage is . . .' And if we try to define Good as *X*, we have to add that we mean of course a good *X*. If we say that Good is Reason, we have to talk about good judgement. If we say that Good is Love, we have to explain that there are different kinds of love. Even the concept of Truth has it ambiguities and it is really only of Good that we can say 'it is the trial of itself and needs no other touch'. And with this I agree. It is also argued that all things which are capable of showing degrees of excellence show it in their own way. The idea of perfection can only be exemplified in particular cases in terms of the kind of perfection which is appropriate. So one could not say in general what perfection is, in the way in which one could talk about generosity or good painting. In any case, opinions differ and the truth of judgements of value cannot be demonstrated. This line of argument is sometimes used to support a view of Good as empty and almost trivial, a mere word, 'the most general adjective of commendation', a flag used by the questing will, a term which could with greater clarity be replaced by 'I'm for this.' This argument and its conclusion seem to me to be wrong for reasons which I have already given: excellence has a kind of unity and there are facts about our condition from which lines converge in a definite direction; and also for other reasons which I will now suggest.

A genuine mysteriousness attaches to the idea of goodness and the Good. This is a mystery with several aspects. The indefinability of Good is connected with the unsystematic and inexhaustible variety of the world and the pointlessness of virtue. In this respect there is a special link between the concept of Good and the ideas of Death and Chance. (One might say that Chance is really a subdivision of Death. It is certainly our most effective *memento mori.*) A genuine sense of mortality enables us to see virtue as the only thing of worth; and it is impossible to limit and foresee the ways in which it will be required of us. That we cannot dominate the world may be put in a more positive way. Good is mysterious because of human frailty, because of the immense distance which is involved. If there were angels they might be able to define good but we would not understand the definition. We are largely mechanical creatures, the slaves of relentlessly strong selfish forces the nature of which we scarcely comprehend. At best, as decent persons, we are usually very specialized. We behave well in areas where this can be done fairly easily and let other areas of possible virtue remain undeveloped. There are perhaps in the case of every human being insuperable psychological barriers to goodness. The self is a divided thing and the whole of it cannot be redeemed any more than it can be known. And if we look outside the self what we see are scattered intimations of Good. There are few places where virtue plainly shines: great art, humble people who serve others. And can we, without improving ourselves, really see these things clearly? It is in the context of such limitations that we should picture our freedom. Freedom is, I think, a mixed concept. The true half of it is simply a name of an aspect of virtue concerned especially with the clarification of vision and the domination of selfish impulse. The false and more popular half is a name for the self-assertive movements of deluded selfish will which because of our ignorance we take to be something autonomous.

We cannot then sum up human excellence for these reasons: the world is aimless, chancy, and huge, and we are blinded by self. There is a third consideration which is a relation of the other two. It is *difficult* to look at the sun: it is not like looking at other things. We somehow retain the idea, and art both expresses and symbolizes it, that the lines really do converge. There is a magnetic centre. But it is easier to look at the converging edges than to look at the centre itself. We do not and probably cannot know, conceptualize, what it is like in the centre. It may be said that since we cannot see anything there why try to look? And is there not a danger of damaging our ability to focus on the sides? I think there is a sense in trying to look, though the occupation is perilous for reasons connected with masochism and other obscure devices of the psyche. The impulse to worship is deep and ambiguous and old. There are false suns, easier to gaze upon and far more comforting than the true one.

Plato has given us the image of this deluded worship in his great allegory. The prisoners in the cave at first face the back wall. Behind them a fire is burning in the light of which they see upon the wall the shadows of puppets which are carried between them and the fire and they take these shadows to be the whole of reality. When they turn round they can see the fire, which they have to pass in order to get out of the cave. The fire, I take it, represents the self, the old unregenerate psyche, that great source of energy and warmth. The prisoners in the second stage of enlightenment have gained the kind of self-awareness which is nowadays a matter of so much interest to us. They can see in themselves the sources of what was formerly blind selfish instinct. They see the flames which threw the shadows which they used to think were real, and they can see the puppets, imitations of things in the real world, whose shadows they used to recognize. They do not yet dream that there is anything else to see. What is more likely than that they should settle down beside the fire, which though its form is flickering and unclear is quite easy to look at and cosy to sit by?

I think Kant was afraid of this when he went to such lengths to draw our attention away from the empirical psyche. This powerful thing is indeed an object of fascination, and those who study its power to cast shadows are studying something which is real. A recognition of its power may be a step towards escape from the cave; but it may equally be taken as an end point. The fire may be mistaken for the sun, and self-scrutiny taken for goodness. (Of course not everyone who escapes from the cave need have spent much time by the fire. Perhaps the virtuous peasant has got out of the cave without even noticing the fire.) Any religion or ideology can be degraded by the substitution of self, usually in some disguise, for the true object of veneration. However, in spite of what Kant was so much afraid of, I think there is a place both inside and outside religion for a sort of contemplation of the Good, not just by dedicated experts but by ordinary people: an attention which is not just the planning of particular good actions but an attempt to look right away from self towards a distant transcendent perfection, a source of uncontaminated energy, a source of *new* and quite undreamt-of virtue. This attempt, which is a turning of attention away from the particular, may be the thing that helps most when difficulties seem insoluble, and especially when feelings of guilt keep attracting the gaze back towards the self. This is the true mysticism which is morality, a kind of undogmatic prayer which is real and important, though perhaps also difficult and easily corrupted.

I have been speaking of the indefinability of the Good; but is there really nothing else that we can say about it? Even if we cannot find it another name, even if it must be thought of as above and alone, are there not other concepts, or another concept, with which it has some quite special relation? Philosophers have often tried to discern such a relationship: Freedom, Reason, Happiness, Courage, History have recently been tried in the role. I do not find any of these candidates convincing. They seem to represent in each case the philosopher's admiration for some specialized aspect of human conduct which is much less than the whole of excellence and sometimes dubious in itself. I have already mentioned a concept with a certain claim and I will return to that in conclusion. I want now to speak of what is perhaps the most obvious as well as the most ancient and traditional claimant, though one which is rarely mentioned by our contemporary philosophers, and that is Love. Of course Good is sovereign over Love, as it is sovereign over other concepts, because Love can name something bad. But is there not nevertheless something about the conception of a refined love which is practically identical with goodness? Will not 'Act lovingly' translate 'Act perfectly', whereas 'Act rationally' will not? It is tempting to say so.

However, I think that Good and Love should not be identified, and not only because human love is usually self-assertive. The concepts, even when the idea of love is purified, still play different roles. We are dealing here with very difficult metaphors. Good is the magnetic centre towards which love naturally moves. False love moves to false good. False love embraces false death. When true good is loved, even impurely or by accident, the quality of the love is automatically refined, and when the soul is turned towards Good the highest part of the soul is enlivened. Love is the tension between the imperfect soul and the magnetic perfection which is conceived of as lying beyond it. (In the *Symposium* Plato pictures Love as being poor and needy.) And when we try perfectly to love what is imperfect, our love goes to its object *via* the Good to be thus purified and made unselfish and just. The mother loving the retarded child or loving the tiresome elderly relation. Love is the general name of the quality of attachment and it is capable of infinite degradation and is the source of our greatest errors; but when it is even partially refined it is the energy and passion of the soul in its search for Good, the force that joins us to Good and joins us to the world through Good. Its existence is the unmistakable sign that we are spiritual creatures, attracted by excellence and made for the Good. It is a reflection of the warmth and light of the sun.

Perhaps the finding of other names for Good or the establishing of special relationships cannot be more than a sort of personal game. However, I want in conclusion to make just one more move. Goodness is connected with the acceptance of real death and real chance and real transience and only against the background of this acceptance, which is psychologically so difficult, can we understand the full extent of what virtue is like. The acceptance of death is an acceptance of our own nothingness which is an automatic spur to our concern with what is not ourselves. The good man is humble; he is very unlike the big neo-Kantian Lucifer. He is much more like Kierkegaard's tax collector. Humility is a rare virtue and an unfashionable one and one which is often hard to discern. Only rarely does one meet somebody in whom it positively shines, in whom one apprehends with amazement the absence of the anxious avaricious tentacles of the self. In fact any other name for Good must be a partial name; but names of virtues suggest directions of thought, and this direction seems to me a better one than that suggested by more popular concepts such as freedom and courage. The humble man, because he sees himself as nothing, can see other things as they are. He sees the pointlessness of virtue and its unique value and the endless extent of its demand. Simone Weil tells us that the exposure of the soul to God condemns the selfish part of it not to suffering but to death. The humble man perceives the distance between suffering and death. And although he is not by definition the good man, perhaps he is the kind of man who is most likely of all to become good.

6

THE NATURE OF THE VIRTUES

ALASDAIR MACINTYRE

One response to the history which I have narrated so far might well be to suggest that even within the relatively coherent tradition of thought which I have sketched there are just too many different and incompatible conceptions of virtue for there to be any real unity to the concept or indeed to the history. Homer, Sophocles, Aristotle, the New Testament and medieval thinkers differ from each other in too many ways. They offer us different and incompatible lists of the virtues; they give a different rank order of importance to different virtues; and they have different and incompatible theories of the virtues. If we were to consider later Western writers on the virtues, the list of differences and incompatibilities would be enlarged still further; and if we extended our enquiry to Japanese, say, or American Indian cultures, the differences would become greater still. It would be all too easy to conclude that there are a number of rival and alternative conceptions of the virtues, but, even within the tradition which I have been delineating, no single core conception.

The case for such a conclusion could not be better constructed than by beginning from a consideration of the very different lists of items which different authors in different times and places have included in their catalogues of virtues. Some of these catalogues—Homer's, Aristotle's, and the New Testament's—I have already noticed at greater or lesser length. Let me at the risk of some repetition recall some of their key features and then introduce for further comparison the catalogues of two later Western writers, Benjamin Franklin and Jane Austen.

The first example is that of Homer. At least some of the items in a Homeric list of the *aretai* would clearly not be counted by most of us nowadays as virtues at all, physical strength being the most obvious example. To this it might be replied that perhaps we ought not to translate the word *aretē* in Homer by our word 'virtue', but instead by our word

From Alasdair MacIntyre, *After Virtue* (London: Duckworth, 1985), 169–89. Reprinted by permission of Gerald Duckworth & Co Ltd.

'excellence'; and perhaps, if we were so to translate it, the apparently surprising difference between Homer and ourselves would at first sight have been removed. For we could allow without any kind of oddity that the possession of physical strength is the possession of an excellence. But in fact we would not have removed, but instead would merely have relocated, the difference between Homer and ourselves. For we would now seem to be saying that Homer's concept of an *aretē*, an excellence, is one thing and that our concept of a virtue is quite another, since a particular quality can be an excellence in Homer's eyes, but not a virtue in ours and *vice versa*.

But of course it is not that Homer's list of virtues differs only from our own; it also notably differs from Aristotle's. And Aristotle's of course also differs from our own. For one thing, as I noticed earlier, some Greek virtue-words are not easily translatable into English or rather out of Greek. Moreover, consider the importance of friendship as a virtue in Aristotle's list—how different from us! Or the place of *phronēsis*—how different from Homer and from us! The mind receives from Aristotle the kind of tribute which the body receives from Homer. But it is not just the case that the difference between Aristotle and Homer lies in the inclusion of some items and the omission of others in their respective catalogues. It turns out also in the way in which those catalogues are ordered, in which items are ranked as relatively central to human excellence and which marginal.

Moreover, the relationship of virtues to the social order has changed. For Homer the paradigm of human excellence is the warrior; for Aristotle it is the Athenian gentleman. Indeed according to Aristotle certain virtues are only available to those of great riches and of high social status; there are virtues which are unavailable to the poor man, even if he is a free man. And those virtues are on Aristotle's view ones central to human life; magnanimity—and once again, any translation of *megalopsuchia* is unsatisfactory—and munificence are not just virtues, but important virtues within the Aristotelian scheme.

At once it is impossible to delay the remark that the most striking contrast with Aristotle's catalogue is to be found neither in Homer's nor in our own, but in the New Testament's. For the New Testament not only praises virtues of which Aristotle knows nothing—faith, hope, and love—and says nothing about virtues such as *phronēsis* which are crucial for Aristotle, but it praises at least one quality as a virtue which Aristotle seems to count as one of the vices relative to magnanimity, namely humility. Moreover, since the New Testament quite clearly sees the rich as destined for the pains of Hell, it is clear that the key virtues cannot be available to them; yet they *are* available to slaves. And the New Testament of course differs from both Homer and Aristotle not only in the items included in its catalogue, but once again in its rank ordering of the virtues.

Turn now to compare all three lists of virtues considered so far—the Homeric, the Aristotelian, and the New Testament's—with two much later lists, one which can be compiled from Jane Austen's novels and the other which Benjamin Franklin constructed for himself. Two features stand out in Jane Austen's list. The first is the importance that she allots to the virtue which she calls 'constancy'. In some ways constancy plays a role in Jane Austen analogous to that of *phronēsis* in Aristotle; it is a virtue the possession of which is a prerequisite for the possession of other virtues. The second is the fact that what Aristotle treats as the virtue of agreeableness (a virtue for which he says there is no name) she treats as only the simulacrum of a genuine virtue—the genuine virtue in question is the one she calls amiability. For the man who practises agreeableness does so from considerations of honour and expediency, according to Aristotle; whereas Jane Austen thought it possible and necessary for the possessor of that virtue to have a certain real affection for people as such. (It matters here that Jane Austen is a Christian.) Remember that Aristotle himself had treated military courage as a simulacrum of true courage. Thus we find here yet another type of disagreement over the virtues; namely, one as to which human qualities are genuine virtues and which mere simulacra.

In Benjamin Franklin's list we find almost all the types of difference from at least one of the other catalogues we have considered and one more. Franklin includes virtues which are new to our consideration such as cleanliness, silence, and industry; he clearly considers the drive to acquire itself a part of virtue, whereas for most ancient Greeks this is the vice of *pleonexia*; he treats some virtues which earlier ages had considered minor as major; but he also redefines some familiar virtues. In the list of thirteen virtues which Franklin compiled as part of his system of private moral accounting, he elucidates each virtue by citing a maxim obedience to which *is* the virtue in question. In the case of chastity the maxim is 'Rarely use venery but for health or offspring—never to dullness, weakness or the injury of your own or another's peace or reputation.' This is clearly not what earlier writers had meant by 'chastity'.

We have therefore accumulated a startling number of differences and incompatibilities in the five stated and implied accounts of the virtues. So the question which I raised at the outset becomes more urgent. If different writers in different times and places, but all within the history of Western culture, include such different sets and types of items in their lists, what grounds have we for supposing that they do indeed aspire to list items of one and the same kind, that there is any shared concept at all? A second kind of consideration reinforces the presumption of a negative answer to this question. It is not just that each of these five writers lists different and differing kinds of items; it is also that each of these lists embodies, is the expression of a different theory about what a virtue is.

In the Homeric poems a virtue is a quality the manifestation of which enables someone to do exactly what their well-defined social role requires. The primary role is that of the warrior king and that Homer lists those virtues which he does becomes intelligible at once when we recognize that the key virtues therefore must be those which enable a man to excel in combat and in the games. It follows that we cannot identify the Homeric virtues until we have first identified the key social roles in Homeric society and the requirements of each of them. The concept of *what anyone filling such-and-such a role ought to do* is prior to the concept of a virtue; the latter concept has application only via the former.

On Aristotle's account matters are very different. Even though some virtues are available only to certain types of people, none the less virtues attach not to men as inhabiting social roles, but to man as such. It is the *telos* of man as a species which determines what human qualities are virtues. We need to remember, however, that although Aristotle treats the acquisition and exercise of the virtues as means to an end, the relationship of means to end is internal and not external. I call a means internal to a given end when the end cannot be adequately characterized independently of a characterization of the means. So it is with the virtues and the *telos* which is the good life for man on Aristotle's account. The exercise of the virtues is itself a crucial component of the good life for man. This distinction between internal and external means to an end is not drawn by Aristotle himself in the *Nicomachean Ethics*, but it is an essential distinction to be drawn if we are to understand what Aristotle intended. The distinction *is* drawn explicitly by Aquinas in the course of his defence of St Augustine's definition of a virtue, and it is clear that Aquinas understood that in drawing it he was maintaining an Aristotelian point of view.

The New Testament's account of the virtues, even if it differs as much as it does in content from Aristotle's—Aristotle would certainly not have admired Jesus Christ and he would have been horrified by St Paul—does have the same logical and conceptual structure as Aristotle's account. A virtue is, as with Aristotle, a quality the exercise of which leads to the achievement of the human telos. *The* good for man is of course a supernatural and not only a natural good, but supernature redeems and completes nature. Moreover, the relationship of virtues as means to the end which is human incorporation in the divine kingdom of the age to come is internal and not external, just as it is in Aristotle. It is of course this parallelism which allows Aquinas to synthesize Aristotle and the New Testament. A key feature of this parallelism is the way in which the concept of *the good life for man* is prior to the concept of a virtue in just the way in which on the Homeric account the concept of a social role was prior. Once again it is the way in which the former concept is applied which determines how the latter is to be applied. In both cases the concept of a virtue is a secondary concept.

The intent of Jane Austen's theory of the virtues is of another kind. C. S. Lewis has rightly emphasized how profoundly Christian her moral vision is and Gilbert Ryle has equally rightly emphasized her inheritance from Shaftesbury and from Aristotle. In fact her views combine elements from Homer as well, since she is concerned with social roles in a way that neither the New Testament nor Aristotle are. She is therefore important for the way in which she finds it possible to combine what are at first sight disparate theoretical accounts of the virtues. But for the moment any attempt to assess the significance of Jane Austen's synthesis must be delayed. Instead we must notice the quite different style of theory articulated in Benjamin Franklin's account of the virtues.

Franklin's account, like Aristotle's, is teleological; but unlike Aristotle's, it is utilitarian. According to Franklin in his *Autobiography* the virtues are means to an end, but he envisages the means–ends relationship as external rather than internal. The end to which the cultivation of the virtues ministers is happiness, but happiness understood as success, prosperity in Philadelphia and ultimately in heaven. The virtues are to be useful and Franklin's account continuously stresses utility as a criterion in individual cases: 'Make no expence but to do good to others or yourself; i.e. waste nothing', 'Speak not but what may benefit others or yourself. Avoid trifling conversation', and, as we have already seen, 'Rarely use venery but for health or offspring . . .'. When Franklin was in Paris he was horrified by Parisian architecture: 'Marble, porcelain and gilt are squandered without utility.'

We thus have at least three very different conceptions of a virtue to confront: a virtue is a quality which enables an individual to discharge his or her social role (Homer); a virtue is a quality which enables an individual to move towards the achievement of the specifically human *telos*, whether natural or supernatural (Aristotle, the New Testament, and Aquinas); a virtue is a quality which has utility in achieving earthly and heavenly success (Franklin). Are we to take these as three rival accounts of the same thing? Or are they instead accounts of three different things? Perhaps the moral structures in archaic Greece, in fourth-century Greece, and in eighteenth-century Pennsylvania were so different from each other that we should treat them as embodying quite different concepts, whose difference is initially disguised from us by the historical accident of an inherited vocabulary which misleads us by linguistic resemblance long after conceptual identity and similarity have failed. Our initial question has come back to us with redoubled force.

Yet although I have dwelt upon the *prima-facie* case for holding that the differences and incompatibilities between different accounts at least suggest that there is no single, central, core conception of the virtues which might make a claim for universal allegiance, I ought also to point out that each of the five moral accounts which I have sketched so summarily does embody just such a claim. It is indeed just this feature of those accounts that makes them of more than sociological or antiquarian interest. Every one of these accounts claims not only theoretical, but also an institutional hegemony. For Odysseus the Cyclopes stand condemned because they lack agriculture, on *agora* and *themis*. For Aristotle the barbarians stand condemned because they lack the *polis* and are therefore incapable of politics. For New Testament Christians there is no salvation outside the apostolic church. And we know that Benjamin Franklin found the virtues more at home in Philadelphia than in Paris and that for Jane Austen the touchstone of the virtues is a certain kind of marriage and indeed a certain kind of naval officer (that is, a certain kind of *English* naval officer).

The question can therefore now be posed directly: are we or are we not able to disentangle from these rival and various claims a unitary core concept of the virtues of which we can give a more compelling account than any of the other accounts so far? I am going to argue that we can in fact discover such a core concept and that it turns out to provide the tradition of which I have written the history with its conceptual unity. It will indeed enable us to distinguish in a clear way those beliefs about the virtues which genuinely belong to the tradition from those which do not. Unsurprisingly perhaps it is a complex concept, different parts of which derive from different stages in the development of the tradition. Thus the concept itself in some sense embodies the history of which it is the outcome.

One of the features of the concept of a virtue which has emerged with some clarity from the argument so far is that it always requires for its application the acceptance of some prior account of certain features of social and moral life in terms of which it has to be defined and explained. So in the Homeric account the concept of a virtue is secondary to that of *a social role*, in Aristotle's account it is secondary to that of *the good life for man* conceived as the *telos* of human action and in Franklin's much later account it is secondary to that of utility. What is it in the account which I am about to give which provides in a similar way the necessary background against which the concept of a virtue has to be made intelligible? It is in answering this question that the complex, historical, multilayered character of the core concept of virtue becomes clear. For there are no less than three stages in the logical development of the concept which have to be identified in order, if the core conception of a virtue is to be understood, and each of these stages has its own conceptual background. The first stage requires a background account of what I shall call a practice, the second an account of the narrative order of a single human life, and the third an account of what constitutes a moral tradition. Each later stage presupposes the earlier, but not *vice versa*. Each earlier stage is both modified by and reinterpreted in the light of, but also provides an essential constituent of each later stage. The progress in the development of the concept is closely related to, although it does not recapitulate in any straightforward way, the history of the tradition of which it forms the core.

In the Homeric account of the virtues—and in heroic societies more generally—the exercise of a virtue exhibits qualities which are required for sustaining a social role and for exhibiting excellence in some well-marked area of social practice: to excel is to excel at war or in the games, as Achilles does, in sustaining a household, as Penelope does, in giving counsel in the assembly, as Nestor does, in the telling of a tale, as Homer himself does. When Aristotle speaks of excellence in human activity, he sometimes, though not always, refers to some well-defined type of human practice: flute-playing, or war, or geometry. I am going to suggest that this notion of a particular type of practice as providing the arena in which the virtues are exhibited and in terms of which they are to receive their primary, if incomplete, definition is crucial to the whole enterprise of identifying a core concept of the virtues. I hasten to add two *caveats* however.

The first is to point out that my argument will not in any way imply that virtues are *only* exercised in the course of what I am calling practices. The second is to warn that I shall be using the word 'practice' in a specially defined way which does not completely agree with current ordinary usage, including my own previous use of that word. What am I going to mean by it?

By a 'practice' I am going to mean any coherent and complex form of socially established cooperative human activity through which goods internal to that form of activity are realized in the course of trying to achieve those standards of excellence which are appropriate to, and partially definitive of, that form of activity, with the result that human powers to achieve excellence, and human conceptions of the ends and goods involved, are systematically extended. Tic-tac-toe is not an example of a practice in this sense, nor is throwing a football with skill; but the game of football is, and so is chess. Bricklaying is not a practice; architecture is. Planting turnips is not a practice; farming is. So are the enquiries of physics, chemistry, and biology, and so is the work of the historian, and so are painting and music. In the ancient and medieval worlds the creation and sustaining of human communities—of households, cities, nations—are generally taken to be a practice in the sense in which I have defined it. Thus the range of practices is wide: arts, sciences, games, politics in the Aristotelian sense, the making and sustaining of family life, all fall under the concept. But the question of the precise range of practices is not at this stage of the first importance. Instead let me explain some of the key terms involved in my definition, beginning with the notion of goods internal to a practice.

Consider the example of a highly intelligent 7-year-old child whom I wish to teach to play chess, although the child has no particular desire to learn the game. The child does, however, have a very strong desire for candy and little chance of obtaining it. I therefore tell the child that if the child will play chess with me once a week I will give the child 50¢ worth of candy; moreover I tell the child that I will always play in such a way that it will be difficult, but not impossible, for the child to win and that, if the child wins, the child will receive an extra 50¢ worth of candy. Thus motivated the child plays and plays to win. Notice, however, that, so long as it is the candy alone which provides the child with a good reason for playing chess, the child has no reason not to cheat and every reason to cheat, provided he or she can do so successfully. But, so we may hope, there will come a time when the child will find in those goods specific to chess, in the achievement of a certain highly particular kind of analytical skill, strategic imagination and competitive intensity, a new set of reasons, reasons now not just for winning on a particular occasion, but for trying to excel in whatever way the game of chess demands. Now if the child cheats, he or she will be defeating not me, but himself or herself.

There are thus two kinds of good possibly to be gained by playing chess. On the one hand there are those goods externally and contingently attached to chess-playing and to other practices by the accidents of social circumstance—in the case of the imaginary child candy, in the case of real adults such goods as prestige, status, and money. There are always alternative ways for achieving such goods, and their achievement is never to be had *only* by engaging in some particular kind of practice. On the other hand there are the goods internal to the practice of chess which cannot be had in any way but by playing chess or some other game of that specific kind. We call them internal for two reasons: first, as I have already suggested, because we can only specify them in terms of chess or some other game of that specific kind and by means of examples from such games (otherwise the meagreness of our vocabulary for speaking of such goods forces us into such devices as my own resort to writing of 'a certain highly particular king of'); and secondly because they can only be identified and recognized by the experience of participating in the practice in question. Those who lack the relevant experience are incompetent thereby as judges of internal goods.

This is clearly the case with all the major examples of practices: consider for example—even if briefly and inadequately—the practice of portrait-painting as it developed in Western Europe from the late middle ages to the eighteenth century. The successful portrait painter is able to achieve many goods which are in the sense just defined external to the practice of portrait-painting—fame, wealth, social status, even a measure of power and influence at courts upon occasion. But those external goods are not to be confused with the goods which are internal to the practice. The internal goods are those which result from an extended attempt to show how Wittgenstein's dictum 'The human body is the best picture of the human soul' (*Investigations*, 178e) might be made to become true by teaching us 'to regard . . . the picture on our wall as the object itself (the men, landscape and so on) depicted there' (p. 205e) in a quite new way. What is misleading about Wittgenstein's dictum as it stands is its neglect of the truth in George Orwell's thesis 'At 50 everyone has the face he deserves'. What painters from Giotto to Rembrandt learnt to show was how the face at any age may be revealed as the face that the subject of a portrait deserves.

Originally in medieval paintings of the saints the face was an icon; the question of a resemblance between the depicted face of Christ or St Peter and the face that Jesus or Peter actually possessed at some particular age did not even arise. The antithesis to this iconography was the relative naturalism of certain fifteenth-century Flemish and German painting. The heavy eyelids, the coifed hair, the lines around the mouth undeniably represent some particular woman, either actual or envisaged. Resemblance has usurped the iconic relationship. But with Rembrandt there is, so to speak, synthesis: the naturalistic portrait is now rendered as an icon, but an icon of a new and hitherto inconceivable kind. Similarly in a very different kind of sequence mythological faces in a certain kind of seventeenth-century French painting become aristocratic faces in the eighteenth century. Within each of these sequences at least two different kinds of good internal to the painting of human faces and bodies are achieved.

There is first of all the excellence of the products, both the excellence in performance by the painters and that of each portrait itself. This excellence—the very verb 'excel' suggests it—has to be understood historically. The sequences of development find their point and purpose in a progress towards and beyond a variety of types and modes of excellence. There are of course sequences of decline as well as of progress, and progress is rarely to be understood as straightforwardly linear. But it is in participation in the attempts to sustain progress and to respond creatively to moments that the second kind of good internal to the practices of portrait-painting is to be found. For what the artist discovers within the pursuit of excellence in portrait-painting—and what is true of portrait-painting is true of the practice of the fine arts in general—is the good of a certain kind of life. That life may not constitute the whole of life for someone who is a painter by a very long way or it may at least for a period, Gauguin-like, absorb him or her at the expense of almost everything else. But it is the painter's living out of a greater or lesser part of his or her life *as a painter* that is the second kind of good internal to painting. And judgement upon these goods requires at the very least the kind of competence that is only to be acquired either as a painter or as someone willing to learn systematically what the portrait painter has to teach.

A practice involves standards of excellence and obedience to rules as well as the achievement of goods. To enter into a practice is to accept the authority of those standards and the inadequacy of my own performance as judged by them. It is to subject my own attitudes, choices, preferences, and tastes to the standards which currently and partially define the practice. Practices of course, as I have just noticed, have a history: games, sciences, and arts all have histories. Thus the standards are not themselves immune from criticism, but none the less we cannot be initiated into a practice without accepting the authority of the best standards realized so far. If, on starting to listen to music, I do not accept my own incapacity to judge correctly, I will never learn to hear, let alone to appreciate, Bartok's last quartets. If, on starting to play baseball, I do not accept that others know better than I when to throw a fast ball and when not, I will never learn to appreciate good pitching let alone to pitch. In the realm of practices the authority of both goods and standards operates in such a way as to rule out all subjectivist and emotivist analyses of judgement. De gustibus *est* disputandum.

We are now in a position to notice an important difference between what I have called internal and what I have called external goods. It is characteristic of what I have called external goods that when achieved they are always some individual's property and possession. Moreover, characteristically they are such that the more someone has of them, the less there is for other people. This is sometimes necessarily the case, as with power and fame, and sometimes the case by reason of contingent circumstance as with money. External goods are therefore characteristically objects of competition in which there must be losers as well as winners. Internal goods are indeed the outcome of competition to excel, but it is characteristic of them that their achievement is a good for the whole community who participate in the practice. So when Turner transformed the seascape in painting or W. G. Grace advanced the art of batting in cricket in a quite new way their achievement enriched the whole relevant community.

But what does all or any of this have to do with the concept of the virtues? It turns out that we are now in a position to formulate a first, even if partial and tentative definition of a virtue: *A virtue is an acquired human quality the possession and exercise of which tends to enable us to achieve those goods which are internal to practices and the lack of which effectively prevents us from achieving any such goods.* Later this definition will need amplification and amendment. But as a first approximation to an adequate definition it already illuminates the place of the virtues in human life. For it is not difficult to show for a whole range of key virtues that without them the goods internal to practices are barred to us, but not just barred to us generally, barred in a very particular way.

It belongs to the concept of a practice as I have outlined it—and as we are all familiar with it already in our actual lives, whether we are painters or physicists or quarterbacks or indeed just lovers of good painting or first-rate experiments or a well-thrown pass—that its goods can only be achieved by subordinating ourselves to the best standard so far achieved, and that entails subordinating ourselves within the practice in our relationship to other practitioners. We have to learn to recognize what is due to whom; we have to be prepared to take whatever self-endangering risks are demanded along the way; and we have to listen carefully to what we are told about our own inadequacies and to reply with the same carefulness for the facts. In other words we have to accept as necessary components of any practice with internal goods and standards of excellence the virtues of justice, courage, and honesty. For not to accept these, to be willing to cheat as our imagined child was willing to cheat in his or her early days at chess, so far bars us from achieving the standards of excellence or the goods internal to the practice that it renders the practice pointless except as a device for achieving external goods.

We can put the same point in another way. Every practice requires a certain kind of relationship between those who participate in it. Now the virtues are those goods by reference to which, whether we like it or not, we define our relationships to those other people with whom we share the kind of purposes and standards which inform practices. Consider an example of how reference to the virtues has to be made in certain kinds of human relationship.

A, *B*, *C* and *D* are friends in that sense of friendship which Aristotle takes to be primary: they share in the pursuit of certain goods. In my terms they share in a practice. *D* dies in obscure circumstances, *A* discovers how *D* died and tells the truth about it to *B* while lying to *C*. *C* discovers the lie. What *A* cannot then intelligibly claim is that he stands in the same relationship of friendship to both *B* and *C*. By telling the truth to one and lying to the other he has partially defined a difference in the relationship. Of course it is open to *A* to explain this difference in a number of ways; perhaps he was trying to spare *C* pain or perhaps he is simply cheating *C*. But some difference in the relationship now exists as a result of the lie. For their allegiance to each other in the pursuit of common goods has been put in question.

Just as, so long as we share the standards and purposes characteristic of practices, we define our relationships to each other, whether we acknowledge it or not, by reference to standards of truthfulness and trust, so we define them too by reference to standards of justice and of courage. If *A*, a professor, gives *B* and *C* the grades that their papers deserve, but grades *D* because he is attracted by *D*'s blue eyes or is repelled by *D*'s dandruff, he has defined his relationship to *D* differently from his relationship to the other members of the class, whether he wishes it or not. Justice requires that we treat others in respect of merit or desert according to uniform and impersonal standards; to depart from the standards of justice in some particular instance defines our relationship with the relevant person as in some way special or distinctive.

The case with courage is a little different. We hold courage to be a virtue because the care and concern for individuals, communities, and causes which is so crucial to so much in practices requires the existence of such a virtue. If someone says that he cares for some individual, community, or cause, but is unwilling to risk harm or danger on his, her, or its own behalf, he puts in question the genuineness of his care and concern. Courage, the capacity to risk harm or danger to oneself, has its role in human life because of this connection with care and concern. This is not to say that a man cannot genuinely care and also be a coward. It is in part to say that a man who genuinely cares and has not the capacity for risking harm or danger has to define himself, both to himself and to others, as a coward.

I take it then that from the standpoint of those types of relationship without which practices cannot be sustained truthfulness, justice, and courage—and perhaps some others—are genuine excellences, are virtues in the light of which we have to characterize ourselves and others, whatever our private moral standpoint or our society's particular codes may be. For this recognition that we cannot escape the definition of our relationships in terms of such goods is perfectly compatible with the acknowledgement that different societies have and have had different codes of truthfulness, justice and courage. Lutheran pietists brought up their children to believe that one ought to tell the truth to everybody at all times, whatever the circumstances or consequences, and Kant was one of their children. Traditional Bantu parents brought up their children not to tell the truth to unknown strangers, since they believed that this could render the family vulnerable to witchcraft. In our culture many of us have been brought up not to tell the truth to elderly great-aunts who invite us to admire their new hats. But each of these codes embodies an acknowledgement of the virtue of truthfulness. So it is also with varying codes of justice and of courage.

Practices then might flourish in societies with very different codes; what they could not do is flourish in societies in which the virtues were not valued, although institutions and technical skills serving unified purposes might well continue to flourish. (I shall have more to say about the contrast between institutions and technical skills mobilized for a unified end, on the one hand, and practices on the other, in a moment.) For the kind of cooperation, the kind of recognition of authority and of achievement, the kind of respect for standards and the kind of risk-taking which are characteristically involved in practices demand for example fairness in judging oneself and others—the kind of fairness absent in my example of the professor, a ruthless truthfulness without which fairness cannot find application—the kind of truthfulness absent in my example of *A*, *B*, *C*, and *D*—and willingness to trust the judgements of those whose achievements in the practice give them an authority to judge which presupposes fairness and truthfulness in those judgements, and from time to time the taking of self-endangering, reputation-endangering, and even achievement-endangering risks. It is no part of my thesis that great violinists cannot be vicious or great chess-players mean-spirited. Where the virtues are required, the vices also may flourish. It is just that the vicious and mean-spirited necessarily rely on the virtues of others for the practices in which they engage to flourish and also deny themselves the experience of achieving those internal goods which may reward even not very good chess-players and violinists.

To situate the virtues any further within practices it is necessary now to clarify a little further the nature of a practice by drawing two important contrasts. The discussion so far I hope makes it clear that a practice, in the sense intended, is never just a set of technical skills, even when directed towards some unified purpose and even if the exercise of those skills can on occasion be valued or enjoyed for their own sake. What is distinctive of a practice is in part the way in which conceptions of the relevant goods and ends which the technical skills serve—and every practice does require the exercise of technical skills—are transformed and enriched by these extensions of human powers and by that regard for its own internal goods which are partially definitive of each particular practice or type of practice. Practices never have a goal or goals fixed for all time—painting has no such goal nor has physics—but the goals themselves are transmuted by the history of the activity. It therefore turns out not to be accidental that every practice has its own history and a history which is more and other than that of the improvement of the relevant technical skills. This historical dimension is crucial in relation to the virtues.

To enter into a practice is to enter into a relationship not only with its contemporary practitioners, but also with those who have preceded us in the practice, particularly those whose achievements extended the reach of the practice to its present point. It is thus the achievement, and *a fortiori* the authority, of a tradition which I then confront and from which I have to learn. And for this learning and the relationship to the past which it embodies the virtues of justice, courage, and truthfulness are prerequisite in precisely the same way and for precisely the same reasons as they are in sustaining present relationships within practices.

It is not only of course with sets of technical skills that practices ought to be contrasted. Practices must not be confused with institutions. Chess, physics, and medicine are practices; chess clubs, laboratories, universities, and hospitals are institutions. Institutions are characteristically and necessarily concerned with what I have called external goods. They are involved in acquiring money and other material goods; they are structured in terms of power and status, and they distribute money, power, and status as rewards. Nor could they do otherwise if they are to sustain not only themselves, but also the practices of which they are the bearers. For no practices can survive for any length of time unsustained by institutions. Indeed so intimate is the relationship of practices to institutions—and consequently of the goods external to the goods internal to the practices in question—that institutions and practices characteristically form a single causal order in which the ideals and the creativity of the practice are always vulnerable to the acquisitiveness of the institution, in which the cooperative care for common goods of the practice is always vulnerable to the competitiveness of the institution. In this context the essential function of the virtues is clear. Without them, without justice, courage, and truthfulness, practices could not resist the corrupting power of institutions.

Yet if institutions do have corrupting power, the making and sustaining of forms of human community—and therefore of institutions—itself has all the characteristics of a practice, and moreover of a practice which stands in a peculiarly close relationship to the exercise of the virtues in two important ways. The exercise of the virtues is itself apt to require a highly determinate attitude to social and political issues; and it is always within some particular community with its own specific institutional forms that we learn or fail to learn to exercise the virtues. There is of course a crucial difference between the way in which the relationship between moral character and political community is envisaged from the standpoint of liberal individualist modernity and the way in which that relationship was envisaged from the standpoint of the type of ancient and medieval tradition of the virtues which I have sketched. For liberal individualism a community is simply an arena in which individuals each pursue their own self-chosen conception of the good life, and political institutions exist to provide that degree of order which makes such self-determined activity possible. Government and law are, or ought to be, neutral between rival conceptions of the good life for man, and hence, although it is the task of government to promote law-abidingness, it is on the liberal view no part of the legitimate function of government to inculcate any one moral outlook.

By contrast, on the particular ancient and medieval view which I have sketched political community not only requires the exercise of the virtues for its own sustenance, but it is one of the tasks of government to make its citizens virtuous, just as it is one of the tasks of parental authority to make children grow up so as to be virtuous adults. The classical statement of this analogy is by Socrates in the *Crito*. It does not of course follow from an acceptance of the Socratic view of political community and political authority that we ought to assign to the modern state the moral function which Socrates assigned to the city and its laws. Indeed the power of the liberal individualist standpoint partly derives from the evident fact that the modern state is indeed totally unfitted to act as moral educator of any community. But the history of how the modern state emerged is of course itself a moral history. If my account of the complex relationship of virtues to practices and to institutions is correct, it follows that we shall be unable to write a true history of practices and institutions unless that history is also one of the virtues and vices. For the ability of a practice to retain its integrity will depend on the way in which the virtues can be and are exercised in sustaining the institutional forms which are the social bearers of the practice. The integrity of a practice causally requires the exercise of the virtues by at least some of the individuals who embody it in their activities; and conversely the corruption of institutions is always in part at least an effect of the vices.

The virtues are of course themselves in turn fostered by certain types of social institution and endangered by others. Thomas Jefferson thought that only in a society of small farmers could the virtues flourish; and Adam Ferguson with a good deal more sophistication saw the institutions of modern commercial society as endangering at least some traditional virtues. It is Ferguson's type of sociology which is the empirical counterpart of the conceptual account of the virtues which I have given, a sociology which aspires to lay bare the empirical, causal connection between virtues, practices, and institutions. For this kind of conceptual account has strong empirical implications; it provides an explanatory scheme which can be tested in particular cases. Moreover my thesis has empirical content in another way; it does entail that without the virtues there could be a recognition only of what I have called external goods and not at all of internal goods in the context of practices. And in any society which recognized only external goods competitiveness would be the dominant and even exclusive feature. We have a brilliant portrait of such a society in Hobbes's account of the state of nature; and Professor Turnbull's report of the fate of the Ik suggests that social reality does in the most horrifying way confirm both my thesis and Hobbes's.

Virtues then stand in a different relationship to external and to internal goods. The possession of the virtues—and not only of their semblance and simulacra—is necessary to achieve the latter; yet the possession of the virtues may perfectly well hinder us in achieving external goods. I need to emphasize at this point that external goods genuinely are goods. Not only are they characteristic objects of human desire, whose allocation is what gives point to the virtues of justice and of generosity, but no one can despise them altogether without a certain hypocrisy. Yet notoriously the cultivation of truthfulness, justice, and courage will often, the world being what it contingently is, bar us from being rich or famous or powerful. Thus although we may hope that we can not only achieve the standards of excellence and the internal goods of certain practices by possessing the virtues *and* become rich, famous, and powerful, the virtues are always a potential stumbling block to this comfortable ambition. We should therefore expect that, if in a particular society the pursuit of external goods were to become dominant, the concept of the virtues might suffer first attrition and then perhaps something near total effacement, although simulacra might abound.

The time has come to ask the question of how far this partial account of a core conception of the virtues—and I need to emphasize that all that I have offered so far is the first stage of such an account—is faithful to the tradition which I delineated. How far, for example, and in what ways is it Aristotelian? It is—happily—not Aristotelian in two ways in which a good deal of the rest of the tradition also dissents from Aristotle. First, although this account of the virtues is teleological, it does not require the identification of any teleology in nature, and hence it does not require any allegiance to Aristotle's metaphysical biology. And secondly, just because of the multiplicity of human practices and the consequent multiplicity of goods in the pursuit of which the virtues may be exercised—goods which will often be contingently incompatible and which will therefore make rival claims upon our allegiance—conflict will not spring solely from flaws in individual character. But it was just on these two matters that Aristotle's account of the virtues seemed most vulnerable; hence if it turns out to be the case that this socially teleological account can support Aristotle's general account of the virtues as well as does his own biologically teleological account, these differences from Aristotle himself may well be regarded as strengthening rather than weakening the case for a generally Aristotelian standpoint.

There are at least three ways in which the account that I have given *is* clearly Aristotelian. First it requires for its completion a cogent elaboration of just those distinctions and concepts which Aristotle's account requires: voluntariness, the distinction between the intellectual virtues and the virtues of character, the relationship of both to natural abilities and to the passions and the structure of practical reasoning. On every one of these topics something very like Aristotle's view has to be defended, if my own account is to be plausible.

Secondly my account can accommodate an Aristotelian view of pleasure and enjoyment, whereas it is interestingly irreconcilable with any utilitarian view and more particularly with Franklin's account of the virtues. We can approach these questions by considering how to reply to someone who, having considered my account of the differences between goods internal to and goods external to a practice, inquired into which class, if either, does pleasure or enjoyment fall? The answer is, 'Some types of pleasure into one, some into the other.'

Someone who achieves excellence in a practice, who plays chess or football well, or who carries through an enquiry in physics or an experimental mode in painting with success characteristically enjoys his achievement and his activity in achieving. So does someone who, although not breaking the limit of achievement, plays or thinks or acts in a way that leads towards such a breaking of limit. As Aristotle says, the enjoyment of the activity and the enjoyment of achievement are not the ends at which the agent aims, but the enjoyment supervenes upon the successful activity in such a way that the activity achieved and the activity enjoyed are one and the same state. Hence to aim at the one is to aim at the other; and hence also it is easy to confuse the pursuit of excellence with the pursuit of enjoyment *in this specific sense.* This particular confusion is harmless enough; what is not harmless is the confusion of enjoyment *in this specific sense* with other forms of pleasure.

For certain kinds of pleasure are of course external goods along with prestige, status, power, and money. Not all pleasure is the enjoyment supervening upon achieved activity; some is the pleasure of psychological or physical states independent of all activity. Such states—for example that produced on a normal palate by the closely successive and thereby blended sensations of Colchester oyster, cayenne pepper, and Veuve Cliquot—may be sought as external goods, as external rewards which may be purchased by money or received in virtue of prestige. Hence the pleasures are categorized neatly and appropriately by the classification into internal and external goods.

It is just this classification which can find no place within Franklin's account of the virtues, which is formed entirely in terms of external relationships and external goods. Thus although by this stage of the argument it is possible to claim that my account does capture a conception of the virtues which is at the core of the particular ancient and medieval tradition which I have delineated, it is equally clear that there is more than one possible conception of the virtues and that Franklin's standpoint and indeed any utilitarian standpoint is such that to accept it will entail rejecting the tradition and *vice versa.*

One crucial point of incompatibility was noted long ago by D. H. Lawrence. When Franklin asserts, 'Rarely use venery but for health or offspring . . .', Lawrence replies, 'Never *use* venery.' It is of the character of a virtue that in order that it be effective in producing the internal goods which are the rewards of the virtues it should be exercised without regard to consequences. For it turns out to be the case that—and this is in part at least one more empirical factual claim—although the virtues are just those qualities which tend to lead to the achievement of a certain class of goods, none the less unless we practise them irrespective of whether in any particular set of contingent circumstances they will produce those goods or not, we cannot possess them at all. We cannot be genuinely courageous or truthful and be so only on occasion. Moreover, as we have seen, cultivation of the virtues always may and often does hinder the achievement of those external goods which are the mark of worldly success. The road to success in Philadelphia and the road to heaven may not coincide after all.

Furthermore we are now able to specify one crucial difficulty for *any* version of utilitarianism—in addition to those which I noticed earlier. Utilitarianism cannot accommodate the distinction between goods internal to and goods external to a practice. Not only is that distinction marked by none of the classical utilitarians—it cannot be found in Bentham's writings nor in those of either of the Mills or of Sidgwick—but internal goods and external goods are not commensurable with each other. Hence the notion of summing goods—and *a fortiori* in the light of what I have said about kinds of pleasure and enjoyment the notion of summing happiness—in terms of one single formula or conception of utility, whether it is Franklin's or Bentham's or Mill's, makes no sense. None the less we ought to note that although *this* distinction is alien to J. S. Mill's thought, it is plausible and in no way patronizing to suppose that something like this is the distinction which he was trying to make in *Utilitarianism* when he distinguished between 'higher' and 'lower' pleasures. At the most we can say 'something like this'; for J. S. Mill's upbringing had given him a limited view of human life and powers, had unfitted him, for example, for appreciating games just because of the way it had fitted him for appreciating philosophy. None the less the notion that the pursuit of excellence in a way that extends human powers is at the heart of human life is instantly recognizable as at home in not only J. S. Mill's political and social thought, but also in his and Mrs Taylor's life. Were I to choose human exemplars of certain of the virtues as I understand them, there would of course be many names to name, those of St Benedict and St Francis of Assisi and St Theresa *and* those of Frederick Engels and Eleanor Marx and Leon Trotsky among them. But that of John Stuart Mill would have to be there as certainly as any other.

Thirdly, my account is Aristotelian in that it links evaluation and explanation in a characteristically Aristotelian way. From an Aristotelian standpoint to identify certain actions as manifesting or failing to manifest a virtue or virtues is never only to evaluate; it is also to take the first step towards explaining why those actions rather than some others were performed. Hence for an Aristotelian quite as much as for a Platonist the fate of a city or an individual can be explained by citing the injustice of a tyrant or the courage of its defenders. Indeed without allusion to the place that justice and injustice, courage and cowardice play in human life, very little will be genuinely explicable. It follows that many of the explanatory projects of the modern social sciences, a methodological canon of which is the separation of 'the facts' from all evaluation, are bound to fail. For the fact that someone was or failed to be courageous or just cannot be recognized as 'a fact' by those who accept that methodological canon. The account of the virtues which I have given is completely at one with Aristotle's on this point. But now the question may be raised: your account may be in many respects Aristotelian, but is it not in some respects false? Consider the following important objection.

I have defined the virtues partly in terms of their place in practices. But surely, it may be suggested, some practices—that is, some coherent human activities which answer to the description of what I have called a practice—are evil. So in discussions by some moral philosophers of this type of account of the virtues it has been suggested that torture and sado-masochistic sexual activities might be examples of practices. But how can a disposition be a virtue if it is the kind of disposition which sustains practices and some practices issue in evil? My answer to this objection falls into two parts.

First I want to allow that there *may* be practices—in the sense in which I understand the concept—which simply *are* evil. I am far from convinced that there are, and I do not in fact believe that either torture or sado-masochistic sexuality answers to the description of a practice which my account of the virtues employs. But I do not want to rest my case on this lack of conviction, especially since it is plain that as a matter of contingent fact many types of practice may on particular occasions be productive of evil. For the range of practices includes the arts, the sciences, and certain types of intellectual and athletic game. And it is at once obvious that any of these may under certain conditions be a source of evil: the desire to excel and to win can corrupt, a man may be so engrossed by his painting that he neglects his family, what was initially an honourable resort to war can issue in savage cruelty. But what follows from this?

It certainly is not the case that my account entails *either* that we ought to excuse or condone such evils *or* that whatever flows from a virtue is right. I do have to allow that courage sometimes sustains injustice, that loyalty has been known to strengthen a murderous aggressor and that generosity has sometimes weakened the capacity to do good. But to deny this would be to fly in the face of just those empirical facts which I invoked in criticizing Aquinas' account of the unity of the virtues. That the virtues need initially to be defined and explained with reference to the notion of a practice thus in no way entails approval of all practices in all circumstances. That the virtues—as the objection itself presupposed—*are* defined not in terms of good and right practices, but of practices, does not entail or imply that practices as actually carried through at particular times and places do not stand in need of moral criticism. And the resources for such criticism are not lacking. There is in the first place no inconsistency in appealing to the requirements of a virtue to criticise a practice. Justice may be initially defined as a disposition which in its particular way is necessary to sustain practices; it does not follow that in pursuing the requirements of a practice violations of justice are not to be condemned. Moreover a morality of virtues requires as its counterpart a conception of moral law. Its requirements too have to be met by practices. But, it may be asked, does not all this imply that more needs to be said about the place of practices in some larger moral context? Does not this at least suggest that there is more to the core concept of a virtue than can be spelled out in terms of practices? I have after all emphasized that the scope of any virtue in human life extends beyond the practices in terms of which it is initially defined. What then is the place of the virtues in the larger arenas of human life?

I stressed earlier that any account of the virtues in terms of practices could only be a partial and first account. What is required to complement it? The most notable difference so far between my account and any account that could be called Aristotelian is that although I have in no way restricted the exercise of the virtues to the context of practices, it is in terms of practices that I have located their point and function. Whereas Aristotle locates that point and function in terms of the notion of a type of whole human life which can be called good. And it does seem that the question 'What would a human being lack who lacked the virtues?' must be given a kind of answer which goes beyond anything which I have said so far. For such an individual would not merely fail *in a variety of particular ways* in respect of the kind of excellence which can be achieved through participation in practices and in respect of the kind of human relationship required to sustain such excellence. His own life *viewed as a whole* would perhaps be defective; it would not be the kind of life which someone would describe in trying to answer the question 'What is the best kind of life for this kind of man or woman to live?' And that question cannot be answered without at least raising Aristotle's own question, 'What is the good life for man?' Consider three ways in which a human life informed only by the conception of the virtues sketched so far would be defective.

It would be pervaded, first of all, by *too many* conflicts and *too much* arbitrariness. I argued earlier that it is a merit of an account of the virtues in terms of a multiplicity of goods that it allows for the possibility of tragic conflict in a way in which Aristotle's does not. But it may also produce even in the life of someone who is virtuous and disciplined too many occasions when one allegiance points in one direction, another in another. The claims of one practice may be incompatible with another in such a way that one may find oneself oscillating in an arbitrary way, rather than making rational choices. So it seems to have been with T. E. Lawrence. Commitment to sustaining the kind of community in which the virtues can flourish may be incompatible with the devotion which a particular practice—of the arts, for example—requires. So there may be tensions between the claims of family life and those of the arts—the problem that Gauguin solved or failed to solve by fleeing to Polynesia, or between the claims of politics and those of the arts—the problem that Lenin solved or failed to solve by refusing to listen to Beethoven.

If the life of the virtues is continuously fractured by choices in which one allegiance entails the apparently arbitrary renunciation of another, it may seem that the goods internal to practices do after all derive their authority from our individual choices; for when different goods summon in different and in incompatible directions, 'I' have to choose between their rival claims. The modern self with its criterionless choices apparently reappears in the alien context of what was claimed to be an Aristotelian world. This accusation might be rebutted in part by returning to the question of why both goods and virtues do have authority in our lives and repeating what was said earlier in this chapter. But this reply would only be partly successful; the distinctively modern notion of choice would indeed have reappeared, even if with a more limited scope for its exercise than it has usually claimed.

Secondly, without an overriding conception of the *telos* of a whole human life, conceived as a unity, our conception of certain individual virtues has to remain partial and incomplete. Consider two examples. Justice, on an Aristotelian view, is defined in terms of giving each person his or her due or desert. To deserve well is to have contributed in some substantial way to the achievement of those goods, the sharing of which and the common pursuit of which provide foundations for human community. But the goods internal to practices, including the goods internal to the practice of making and sustaining forms of community, need to be ordered and evaluated in some way if we are to assess relative desert. Thus only substantive application of an Aristotelian concept of justice requires an understanding of goods and of the good that goes beyond the multiplicity of goods which inform practices. As with justice, so also with patience. Patience is the virtue of waiting attentively without complaint, but not of waiting thus for anything at all. To treat patience as a virtue presupposes some adequate answer to the question: waiting for what? Within the context of practices a partial, although for many purposes adequate, answer can be given: the patience of a craftsman with refractory material, of a teacher with a slow pupil, of a politician in negotiations, are all species of patience. But what if the material is just too refractory, the pupil too slow, the negotiations too frustrating? Ought we always at a certain point just to give up in the interests of the practice itself? The medieval exponents of the virtue of patience claimed that there are certain types of situation in which the virtue of patience requires that I do not ever give up on some person or task, situations in which, as they would have put it, I am required to embody in my attitude to that person or task something of the patient attitude of God towards his creation. But this could only be so if patience served some overriding good, some *telos* which warranted putting other goods in a subordinate place. Thus it turns out that the content of the virtue of patience depends upon how we order various goods in a hierarchy and *a fortiori* on whether we are able rationally so to order these particular goods.

I have suggested so far that unless there is a *telos* which transcends the limited goods of practices by constituting the good of a whole human life, the good of a human life conceived as a unity, it will *both* be the case that a certain subversive arbitrariness will invade the moral life *and* that we shall be unable to specify the context of certain virtues adequately. These two considerations are reinforced by a third: that there is at least one virtue recognized by the tradition which cannot be specified at all except with reference to the wholeness of a human life—the virtue of integrity or constancy. 'Purity of heart', said Kierkegaard, 'is to will one thing.' This notion of singleness of purpose in a whole life can have no application unless that of a whole life does.

It is clear therefore that my preliminary account of the virtues in terms of practices captures much, but very far from all, of what the Aristotelian tradition taught about the virtues. It is also clear that to give an account that is at once more fully adequate to the tradition and rationally defensible, it is necessary to raise a question to which the Aristotelian tradition presupposed an answer, an answer so widely shared in the pre-modern world that it never had to be formulated explicitly in any detailed way. This question is: is it rationally justifiable to conceive of each human life as a unity, so that we may try to specify each such life as having its good and so that we may understand the virtues as having their function in enabling an individual to make of his or her life one kind of unity rather than another?

7

VIRTUE AND REASON

JOHN MCDOWELL

I

Presumably the point of, say, inculcating a moral outlook lies in a concern with how people live. It may seem that the very idea of a moral outlook makes room for, and requires, the existence of moral theory, conceived as a discipline which seeks to formulate acceptable principles of conduct. It is then natural to think of ethics as a branch of philosophy related to moral theory, so conceived, rather as the philosophy of science is related to science. On this view, the primary topic of ethics is the concept of right conduct, and the nature and justification of principles of behaviour. If there is a place for an interest in the concept of virtue, it is a secondary place. Virtue is a disposition (perhaps of a specially rational and self-conscious kind) to behave rightly; the nature of virtue is explained, as it were, from the outside in.

My aim is to sketch the outlines of a different view, to be found in the philosophical tradition which flowers in Aristotle's ethics. According to this different view, although the point of engaging in ethical reflection still lies in the interest of the question 'How should one live?',[1] that question is necessarily approached *via* the notion of a virtuous person. A conception of right conduct is grasped, as it were, from the inside out.

II

I shall begin with some considerations which make it attractive to say, with Socrates, that virtue is knowledge.

What is it for someone to possess a virtue? 'Knowledge' implies that he

John McDowell, 'Virtue and Reason', *The Monist*, 62 (1979), 331–50.

[1] Aristotle, *Nicomachean Ethics* (henceforth cited as *NE*), e.g. 1103^b26–31; cf. Plato, *Republic* 352^d5–6.

gets things right; if we are to go any distance towards finding plausibility in the Socratic thesis, it is necessary to start with examples whose status as virtues, and hence as states of character whose possessor arrives at right answers to a certain range of questions about how to behave, is not likely to be queried. I shall use the example of kindness; anyone who disputes its claim to be a virtue should substitute a better example of his own. (The objectivity which 'knowledge' implies will recur later.)

A kind person can be relied on to behave kindly when that is what the situation requires. Moreover, his reliably kind behaviour is not the outcome of a blind, non-rational habit or instinct, like the courageous behaviour—so called only by courtesy—of a lioness defending her cubs.[2] Rather, that the situation requires a certain sort of behaviour is (one way of formulating) his reason for behaving in that way, on each of the relevant occasions. So it must be something of which, on each of the relevant occasions, he is aware. A kind person has a reliable sensitivity to a certain sort of requirement which situations impose on behaviour. The deliverances of a reliable sensitivity are cases of knowledge; and there are idioms according to which the sensitivity itself can appropriately be described as knowledge: a kind person knows what it is like to be confronted with a requirement of kindness. The sensitivity is, we might say, a sort of perceptual capacity.[3]

(Of course a kind person need not himself classify the behaviour he sees to be called for, on one of the relevant occasions, as kind. He need not be articulate enough to possess concepts of the particular virtues; and even if he does, the concepts need not enter his reasons for the actions which manifest those particular virtues. It is enough if he thinks of what he does, when—as we put it—he shows himself to be kind, under some such description as 'the thing to do'. The description need not differ from that under which he thinks of other actions of his, which we regard as manifesting different virtues; the division into actions which manifest kindness and actions which manifest other virtues can be imposed, not by the agent himself, but by a possibly more articulate, and more theoretically oriented, observer.)

The considerations adduced so far suggest that the knowledge constituted by the reliable sensitivity is a necessary condition for possession of the virtue. But they do not show that the knowledge is, as in the Socratic thesis, to be identified with the virtue. A preliminary case for the identification might go as follows. On each of the relevant occasions, the require-

[2] Cf. *NE* VI. 13 on the distinction between 'natural virtue' and 'virtue strictly so called'.

[3] Non-cognitivist objections to this sort of talk will be considered later.

ment imposed by the situation, and detected by the agent's sensitivity to such requirements, must exhaust his reason for acting as he does. It would disqualify an action from counting as a manifestation of kindness if its agent needed some extraneous incentive to compliance with the requirement—say, the rewards of a good reputation. So the deliverances of his sensitivity constitute, one by one, complete explanations of the actions which manifest the virtue. Hence, since the sensitivity fully accounts for its deliverances, the sensitivity fully accounts for the actions. But the concept of the virtue is the concept of a state whose possession accounts for the actions which manifest it. Since that explanatory role is filled by the sensitivity, the sensitivity turns out to be what the virtue is.[4]

That is a preliminary case for the identification of particular virtues with, as it were, specialized sensitivities to requirements. *Mutatis mutandis*, a similar argument applies to virtue in general. Indeed, in the context of another Socratic thesis, that of the unity of virtue, virtue in general is what the argument for identification with knowledge really concerns; the specialized sensitivities which are to be equated with particular virtues, according to the argument considered so far, are actually not available one by one for a series of separate identifications.

What makes this plausible is the attractive idea that a virtue issues in nothing but right conduct. Suppose the relevant range of behaviour, in the case of kindness, is marked out by the notion of proper attentiveness to others' feelings. Now sometimes acting in such a way as to indulge someone's feelings is not acting rightly: the morally important fact about the situation is not that *A* will be upset by a projected action (though he will), but, say, that *B* has a right—a consideration of a sort, sensitivity to which might be thought of as constituting fairness. In such a case, a straightforward propensity to be gentle to others' feelings would not lead to right conduct. If a genuine virtue is to produce nothing but right conduct, a simple propensity to be gentle cannot be identified with the virtue of kindness. Possession of the virtue must involve not only sensitivity to facts about others' feelings as reasons for acting in certain ways, but also sensitivity to facts about rights as reasons for acting in certain ways; and when

[4] There is a gap here. Even if it is conceded that the virtuous person has no further *reason* for what he does than the deliverance of his sensitivity, still, it may be said, two people can have the same reason for acting in a certain way, but only one of them acts in that way. There must then be some further *explanation* of this difference between them: if not that the one who acts has a further reason, then perhaps that the one who does not is in some state, standing or temporary, which undermines the efficacy of reasons, or perhaps of reasons of the particular kind in question, in producing action. This suggests that if we are to think of virtue as guaranteeing action, virtue must consist not in the sensitivity alone but in the sensitivity together with freedom from such obstructive states. These issues recur in § 3 below.

circumstances of both sorts obtain, and circumstance of the second sort is the one that should be acted on, a possessor of the virtue of kindness must be able to tell that that is so.[5] So we cannot disentangle genuine possession of kindness from the sensitivity which constitutes fairness. And since there are obviously no limits on the possibilities for compresence, in the same situation, of circumstances of the sorts proper sensitivities to which constitute all the virtues, the argument can be generalized: no one virtue can be fully possessed except by a possessor of all of them, that is, a possessor of virtue in general. Thus the particular virtues are not a batch of independent sensitivities. Rather, we use the concepts of the particular virtues to mark similarities and dissimilarities among the manifestations of a single sensitivity which is what virtue, in general, is: an ability to recognize requirements which situations impose on one's behaviour. It is a single complex sensitivity of this sort which we are aiming to instil when we aim to inculcate a moral outlook.

III

There is an apparent obstacle to the identification of virtue with knowledge. The argument for the identification requires that the deliverances of the sensitivity—the particular pieces of knowledge with which it equips its possessor—should fully explain the actions which manifest virtue. But it is plausible that appropriate action need not be elicited by a consideration apprehended as a reason—even a conclusive reason—for acting in a certain way. That may seem to open the following possibility: a person's perception of a situation may precisely match what a virtuous person's perception of it would be, although he does not act as the virtuous person would. But if a perception which corresponds to the virtuous person's does not call forth a virtuous action from this non-virtuous person, then the virtuous person's matching perception—the deliverance of his sensitivity—cannot, after all, fully account for the virtuous action which it does elicit from him. Whatever is missing, in the case of the person who does not act virtuously, must be present as an extra component, over and above the deliverance of the sensitivity, in a complete specification of the reason why the virtuous person acts as he does.[6] That destroys the identification of

[5] I do not mean to suggest that there is always a way of acting satisfactorily (as opposed to making the best of a bad job); nor that there is always one right answer to the question what one should do. But when there is a right answer, a virtuous person should be able to tell what it is.

[6] If we distinguish the reason why he acts from his reason for acting, this is the objection of n. 4.

virtue with the sensitivity. According to this line of argument, the sensitivity can be at most an ingredient in a composite state which is what virtue really is.

If we are to retain the identification of virtue with knowledge, then, by contraposition, we are committed to denying that a virtuous person's perception of a situation can be precisely matched in someone who, in that situation, acts otherwise than virtuously. Socrates seems to have supposed that the only way to embrace this commitment is in terms of ignorance, so that, paradoxically, failure to act as a virtuous person would cannot be voluntary, at least under that description. But there is a less extreme possibility, sketched by Aristotle.[7] This is to allow that someone who fails to act virtuously may, in a way, perceive what a virtuous person would, so that his failure to do the right thing is not inadvertent; but to insist that his failure occurs only because his appreciation of what he perceives is clouded, or unfocused, by the impact of a desire to do otherwise. This preserves the identification of virtue with a sensitivity; contrary to the counter-argument, nothing over and above the unclouded deliverances of the sensitivity is needed to explain the actions which manifest virtue. It is not that some extra explanatory factor, over and above the deliverances of the sensitivity, conspires with them to elicit action from the virtuous person, but rather that the other person's failure to act in that way is accounted for by a defectiveness in the approximations to those deliverances which he has.

It would be a mistake to protest that one can fail to act on a reason, and even on a reason judged by oneself to be better than any reason which one has for acting otherwise, without there needing to be any clouding or distortion in one's appreciation of the reason which one flouts.[8] That is true; but to suppose it constitutes an objection to Aristotle is to fail to understand the special nature of the conception of virtue which generates Aristotle's interest in incontinence.

One way to bring out the special nature of the conception is to note that, for Aristotle, continence is distinct from virtue, and just as problematic as incontinence. If someone needs to overcome an inclination to act otherwise, in getting himself to act as, say, temperance or courage demands, then he shows not virtue but (mere) continence. Suppose we take it that a virtuous person's judgement as to what he should do is arrived at by weighing, on the one side, some reason for acting in a way that will in fact manifest, say, courage, and, on the other side, a reason for doing something

[7] *NE* VII. 3.

[8] Cf. Donald Davidson, 'How is Weakness of Will Possible?', in Joel Feinberg (ed.), *Moral Concepts* (Oxford, 1969), 93–113, at pp. 99–100.

else (say a risk to life and limb, as a reason for running away), and deciding that on balance the former reason is the better. In that case, the distinction between virtue and continence will seem unintelligible. If the virtuous person allows himself to weigh the present danger, as a reason for running away, why should we not picture the weighing as his allowing himself to feel an inclination to run away, of a strength proportional to the weight which he allows to the reason? So long as he keeps the strength of his inclinations in line with the weight which he assigns to the reasons, his actions will conform to his judgement as to where, on balance, the better reason lies; what more can we require for virtue? (Perhaps that the genuinely courageous person simply does not care about his own survival? But Aristotle is rightly anxious to avert this misconception.[9]) The distinction becomes intelligible if we stop assuming that the virtuous person's judgement is a balancing of reasons for and against. The view of a situation which he arrives at by exercising his sensitivity is one in which some aspect of the situation is seen as constituting a reason for acting in some way; this reason is apprehended, not as outweighing or overriding any reasons for acting in other ways which would otherwise be constituted by other aspects of the situation (the present danger, say), but as silencing them. Here and now the risk to life and limb is not seen as any reason for removing himself. Aristotle's problem about incontinence is not 'How can one weigh considerations in favour of actions *X* and *Y*, decide that on balance the better reasons are in favour of *X*, but nevertheless perform *Y*?' (a question which, no doubt, does not require the idea of clouded judgement for its answer); but rather (a problem equally about continence) 'How can one have a view of a situation in which considerations which would otherwise appeal to one's will are silenced, but nevertheless allow those considerations to make themselves heard by one's will?'—a question which clearly is answerable, if at all, only by supposing that the incontinent or continent person does not fully share the virtuous person's perception of the situation.[10]

A more pressing objection is directed against the special conception of

[9] *NE* III. 9.

[10] On this view, genuine deliverances of the sensitivity involved in virtue would necessitate action. It is not that action requires not only a deliverance of the sensitivity but also, say, freedom from possibly obstructive factors, for instance distracting desires. An obstructive factor would not interfere with the efficacy of a deliverance of the sensitivity, but rather preclude genuine achievement of that view of the situation. This fills the gap mentioned in n. 4 above. (My discussion of incontinence here is meant to do no more than suggest that the identification of virtue with knowledge should not be dismissed out of hand, on the ground that it poses a problem about incontinence. I have said a little more in §§ 9, 10 of my 'Are Moral Requirements Hypothetical Imperatives?', *Proceedings of the Aristotelian Society Supplementary Volume 52* (1978), 13–29; but a great deal more would be needed in a full treatment.)

virtue: in particular, the use of cognitive notions in characterizing it. According to this objection, it must be a misuse of the notion of perception to suppose that an unclouded perception might suffice, on its own, to constitute a reason for acting in a certain way. An exercise of a genuinely cognitive capacity can yield at most part of a reason for acting; something appetitive is needed as well. To talk of virtue—a propensity to act in certain ways for certain reasons—as consisting in a sensitivity, a perceptual capacity, is to amalgamate the required appetitive component into the putative sensitivity. But all that is achieved thereby is a projection of human purposes into the world. (Here it becomes apparent how the objection touches on the issue of objectivity.) How one's will is disposed is a fact about oneself; whereas a genuinely cognitive faculty discloses to one how the world is independently of oneself, and in particular independently of one's will. Cognition and volition are distinct: the world—the proper sphere of cognitive capacities—is in itself an object of purely theoretical contemplation, capable of moving one to action only in conjunction with an extra factor—a state of will—contributed by oneself. I shall return to this objection.

IV

Presented with an identification of virtue with knowledge, it is natural to ask for a formulation of the knowledge which virtue is. We tend to assume that the knowledge must have a stateable propositional content (perhaps not capable of immediate expression by the knower). Then the virtuous person's reliably right judgements as to what he should do, occasion by occasion, can be explained in terms of interaction between this universal knowledge and some appropriate piece of particular knowledge about the situation at hand; and the explanation can take the form of a 'practical syllogism', with the content of the universal knowledge, or some suitable part of it, as major premiss, the relevant particular knowledge as minor premiss, and the judgement about what is to be done as deductive conclusion.

This picture is congenial to the objection mentioned at the end of §3. According to this picture, the problematic concept of a requirement figures only in the major premiss, and the conclusion, of the syllogism which reconstructs the virtuous person's reason for acting. Knowledge of the major premiss, the objector might say, is none other than the disposition of the will which is required, according to the objection, as a further component in the relevant reasons for acting, and hence as a further component in virtue, over and above any strictly cognitive state. (We call it 'knowledge' to endorse it, not to indicate that it is genuinely cognitive.) What a virtuous person really perceives is only what is stated in the minor premiss of the syllogism: that is, a straightforward fact about the situation at hand, which—as the objection requires—would be incapable of eliciting action on its own.

This picture fits only if the virtuous person's views about how, in general, one should behave are susceptible of codification, in principles apt for serving as major premisses in syllogisms of the sort envisaged. But to an unprejudiced eye it should seem quite implausible that any reasonably adult moral outlook admits of any such codification. As Aristotle consistently says, the best generalizations about how one should behave hold only for the most part.[11] If one attempted to reduce one's conception of what virtue requires to a set of rules, then, however subtle and thoughtful one was in drawing up the code, cases would inevitably turn up in which a mechanical application of the rules would strike one as wrong—and not necessarily because one had changed one's mind; rather, one's mind on the matter was not susceptible of capture in any universal formula.[12]

A deep-rooted prejudice about rationality blocks ready acceptance of this. A moral outlook is a specific determination of one's practical rationality: it shapes one's views about what reasons one has for acting. Rationality requires consistency; a specific conception of rationality in a particular area imposes a specific form on the abstract requirement of consistency—a specific view of what counts as going on doing the same thing here. The prejudice is the idea that acting in the light of a specific conception of rationality must be explicable in terms of being guided by a formulable universal principle. This prejudice comes under radical attack in Wittgenstein's discussion, in the *Philosophical Investigations*, of the concept of following a rule.

Consider an exercise of rationality in which there *is* a formulable rule, of which each successive action can be regarded as an application, appropriate in the circumstances arrived at: say (Wittgenstein's example) the extending of a series of numbers. We tend to picture the understanding of the instruction 'Add 2'—command of the rule for extending the series 2, 4, 6, 8, . . .—as a psychological mechanism which, aside from lapses of attention and so forth, churns out the appropriate behaviour with the sort of reliability which a physical mechanism, say a piece of clockwork, might have. If someone is extending the series correctly, and one takes his behaviour to

[11] See, e.g., *NE* I. 3.
[12] See *NE* V. 10, especially 1137^{b}19–24.

be compliance with the understood instruction, then, according to this picture, one has postulated such a psychological mechanism, underlying his behaviour, by an inference analogous to that whereby one might hypothesize a physical structure underlying the observable motions of some inanimate object. But this picture is profoundly suspect.

What manifests the pictured state of understanding? Suppose the person says, when asked what he is doing, 'Look, I'm adding 2 each time.' This apparent manifestation of understanding (or any other) will have been accompanied, at any point, by at most a finite fragment of the potentially infinite range of behaviour which we want to say the rule dictates. Thus the evidence for the presence of the pictured state is always compatible with the supposition that, on some future occasion for its exercise, the behaviour elicited by the occasion will diverge from what we would count as correct. Wittgenstein dramatizes this with the example of the man who continues the series, after 1,000, with 1,004, 1,008, . . .[13] If a possibility of the 1,004, 1,008, . . . type were to be realized (and we could not bring the person to concede that he had simply made a mistake), that would show that the behaviour hitherto was not guided by the psychological conformation which we were picturing as guiding it. The pictured state, then, always transcends the grounds on which it is allegedly postulated.

There may be an inclination to protest: 'This is merely inductive scepticism about other minds. After all, one knows in one's own case that one's behaviour will not come adrift like that.' But this misses the point of the argument.

First, if what it is for one's behaviour to come adrift is for it suddenly to seem that everyone else is out of step, then clearly the argument bears on one's own case just as much as on the case of others. (Imagine that the person who goes on with 1,004, 1,008, . . . had said, in advance, 'I know in my own case that my behaviour will not come adrift.')

Second, it is a mistake to interpret the argument as making a sceptical point: that one does not know, in the case of another person (or in one's own case either, once we have made the first correction), that the behaviour will not come adrift. The argument is not meant to suggest that we should be in a state of constant trepidation lest possibilities of the 1,004, 1,008, . . . type be realized.[14] We are confident that they will not: the argument aims, not at all to undermine this confidence, but to change our conception of its ground and nature. We tend to picture our transition to this confident expectation, from such grounds as we have, as being medi-

[13] Wittgenstein, *Philosophical Investigations* (Oxford, 1953), § 185.

[14] Nor even that we really *understand* the supposition that such a thing might happen. See Barry Stroud, 'Wittgenstein and Logical Necessity', *Philosophical Review*, 74 (1965), 504–18.

ated by the postulated psychological mechanism. But we can no more find the putatively mediating state manifested in the grounds for our expectation than we can find manifested there the very future occurrences we expect. Postulation of the mediating state is an idle intervening step; it does nothing to underwrite the confidence of the expectation.

(The content of the expectation is not purely behavioural. We might have a good scientific argument, mediated by postulation of a physiological mechanism, for not expecting any particular train of behaviour, of the 1,004, 1,008, . . . type, which we might contemplate. Here postulation of the mediating physiological state would not be an idle intervening step. But the parallel is misleading. We can bring this out by considering a variant of Wittgenstein's example, in which, on reaching 1,000, the person goes on as we expect, with 1,002, 1,004, . . . , but with a sense of dissociation from what he is doing. What he does no longer strikes him as going on in the same way; it feels as if a sheer habit has usurped his reason in controlling his behaviour. We confidently expect that this sort of thing will not happen; once again, postulation of a psychological mechanism does nothing to underwrite this confidence.)

What *is* the ground and nature of our confidence? About the competent use of words, Stanley Cavell writes:

> We learn and teach words in certain contexts, and then we are expected, and expect others, to be able to project them into further contexts. Nothing insures that this projection will take place (in particular, not the grasping of universals nor the grasping of books of rules), just as nothing insures that we will make, and understand, the same projections. That on the whole we do is a matter of our sharing routes of interest and feeling, modes of response, senses of humour and of significance and of fulfilment, of what is outrageous, of what is similar to what else, what a rebuke, what forgiveness, of when an utterance is an assertion, when an appeal, when an explanation—all the whirl of organism Wittgenstein calls 'forms of life.' Human speech and activity, sanity and community, rest upon nothing more, but nothing less, than this. It is a vision as simple as it is difficult, and as difficult as it is (and because it is) terrifying.[15]

The terror of which Cavell speaks at the end of this marvellous passage is a sort of vertigo, induced by the thought that there is nothing but shared forms of life to keep us, as it were, on the rails. We are inclined to think that that is an insufficient foundation for a conviction that when we, say, extend a number series, we really are, at each stage, doing the same thing as before. In this mood, it seems to us that what Cavell describes cannot be a shared conceptual framework within which something is, given the circumstances, objectively the correct move;[16] it looks, rather, like a congru-

[15] Stanley Cavell, *Must We Mean What We Say*? (New York, 1969), 52.

[16] Locating the desired objectivity *within* the conceptual framework is intended to leave open,

ence of subjectivities, with the congruence not grounded as it would need to be to amount to an objectivity. So we feel we have lost the objectivity of (in our case) mathematics (and similarly in other cases). We recoil from this vertigo into the idea that we are kept on the rails by our grasp of rules. This idea has a pair of twin components: first, the idea (as above) that grasp of the rules is a psychological mechanism which (apart from mechanical failure, which is how we picture mistakes and so forth) guarantees that we stay in the straight and narrow; and, second, the idea that the rails—what we engage our mental wheels with when we come to grasp the rules—are objectively there, in a way which transcends the 'mere' sharing of forms of life (hence, for instance, platonism about numbers). This composite idea is not the perception of some truth, but a consoling myth, elicited from us by our inability to endure the vertigo.

Of course, this casts no doubt on the possibility of putting explanations of particular moves, in the extending of a number series, in a syllogistic form: universal knowledge of how to extend the series interacts with particular knowledge of where one is in it, to produce a non-accidentally correct judgement as to what the next number is. In this case we can formulate the explanation so as to confer on the judgement explained the compellingness possessed by the conclusion of a proof. What is wrong is to take that fact to indicate that the explanation lays bare the inexorable workings of a machine: something whose operations, with our understanding of them, would not depend on the deliverances, in particular cases, of (for instance, and centrally) that shared sense of what is similar to what else which Cavell mentions. The truth is that it is only because of our own involvement in our 'whirl of organism' that we can understand the words we produce as conferring that special compellingness on the judgement explained.

Now it is only this misconception of the deductive paradigm which leads us to suppose that the operations of any specific conception of rationality in a particular area—any specific conception of what counts as doing the same thing—must be deductively explicable; that is, that there must be a formulable universal principle suited to serve as major premiss in syllogistic explanations of the sort considered above.

Consider, for instance, a concept whose application gives rise to hard cases, in this sense: there are disagreements which resist resolution by

here, the possibility of querying whether the conceptual framework itself is objectively the right one. If someone wants to reject the question whether this rather than that moral outlook is objectively correct, he will still want it to be an objective matter whether one has, say, succeeded in inculcating a particular moral outlook in someone else; so he will still be susceptible to the vertigo I am describing.

argument, as to whether or not the concept applies. Convinced that one is in the right on a hard case, one will find oneself saying, as one's arguments tail off without securing assent, 'You simply aren't seeing it,' or 'But don't you see?' In such cases the prejudice takes the form of a dilemma. One horn is that the inconclusiveness of one's arguments stems merely from an inability, in principle remediable, to articulate what one knows. It is possible, in principle, to spell out a universal formula which specifies the conditions under which the concept, in that use of it which one has mastered, is correctly applied. That would elevate one's argument to deductiveness. (If one's opponent refused to accept the deductive argument's major premiss, that would show that he had not mastered the same use of the concept, so that there would be, after all, no substantive disagreement.) If this assimilation to the deductive paradigm is not possible, then—this is the other horn of the dilemma—one's conviction that one is genuinely making a correct application of a concept (genuinely going on in the same way as before) must be an illusion. The case is revealed as one which calls, not for finding (seeing) the right answer to a question about how things are, but (perhaps) for a creative decision as to what to say.[17] Thus: either the case is not really a hard case, since sufficient ingenuity in the construction of arguments will resolve it; or, if its hardness is ineliminable, that shows that the issue cannot, after all, be one about whether an application of a concept is correct.

In a hard case, the issue turns on that appreciation of the particular instance whose absence is deplored, in 'You simply aren't seeing it,' or which is unsuccessfully appealed to, in 'But don't you see?' The dilemma reflects the view that a putative judgement which is grounded in nothing firmer than that cannot really be going on in the same way as before. This is an avoidance of vertigo. The thought is: there is not enough there to constitute the rails on which a genuine series of consistent applications of a concept must run. But in fact it is an illusion to suppose that the first horn of the dilemma yields a way of preserving from risk of vertigo the conviction that we are dealing with genuine concept-application. The illusion is the misconception of the deductive paradigm: the idea that deductive explicability characterizes an exercise of reason in which it is, as it were, automatically compelling, without dependence on our partially shared 'whirl of organism'. The dilemma registers a refusal to accept that when the dependence which induces vertigo is out in the open, in

[17] Why not abandon the whole practice as fraudulent? In some cases something may need to be said: for instance by a judge, in a lawsuit. Against the view that in legal hard cases judges are free to *make* the law, see Ronald Dworkin, 'Hard Cases', in *Taking Rights Seriously* (London, 1977), 81–130.

the appeal to appreciation, we can genuinely be going on in the same way; but the paradigm of a genuine case, that with which the rejected case is unfavourably compared, has the same dependence, only less obviously.[18]

Contemplating the dependence should not induce vertigo at all. We cannot be whole-heartedly engaged in the relevant parts of the 'whirl of organism', and at the same time achieve the detachment necessary in order to query whether our unreflective view of what we are doing is illusory. The cure for the vertigo, then, is to give up the idea that philosophical thought, about the sorts of practice in question, should be undertaken at some external standpoint, outside our immersion in our familiar forms of life.[19] If this cure works where explanations of exercises of rationality conform to the deductive paradigm, it should be no less efficacious where we explicitly appeal to appreciation of the particular instance in inviting acceptance of our judgements. And its efficacy in cases of the second kind is direct. Only the illusion that the deductive cases are immune can make it seem that, in order to effect the cure in cases of the second kind, we must first eliminate explicit dependence on appreciation, by assimilating them, as the prejudice requires, to the deductive paradigm.

If we make the assimilation, we adopt a position in which it is especially clear that our picture of a psychological mechanism, underlying a series of exercises of rationality, is a picture of something which transcends the grounds on which it is ascribed to anyone. In the cases in question, no one can express the envisaged universal formula. This transcendence poses difficulties about the acquisition of the pictured state. We are inclined to be impressed by the sparseness of the teaching which leaves someone capable of autonomously going on in the same way. All that happens is that the pupil is told, or shown, what to do in a few instances, with some surrounding talk about why that is the thing to do; the surrounding talk, *ex hypothesi* given that we are dealing with a case of the second kind, falls short of including actual enunciation of a universal principle, mechanical application of which would constitute correct behaviour in the practice in question. Yet pupils do acquire a capacity to go on, without further advice, to novel instances. Impressed by the sparseness of the teaching, we find this remarkable. But assimilation to the deductive paradigm leaves it no less remarkable. The assimilation replaces the question 'How is it that the

[18] In the rejected case, the dependence is out in the open in an especially perturbing form, in that the occasional failure of the appeal to appreciation brings out how the 'whirl of organism' is only partly shared; whereas there are no hard cases in mathematics. This is indeed a significant fact about mathematics. But its significance is not that mathematics is immune from the dependence.

[19] I am not suggesting that effecting this cure is a simple matter.

pupil, given that sparse instruction, goes on to new instances in the right way?' with the question 'How is it that the pupil, given that sparse instruction, divines from it a universal formula with the right deductive powers?' The second question is, if anything, less tractable. Addressing the first, we can say: it is a fact (no doubt a remarkable fact) that, against a background of common human nature and shared forms of life, one's sensitivities to kinds of similarities between situations can be altered and enriched by just this sort of instruction. This attributes no guesswork to the learner; whereas no amount of appealing to common human nature and shared forms of life will free the second question from its presupposition—inevitably imported by assimilation to the deductive—that the learner is required to make a leap of divination.[20]

It is not to be supposed that the appreciation of the particular instance, explicitly appealed to in the second kind of case, is a straightforward or easy attainment on the part of those who have it; that either, on casual contemplation of an instance, one sees it in the right light, or else one does not, and is then unreachable by argument. First, 'Don't you see?' can often be supplemented with words aimed at persuasion. A skilfully presented characterization of an instance will sometimes bring someone to see it as one wants; or one can adduce general considerations, for instance about the point of the concept a particular application of which is in dispute. Given that the case is one of the second kind, any such arguments will fall short of rationally necessitating acceptance of their conclusion in the way a proof does.[21] But it is only the prejudice I am attacking which makes this seem to cast doubt on their status as arguments: that is, appeals to reason. Second, if effort can induce the needed appreciation in someone else, it can also take effort to acquire it oneself. Admitting the dependence on appreciation does not imply that, if someone has the sort of specific determination of rationality we are considering, the right way to handle a given situation will always be clear to him on unreflective inspection of it.

V

If we resist the prejudice, and respect Aristotle's belief that a view of how one should live is not codifiable, what happens to our explanations of a virtuous person's reliably right judgements as to what he should do on

[20] See Wittgenstein, *Philosophical Investigations*, e.g., §210.

[21] If general considerations recommend a universal formula, it will employ terms which themselves give rise to hard cases.

particular occasions? Aristotle's notion of the practical syllogism is obviously meant to apply here; we need to consider how.

The explanations, so far treated as explanations of judgements about what to do, are equally explanations of actions. The point of analogy which motivates the quasi-logical label 'practical syllogism' is this. If something might serve as an argument for a theoretical conclusion, then it can equally figure in an account of someone's reasons for believing that conclusion, with the premisses of the argument giving the content of the psychological states—beliefs, in the theoretical case—which we cite in the reason-giving explanation. Now actions too are explained by reasons; that is, by citing psychological states in the light of which we can see how acting in the way explained would have struck the agent as in some way rational. The idea of a practical syllogism is the idea of an argument-like schema for explanations of actions, with the 'premisses', as in the theoretical case, giving the content of the psychological states cited in the explanation.[22]

David Wiggins has given this account of the general shape of a practical syllogism:

> The first or major premiss mentions something of which there could be a desire, *orexis*, transmissible to some practical conclusion (i.e., a desire convertible *via* some available minor premiss into an action). The second premiss pertains to the feasibility in the particular situation to which the syllogism is applied of what must be done if the claim of the major premiss is to be heeded.[23]

This schema fits most straightforwardly when reasons are (in a broad sense) technical: the major premiss specifies a determinate goal, and the minor premiss marks out some action as a means to it.[24]

The role played by the major premiss, in these straightforward applications of the schema, is to give the content of an orectic psychological state: something we might conceive as providing the motivating energy for the

[22] I distinguish practical reason from practical reasoning. From *NE* 1105ᵃ28–33, with 1111ᵃ15–16, it might seem that virtuous action, in Aristotle's view, must be the outcome of reasoning. But this doctrine is both incredible in itself and inconsistent with 1117ᵃ17–22. So I construe Aristotle's discussion of deliberation as aimed at the reconstruction of reasons for action not necessarily thought out in advance; where they were not thought out in advance, the concept of deliberation applies in an 'as if' style. See John M. Cooper, *Reason and Human Good in Aristotle* (Cambridge, Mass., 1975), 5–10. (It will be apparent that what I say about Aristotle's views on practical reason runs counter to Cooper's interpretation at many points. I am less concerned here with what Aristotle actually thought than with certain philosophical issues; so I have not encumbered this paper with scholarly controversy.)

[23] David Wiggins, 'Deliberation and Practical Reason', *Proceedings of the Aristotelian Society*, 76 (1975–6), 29–51, at p. 40. The quoted passage is an explanation of Aristotle, *De Motu Animalium* 701ᵃ9 ff. My debt to Wiggins's paper will be apparent.

[24] There is an inclination to insist on the only, or best, means. But this is the outcome of a suspect desire to have instances of the schema which *prove* that the action explained is the thing to do.

actions explained. Aristotle's idea seems to be that what fills an analogous role in the explanation of virtuous actions is the virtuous person's conception of the sort of life a human being should lead.[25] If that conception were codifiable in universal principles, the explanations would take the deductive shape insisted on by the prejudice discussed in § 4. But the thesis of uncodifiability means that the envisaged major premiss, in a virtue syllogism, cannot be definitively written down.[26] Any attempt to capture it in words will recapitulate the character of the teaching whereby it might be instilled: generalizations will be approximate at best, and examples will need to be taken with the sort of 'and so on' which appeals to the cooperation of a hearer who has cottoned on.[27]

If someone guides his life by a certain conception of how to live, then he acts, on particular occasions, so as to fulfil suitable concerns.[28] A concern can mesh with a noticed fact about a situation, so as to account for an action: as, for instance, a concern for the welfare of one's friends, together with awareness that a friend is in trouble and open to being comforted, can explain missing a pleasant party in order to talk to the friend. On a suitable occasion, that pair of psychological states might constitute the core of a satisfying explanation of an action which is in fact virtuous. Nothing more need be mentioned for the action to have been given a completely intelligible motivation. In Aristotle's view, the orectic state cited in an explanation of a virtuous action is the agent's entire conception of how to live, rather than just whatever concern it happened to be; and this may now seem mysterious. But the core explanation, as so far envisaged, lacks any indication that the action explained conformed to the agent's conception of how to live. The core explanation would apply equally to a case of helping one's friend because one thought it was, in the circumstances, the thing to do, and to a case of helping one's friend in spite of thinking it was not, in the circumstances, the thing to do.

A conception of how one should live is not simply an unorganized collection of propensities to act, on this or that occasion, in pursuit of this or that concern. Sometimes there are several concerns, fulfilment of any

[25] *NE* 1144a31–3.

[26] This is distinct from the claim that a person may at any stage be prone to change his mind (cf. § 3 above). Wiggins ('Deliberation and Practical Reason') appears at some points to run the two claims together, no doubt because he is concerned with practical reason generally, and not, as I am, with the expression in action of a specific conception of how to live. The line between realizing that one's antecedent conception of how to live requires something which one had not previously seen it to require, on the one hand, and modifying one's conception of how to live, on the other, is not a sharp one. But I do not want to exploit cases most happily described in the second way.

[27] Cf. Wittgenstein, *Philosophical Investigations*, § 208.

[28] I borrow this excellent term from Wiggins, 'Deliberation and Practical Reason', 43 ff.

one of which might, on a suitable occasion, constitute acting as a certain conception of how to live would dictate, and each of which, on the occasion at hand, is capable of engaging with a known fact about the situation and issuing in action. Acting in the light of a conception of how to live requires selecting and acting on the right concern. (Compare the end of § 1, on the unity of virtue.) So if an action whose motivation is spelled out in our core explanation is a manifestation of virtue, more must be true of its agent than just that on this occasion he acted with that motivation. The core explanation must at least be seen against the background of the agent's conception of how to live; and if the situation is one of those on which any of several concerns might impinge, the conception of how to live must be capable of actually entering our understanding of the action, explaining why it was this concern rather than any other which was drawn into operation.

How does it enter? If the conception of how to live involved a ranking of concerns, or perhaps a set of rankings each relativized to some type of situation, the explanation of why one concern was operative rather than another would be straightforward. But uncodifiability rules out laying down such general rankings in advance of all the predicaments with which life may confront one.

What I have described as selecting the right concern might equally be described in terms of the minor premiss of the core explanation. If there is more than one concern which might impinge on the situation, there is more than one fact about the situation which the agent might, say, dwell on, in such a way as to summon an appropriate concern into operation. It is by virtue of his seeing this particular fact rather than that one as the salient fact about the situation that he is moved to act by this concern rather than that one.[29] This perception of saliences is the shape taken here by the appreciation of particular cases which I discussed in § 5: something to which the uncodifiability of an exercise of rationality sometimes compels explicit appeal when we aim to represent actions as instances of it. A conception of how to live shows itself, when more than one concern might issue in action, in one's seeing, or being able to be brought to see, one fact rather than another as salient. And our understanding of such a conception enters into our understanding of actions—the supplementation which the core explanation needs—by enabling us to share, or at least comprehend, the agent's perception of saliences.[30]

It is not wrong to think of the virtuous person's judgements about what

[29] This use of 'salient' follows Wiggins, ibid. 45.

[30] On the importance of the appreciation of the particular case, see *NE* 1142^{a}23–30, 1143^{a}25–^{b}5; discussed by Wiggins, 'Deliberation and Practical Reason', 46–9. (For the point of 'or at least comprehend', see n. 33 below.)

to do, or his actions, as explicable by interaction between knowledge of how to live and particular knowledge about the situation at hand. (Compare the beginning of §4.) But the thought needs a more subtle construal than the deductive paradigm allows. With the core explanations and their supplementations, I have in effect been treating the complete explanations as coming in two stages. It is at the first stage—hitherto the supplementation—that knowledge of how to live interacts with particular knowledge: knowledge, namely, of all the particular facts capable of engaging with concerns whose fulfilment would, on occasion, be virtuous. This interaction yields, in a way essentially dependent on appreciation of the particular case, a view of the situation with one such fact, as it were, in the foreground. Seen as salient, that fact serves, at the second stage, as minor premiss in a core explanation.[31]

VI

We can go back now to the non-cognitivist objection outlined at the end of §3. Awareness that one's friend is in trouble and open to being comforted—the psychological state whose content is the minor premiss of our core explanation—can perhaps, for the sake of argument, be conceded to be the sort of thing which the objection insists cognitive states must be: something capable of eliciting action only in conjunction with a non-cognitive state, namely, in our example, a concern for one's friends.[32] But if someone takes that fact to be the salient fact about the situation, he is in a psychological state which is essentially practical. The relevant notion of salience cannot be understood except in terms of seeing something as a reason for acting which silences all others (compare §3). So classifying that state as a cognitive state is just the sort of thing which the objection attacks.

The most natural way to press the objection is to insist on purifying the content of what is genuinely known down to something which is, in itself, motivationally inert (namely, given the concession above, that one's friend is in trouble and open to being comforted); and then to represent the 'perception' of a salience as an amalgam of the purified awareness with an

[31] That the interaction, at the first stage, is with *all* the potentially reason-yielding facts about the situation allows us to register that, in the case of, say, courage, the gravity of the risk, in comparison to the importance of the end to be achieved by facing it, makes a difference to whether virtue really does require facing the risk; even though at the second stage, if the risk is not seen as salient, it is seen as no reason at all for running away. I am indebted here to a version of Wiggins's (f) (cited in 'Deliberation and Practical Reason', 45), importantly modified for a revised excerpt from his paper in Joseph Raz (ed.), *Practical Reasoning* (Oxford, 1978).

[32] Actually this is open to question, because of special properties of the concept of a friend.

additional appetitive state. But what appetitive state? Concern for one's friends yields only the core explanation, not the explanation in which the 'perception' of salience was to figure. Perhaps the conception of how to live? That is certainly an orectic state. But, given the thesis of uncodifiability, it is not intelligible independently of just such appreciation of particular situations as is involved in the present 'perception' of a salience; so it is not suitable to serve as an element into which, together with some genuine awareness, the 'perception' could be regarded as analysable. (This non-cognitivist strategy is reflected in assimilation to the deductive paradigm: that the assimilation is congenial to the non-cognitivist objection was noted early in §4. The failure of the strategy is reflected in the failure of the assimilation, given the thesis of uncodifiability.)

If we feel the vertigo discussed in § 4, it is out of distaste for the idea that a manifestation of reason might be recognizable as such only from within the practice whose status is in question. We are inclined to think there ought to be a neutral external standpoint from which the rationality of any genuine exercise of reason could be demonstrated. Now we might understand the objection to be demanding a non-cognitive extra which would be analogous to hunger: an appetitive state whose possession by anyone is intelligible in its own right, not itself open to assessment as rational or irrational, but conferring an obvious rationality, recognizable from outside, on behaviour engaged in with a view to its gratification. In that case it is clear how the objection is an expression of the craving for a kind of rationality independently demonstrable as such. However, it is highly implausible that all the concerns which motivate virtuous actions are intelligible, one by one, independently of appreciating a virtuous person's distinctive way of seeing situations. And even if they were, the various particular concerns figure only in the core explanation. We do not fully understand a virtuous person's actions—we do not see the consistency in them—unless we can supplement the core explanations with a grasp of his conception of how to live. And though this is to credit him with an orectic state, it is not to credit him with an externally intelligible overarching desire; for we cannot understand the content of the orectic state from the envisaged external standpoint. It is, rather, to comprehend, essentially from within, the virtuous person's distinctive way of viewing particular situations.[33]

[33] The qualification 'essentially' is to allow for the possibility of appreciating what it is like to be inside a way of thinking without actually being inside it, on the basis of a sufficient affinity between it and a way of thinking of one's own. These considerations about externally intelligible desires bear on Philippa Foot's thesis, in 'Morality as a System of Hypothetical Imperatives',

The rationality of virtue, then, is not demonstrable from an external standpoint. But to suppose that it ought to be is only a version of the prejudice discussed in § 4. It is only an illusion that our paradigm of reason, deductive argument, has its rationality discernible from a standpoint not necessarily located within the practice itself.

VII

Although perceptions of saliences resist decomposition into 'pure' awareness together with appetitive states, there is an inclination to insist, nevertheless, that they cannot be genuinely cognitive states. We can be got into a cast of mind in which—as it seems to us—we have these problematic perceptions, only because we can be brought to care about certain things; hence, ultimately, only because of certain antecedent facts about our emotional and appetitive make-up. This can seem to justify a more subtle non-cognitivism: one which abandons the claim that the problematic perceptions can be analysed into cognitive and appetitive components, but insists that, because of the anthropocentricity of the conceptual apparatus involved, they are not judgements, true or false, as to how things are in an independent reality; and that is what cognitive states are.[34]

I cannot tackle this subtle non-cognitivism properly now. I suspect that its origin is a philistine scientism, probably based on the misleading idea that the right of scientific method to rational acceptance is discernible from a more objective standpoint than that from which we seem to perceive the saliences. A scientistic conception of reality is eminently open to dispute. When we ask the metaphysical question whether reality is what science can find out about, we cannot, without begging the question, restrict the materials for an answer to those which science can countenance. Let the question be an empirical question, by all means; but the empirical data which would be collected by a careful and sensitive

Philosophical Review, 81 (1972), 305–16, that morality should be construed, or recast, in terms of hypothetical imperatives, on pain of being fraudulent. Her negative arguments seem to me to be analogous to an exposé of the emptiness of platonism, as affording a foundation for mathematical practice external to the practice itself. In the mathematical case it is not a correct response to look for another external guarantee of the rationality of the practice, but that seems to me just what Mrs Foot's positive suggestion amounts to in the moral case. (If the desires are not externally intelligible, the label 'hypothetical imperative' loses its point.) See, further, my 'Are Moral Requirements Hypothetical Imperatives?'.

[34] On anthropocentricity, see David Wiggins, 'Truth, Invention, and the Meaning of Life', *Proceedings of the British Academy*, 62 (1976), 331–78, at pp. 348–9, 360–3.

moral phenomenology—no doubt not a scientific enterprise—are handled quite unsatisfyingly by non-cognitivism.[35]

It would be a mistake to object that stress on appreciation of the particular, and the absence of a decision procedure, encourages everyone to pontificate about particular cases. In fact resistance to non-cognitivism, about the perception of saliences, recommends humility. If we resist non-cognitivism, we can equate the conceptual equipment which forms the framework of anything recognizable as a moral outlook with a capacity to be impressed by certain aspects of reality. But ethical reality is immensely difficult to see clearly. (Compare the end of §4.) If we are aware of how, for instance, selfish fantasy distorts our vision, we shall not be inclined to be confident that we have got things right.[36]

It seems plausible that Plato's ethical Forms are, in part at least, a response to uncodifiability: if one cannot formulate what someone has come to know when he cottons onto a practice, say one of concept-application, it is natural to say that he has seen something. Now in the passage quoted in §4, Cavell mentions two ways of avoiding vertigo: 'the grasping of universals' as well as what we have been concerned with so far, 'the grasping of books of rules'. But though Plato's Forms are a myth, they are not a consolation, a mere avoidance of vertigo; vision of them is portrayed as too difficult an attainment for that to be so. The remoteness of the Form of the Good is a metaphorical version of the thesis that value is not in the world, utterly distinct from the dreary literal version which has obsessed recent moral philosophy. The point of the metaphor is the colossal difficulty of attaining a capacity to cope clear-sightedly with the ethical reality which *is* part of our world. Unlike other philosophical responses to uncodifiability, this one may actually work towards moral improvement; negatively, by inducing humility, and positively, by an inspiring effect akin to that of a religious conversion.[37]

VIII

If the question 'How should one live?' could be given a direct answer in universal terms, the concept of virtue would have only a secondary place in moral philosophy. But the thesis of uncodifiability excludes a head-on approach to the question whose urgency gives ethics its interest. Occasion

[35] See ibid. and Iris Murdoch, *The Sovereignty of Good* (London, 1970).
[36] Cf. ibid. I am indebted here to Mark Platts.
[37] This view of Plato is beautifully elaborated by Iris Murdoch.

by occasion, one knows what to do, if one does, not by applying universal principles but by being a certain kind of person: one who sees situations in a certain distinctive way. And there is no dislodging, from the central position they occupy in the ethical reflection of Plato and Aristotle, questions about the nature and (hardly discussed in this paper) the acquisition of virtue.

It is sometimes complained that Aristotle does not attempt to outline a decision procedure for questions about how to behave. But we have good reason to be suspicious of the assumption that there must be something to be found along the route he does not follow.[38] And there is plenty for us to do in the area of philosophy of mind where his different approach locates ethics.

[38] The idea, for instance, that something like utilitarianism *must* be right looks like a double avoidance of vertigo: first, in the thought that there must be a decision procedure; and second, in the reduction of practical rationality to the pursuit of neutrally intelligible desires.

8

VIRTUES AND VICES

PHILIPPA FOOT

I

For many years the subject of the virtues and vices was strangely neglected by moralists working within the school of analytic philosophy. The tacitly accepted opinion was that a study of the topic would form no part of the fundamental work of ethics; and since this opinion was apparently shared by philosophers such as Hume, Kant, Mill, G. E. Moore, W. D. Ross, and H. A. Prichard, from whom much contemporary moral philosophy has been derived, perhaps the neglect is not so surprising after all.* However that may be, things have recently been changing. During the past few decades several philosophers have turned their attention to the subject; notably G. H. von Wright and Peter Geach. Von Wright devoted a not at all perfunctory chapter to the virtues in his book *The Varieties of Goodness*[1] published in 1963, and Peter Geach's book called *The Virtues*[2] appeared in 1977. Meanwhile a number of interesting articles on the topic have come out in the journals.

In spite of this modern work, it perhaps is best when considering the virtues and vices to go back to Aristotle and Aquinas. I myself have found Plato less helpful, because the individual virtues and vices are not so clearly or consistently distinguished in his work. It is certain, in any case, that the most systematic account is found in Aristotle, and in the blending of Aristotelian and Christian philosophy found in St Thomas. By and large Aquinas followed Aristotle—sometimes even heroically—where Aristotle gave an opinion, and where St Thomas is on his own, as in developing the doctrine of the theological virtues of faith, hope, and charity, and in his theocentric doctrine of happiness, he still uses an Aristotelian framework

From Philippa Foot, *Virtues and Vices and Other Essays in Moral Philosophy* (Oxford: Blackwell, 1978), 1–18. Reprinted by permission of the author.

* Here and elsewhere small stylistic changes have been made in the present text.

[1] G. H. von Wright, *The Varieties of Goodness* (London, 1963).

[2] Peter Geach, *The Virtues* (Cambridge, 1977).

where he can: as for instance in speaking of happiness as man's last end. However, there are different emphases and new elements in Aquinas's ethics: often he works things out in far more detail than Aristotle did, and it is possible to learn a great deal from Aquinas that one could not have got from Aristotle. It is my opinion that the *Summa Theologica* is one of the best sources we have for moral philosophy, and moreover that St Thomas's ethical writings are as useful to the atheist as to the Catholic or other Christian believer.

There is, however, one minor obstacle to be overcome when one goes back to Aristotle and Aquinas for help in constructing a theory of virtues, namely a lack of coincidence between their terminology and our own. For when we talk about the virtues we are not taking as our subject everything to which Aristotle gave the name *aretē* or Aquinas *virtus*, and consequently not everything called a virtue in translations of these authors. 'The virtues' to us are the moral virtues whereas *aretē* and *virtus* refer also to arts, and even to excellences of the speculative intellect whose domain is theory rather than practice. And to make things more confusing we find some dispositions called moral virtues in translations from the Greek and Latin, although the class of virtues that Aristotle calls *aretai ēthikai* and Aquinas *virtutes morales* does not exactly correspond with our class of moral virtues. For us there are four cardinal moral virtues: courage, temperance, wisdom, and justice. But Aristotle and Aquinas call only three of these virtues moral virtues; practical wisdom (Aristotle's *phronēsis* and Aquinas's *prudentia*) they class with the intellectual virtues, though they point out the close connections between practical wisdom and what they call moral virtues; and sometimes they even use *aretē* and *virtus* very much as we use 'virtue'.

I will come back to Aristotle and Aquinas, and shall indeed refer to them frequently in this paper. But I want to start by making some remarks, admittedly fragmentary, about the concept of a moral virtue as we understand the idea.

First of all it seems clear that virtues are, in some general way, beneficial. Human beings do not get on well without them. Nobody can get on well if he lacks courage, and does not have some measure of temperance and wisdom, while communities where justice and charity are lacking are apt to be wretched places to live, as Russia was under the Stalinist terror, or Sicily under the Mafia. But now we must ask to whom the benefit goes, whether to the one who has the virtue or rather to those who have to do with him? In the case of some of the virtues the answer seems clear. Courage, temperance and wisdom benefit both the person who has these dispositions and other people as well; and moral failings such as pride, vanity, worldliness, and avarice harm both their possessor and others, though chiefly perhaps the former. But what about the virtues of charity and justice? These are directly concerned with the welfare of others, and with what is owed to them; and since each may require sacrifice of interest on the part of the virtuous man both may seem to be deleterious to their possessor and beneficial to others. Whether in fact it is so has, of course, been a matter of controversy since Plato's time or earlier. It is a reasonable opinion that on the whole anyone is better off for being charitable and just, but this is not to say that circumstances may not arise in which he will have to sacrifice everything for charity or justice.

Nor is this the only problem about the relation between virtue and human good. For one very difficult question concerns the relation between justice and the common good. Justice, in the wide sense in which it is understood in discussions of the cardinal virtues, and in this paper, has to do with that to which someone has a right—that which he is owed in respect of non-interference and positive service—and rights may stand in the way of the pursuit of the common good. Or so at least it seems to those who reject utilitarian doctrines. This dispute cannot be settled here, but I shall treat justice as a virtue independent of charity, and standing as a possible limit on the scope of that virtue.

Let us say then, leaving unsolved problems behind us, that virtues are in general beneficial characteristics, and indeed ones that a human being needs to have, for his own sake and that of his fellows. This will not, however, take us far towards a definition of a virtue, since there are many other qualities of a man that may be similarly beneficial, as for instance bodily characteristics such as health and physical strength, and mental powers such as those of memory and concentration. What is it, we must ask, that differentiates virtues from such things?

As a first approximation to an answer we might say that while health and strength are excellences of the body, and memory and concentration of the mind, it is the will that is good in a man of virtue. But this suggestion is worth only as much as the explanation that follows it. What might we mean by saying that virtue belongs to the will?

In the first place we observe that it is primarily by his intentions that a man's moral dispositions are judged. If he does something unintentionally, this is usually irrelevant to our estimate of virtue. But of course this thesis must be qualified, because failures in performance rather than intention may show a lack of virtue. This will be so when, for instance, one man brings harm to another without realizing he is doing it, but where his ignorance is itself culpable. Sometimes in such cases there will be a previous act or omission to which we can point as the source of the ignorance.

Charity requires that we take care to find out how to render assistance where we are likely to be called on to do so, and thus, for example, it is contrary to charity to fail to find out about elementary first aid. But in an interesting class of cases in which it seems again to be performance rather than intention that counts in judging a man's virtue there is no possibility of shifting the judgement to previous intentions. For sometimes one man succeeds where another fails not because there is some specific difference in their previous conduct but rather because his heart lies in a different place; and the disposition of the heart is part of virtue.

Thus it seems right to attribute a kind of moral failing to some deeply discouraging and debilitating people who say, without lying, that they mean to be helpful; and on the other side to see virtue *par excellence* in one who is prompt and resourceful in doing good. In his novel *A Single Pebble* John Hersey describes such a man, speaking of a rescue in a swift flowing river:

> It was the head tracker's marvellous swift response that captured my admiration at first, his split second solicitousness when he heard a cry of pain, his finding in mid-air, as it were, the only way to save the injured boy. But there was more to it than that. His action, which could not have been mulled over in his mind, showed a deep, instinctive love of life, a compassion, an optimism, which made me feel very good . . .

What this suggests is that a man's virtue may be judged by his innermost desires as well as by his intentions; and this fits with our idea that a virtue such as generosity lies as much in someone's attitudes as in his actions. Pleasure in the good fortune of others is, one thinks, the sign of a generous spirit; and small reactions of pleasure and displeasure often the surest signs of a man's moral disposition.

None of this shows that it is wrong to think of virtues as belonging to the will; what it does show is that 'will' must here be understood in its widest sense, to cover what is wished for as well as what is sought.

A different set of considerations will, however, force us to give up any simple statement about the relation between virtue and will, and these considerations have to do with the virtue of wisdom. Practical wisdom, we said, was counted by Aristotle among the intellectual virtues, and while our *wisdom* is not quite the same as *phronēsis* or *prudentia*, it too might seem to belong to the intellect rather than the will. Is not wisdom a matter of knowledge, and how can knowledge be a matter of intention or desire? The answer is that it isn't, so that there is good reason for thinking of wisdom as an intellectual virtue. But on the other hand wisdom has special connections with the will, meeting it at more than one point.

In order to get this rather complex picture in focus we must pause for a little and ask what it is that we ourselves understand by wisdom: what the wise man knows and what he does. Wisdom, as I see it, has two parts. In the first place the wise man knows the means to certain good ends; and secondly he knows how much particular ends are worth. Wisdom in its first part is relatively easy to understand. It seems that there are some ends belonging to human life in general rather than to particular skills such as medicine or boatbuilding, ends having to do with such matters as friendship, marriage, the bringing-up of children, or the choice of ways of life; and it seems that knowledge of how to act well in these matters belongs to some people but not to others. We call those who have this knowledge wise, while those who do not have it are seen as lacking wisdom. So, as both Aristotle and Aquinas insisted, wisdom is to be contrasted with cleverness because cleverness is the ability to take the right steps to any end, whereas wisdom is related only to good ends, and to human life in general rather than to the ends of particular arts.

Moreover, we should add, there belongs to wisdom only that part of knowledge which is within the reach of any ordinary adult human being: knowledge that can be acquired only by someone who is clever or who has access to special training is not counted as part of wisdom, and would not be so counted even if it could serve the ends that wisdom serves. It is therefore quite wrong to suggest that wisdom cannot be a moral virtue because virtue must be within the reach of anyone who really wants it and some people are too stupid to be anything but ignorant even about the most fundamental matters of human life. Some people are wise without being at all clever or well informed: they make good decisions and they know, as we say, 'what's what'.

In short wisdom, in what we called its first part, is connected with the will in the following ways. To begin with it presupposes good ends: the man who is wise does not merely know *how* to do good things such as looking after his children well, or strengthening someone in trouble, but must also want to do them. And then wisdom, in so far as it consists of knowledge which anyone can gain in the course of an ordinary life, is available to anyone who really wants it. As Aquinas put it, it belongs 'to a power under the direction of the will'.[3]

The second part of wisdom, which has to do with values, is much harder to describe, because here we meet ideas which are curiously elusive, such as the thought that some pursuits are more worthwhile than others, and some matters trivial and some important in human life. Since it makes good sense to say that most men waste a lot of their lives in ardent pursuit

[3] Aquinas, *Summa Theologica* 1a2ae Q.56 a.3.

of what is trivial and unimportant, it is not possible to explain the important and the trivial in terms of the amount of attention given to different subjects by the average man. But I have never seen, or been able to think out, a true account of this matter, and I believe that a complete account of wisdom, and of certain other virtues and vices, must wait until this gap can be filled. What we can see is that one of the things a wise man knows and a foolish man does not is that such things as social position, and wealth, and the good opinion of the world, are too dearly bought at the cost of health or friendship or family ties. So we may say that a man who lacks wisdom 'has false values', and that vices such as vanity and worldliness and avarice are contrary to wisdom in a special way. There is always an element of false judgement about these vices, since the man who is vain for instance sees admiration as more important than it is, while the worldly man is apt to see the good life as one of wealth and power. Adapting Aristotle's distinction between the weak-willed man (the *akratēs*) who follows pleasure though he knows, in some sense, that he should not, and the licentious man (the *akolastos*) who sees the life of pleasure as the good life,[4] we may say that moral failings such as these are never purely 'akratic'. It is true that a man may criticize himself for his worldliness or vanity or love of money, but then it is his values that are the subject of his criticism.

Wisdom in this second part is, therefore, partly to be described in terms of apprehension, and even judgement, but since it has to do with a man's attachments it also characterizes his will.

The idea that virtues belong to the will, and that this helps to distinguish them from such things as bodily strength or intellectual ability, has, then, survived the consideration of the virtue of wisdom, albeit in a fairly complex and slightly attenuated form. And we shall find this idea useful again if we turn to another important distinction that must be made, namely that between virtues and other practical excellences such as arts and skills.

Aristotle has sometimes been accused, for instance by von Wright, of failing to see how different virtues are from arts or skills;[5] but in fact one finds, among the many things that Aristotle and Aquinas say about this difference, the observation that seems to go to the heart of the matter. In the matter of arts and skills, they say, voluntary error is preferable to involuntary error, while in the matter of virtues (what we call virtues) it is the reverse.[6] The last part of the thesis is actually rather hard to interpret, because it is not clear what is meant by the idea of involuntary viciousness. But we can leave this aside and still have all we need in order to distinguish

[4] Aristotle, *Nicomachean Ethics*, especially bk. VII.
[5] Von Wright, *The Varieties of Goodness*, ch. VIII.
[6] Aristotle, *Nicomachean Ethics* $1140^{b}22$–5. Aquinas, *Summa Theologica* 1a2ae Q.57 a.4.

arts or skills from virtues. If we think, for instance, of someone who deliberately makes a spelling mistake (perhaps when writing on the blackboard in order to explain this particular point), we see that this does not in any way count against his skill as a speller: 'I did it deliberately' rebuts an accusation of this kind. And what we can say without running into any difficulties is that there is no comparable rebuttal in the case of an accusation relating to lack of virtue. If a man acts unjustly or uncharitably, or in a cowardly or intemperate manner, 'I did it deliberately' cannot on any interpretation lead to exculpation. So, we may say, a virtue is not, like a skill or an art, a mere capacity: it must actually engage the will.

II

I shall now turn to another thesis about the virtues, which I might express by saying that they are *corrective*, each one standing at a point at which there is some temptation to be resisted or deficiency of motivation to be made good. As Aristotle put it, virtues are about what is difficult for men, and I want to see in what sense this is true, and then to consider a problem in Kant's moral philosophy in the light of what has been said.

Let us first think about courage and temperance. Aristotle and Aquinas contrasted these virtues with justice in the following respect. Justice was concerned with operations, and courage and temperance with passions.[7] What they meant by this seems to have been, primarily, that the man of courage does not fear immoderately nor the man of temperance have immoderate desires for pleasure, and that there was no corresponding moderation of a passion implied in the idea of justice. This particular account of courage and temperance might be disputed on the ground that a man's courage is measured by his action and not by anything as uncontrollable as fear; and similarly that the temperate man who must on occasion refuse pleasures need not *desire* them any less than the intemperate man. Be that as it may (and something will be said about it later), it is obviously true that courage and temperance have to do with particular springs of action as justice does not. Almost any desire can lead a man to act unjustly, not even excluding the desire to help a friend or to save a life, whereas a cowardly act must be motivated by fear or a desire for safety, and an act of intemperance by a desire for pleasure, perhaps even for a particular range of pleasures such as those of eating or drinking or sex.

[7] Aristotle, *Nicomachean Ethics* 1106^{b}15 and 1129^{a}4, has this implication; but Aquinas is more explicit in *Summa Theologica* 1a2ae Q.60 a.2.

And now, going back to the idea of virtues as correctives, one may say that it is only because fear and the desire for pleasure often operate as temptations that courage and temperance exist as virtues at all. As things are, we often want to run away not only where that is the right thing to do but also where we should stand firm; and we want pleasure not only where we should seek pleasure but also where we should not. If human nature had been different there would have been no need of a corrective disposition in either place, as fear and pleasure would have been good guides to conduct throughout life. So Aquinas says, about the passions

> They may incite us to something against reason, and so we need a curb, which we name *temperance*. Or they may make us shirk a course of action dictated by reason, through fear of dangers or hardships. Then a person needs to be steadfast and not run away from what is right; and for this *courage* is named.[8]

As with courage and temperance so with many other virtues: there is, for instance, a virtue of industriousness only because idleness is a temptation; and of humility only because men tend to think too well of themselves. Hope is a virtue because despair too is a temptation; it might have been that no one cried that all was lost except where he could really see it to be so, and in this case there would have been no virtue of hope.

With virtues such as justice and charity it is a little different, because they correspond not to any particular desire or tendency that has to be kept in check but rather to a deficiency of motivation; and it is this that they must make good. If people were as much attached to the good of others as they are to their own good there would no more be a general virtue of benevolence than there is a general virtue of self-love. And if people cared about the rights of others as they care about their own rights, no virtue of justice would be needed to look after the matter, and rules about such things as contracts and promises would only need to be made public, like the rules of a game that everyone was eager to play.

On this view of the virtues and vices everything is seen to depend on what human nature is like, and the traditional catalogue of the two kinds of dispositions is not hard to understand. Nevertheless it may be defective, and anyone who accepts the thesis that I am putting forward will feel free to ask himself where the temptations and deficiencies that need correcting are really to be found. It is possible, for example, that the theory of human nature lying behind the traditional list of the virtues and vices puts too much emphasis on hedonistic and sensual impulses, and does not sufficiently take account of less straightforward inclinations such as the desire

[8] Aquinas, *Summa Theologica* 1a2ae Q.61 a.3.

to be put upon and dissatisfied, or the unwillingness to accept good things as they come along.

It should now be clear why I said that virtues should be seen as correctives; and part of what is meant by saying that virtue is about things that are difficult for men should also have appeared. The further application of this idea is, however, controversial, and the following difficulty presents itself: that we both are and are not inclined to think that the harder a man finds it to act virtuously the more virtue he shows if he does act well. For on the one hand great virtue is needed where it is particularly hard to act virtuously; yet on the other it could be argued that difficulty in acting virtuously shows that the agent is imperfect in virtue: according to Aristotle to take pleasure in virtuous action is the mark of true virtue, with the self-mastery of the one who finds virtue difficult only a second best. How then is this conflict to be decided? Who shows most courage, the one who wants to run away but does not, or the one who does not even want to run away? Who shows most charity, the one who finds it easy to make the good of others his object, or the one who finds it hard?

What is certain is that the thought that virtues are corrective does not constrain us to relate virtue to difficulty in each individual man. Since men in general find it hard to face great dangers or evils, and even small ones, we may count as courageous those few who without blindness or indifference are nevertheless fearless even in terrible circumstances. And when someone has a natural charity or generosity it is at least part of the virtue that he has; if natural virtue cannot be the whole of virtue this is because a kindly or fearless disposition could be disastrous without justice and wisdom, and because these virtues have to be learned, not because natural virtue is too easily acquired. I have argued that the virtues can be seen as correctives in relation to human nature in general but not that each virtue must present a difficulty to each and every man.

Nevertheless many people feel strongly inclined to say that it is for moral effort that moral praise is to be bestowed, and that in proportion as someone finds it easy to be virtuous so much the less is he to be morally admired for his good actions. The dilemma can be resolved only when we stop talking about difficulties standing in the way of virtuous action as if they were of only one kind. The fact is that some kinds of difficulties do indeed provide an occasion for much virtue, but that others rather show that virtue is incomplete.

To illustrate this point I shall first consider an example of honest action. We may suppose for instance that a person has an opportunity to steal, in circumstances where stealing is not morally permissible, but refrains. And now let us ask our old question. For one it is hard to refrain from stealing and for another it is not: which shows the greater virtue in acting as he should? It is not difficult to see in this case that it makes all the difference whether the difficulty comes from circumstances, as that someone is poor, or that his theft is unlikely to be detected, or whether it comes from something that belongs to his own character. The fact that a man is *tempted* to steal is something about him that shows a certain lack of honesty: of one thoroughly honest we say that it 'never entered his head', meaning that it was never a real possibility for him. But the fact that he is poor is something that makes the occasion more *tempting*, and difficulties of this kind make honest action all the more virtuous.

A similar distinction can be made between different obstacles standing in the way of charitable action. Some circumstances, as that great sacrifice is needed, or that the one to be helped is a rival, give an occasion on which charity is severely tested. Yet in given circumstances of this kind it is the man who acts easily rather than the one who finds it hard who shows the most charity. Charity is a virtue of attachment, and that sympathy for others which makes it easier to help them is part of the virtue itself.

These are fairly simple cases, but I am not supposing that it is always easy to say where the relevant distinction is to be drawn. What, for instance, should we say about the emotion of fear as an obstacle to action? Is someone more courageous if he fears much and nevertheless acts, or if he is relatively fearless? Several things must be said about this. In the first place it seems that the emotion of fear is not a necessary condition for the display of courage; in face of a great evil such as death or injury one may show courage even if one does not tremble. On the other hand even irrational fears may give an occasion for courage: if someone suffers from claustrophobia or a dread of heights he may require courage to do that which would not be a courageous action for others. But not all fears belong from this point of view to the circumstances rather than to character. For while we do not think of claustrophobia or a dread of heights as features of character, a general timorousness may be. Thus, although pathological fears are not the result of one's choices and values, some fears may be. The fears that count against courage are those that we think should be overcome, and among them, in a special class, those that reflect the fact that safety is valued too much.

In spite of problems such as these, which have certainly not all been solved, both the distinction between different kinds of obstacles to virtuous action and the general idea that virtues are correctives will be useful in resolving a difficulty in Kant's moral philosophy closely related to the issues discussed in the preceding paragraphs. In a passage in the first section of the *Groundwork of the Metaphysics of Morals* Kant notoriously tied himself into a knot in trying to give an account of those actions which have as he put it 'positive moral worth'. Arguing that only actions done out of a sense of duty have this worth, he contrasts a philanthropist who 'takes pleasure in spreading happiness around him' with one who acts out of respect for duty, saying that the actions of the latter but not the former have moral worth. Much scorn has been poured on Kant for this curious doctrine, and indeed it does seem that something has gone wrong, but perhaps we are not in a position to scoff unless we can give our own account of the idea on which Kant is working. After all it does seem that he is right in saying that some actions are in accordance with duty, and even required by duty, without being the subjects of moral praise, like those of the honest trader who deals honestly in a situation in which it is in his interest to do so.

It was this kind of example that drove Kant to his strange conclusion. He added another example, however, in discussing acts of self-preservation; these he said, while they normally have no positive moral worth, may have it when a man preserves his life not from inclination but without inclination and from a sense of duty. Is he not right in saying that acts of self-preservation normally have no moral significance but that they may have it, and how do we ourselves explain this fact?

To anyone who approaches this topic from a consideration of the virtues the solution readily suggests itself. Some actions are in accordance with virtue without requiring virtue for their performance, whereas others are both in accordance with virtue and such as to show possession of a virtue. So Kant's trader was dealing honestly in a situation in which the virtue of honesty is not required for honest dealing, and it is for this reason that his action did not have 'positive moral worth'. Similarly, the care that one ordinarily takes for one's life, as for instance on some ordinary morning in eating one's breakfast and keeping out of the way of a car on the road, is something for which no virtue is required. As we said earlier, there is no general virtue of self-love as there is a virtue of benevolence or charity, because men are generally attached sufficiently to their own good. Nevertheless in special circumstances virtues such as temperance, courage, fortitude, and hope may be needed if someone is to preserve his life. Are these circumstances in which the preservation of one's own life is a duty? Sometimes it is so, for sometimes it is what is owed to others that should keep a man from destroying himself, and then he may act out of a sense of duty. But not all cases in which acts of self-preservation show virtue are like this. For a man may display each of the virtues just listed even where he does not do any harm to others if he kills himself or fails to preserve his life. And it is this that explains why there may be a moral aspect to suicide which does not depend on possible injury to other people. It is not that suicide is 'always wrong', whatever that would mean, but that suicide is *sometimes* contrary to virtues such as courage and hope.

Let us now return to Kant's philanthropists, with the thought that it is action that is in accordance with virtue and also displays a virtue that has moral worth. We see at once that Kant's difficulties are avoided, and the happy philanthropist reinstated in the position which belongs to him. For charity is, as we said, a virtue of attachment as well as action, and the sympathy that makes it easier to act with charity is part of the virtue. The man who acts charitably out of a sense of duty is not to be undervalued, but it is the other who most shows virtue and therefore to the other that most moral worth is attributed. Only a detail of Kant's presentation of the case of the dutiful philanthropist tells on the other side. For what he actually said was that this man felt no sympathy and took no pleasure in the good of others because 'his mind was clouded by some sorrow of his own', and this is the kind of circumstance that increases the virtue that is needed if a man is to act well.

III

It was suggested above that an action with 'positive moral worth', or as we might say a positively good action, was to be seen as one which was in accordance with virtue, by which I mean contrary to no virtue, and moreover one for which a virtue was required. Nothing has so far been said about another case, excluded by the formula, in which it might seem that an act displaying one virtue was nevertheless contrary to another. In giving this last description I am thinking not of two virtues with competing claims, as if what were required by justice could nevertheless be demanded by charity, or something of that kind, but rather of the possibility that a virtue such as courage or temperance or industry which overcomes a special temptation might be displayed in an act of folly or villainy. Is this something that we must allow for, or is it only good or innocent actions which can be acts of these virtues? Aquinas, in his definition of virtue, said that virtues can produce only good actions, and that they are dispositions 'of which no one can make bad use',[9] except when they are treated as objects, as in being the subject of hatred or pride. The common opinion nowadays is, however, quite different. With the notable exception of Peter Geach,

[9] Aquinas op. cit. 1a2ae Q.56 a.5.

hardly anyone sees any difficulty in the thought that virtues may sometimes be displayed in bad actions. Von Wright, for instance, speaks of the courage of the villain as if this were a quite unproblematic idea, and most people take it for granted that the virtues of courage and temperance may aid a bad man in his evil work. It is also supposed that charity may lead a man to act badly, as when someone does what he has no right to do, but does it for the sake of a friend.

There are, however, reasons for thinking that the matter is not so simple as this. If a man who is willing to do an act of injustice to help a friend, or for the common good, is supposed to act out of charity, and he so acts where a just man will not, it should be said that the unjust man has more charity than the just man. But do we not think that someone not ready to act unjustly may yet be perfect in charity, the virtue having done its whole work in prompting him to do the acts that are permissible? And is there not more difficulty than might appear in the idea of an act of injustice which is nevertheless an act of courage? Suppose for instance that a sordid murder were in question, say a murder done for gain or to get an inconvenient person out of the way, but that this murder had to be done in alarming circumstances or in the face of real danger; should we be happy to say that such an action was an act of courage or a courageous act? Did the murderer, who certainly acted boldly, or with intrepidity, if he did the murder, also act courageously? Some people insist that they are ready to say this, but I have noticed that they like to move over to a murder for the sake of conscience, or to some other act done in the course of a villainous enterprise but whose immediate end is innocent or positively good. On their hypothesis, which is that bad acts can easily be seen as courageous acts or acts of courage, my original example should be just as good.

What are we to say about this difficult matter? There is no doubt that the murderer who murdered for gain was *not a coward*: he did not have a second moral defect which another villain might have had. There is no difficulty about this because it is clear that one defect may neutralize another. As Aquinas remarked, it is better for a blind horse if it is slow.[10] It does not follow, however, that an act of villainy can be courageous; we are inclined to say that it 'took courage', and yet it seems wrong to think of courage as equally connected with good actions and bad.

One way out of this difficulty might be to say that the man who is ready to pursue bad ends does indeed have courage, and shows courage in his action, but that in him courage is not a virtue. Later I shall consider some cases in which this might be the right thing to say, but in this instance it

[10] Ibid. 1a2ae Q.58 a.4.

does not seem to be. For unless the murderer consistently pursues bad ends, his courage will often result in good; it may enable him to do many innocent or positively good things for himself or for his family and friends. On the strength of an individual bad action we can hardly say that in him courage is not a virtue. Nevertheless there is something to be said even about the individual action to distinguish it from one that would readily be called an act of courage or a courageous act. Perhaps the following analogy may help us to see what it is. We might think of words such as 'courage' as naming characteristics of human beings in respect of a certain power, as words such as 'poison' and 'solvent' and 'corrosive' so name the properties of physical things. The power to which virtue-words are so related is the power of producing good action, and good desires. But just as poisons, solvents, and corrosives do not always operate characteristically, so it could be with virtues. If *P* (say arsenic) is a poison it does not follow that *P* acts as a poison wherever it is found. It is quite natural to say on occasion '*P* does not act as a poison here' though *P* is a poison and it is *P* that is acting here. Similarly courage is not operating as a virtue when the murderer turns his courage, which is a virtue, to bad ends. Not surprisingly the resistance that some of us registered was not to the expression 'the courage of the murderer' or to the assertion that what he did 'took courage' but rather to the description of that action as an act of courage or a courageous act. It is not that the action *could* not be so described, but that the fact that courage does not here have its characteristic operation is a reason for finding the description strange.

In this example we were considering an action in which courage was not operating as a virtue, without suggesting that in that agent it generally failed to do so. But the latter is also a possibility. If someone is both wicked and foolhardy this may be the case with courage, and it is even easier to find examples of a general connection with evil rather than good in the case of some other virtues. Suppose, for instance, that we think of someone who is over-industrious, or too ready to refuse pleasure, and this is characteristic of him rather than something we find on one particular occasion. In this case the virtue of industry, or the virtue of temperance, has a systematic connection with defective action rather than good action; and it might be said in either case that the virtue did not operate as a virtue in this man. Just as we might say in a certain setting '*P* is not a poison here' though *P* is a poison and *P* is here, so we might say that industriousness, or temperance, is not a virtue in some. Similarly in a man habitually given to wishful thinking, who clings to false hopes, hope does not operate as a virtue and we may say that it is not a virtue in him.

The thought developed in the last paragraph, to the effect that not every man who has a virtue has something that is a virtue in him, may help to explain a certain discomfort that one may feel when discussing the virtues. It is not easy to put one's finger on what is wrong, but it has something to do with a disparity between the moral ideals that may seem to be implied in our talk about the virtues, and the moral judgements that we actually make. Someone reading the foregoing pages might, for instance, think that the author of this paper always admired most those people who had all the virtues, being wise and temperate as well as courageous, charitable, and just. And indeed it is sometimes so. There are some people who do possess all these virtues and who are loved and admired by all the world, as Pope John XXIII was loved and admired. Yet the fact is that many of us look up to some people whose chaotic lives contain rather little of wisdom or temperance, rather than to some others who possess these virtues. And while it may be that this is just romantic nonsense I suspect that it is not. For while wisdom always operates as a virtue, its close relation prudence does not, and it is prudence rather than wisdom that inspires many a careful life. Prudence is not a virtue in everyone, any more than industriousness is, for in some it is rather an over-anxious concern for safety and propriety, and a determination to keep away from people or situations which are apt to bring trouble with them; and by such defensiveness much good is lost. It is the same with temperance. Intemperance can be an appalling thing, as it was with Henry VIII of whom Wolsey remarked that 'rather than he will either miss or want any part of his will or appetite, he will put the loss of one half of his realm in danger'. Nevertheless in some people temperance is not a virtue, but is rather connected with timidity or with a grudging attitude to the acceptance of good things. Of course what is best is to live boldly yet without imprudence or intemperance, but the fact is that rather few can manage that.[11]

[11] I am indebted to friends in many universities for their help in forming my views on this subject; and particularly to John Giuliano of UCLA, whose unpublished work on the unity of the virtues I have consulted with profit, and to Rosalind Hursthouse, who commented on a draft of the middle period.

9

THE MISFORTUNES OF VIRTUE

J. B. SCHNEEWIND

In recent years a number of moral philosophers have been critical of what they take to be the striking neglect by their predecessors of the topic of virtue and the virtues. It is not always clear exactly what period is meant to be covered in this indictment, but a statement by Philippa Foot gives us a clue: 'For many years the subject of the virtues and vices was strangely neglected by moralists within the school of analytic philosophy. The tacitly accepted opinion was that a study of the topic would form no part of the fundamental work of ethics; and since this opinion was apparently shared by philosophers such as Hume, Kant, Mill, G. E. Moore, W. D. Ross, and H. A. Prichard, from whom contemporary moral philosophy has mostly been derived, perhaps the neglect was not so surprising after all.'[1] Another of the friends of virtue, G. H. von Wright, shares Foot's view. 'Virtue is a neglected topic in modern ethics,' he says, and implies that Kant is one of the culprits.[2] The suggestion is that virtue has been neglected ever since the period of moral philosophy that culminated in the theories of Hume and Kant. Such widespread and protracted indifference would indeed have to count as a misfortune for virtue; if it actually occurred a historian of ethics might well be expected to try to explain why. But I doubt very much that it did occur. In this article I shall argue that at least during the seventeenth and eighteenth centuries, the formative period for modern moral philosophy, virtue did not suffer from neglect. Its misfortune was something rather different.

[1] Philippa Foot, 'Virtues and Vices', Chapter 8 in this volume. This passage is quoted from the original version.

[2] G. H. von Wright, *The Varieties of Goodness* (London, 1963), 136. Von Wright continues: 'Kant's famous *dictum* that formal logic had made no appreciable progress since Aristotle, could be paraphrased and applied—with at least equally good justification—to the ethics of virtue.'

I

It is not easy to collect from present exponents of virtue-centred views of morality an agreement about what distinguishes their position from others. Some idea of the difference is, however, necessary if we are to discuss virtue's misfortunes. At the risk of oversimplification, I will lay out a set of differences between virtue-centred views, on the one hand, and what I shall call 'act-centred' or 'rule-centred' views on the other.[3]

It seems to be commonly agreed that a virtue-centred view sees character at the core of morality and supposes that the central moral question is not 'What ought I to do?' but 'What sort of person am I to be?' The first point about a virtue-centred view is that the primary or central moral judgements are judgements about the character of agents. The virtuous person, as one commentator put it, is someone 'for whom proper conduct emanates characteristically from a fixed disposition'.[4] There is not much agreement on exactly what sort of disposition a virtue is, but this much at least we might take as common ground: that virtuous dispositions lead virtuous agents to be sensitive to the goods and ills to which people are exposed in particular situations and to respond by bringing about good and preventing harm.

Second, on the epistemological side, the virtue theorist holds that the perceptions of the virtuous person are the original and central source of knowledge of how much good to pursue, for whom, in what circumstances, and how vigorously. We may be able to formulate rules which crudely map the decisions of the virtuous person, but no set of rules will exactly capture them or anticipate every decision in a new situation. Nor does the virtuous person have any algorithm.[5] We may educate children into virtue by teaching them some simple rules, but mature moral agents do not need them.

Third, virtue is natural to humans, not in the sense that it need not be learned or that it is easy to acquire, but in the sense that virtuous agents individually, as well as the community they compose, benefit from virtue. This fact indicates our social nature. Living alone, and living without virtue, are both harmful to us.

[3] I take rules (and laws) to require acts, and therefore, for the purposes of this article, do not consider the differences between the names I assign to be significant.

[4] L. A. Kosman, 'Being Properly Affected: Virtues and Feelings in Aristotle's Ethics', in Amélie O. Rorty (ed.), *Essays on Aristotle's Ethics* (Berkeley and Los Angeles, 1980), 103.

[5] 'If one were to ask Aristotle how to decide how to act on particular occasions, his initial answer would be that one must do so by bringing to bear the intellectual excellence of (practical) wisdom. If we then ask in what wisdom consists, we shall get a long answer. . . . There is no simple decision procedure for the wise man to use' (J. O. Urmson, 'Aristotle's Doctrine of the Mean', in Rorty (ed.), *Essays*, 162).

By contrast to virtue-centred views of morality, act-centred views see the point of morality as directing what we do. We may acquire habits of acting in the right ways, and these habits may be called virtues. But their value lies in their ensuring correct action, and if we are praised as virtuous, the praise derives from the value placed on what we do.[6]

The act-centred theorist then explains how we can know what to do by appealing to rules, laws, or principles which spell out or give us a method for finding out what is right, or permitted, or obligatory. The rules or principles can be known and applied by someone who has no desire or concern for acting on them. Such a person could mimic the actions of someone who had, behaving correctly without valuing such behaviour for itself. There is thus no counterpart in an act-centred theory for the epistemological privilege of the virtuous agent in a virtue-centred view.

Finally, since the principles of morality provide the structure of morally decent common life, virtuous people will tend to contribute to the common good. How well each individual will fare in so doing is to some extent an open question, though it seems obvious that everyone has a better chance of living a good life in a society dominated by virtuous people than in one where there are few.

An act-centred morality will naturally welcome the virtues, construed in its own way, as subordinate to the explicit rules or laws that require specific actions. So if a virtue-centred ethic is to be significantly different from an act-centred ethic, it needs to show that the virtues which are most important to morality have a life of their own, which is independent of rules or laws.

II

It is sometimes suggested that the first misfortune of virtue was the collapse of Aristotelian teleological thinking as a result of the rise of the new science in the sixteenth and seventeenth centuries. But Christian teleology was available to replace Aristotle's, and in any case this diagnosis overlooks a much earlier misfortune: Christianity itself. Thomas Reid reminds us of the opposition between virtue ethics and Christian ethics. 'Morals have been methodized in different ways,' he remarks. 'The Ancients commonly arranged them under the four cardinal virtues of prudence, temperance, fortitude, and justice. Christian writers, I think more properly, under

[6] Or on the results of what we do.

the three heads of the duty we owe to God, to ourselves, and to our neighbor.'[7] Christianity, as Reid indicates, teaches a morality of duty, not of virtue, and it understands duty in terms of acts complying with law. A contemporary authority agrees with this point. 'Any consideration of Christian morality', he remarks, 'must acknowledge that the idea and the connotations of law are all-pervading and appear all but indispensable to the subject.'[8] From the earliest days of the practice of confession in the sixth century through the great flowering of casuistry in the sixteenth and seventeenth centuries, Catholic moralists were preoccupied with specific acts which might or might not be sins, and with the appropriate penalties for them if they were.[9] If ever there was an ethics of acts and quandaries,[10] it was here.

It is no surprise to find, therefore, that there is a commonly accepted understanding of virtue and the virtues in the seventeenth century which makes them secondary to laws or rules. Though many sources might be cited, I will let John Locke articulate what had long been a commonplace: 'By whatever standard soever we frame in our minds the ideas of virtues or vices . . . their rectitude, or obliquity, consists in the agreement with those patterns prescribed by some law.'[11] In the previous century the Puritan divine William Perkins had the same thing to say: 'Universall justice, is the practise of all vertue: of that, whereby a man observes all the commandements of the Law.'[12] It is arguable that the idea goes back as far as Saint Thomas's attempt to bring classical natural-law doctrine and Aristotelian virtue theory into some kind of union. However that may be, the dominance of an act-centred or legalistic account of morality is to be

[7] Thomas Reid, *Essays on the Active Powers of Man* (Edinburgh: University of Edinburgh Press, 1788), bk. 5, ch. 2. The contrast between Christian and heathen did not end with Reid. 'Many have heard so much of the *danger* of trusting to good works . . . that they . . . consider that the less they think about them the better. The word virtue sounds to them heathenish' (*Miscellaneous Remains from the Commonplace Book of Richard Whately, D.D.*, ed. E. J. Whately (London, 1865), 239). 'It is true that the classic origins of the doctrine of virtue later made Christian critics suspicious of it. They warily regarded it as too philosophical and not Scriptural enough. Thus, they preferred to talk about commandments and duties rather than about virtues' (Josef Pieper, *The Four Cardinal Virtues* (Notre Dame, Ind., 1966), p. x, referring to what he evidently regards as a still-living attitude).

[8] John Mahoney, *The Making of Moral Theology: A Study of the Roman Catholic Tradition* (Oxford, 1987), 224.

[9] See ibid. 30–1 and ch. 1 generally.

[10] See Edmund L. Pincoffs, *Quandaries and Virtues* (Lawrence, Kan., 1986), esp. ch. 2.

[11] John Locke, *Essay concerning Human Understanding*, ed. Peter H. Nidditch (Oxford, 1979), p. 358, 2.28.14.

[12] William Perkins, *The Whole Treatise of Cases of Conscience*, in *William Perkins*, ed. Thomas F. Merrill (Nieuwkoop, 1966), ch. 6, p. 231. Merrill does not give the date of this treatise; Perkins died in 1602.

found in numerous Protestant writings, clerical as well as lay, throughout the period that concerns us.[13] It even affected the way Aristotle was understood, as we can see from a comment in the notes of an early seventeenth-century Cambridge tutor taking his students through the *Nicomachean Ethics*. 'The other day we proposed a definition of virtue,' he says. 'It is a constant disposition of the soul to live according to law.'[14] The assumption almost universally made is that if the virtues are important it is precisely because they are the habits, however formed, of obeying the moral laws—or the moral law, if, as with Cumberland and Samuel Johnson, the writer reduces them all to one.[15] A virtuous person is one whose standing dispositions lead her to do the acts required by the laws of morality.

The natural-law thinkers whose work dominated seventeenth-century moral thinking and exercised a powerful influence well into the eighteenth were not, therefore, introducing a new emphasis into the subject by seeing law as the focal point of the moral life. But their apparent neglect of the topic of virtue makes them look like paradigm cases of act-centred or law-centred theories in which character is assigned no importance. This impression is strengthened when we examine the criticisms of Aristotle on virtue offered by the founder of so-called modern natural law, Hugo Grotius.

In the Prolegomena to his *Law of War and Peace* of 1625, Grotius devotes three paragraphs to a criticism of Aristotle's doctrine that virtue consists in a mean in passion and action. The theory of the mean is a crucial point of difference between virtue-centred and act-centred views of morality, because it is one way of articulating the virtue theorist's belief that no antecedently statable set of rules or laws can substitute for virtuous character in leading people to act properly. Grotius plainly wants nothing to do with it.

[13] Alasdair MacIntyre tells us that Hume's 'treatment of the virtues' contains 'a quite new conception of the relationship of virtues to rules. . . . Virtues are indeed now conceived of . . . as being just those dispositions necessary to produce obedience to the rules of morality' (*After Virtue* (London, 1985), 216). If that were Hume's view—and I argue below that it is not—it would hardly be new.

[14] William S. Costello, SJ, *The Scholastic Curriculum at Early Seventeenth-Century Cambridge* (Cambridge, 1958), 65–6.

[15] Samuel Johnson is a telling case of the general point I wish to make. Although in numerous essays he speaks of the virtues as means between extremes, he has no clear view about them. In the review of Soame Jenyns, *A Free Inquiry into the Nature and Origin of Evil* (1757), he espouses a version of what we call 'rule utilitarianism', and he seems to think of its rules as the laws of nature laid down by God and revealed through conscience. These are at the core of morality for him. He does not mention virtue or the virtues in the 1748 allegory 'The Vision of Theodore, the Hermit of Teneriffe', which he once said he thought was his finest work. That tale shows Reason guiding us with the aid of Conscience, which is the emissary of religion; habits are almost always bad; and it is clear that man's natural dispositions, uncorrected, would do no one any good.

His criticisms are brief. He points out the implausibility of the doctrine of the mean with respect to virtues such as truthfulness (said to be a mean between boastfulness and dissimulation), but his main fire is reserved for justice.[16] Aristotle himself, says Grotius, could not make the doctrine work when it came to this virtue. For he could not point to a mean in any appropriate passion, or any action coming from the passions, which could plausibly be said to constitute justice. So he resorted to making claims about the things justice is concerned with—possessions, honours, security—because only about these would it be reasonable to say that there could be a too much or a too little. And even here, Grotius continues, the doctrine of the mean fails. A single example shows this. It may be a fault not to take what is my own property—for example, if I need it in order to support my child—but it is surely not doing an injustice to another to claim less than is mine. Justice consists wholly in 'abstaining from that which is another's'. And Grotius adds that 'it does not matter whether injustice arises from avarice, from lust, from anger, or from ill-advised compassion'. What matters is only whether one is taking what another has a right to.[17] Grotius concedes that some virtues do keep passions under control, but this is not due to the nature of virtue. It is due, rather, to the fact that 'right reason, which virtue everywhere follows' sometimes prescribes moderation. At other times, as in worshipping God, or in hoping for eternal bliss, it does not. These cannot be excessive, any more than hatred of sin can be too great.[18]

The immediate target of the attack, the doctrine of the mean, need be no part of a virtue-centred theory, but Grotius is rejecting more than that doctrine. He is saying that a central feature of such theories is wrong. The motive of the just agent does not matter. To be just is simply to have the habit of following right reason with respect to the rights of others. It does not matter why the agent has and sustains the habit. And rights are not, for Grotius, the kind of good which virtuous dispositions regard. Rights are or spring from—Grotius is not entirely clear—a special moral attribute attaching to human nature, which even God must respect.[19] They make acts

[16] Hugo Grotius, *On the Law of War and Peace*, trans. Francis W. Kelsey (Oxford, 1925), Prolegomena, sect. 43.

[17] Ibid., sect. 44.

[18] Ibid., sect. 45. Saint Thomas Aquinas, *Summa theologiae* 2a–2ae.27.6, makes the point that the theological virtues faith, hope, and charity cannot be excessive. In *On Charity*, trans. Lottie H. Kendzierski (Milwaukee, 1984), Aquinas says that the theological virtues are not means between extremes and that only the moral virtues are (art. 2, reply to objections 10 and 13, p. 31).

[19] Grotius is here opposing the voluntarist view of the laws of nature. On Grotius on rights, see Richard Tuck, *Natural Rights Theories* (Cambridge, 1979).

required or forbidden regardless of the natural good brought about by respecting them.

Grotius rejects yet another important aspect of an ethics of virtue, its attribution of a privileged status to the insight of the virtuous agent. He does not think the laws of nature determine what we are to do down to the last detail. Where the law is indeterminate, however, what operates is not insight but discretion. In such cases we choose freely among permissible acts. Grotius brings this out in direct confrontation with Aristotelianism. Because so many complexities enter into morals, he says, and circumstances always alter cases, it comes about 'that between what should be done and what it is wrong to do there is a mean, that which is permissible; and this is now closer to the former, now to the latter. . . . This is what Aristotle means when he says: "Oftentimes it is hard to decide what choice one should make."'[20] The virtuous are simply those who obey the law where it is specific, and stay within the bounds of the permissible where it leaves room for choice. In the Grotian morality of rule and act there is no room for any special cognitive ability arising from virtue.

Grotius was accepted as a major authority on morality and law. His followers saw him as the founder of a new school of thought, and even Dugald Stewart, who did not admire natural-law theory, allowed that Grotius 'gave a new direction to the studies of the learned'.[21] His most important successor was Samuel Pufendorf, by far the most widely disseminated of the natural-law writers of the seventeenth century, and the most widely and persistently taught.[22] Like Grotius he claimed that there is a methodical, non-intuitive, way of deriving knowledge of the rules of morality.[23] He went even further than his master in actually spelling out these rules in considerable detail. To read his treatise, or the treatises of his imitators and commentators, is to see how the moral life looks as if it is viewed as overwhelmingly a matter of learning the rules and acting as they direct.

There were of course critics, among them those who defended Aristotle

[20] Grotius, 2.23.1.

[21] Dugald Stewart, *Dissertation Exhibiting the Progress of Metaphysical, Ethical and Political Philosophy* (1815), in *Works*, ed. Sir William Hamilton (Edinburgh, 1854), i. 170.

[22] Horst Denzer, *Moralphilosophie und Naturrecht bei Samuel Pufendorf* (Munich, 1972), lists nearly forty editions of Pufendorf's major work, the *de Jure Naturae et Gentium* (1672), in Latin, French, English, and German, and nearly a hundred of the shorter work, *de Officio Hominis et Civis* (1673), in every major European language. His figures are probably quite low. See also Sieglinde C. Othmer, *Berlin und die Verbreitung des Naturrechts in Europa* (Berlin, 1970), 136–42, for tabular information about translations and editions.

[23] See J. B. Schneewind, 'Pufendorf's Place in the History of Ethics', *Synthèse*, 73 (1987), 122–55, for fuller discussion.

and his theory of virtue against the Grotian attacks.[24] But the defences, however justified, seemed to have had little effect. We need not think that Grotius and Pufendorf had refuted Aristotle; we must allow that for the cultivated Europe of their age and much of the eighteenth century they displaced his understanding of morality with another one. The culture seems to have been hungry for a morality giving the kind of explicit guidance that rules and laws provide. The triumph of the Grotian version of natural-law theory thus seems to constitute exactly the kind of misfortune that the friends of virtue suppose must have happened at some point during this period.

III

The triumph of natural law was not, however, an unmitigated misfortune for virtue. The natural lawyers provided in their own way for an aspect of the moral life where action is not governed by rules and where the agent's character and motives are central. Nor was this an unimportant aspect of morality. On the contrary, it was here that the lawyers, who with the exception of Hobbes were serious Christians, made room for the operations of that love which their religion made so important to them. Constructing natural-law theory, they could not appeal to revelation: all the more significant, then, their insistence that there is a requirement of love which cannot be understood in the ways in which other kinds of requirement are. It was by means of their distinction between perfect and imperfect rights and duties that they made room for love in their general theory. And because they understood imperfect duties as they did, the discussions of them covered much of the ground which in the vocabulary they rejected was discussed in terms of virtue.

This now familiar distinction was first made by Grotius, in terms of rights. Some rights, such as those involved in property ownership or conferred by contract, entitle their possessors to use force to obtain that to which they have the right if it is not otherwise forthcoming. Other rights, such as the right of a beggar to your alms, do not carry this entitlement: they are thus 'imperfect', that is, not full and complete.[25] Pufendorf develops the distinction in terms of duties. He sees perfect

[24] For example, Samuel Rachel, *Dissertations on the Law of Nature and of Nations* (1676), trans. John Pawley Bate (Oxford, 1916), devotes some seventeen pages in 'Of Moral Virtue' (sects. 17–44) to defending Aristotle and showing that Grotius's criticisms can all be answered.

[25] Grotius, 1.1.4–8, pp. 35–7.

duties as those whose performance could be compelled, either by force (prior to the existence of political society) or through court action. He adds that what is owed under a perfect duty is always quite specific: precisely so much money or such and such services. Imperfect duties, for both Grotius and Pufendorf, are not precisely specifiable. They fall under what Grotius calls the law of love, which tells us to benefit others but does not specify how much, or to whom, one ought to give.[26] Giving must be the expression of one's direct concern for the good of another. To give in order to be rewarded for so doing is to take away an essential element of imperfect duties.

Pufendorf adds an important point to Grotius's sketch. Perfect duties are those which must be carried out if society is to exist at all. Imperfect duties serve to improve the quality of life, but society could continue to exist even if they were ignored. But if performance of the former is more urgent, it does not entitle the agent to merit, whereas genuine execution of imperfect duty is meritorious.[27] Functionally speaking, perfect and imperfect duties thus have complementary roles in facilitating social life. As Pufendorf puts it, 'The law of humanity or charity, and the agreements of men, mutually supplement each other by way of their duties and guarantees, in that what is not or cannot be secured by charity is secured by agreements, while in cases where agreements are not possible, charity offers its services.'[28]

It is significant that Pufendorf uses the term 'charity' here. He is following Grotius in transforming the theological virtue of charity into a secular virtue, detaching it from its Thomistic sense of friendship with God, and seeing its importance not in its role in personal salvation,[29] but in its ability to improve social life. It is equally important that he does not say that love should infuse the other areas of the moral life. Perfect duties, or duties of justice, need not be carried out in a loving spirit. They are fully executed when a perfect right is respected, and the man who regularly carries out all his perfect duties is a just man even if he dislikes acting justly. What matters is the performance, not the spirit behind it.[30]

[26] Grotius, 3.13.4, p. 759; 2.25.3, sects. 2–3, pp. 579–80; 1.2.8, sect. 10, p. 75; 2.12.9, sect. 2, p. 347.

[27] Samuel Pufendorf, *The Law of Nature and of Nations*, trans. C. H. Oldfather and W. A. Oldfather (Oxford, 1934), 1.1.19–20, pp. 18–20; 1.7.7–9, pp. 118–21.

[28] Ibid. 3.4.1, p. 380.

[29] Or not only so: he thinks the merit one acquires from performing imperfect duties will count with God.

[30] Moreover it is not the case, as it is in Luther, that only those given divine grace are expected to act from love, while the rest are subjected to compulsion. In the state of nature as well as in political society everyone is expected to perform some imperfect duties, and everyone is under laws which threaten the use of force to exact compliance.

IV

The idea of imperfect duties allowed for the accommodation within natural-law theory of many of the features of the moral life stressed by virtue-centred outlooks. So although the friends of virtue will of course protest that much is altered or omitted, I think that they cannot fairly say that natural-law theory involved the complete neglect of virtue. The distinction between perfect and imperfect duty has another importance for virtue as well. It provides the context for understanding the two most original and profound of the modern discussions of the subject—the theories of Hume and of Kant.

Hume acknowledges a debt to Grotius in his second *Enquiry*, and there is no doubt that he was familiar with Pufendorf and other natural-law writers as well.[31] A full analysis of his debt to them remains to be made. Here I will suggest only that his distinction between the artificial and the natural virtues is clarified by seeing it in connection with the distinction between perfect and imperfect duties. We should see Hume as trying to show that a theory making virtue rather than law the central concept of ethics can give a better account of the distinction than that given by the natural lawyers who invented it.

Hume tells us that in explaining morality, as in explaining anything else, one must account for the data by the smallest number of laws possible.[32] He seems to have been convinced that the Grotian tradition, in distinguishing between perfect and imperfect duties, had correctly located a definite pattern in the moral approvals and disapprovals constituting his data and that the pattern had to be explained. This becomes clear when we note which approvals Hume links to the different types of virtue. The coincidence between his two patterns and the Grotian dichotomy is striking.

The artificial virtues, for Hume, include justice, fidelity to promises, and allegiance to government. Of the natural virtues Hume gives several lists: in one place he includes 'generosity, humanity, compassion, gratitude, friendship, fidelity, zeal, disinterestedness, liberality', which he sums up as beneficence (*T.* 603). Elsewhere he lists meekness, charity, clemency, moderation, and equity as natural virtues (*T.* 578). These lists make it evident that Hume's artificial virtues, like perfect duties, cover the domain of clear and definite claims which may be enforced by law. This is obvious in the

[31] See the discussion in Duncan Forbes, *Hume's Philosophical Politics* (Cambridge, 1975), esp. ch. 1.

[32] David Hume, *Treatise of Human Nature*, ed. L. A. Selby-Bigge and Peter H. Nidditch (Oxford, 1978), 473, 578. References will hereafter be given in the text, identified as *T.*

case of justice and of duties owed to government in Hume's view of them, and becomes so with regard to promising when we note that Hume views it chiefly as concerned with 'the interested commerce of mankind' (*T.* 522), that is, with contracts.

One of the arguments Hume uses to show that justice must be 'artificial' appeals explicitly to the fact that in its domain clear and sharp distinctions are required: 'All natural qualities', Hume says, 'run insensibly into each other, and are, on many occasions, indistinguishable' (*T.* 530). This is true of 'all kinds of vice and virtue' as well—or almost all kinds: 'Whatever may be the case, with regard to all kinds of vice and virtue, 'tis certain, that rights, and obligations, and property, admit of no such insensible gradation, but that a man either has a full and perfect property, or none at all, and is either entirely obliged to perform any action, or lies under no manner of obligation' (*T.* 529). So if you admit that justice has this preciseness, Hume holds, you must agree that it is artificial, not natural.

Finally, Hume takes over yet a further aspect of the Grotian tradition. As for Pufendorf the perfect duties are those which are indispensable for the existence of society, so for Hume the artificial virtues are the ones required if society is to exist, that of justice, concerning itself with property, being the most important of all (*T.* 491). Hume's natural virtues plainly map the imperfect duties, which serve rather to ameliorate or embellish social life. Both sorts of virtue, like both sorts of duty, produce good results. But instead of taking the distinction between the precise and the imprecise, or that between the enforceable and the unenforceable, to be the core of the difference between the artificial and the natural virtues, Hume takes the distinction to be that the good arising from the natural virtues is normally brought about in every case of their exercise, while the good arising from the artificial virtues comes about only as a result of the existence of a general practice of exercising them, and so may not come about in each particular case.[33]

Hume's distinction of kinds of virtue has often been taken as showing that he anticipated the distinction between act and rule utilitarianism, and opted for the latter. From a historical perspective it is more accurate to describe it as Hume's attempt to show how perfect as well as imperfect rights and duties can be explained by a non-teleological virtue-centred theory. His larger aim in doing this is to free our understanding of morality throughout from any need of appeal to supernatural origins or main-

[33] This is one important reason for calling them 'artificial'. Their exercise involves in each case the thought that others will similarly exercise them and that these others will have the thought that I and others will exercise them, and so on. This is not true of the natural virtues, which need not involve the virtuous person's awareness of participating in a social practice.

tenance. Natural-law theory, even when it was not voluntaristic as Pufendorf's was, tended to invoke divine wisdom to explain the fit between moral laws and human good, and divine sanctions to explain the nature of obligation. Hume argues that a narrative of natural development will explain both of these features. And the key to his narrative is the adequacy of human nature to evolve its own directives and controls. Hume's point is that morality need not be imposed upon us from without. It is our own creation, though not, to be sure, our *conscious* doing until fairly late in the game.

In his effort to show how much human nature 'can do by itself',[34] Hume, looking back to classical antiquity for an alternative to natural-law theory, portrays morality as emerging from character unaided by supernatural forces. This is the point of his insistence that the motive determines the moral character of action. 'No action can be virtuous, or morally good,' he famously says, 'unless there be in human nature some motive to produce it, distinct from the sense of its morality' (*T.* 479; cf. p. 518). This principle serves to undermine the natural-law position of Grotius and Pufendorf because it requires a connection between motive and obligatory action which they did not clearly supply for the cases they take as central, perfect duties. Grotius explains the duties in terms of respecting rights but says nothing of the motive that moves us to respond to rights as such. Pufendorf speaks in terms of obligations and is at best unclear about what motive we all always have for carrying them out—other than divine sanctions, which are not only an embarrassment for a natural-law theorist but which, to be justifiable, must also presuppose the obligatoriness of the acts to which they move us. That presupposition is what Hume challenges. Acts, for him, can only be obligatory if there are prior praiseworthy standing motives whose natural expression is doing them, and those motives will be virtues. Only the egoist would see any problem in saying that our natural affections for others are the motives that correspond to imperfect duties. Are there comparable motives which will allow Hume to explain that the perfect duties are morally significant because of the admirable natural dispositions they express?

Hume argues that there are at least no natural motives that will do the trick. There is no natural tendency to respect property, to obey the laws, and to abide by our promises and contracts, as there is a natural tendency to be (say) nice to our children or generous to those in need. Given the

[34] Montaigne, *Essays*, trans. D. Frame (1957; repr. Stanford, Calif., 1976), 3.12, 'Of Physiognomy', pp. 793–4: 'It was he [Socrates] who brought human wisdom back down from the heavens, where she was wasting her time . . . even the simplest can recognize in him their means and their strength; it is impossible to go back further and lower. He did a great favor to human nature by showing how much it can do by itself.'

principle of the priority of virtue in motive to virtue in actions, Hume's problem is to explain why we feel moral approval of acts which display respect for property, obedience to law, and fidelity to contract. His explanation has been discussed many times. I will therefore recall only the nub of it, concentrating on justice, which Hume himself takes as the paradigm.

Justice originates when individuals become aware that stability of possession would be beneficial to each of them individually but is only possible if all and each steadfastly refrain from disturbing one another's transferable goods. As this awareness spreads and becomes more reliably effective in the behaviour of one's fellows, there comes to be what is in effect a convention by which each respects the possessions of others. Only then can the ideas of justice and injustice arise and, with them, the ideas of property, rights, and obligations (*T.* 489–91, 497–8). Self-interest, redirected by the realization that one's own interest cannot be forwarded unless one controls one's avidity for possession when others do so as well, becomes the motive out of which we initially act when we act justly.[35]

The practice called 'justice' arises without any activity of the moral sentiment. Its name acquires positive moral connotations only when agents reflect on their common behaviour and through sympathy with the benefits others enjoy are moved to approve of the disposition in each agent from which such good consequences flow (*T.* 498–500). The man who lacks this socialized sense of his own interests may notice the lack, and hate himself for lacking it. When he does so, he will be able to show respect for the possessions of others out of a hatred for himself for lacking the normal motive, and in that case he will be acting from a sense of duty. This cannot be the standing motive in the case of just actions, any more than it can for other virtuous acts: it is only 'on some occasions' that 'a person will perform an action merely out of regard to its moral obligation'. The standard case is that where there is some definite principle 'capable of producing the action and whose moral beauty renders the action meritorious' (*T.* 479)—and in this case it is the socialized self-interest on which we eventually bestow moral approval.[36]

[35] Knud Haakonssen has provocatively disputed this view and offered an alternative interpretation—admittedly hypothetical—of what Hume has in mind (see his *The Science of a Legislator* (Cambridge, 1981), ch. 2, esp. pp. 33–5).

[36] At one point, Hume expresses indifference about whether we consider the motive to justice a vice or a virtue (*T.* 492). He says this only in order to dismiss the whole question of whether man is innately good or evil: since self-interest controls itself, if self-interest be vicious, then vice controls itself in our nature and makes us social, and if it be good, then a good motive has that effect. In all other contexts Hume makes plain his belief that the settled disposition to respect the possessions of others out of socialized self-interest is a virtue.

Hume certainly sees justice as requiring us to obey the laws or customs concerning property which are current in our society, and one might think this a lapse on his part to a natural-law view. But if individuals may actually possess goods before there are customs or laws, we can see that the latter come to be invented to codify and clarify the convention of respecting possession and to make it more easily transmissible to the young. So what underlies justice is not our ability to form habits of compliance with rules but our ability to extend our sense of self so that self-interest comes to include the interests of others with whom we form a cooperating society. We come, that is, to have an interest in the good of others, which, though mediated and indirect, is akin to the interest the natural virtues lead us to show in their good. When that interest is gratified, not only are our private ends forwarded, but we also receive gratification from the very existence of the institution of justice. Justice by its very nature thus benefits its possessors as well as their society. And if Hume cannot attribute any special cognitive status to the virtuous agent, as Aristotle does, the friends of virtue might think this a small price to pay for a rehabilitation of virtue that does not rely on Aristotelian assumptions we can no longer accept.

Despite its brilliance, however, I think that Hume's view must be considered one of the misfortunes of virtue. It failed to convince those who accepted Grotius's assumptions that it was an adequate alternative to an act-centred or juridical approach to morality. Its weakness becomes apparent if we follow its fortunes in the work of the one major thinker who might be taken as something of a follower of Hume's in ethics, Adam Smith.

V

The eulogy of Grotius as the founder of international law with which Smith concludes *The Theory of the Moral Sentiments* is by no means the only indication of his indebtedness to natural-law thinking.[37] He had a different view of the nature of moral laws or rules and of how they are to be derived, but he shared the Grotian belief that society could not function properly without clear and precise rules for the guidance of action. In working out the implications of this belief he relied extensively on the natural-law distinction between perfect and imperfect duties.

These points stand out sharply in Smith's criticism of the views of virtue

[37] Adam Smith, *The Theory of Moral Sentiments*, ed. D. D. Raphael and A. L. Macfie (Oxford, 1976), 7.4.37, pp. 341–2. Citations hereafter in text as *TMS*. The work appeared first in 1759; the edition I cite, the last edition (1790), was much altered.

he attributes to Plato, Aristotle, the Stoics, Clarke, Wollaston, and Shaftesbury. All of them, he says, place virtue in the propriety of the affections, but 'none of these systems either give, or pretend to give, any precise or distinct measure by which this fitness or propriety can be ascertained or judged of'. Yet to direct such judgements is 'the great purpose of all systems of morality' (*TMS* 7.2.1.1, p. 267; 7.2.1.47–8, p. 293). A natural-law outlook is also plain in his account of the importance of moral rules. These rules are no more than summaries of the judgements which morally sensitive people make of individual cases. They matter because although most people are not able to make delicate moral discriminations they are usually able to 'behave very decently' by acting 'merely from a regard to what they saw were the established rules of behaviour'. Even if one's own sentiments do not make one aware of the proper gratitude to show a patron, one can do everything appropriate simply from the motive of 'reverence for the established rules of duty, a serious and earnest desire of acting, in every respect, according to the law of gratitude'. Even good manners would be rare without explicit guidance; and in a strongly Pufendorfian passage Smith remarks:

> But if without regard to these general rules, even the duties of politeness, which are so easily observed . . . would yet be so frequently violated, what would become of the duties of justice, of truth, of chastity, of fidelity . . . ? But upon the tolerable observance of these duties, depends the very existence of human society, which would crumble into nothing if mankind were not generally impressed with a reverence for those important rules of conduct (*TMS* 3.5.2, p. 163)

If the natural lawyers' stress on actions and on perfect duties is thus apparent in Smith, so too is their preference for the clear and definite over against that which must be left to the discretion of the agent. 'The general rules of almost all the virtues,' he says, 'The general rules which determine what are the offices of prudence, of charity, of generosity, of gratitude, of friendship, are in many respects loose and inaccurate . . . it is scarce possible to regulate our conduct entirely by a regard to them.' Smith here of course refers to Humean natural virtues; and he promptly points out that there is at least one virtue which is not like them: justice.[38] Its rules 'are accurate in the highest degree, and admit of no exceptions or modifications, but such as may be ascertained as accurately as the rules themselves'. The duties of justice must be regarded as sacred, and are best performed when done from 'a reverential and religious regard to those general rules which require them'. The other virtues require us to 'consider the end and

[38] He thinks that of all the imperfect duties, that of gratitude has the most precise rules with the fewest exceptions.

foundation of the rule rather than the rule itself', and to use our judgement accordingly. But in matters of justice, 'the man who refines the least and adheres with the most obstinate steadfastness to the general rules themselves, is the most commendable and the most to be depended upon' (*TMS* 3.6.9–10, pp. 174–5).

Virtue is thus once again discussed in terms of perfect and imperfect duties. The significance of this for Smith shows in two further views of his, one about the importance of examination and discussion of the virtues, the other about the importance of the virtues in society.

Moral philosophy, Smith says, has three parts. One is ethics, whose task is to describe the virtues and vices, pointing out the 'propriety and happiness of the one' and the 'deformity and misery of the other', exhorting us to love the former and refrain from the latter. Ethics can be eloquent but not accurate; it is useful mainly in educating the young (*TMS* 7.4.3–6, pp. 328–9). Next comes jurisprudence, which is 'the endeavour to lay down exact and precise rules for the direction of every circumstance of our behaviour'. It has two branches. Jurisprudence proper considers the person to whom an obligation is owed and asks what he may exact by force. Casuistry considers the person obligated and asks what he ought to think himself bound to do so as neither to wrong his neighbour nor to violate 'the integrity of his own character' (*TMS* 7.4.7–8, pp. 329–30). Now casuistry, says Smith, 'ought to be rejected altogether' (*TMS* 7.4.34, p. 340). In other words, discussions of virtue and character, ethics and casuistry, are either eloquence useful for children or totally useless; and only examination of the rules whose observance is necessary for society is worth one's time. At the very end of *The Theory of the Moral Sentiments* Smith proposes to move on to jurisprudence.

Pufendorf held that imperfect duties did much to ameliorate the life we are enabled to live together when we carry out our perfect duties. In *The Wealth of Nations* Smith did not deny this, but he offered a quite different view of how social existence is enhanced. In a much-quoted passage he remarked:

> It is not from the benevolence of the butcher, the brewer, or the baker, that we expect our dinner, but from their regard to their own interest. We address ourselves, not to their humanity but to their self-love, and never talk to them of our own necessities but of their advantages. . . . It is by treaty, by barter, and by purchase, that we obtain from one another the greater part of those mutual good offices we stand in need of.[39]

[39] Adam Smith, *An Inquiry into the Nature and Causes of the Wealth of Nations*, ed. R. H. Campbell and A. S. Skinner (1976; repr. Oxford, 1979), 1.2.2, pp. 26–7.

If justice establishes the framework for the moral world and self-interest makes life better, the role for the imperfect duties—for what is left of virtue—is small indeed.

VI

Adam Smith shows in a particularly clear way the vulnerability of Hume's virtue-centred ethic when it is faced with a demand for clear and definite moral guidance. I think an awareness of its inability to sustain itself in the face of such a demand enables us to see why Hume's moral philosophy, for all its brilliance, was one of virtue's misfortunes.

Hume presents himself as flouting the naural-law tradition. If we are virtuous, we will not need any moral rules to guide our action (though of course the law of the land is another matter). Hume therefore writes as a theorist bent only on explaining the moral life, not as offering direction nor even as showing us where to get it. He does not claim that his theory gives guidance, still less that it contains a rule book or a single principle which each person could use for decision-making. None the less he has pratical purposes in mind, as his denunciation of the 'monkish virtues' makes clear. The theory is not really neutral with respect to all the data about what people approve.

A Humean moral outlook therefore presents us with a dilemma. If we insist that moral philosophy cannot and should not offer direction, we condemn it to irrelevance in the eyes of those who share Smith's Grotian sense that there is a need for the kind of directive that only laws or rules can give—and the popularity of Pufendorf suggests that there were many who felt this need. But if we allow that moral theory is to provide us with such guides, a still worse problem arises. Hume's drive for Newtonian economy of explanation led him to conclude that natural goods and evils are the ultimate determinant of the content of morality. The core of the virtues, artificial as well as natural, is concern (however, mediated) for the good of others or of oneself. What makes something into a good for someone is that person's desire for it or enjoyment of it. And desires and enjoyments are what they are regardless of morality.[40] Since Hume refuses to believe in the sinfulness of our passions he holds that the content of morality must in the end be determined by facts about what is desired and enjoyed. They automatically carry moral weight because, for Hume, there

[40] I think Hume holds that we have a second-order desire that our own character should be such that others and we ourselves can approve of it. But this is only a minor emendation to the statement in the text.

is no principle in us wholly independent of those facts which might point us in other directions. Take a Grotian approach to Hume's explanatory principle, and what emerges is Benthamism. And Benthamite utilitarianism has, of course, no room for virtues in the traditional sense. It provides a rational decision procedure for every case, so that there is no room for the imprecisions of the imperfect duties, still less for the insight of the virtuous agent, or for any attribution of value to certain kinds of character other than an instrumental value in reliably producing good results. There may or may not be room for moral laws; but the virtues on such a view are at best derivative.

VII

Like Hume, Kant worked in a philosophical culture in which the distinction between perfect and imperfect duties was a commonplace.[41] He himself recurs to it throughout his life. He discusses it as an illustration of his views on negative quantities in an essay of 1763.[42] He reflects on it in marginalia both early and late.[43] In 1766 in *The Dreams of a Spirit Seer* he refers to the distinction as that between the strong law of duty and the weaker law of love (*A*. ii. 335). He brings the problem up in the ethics lectures he gave from 1764 on (*A*. xxvii *passim*). He discusses the matter in the *Groundwork of the Metaphysics of Morals*, and touches on it briefly in the second *Critique*. But until the late *Metaphysics of Morals*, where it is given a major treatment, it played much less of a role in his thinking than I have argued that it did for Hume.

In the *Groundwork* Kant discusses the distinction between perfect and imperfect duties only briefly. In a footnote he remarks that a perfect duty is 'one which allows no exception in the interest of inclination' (*A*. iv. 421 n.), thus suggesting that the sole special feature of imperfect duties is that we may carry them out or not, as we prefer. The other way in which the distinction is drawn is more adequate. Kant distinguishes between maxims which cannot be coherently thought as universal laws, and maxims which can be thought but not willed as laws. Maxims of the first kind are in conflict with strict or narrow or irremissible duty, maxims of the second

[41] In what follows I am much indebted to Wolfgang Kersting, 'Das starke Gesetz der Schuldigkeit und das schwächere der Gütigkeit', *Studia Leibnitiana*, 14 (1982), 184–220.

[42] *Kant's Gesammelte Schriften* (30 vols.; Berlin, 1902), ii. 172, 174. Subsequent references to this *Akademie* edition are in parentheses in the text and are referred to as *A*.

[43] For example, ibid. xix. 10 (#6457), 17 (#6469), 30 (#6498), and 51 (#6517–19), which are all quite early; pp. 94 (#6582), 102 (#6597), 105 (#6603), 125 (#6653), 138 (#6709), and 152 (#6760), probably from the late 1760s and early 1770s, pp. 261 (#7165) and 308 (#7309), late notes.

with broader or meritorious duty. A maxim of not repaying a deliberately contracted debt illustrates the former, a maxim of never helping those in need the latter (*A*. iv. 424). Kant is here clearly restating the traditional perfect/imperfect distinction in his own terms.[44]

At this point in his thinking, however, Kant can make no room for love. Love as inclination or feeling or tender sympathy is dismissed in one sentence. It cannot be commanded. It must be replaced by 'beneficence from duty', which is practical love (*A*. iv. 399). The love commandment of the New Testament is conceptually incoherent if it is understood as requiring a feeling.

I have pointed out that, as traditionally understood, doing one's imperfect duties would earn merit because they go beyond strict obligation and are done from love. In the *Groundwork* Kant calls imperfect duties meritorious but does not explain how they guide us or what motivates us to do them. That we are not to act on a maxim which cannot be willed as a universal law does not tell us what we are to do. I cannot rationally will never to help others, Kant thinks, but this alone will not lead me to think that a given particular act of helping someone is required by the moral law, so that I could then do it solely for that reason. Kant needs to say more about the imperfect duties if he is to retain anything like the traditional distinction.

The additions are made in the *Metaphysics of Morals*. We now have two principles, one governing duties of law or justice (*Rechtspflichten*), the other, duties of virtue or morality (*Tugendpflichten*). Legal duties require us to perform external actions, moral duties to have certain maxims. The principle of legal duties is that we are to act externally only in ways that allow 'the freedom of the will of each to coexist together with the freedom of everyone in accordance with a universal law' (*A*. vi. 230). The principle of virtue is that we are to 'act according to a maxim of *ends* which it can be a universal law for everyone to have' (*A*. vi. 395).[45] These ends, Kant says, are our own perfection and the happiness of others. The idea of compellability, strikingly absent from the *Groundwork*, is tied to the principle of legal duties. We can be compelled to perform external actions, but not to adopt ends; and Kant thinks he is asserting an analytic proposition when he says that acts to which someone has a right may properly be obtained by compulsion. He thus rejects the Pufendorfian way of drawing

[44] In discussing the duty to help others, Kant contrasts duties necessary for the continuation of 'mankind' and duties going beyond that to helpfulness—a version of the Pufendorfian explanation of the distinction (ibid. iv. 430).

[45] Translations of citations from pt. 2 of the *Metaphysics of Morals* are from Mary Gregor, *The Doctrine of Virtue* (New York, 1964).

the distinction between perfect and imperfect duties altogether. It is legality and morality which are distinguished by the propriety or impropriety of using compulsion, not these kinds of duty.

A distinction between the two kinds of duty is however assigned a significant place in morality. The principle of perfect duties enables us to determine a priori with fair precision what action is required, but that of duties of virtue does not. As Kant puts it, when juridical duty is in question, 'then the Mine and the Thine must be determined on the scales of justice with quasi-mathematical precision . . . but so long as this knowledge concerns a mere duty of virtue, this is not necessary' (*A*. vi. 375 n.).[46] We can therefore have perfect duties to ourselves as well as to others, though we can only be compelled to carry out those to others. Imperfect duties to ourselves, like those to others, require us to have certain ends, but we cannot determine on a priori grounds alone what to do in order to achieve them or what acts would best express our attachment to these ends. Consequently, in these cases, 'what is to be done cannot be determined according to rules of morality . . . only judgment can decide this according to rules of prudence (pragmatic rules)' (*A*. vi. 433 n.).[47]

In the *Metaphysics of Morals*, then, an ethic of rule and an ethic of admirable disposition or virtue are presented as dividing the moral life between them, as in the natural-law tradition. Since the ends involved in virtue are generated by obedience to the moral law, they will presumably never lead us to plan acts that would transgress the limits of legaliy; and legality always leaves open more ways than one for us to try to achieve our moral ends. It is worth noting that Kant does not rely on Pufendorf's thesis, which is also Hume's, that the perfect duties are more important for the existence of society than the imperfect. The perfect duties are prior to the imperfect in that they spell out the conditions under which we may act to carry out our imperfect duties. But the imperfect duties are the ones we must carry out to acquire merit, and with it a title to happiness.

The crucial point to be noticed about the new position is that a direct concern for the good of others may now play an immediate motivational role in morality. We do not act with the thought that we are doing our duty when we act to carry out the duties of virtue. If we have performed a duty of virtue, we have made (say) the well-being of a friend our own end. In acting to bring it about, therefore, our purpose is not 'to do our duty', but 'to bring about the well-being of our friend'. If this is not quite acting from love, it can come to be so: 'Helping others to achieve their ends is a duty. If a man practices it often and succeeds in realizing his purpose, he

[46] Ibid. 31. [47] Ibid. 97–8 n.

eventually comes to feel love for those he has helped. Hence the saying: you *ought* to *love* your neighbor . . . means . . . *do good* to your fellow-man, and this will give rise to love of man in you' (*A*. vi. 402).[48]

Kant's reconstruction of virtue seems to be an even more brilliant achievement than Hume's. It does not face the problem which threatened Hume's view of being irrelevant to those who accept the Grotian view of the importance of moral laws because it does contain a directive law, and it argues that there are necessary limits to the range within which such a law can guide our action. It does not have the practical instability of Hume's view because it does not rest morality on some non-moral good to the realization of which character might be merely instrumental. It makes inner motivation to morality central and allows for different kinds of motivation. How then does Kant's late view fit into the story of the misfortunes of virtue?

VIII

If the misfortune is that virtue was neglected by moral philosophers, then part of the answer to this question is that it was the *Groundwork*, not the *Metaphysics of Morals*, that until recently got most of the attention. Perhaps this is because the latter book is so badly written and so hard to understand. Whatever the reason, Kant was almost always seen as arguing that all morality falls under a single principle which is capable of giving guidance over the whole range of the decisions we have to make as moral agents. So discussion of his ethics came to centre on the now familiar questions, Can we really get definite results from the categorical imperative, and if so do we get all and only those we want? If not, will some other principle do the same thing, or are we forced to rely on a plurality of ultimate principles? But in that case, are we not liable to allow convention and prejudice to pass as morality? There was post-Kantian discussion of these issues in Germany, which was much like the controversy in Britain over the Benthamite assertion of the principle of utility as the sole principle of morals; and in similar fashion the terms of the question made the topic of virtue and the virtues unimportant. From this point of view, Kant was one of virtue's misfortunes because he perhaps unintentionally made it uninteresting.

The friends of virtue think that Kant was much more of a misfortune. The virtuous agent, for Kant, has no epistemological privilege: when she

[48] Translations of citations from pt. 2, 62–3. Kant was saying similar things in his ethics lectures at a much earlier stage (see, e.g., xxvii. 417, ll. 10–19; p. 419, ll. 5–7).

exercises her virtue she is simply choosing at her discretion among alternative ways of helping others or improving herself, she is not displaying insight as to the morally best thing to do. Moreover Kant sees virtue in a most un-Aristotelian way, as always a struggle, never a settled principle. Kant's vision of the divided self is the villain here, with morality springing from an impossibly pure reason in conflict with reprobate passions forever calling for discipline. Virtue is not so much the expression of our nature at its most developed as it is the triumph of one part of it over another. The connection between virtue and the agent's own flourishing therefore cannot be made out on Kantian terms except by means of some notoriously questionable postulates. And perhaps worst of all, virtue has at best a partial role to play in morality, dividing the realm with perfect duties which are the archetype of everything the virtue theorist rejects. Kant's theory is a misfortune for virtue, on this view, not because his theory of virtue was ignored but precisely because of what that theory was.

If we take this view—and obviously I cannot assess it here—we must ask just one more question. To what extent is virtue itself involved in creating this misfortune? Here, I think, the history I have been tracing offers us a clue.

If we ask why the project of the Grotians was to establish a law-like code of morals, the answer must be that they took the central difficulties of life to be those arising from disagreement—disagreement involving nations, religious sects, parties to legal disputes, and ordinary people trying to make a living in busy commercial societies. It is not an accident that the very first word in the body of Grotius's text is 'controversiae'.[49] I have tried to show that the natural lawyers did not think this the only morally pertinent problem area. They saw that there is an important part of our lives in which the problem arises not from disagreement but from the scarcity of resources for helping others. No single person, perhaps not even any society, can help everyone who is suffering or in need. But some can be helped even if not all can. The theory of imperfect duties provides one way of thinking about how we are to distribute resources in situations where only some can be helped. The serious issues involved here seemed less urgent to the natural lawyers than the problems arising from disagreement about strict justice, which they took to pose threats to the very existence of society. They therefore gave first priority to what they thought might assist with those controversies.

In tackling these problems, classical virtue theory is of little or no use. Aristotle does not tell us what a virtuous agent (*phronimos*) is to do to convince someone who is not virtuous to agree with him, other than to

[49] Grotius, 1.1.1.

educate him all over again. He does not suggest criteria which anyone and everyone can use to determine who is a virtuous agent and who is not. He does not discuss the situation in which two virtuous agents disagree seriously with one another. And consequently he does not notice what seems to be an implication of his view: that if two allegedly virtuous agents strongly disagree, one of them (at least) must be morally defective.

The Aristotelian theory may have been suited to a society in which there was a recognized class of superior citizens, whose judgement on moral issues would be accepted without question. But the Grotians did not believe they lived in such a world. Moreover, since virtue theory must treat disagreement with the virtuous agent as showing a flaw of character, it discourages parties to a moral dispute from according even prima-facie respect to differing points of view. It encourages each, rather, to impugn the character of the other rather than listen to the other's case. And it gives no distinctive guidance about how to analyse a dispute so as to find the common ground from which agreement can be peacefully reached. Natural-law theory tries to do precisely that. It reminds us of the basic needs we share, and the difficulties, inherent in our nature, to overcoming them. It gives us laws showing us what we have to do to solve the problems. And it instructs us to apply those laws either to resolve our disputes in their terms (in a state of nature) or to construct civil laws which will give us more specific instruments for reaching agreements.

The Grotian approach, in short, leads us to ask how we are to handle serious disagreements among equals. If it is addressing the right problematic, then Kant's moral theory is not one of virtue's misfortunes. He did as well for virtue as could be done, given the deficiencies of classical virtue-centred views. It may well be that the friends of virtue think some other problematic is more relevant to our current situation than the Grotian, or that they see more resources in the classical tradition of virtue-centred ethics than I have noticed. I hope that they will at any rate realize that virtue was not neglected during the seventeenth and eighteenth centuries. It is up to them to show that it was not virtue's own weakness that brought its misfortunes down upon its own head.[50]

[50] A very early version of this paper benefited from the careful scrutiny of William Frankena and from discussion at the University of Michigan. Various revisions were presented at Princeton University, Virginia Commonwealth University, Notre Dame University, Johns Hopkins University (where Michael Slote commented on it), the University of Virginia, the University of Pittsburgh, and the University of California, Berkeley. I am grateful for the many criticisms and suggestions I received at these institutions. I have also received valuable assistance from Richard Rorty, Rüdiger Bittner, and Stephen Hudson, who discussed various versions with me; and I am especially grateful to David Sachs, for insightful suggestions and protracted discussions.

10

ON SOME VICES OF VIRTUE ETHICS

ROBERT B. LOUDEN

It is common knowledge by now that recent philosophical and theological writing about ethics reveals a marked revival of interest in the virtues. But what exactly are the distinctive features of a so-called virtue ethics? Does it have a special contribution to make to our understanding of moral experience? Is there a price to be paid for its different perspective, and if so, is the price worth paying?

Contemporary textbook typologies of ethics still tend to divide the terrain of normative ethical theory into the teleological and deontological. Both types of theory, despite their well-defined differences, have a common focus on acts as opposed to qualities of agents. The fundamental question that both types of theory are designed to answer is: What ought I to do? What is the correct analysis and resolution of morally problematic situations? A second feature shared by teleological and deontological theories is conceptual reductionism. Both types of theory start with a primary irreducible element and then proceed to introduce secondary derivative concepts which are defined in terms of their relations to the beginning element. Modern teleologists (the majority of whom are utilitarians) begin with a concept of the good—here defined with reference to states of affairs rather than persons. After this criterion of the good is established, the remaining ethical categories are defined in terms of this starting-point. Thus, according to the classic maxim, one ought always to promote the greatest good for the greatest number. Duty, in other words, is defined in terms of the element of ends—one ought always to maximize utility. The concepts of virtue and rights are also treated as derivative categories of secondary importance, definable in terms of utility. For the classic utilitarian, a right is upheld 'so long as it is upon the whole advantageous to the society that it should be maintained', while virtue is construed as a 'tendency to give a net

Reprinted by permission from *American Philosophical Quarterly*, 21 (1984), 227–36.

increase to the aggregate quantity of happiness in all its shapes taken together'.[1]

For the deontologist, on the other hand, the concept of duty is the irreducible starting-point, and any attempt to define this root notion of being morally bound to do something in terms of the good to be achieved is rejected from the start. The deontologist is committed to the notion that certain acts are simply inherently right. Here the notion of the good is only a derivative category, definable in terms of the right. The good that we are to promote is right action for its own sake—duty for duty's sake. Similarly, the virtues tend to be defined in terms of pro-attitudes towards one's duties. Virtue is important, but only because it helps us do our duty.

But what about virtue ethics? What are the hallmarks of this approach to normative ethics? One problem confronting anyone who sets out to analyse the new virtue ethics in any detail is that we presently lack fully developed examples of it in the contemporary literature. Most of the work done in this genre has a negative rather than positive thrust—its primary aim is more to criticize the traditions and research programmes to which it is opposed rather than to state positively and precisely what its own alternative is. A second hindrance is that the literature often has a somewhat misty antiquarian air. It is frequently said, for instance, that the Greeks advocated a virtue ethics, though what precisely it is that they were advocating is not always spelled out. In describing contemporary virtue ethics, it is therefore necessary, in my opinion, to do some detective work concerning its conceptual shape, making inferences based on the unfortunately small number of remarks that are available.

For purposes of illustration, I propose briefly to examine and expand on some key remarks made by two contemporary philosophers—Elizabeth Anscombe and Philippa Foot—whose names have often been associated with the revival of virtue movement. Anscombe, in her frequently cited article 'Modern Moral Philosophy', writes: 'you can do ethics without it [viz., the notion of "obligation" or "morally ought"], as is shown by the example of Aristotle. It would be a great improvement if, instead of "morally wrong", one always named a genus such as "untruthful", "unchaste", "unjust".'[2] Here we find an early rallying cry for an ethics of virtue programme, to be based on contemporary efforts in philosophical psychology and action theory. On the Anscombe model, strong, irreducible duty and obligation notions drop out of the picture, and are to be

[1] The rights definition is from Bentham, 'Anarchical Fallacies', repr. in A. I. Melden (ed.), *Human Rights* (Belmont, Calif., 1970), 32. The virtue definition is from Bentham, 'The Nature of Virtue', repr. in Bhiku Parekh (ed.), *Bentham's Political Thought* (New York, 1973), 89.

[2] G. E. M. Anscombe, 'Modern Moral Philosophy'; Chapter 1 in this volume.

replaced by vices such as unchasteness and untruthfulness. But are we to take the assertion literally, and actually attempt to do moral theory without any concept of duty whatsoever? On my reading, Anscombe is not really proposing that we entirely dispose of moral oughts. Suppose one follows her advice, and replaces 'morally wrong' with 'untruthful', 'unchaste', etc. Isn't this merely shorthand for saying that agents *ought* to be truthful and chaste, and that untruthful and unchaste acts are *morally wrong* because good agents don't perform such acts? The concept of the moral ought, in other words, seems now to be explicated in terms of what the good person would do.[3]

A similar strategy is at work in some of Foot's articles. In the Introduction to her recent collection of essays, *Virtues and Vices and Other Essays in Moral Philosophy*, she announces that one of the two major themes running throughout her work is 'the thought that a sound moral philosophy should start from a theory of virtues and vices'.[4] When this thought is considered in conjunction with the central argument in her article 'Morality as a System of Hypothetical Imperatives', the indication is that another virtue-based moral theory is in the making. For in this essay Foot envisions a moral community composed of an 'army of volunteers', composed, that is, of agents who voluntarily commit themselves to such moral ideals as truth, justice, generosity, and kindness.[5] In a moral community of this sort, all moral imperatives become hypothetical rather than categorical: there are things an agent morally ought to do if he or she wants truth, justice, generosity, or kindness, but no things an agent morally ought to do if he or she isn't first committed to these (or other) moral ideals. On the Foot model (as presented in 'Morality as a System'), what distinguishes an ethics of virtue from its competitors is that it construes the ideal moral agent as acting from a direct desire, without first believing that he or she morally ought to perform that action or have that desire. However, in a more recent paper, Foot has expressed doubts about her earlier attempts to articulate the relationship between oughts and desires. In 'William Frankena's Carus Lectures' (1981), she states that '*thoughts* [emphasis added] about what is despicable or contemptible, or low, or again

[3] Anscombe appears to believe also that moral oughts and obligations only make sense in a divine law context, which would mean that only divine command theories of ethics employ valid concepts of obligation. I see no reason to accept such a narrow definition of duty. See ibid. pp. 30–1, 38–40. For one argument against her restrictive divine law approach to moral obligation, see Alan Donagan, *The Theory of Morality* (Chicago, 1977), 3.

[4] Philippa Foot, *Virtues and Vices and Other Essays in Moral Philosophy* (Oxford, 1978), p. xi.

[5] Philippa Foot, 'Morality as a System of Hypothetical Imperatives', *Philosophical Review*, 81 (1972), 305–16; repr. in *Virtues and Vices*, 157–73. See especially the long concluding footnote, added in 1977.

admirable, glorious or honourable may give us the key to the problem of rational moral action'.[6] But regardless of whether she begins with desires or with thoughts, it seems clear her strategy too is not to dispense with oughts entirely, but rather to employ softer, derivative oughts.

In other words, conceptual reductionism is at work in virtue ethics too. Just as its utilitarian and deontological competitors begin with primitive concepts of the good state of affairs and the intrinsically right action respectively and then drive secondary concepts out of their starting-points, so virtue ethics, beginning with a root conception of the morally good person, proceeds to introduce a different set of secondary concepts which are defined in terms of their relationship to the primitive element. Though the ordering of primitive and derivatives differs in each case, the overall strategy remains the same. Viewed from this perspective, virtue ethics is not unique at all. It has adopted the traditional mononomic strategy of normative ethics. What sets it apart from other approaches, again, is its strong agent orientation.

So for virtue ethics, the primary object of moral evaluation is not the act or its consequences, but rather the agent. And the respective conceptual starting-points of agent- and act-centred ethics result in other basic differences as well, which may be briefly summarized as follows. First of all, the two camps are likely to employ different models of practical reasoning. Act theorists, because they focus on discrete acts and moral quandaries, are naturally very interested in formulating decision procedures for making practical choices. The agent, in their conceptual scheme, needs a guide—hopefully a determinate decision procedure—for finding a way out of the quandary. Agent-centered ethics, on the other hand, focuses on long-term characteristic patterns of action, intentionally down-playing atomic acts and particular choice situations in the process. They are not as concerned with portraying practical reason as a rule-governed enterprise which can be applied on a case-by-case basis.

Secondly, their views on moral motivation differ. For the deontological act theorist, the preferred motive for moral action is the concept of duty itself; for the utilitarian act theorist, it is the disposition to seek the happiness of all sentient creatures. But for the virtue theorist, the preferred motivation factor is the virtues themselves (here understood non-reductionistically). The agent who correctly acts from the disposition of charity does so (according to the virtue theorist) not because it maximizes utility or because it is one's duty to do so, but rather out of a commitment to the value of charity for its own sake.

[6] Philippa, Foot, 'William Frankena's Carus Lectures', *The Monist*, 64 (1981), 311.

While I am sympathetic to recent efforts to recover virtue from its longstanding neglect, my purpose in this essay is not to contribute further to the campaign for virtue. Instead, I wish to take a more critical look at the phenomenon, and to ask whether there are certain important features of morality which a virtue-based ethics either handles poorly or ignores entirely. In the remainder of this essay, I shall sketch some objections which (I believe) point to genuine shortcomings of the virtue approach to ethics. My object here is not to offer an exhaustive or even thoroughly systematic critique of virtue ethics, but rather to look at certain mundane regions of the moral field and to ask first what an ethics of virtue might say about them, and second whether what it says about them seems satisfactory.

AGENTS VS. ACTS

As noted earlier, it is a commonplace that virtue theorists focus on good and bad agents rather than on right and wrong acts. In focusing on good and bad agents, virtue theorists are thus forced to de-emphasize discrete acts in favour of long-term, characteristic patterns of behaviour. Several related problems arise for virtue ethics as a result of this particular conceptual commitment.

a. Casuistry and Applied Ethics. It has often been said that for virtue ethics the central question is not 'What ought I to *do*?' but rather 'What sort of person ought I to *be*?'[7] However, people have always expected ethical theory to tell them something about what they ought to do, and it seems to me that virtue ethics is structurally unable to say much of anything about this issue. If I'm right, one consequence of this is that a virtue-based ethics will be particularly weak in the areas of casuistry and applied ethics. A recent reviewer of Foot's *Virtues and Vices*, for instance, notes that 'one must do some shifting to gather her view on the virtues'. 'Surprisingly,' he adds, 'the studies of abortion and euthanasia are not of much use.'[8] And this is odd, when one considers Foot's demonstrated interest in applied ethics in conjunction with her earlier cited prefatory remark that a 'sound moral theory should start from a theory of virtues and vices'. But what can a virtues and vices approach say about specific moral dilemmas?

[7] For background on this 'Being vs. Doing' debate, see Bernard Mayo, *Ethics and the Moral Life* (London, 1958), 211–14, and William K. Frankena, *Ethics* (2nd edn., Englewood Cliffs, NJ, 1973), 65–6.

[8] Arthur Flemming, 'Reviving the Virtues', review of Foot's *Virtues and Vices* and James Wallace's *Virtues and Vices, Ethics*, 90 (1980), 588.

As virtue theorists from Aristotle onward have rightly emphasized, virtues are not simply dispositions to behave in specified ways, for which rules and principles can always be cited. In addition, they involve skills of perception and articulation, situation-specific 'know-how', all of which are developed only through recognizing and acting on what is relevant in concrete moral contexts as they arise. These skills of moral perception and practical reason are not completely routinizable, and so cannot be transferred from agent to agent as any sort of decision procedure 'package deal'. Owing to the very nature of the moral virtues, there is thus a very limited amount of advice on moral quandaries that one can reasonably expect from the virtue-oriented approach. We ought, of course, to do what the virtuous person would do, but it is not always easy to fathom what the hypothetical moral exemplar would do were he in our shoes, and sometimes even he will act out of character. Furthermore, if one asks him why he did what he did, or how he knew what to do, the answer—if one is offered—might not be very enlightening. One would not necessarily expect him to appeal to any rules or principles which might be of use to others.

We can say, à la Aristotle, that the virtuous agent acts for the sake of the noble (*tou kalou heneka*), that he will not do what is base or depraved, etc. But it seems to me that we cannot intelligently say things like: 'The virtuous person (who acts for the sake of the noble) is also one who recognizes that all mentally deficient eight-month-old fetuses should (or should not) be aborted, that the doctor/patient principle of confidentiality must always (or not always) be respected, etc.' The latter simply sound too strange, and their strangeness stems from the fact that motives of virtue and honour cannot be fully routinized.

Virtue theory is not a problem-oriented or quandary approach to ethics: it speaks of rules and principles of action only in a derivative manner. And its derivative oughts are frequently too vague and unhelpful for persons who have not yet acquired the requisite moral insight and sensitivity. Consequently, we cannot expect it to be of great use in applied ethics and casuistry. The increasing importance of these two subfields of ethics in contemporary society is thus a strike against the move to revive virtue ethics.

b. Tragic Humans. Another reason for making sure that our ethical theory allows us to talk about features of acts and their results in abstraction from the agent and his conception of what he is doing is that sometimes even the best person can make the wrong choices. There are cases in which a man's choice is grounded in the best possible information, his motives honourable and his action not at all out of character. And yet his best-laid plans may go sour. Aristotle, in his *Poetics*, suggests that here lies the source of tragedy: we are confronted with an eminent and respected man, 'whose misfortune, however, is brought upon him not by vice (*kakia*) and depravity (*moktheira*) but by some error of judgement (*amartia*)' (1453a8–9). But every human being is morally fallible, for there is a little Oedipus in each of us. So Aristotle's point is that, *regardless of character*, anyone can fall into the sort of mistake of which tragedies are made. Virtue ethics, however, since its conceptual scheme is rooted in the notion of the good person, is unable to assess correctly the occasional (inevitable) tragic outcomes of human action.

Lawrence Becker, in his article 'The Neglect of Virtue', seems at first to draw an opposite conclusion from similar reflections about virtue theory and tragedy, for it is his view that virtue ethics makes an indispensable contribution to our understanding of tragedy. According to him, 'there are times when the issue is not how much harm has been done, or the value to excusing the wrongdoer, or the voluntary nature of the offending behavior, but rather whether the sort of character indicated by the behavior is "acceptable" or not—perhaps even ideal—so that the "wrongful" conduct must be seen simply as an unavoidable defect of it'.[9] As Becker sees it, Oedipus merely comes off as a fool who asked too many questions when viewed from the perspective of act theories. Only a virtue ethics, with its agent perspective, allows us to differentiate tragic heroes from fools, and to view the acts that flow from each character type in their proper light. And the proper light in the case of tragic heroes is that there are unavoidable defects in this character type, even though it represents a human ideal. Becker's point is well taken, but its truth does not cancel out my criticism. My point is that virtue ethics is in danger of blinding itself to the wrongful conduct in Oedipal acts, simply because it views the Oedipuses of the world as honourable persons *and* because its focus is on long-term character manifestations rather than discrete acts. To recognize the wrong in Oedipal behaviour, a theory with the conceptual tools enabling one to focus on discrete acts is needed. (Notice, incidentally, that Becker's own description does just this.)

c. Intolerable Actions. A third reason for insisting that our moral theory enable us to assess acts in abstraction from agents is that we need to be able to identify certain types of action which produce harms of such magnitude that they destroy the bonds of community and render (at least temporarily) the achievement of moral goods impossible. In every traditional moral community one encounters prohibitions or 'barriers to action' which mark off clear boundaries in such areas as the taking of innocent life,

[9] Lawrence Becker, 'The Neglect of Virtue', *Ethics*, 85 (1975), 111.

sexual relations, and the administration of justice according to local laws and customs.[10] Such rules are needed to teach citizens what kinds of actions are to be regarded not simply as bad (a table of vices can handle this) but as intolerable.[11] Theorists must resort to specific lists of offences to emphasize the fact that there are some acts which are absolutely prohibited. We cannot articulate this sense of absolute prohibition by referring merely to characteristic patterns of behaviour.

In rebuttal here, the virtue theorist may reply by saying: 'Virtue ethics does not need to articulate these prohibitions—let the law do it, with its list of do's and don't's.' But the sense of requirement and prohibition referred to above seems to me to be at bottom inescapably moral rather than legal. Morality can (and frequently does) invoke the aid of law in such cases, but when we ask *why* there is a law against, e.g., rape or murder, the proper answer is that it is morally intolerable. To point merely to a legal convention when asked why an act is prohibited or intolerable raises more questions that it answers.

d. Character Change. A fourth reason for insisting that a moral theory be able to assess acts in abstraction from agents and their conception of what they're doing is that peoples' moral characters may sometimes change. Xenophon, towards the beginning of his *Memorabilia* (I.II.21), cites an unknown poet who says: 'Ah, but a good man is at one time noble (*esthlos*), at another wicked (*kakos*).' Xenophon himself agrees with the poet: '. . . many alleged (*phaskonton*) philosophers may say: A just (*dikaios*) man can never become unjust; a self-controlled (*sophron*) man can never become wanton (*hubristes*); in fact no one having learned any kind of knowledge (*mathesis*) can become ignorant of it. I do not hold this view . . . For I see that, just as poetry is forgotten unless it is often repeated, so instruction, when no longer heeded, fades from the mind.'[12]

Xenophon was a practical man who was not often given to speculation, but he arrived at his position on character change in the course of his defence of Socrates. One of the reasons Socrates got into trouble, Xenophon believed, was because of his contact with Critias and Alcibiades during their youth. For of all Athenians, 'none wrought so many evils to the *polis*'. However, Xenophon reached the conclusion that Socrates

[10] Stuart Hampshire (ed.), *Private and Public Morality* (Cambridge, 1978), 7.

[11] Alasdair MacIntyre, *After Virtue* (London, 1985), 142.

[12] It is curious to note that contemporary philosophers as different as Gilbert Ryle and H. G. Gadamer have argued, against Xenophon and myself, that character cannot change. See H. G. Gadamer, 'The Problem of Historical Consciousness', in P. Rabinow and W. M. Sullivan (eds.), *Interpretive Social Science* (Berkeley and Los Angeles, 1979), 140, and Gilbert Ryle, 'On Forgetting the Difference Between Right and Wrong', in A. I. Melden (ed.), *Essays in Moral Philosophy* (Seattle, 1958).

should not be blamed for the disappearance of his good influence once these two had ceased their close contact with him.

If skills can become rusty, it seems to me that virtues can too. Unless we stay in practice we run the risk of losing relative proficiency. We probably can't forget them completely (in part because the opportunities for exercising virtues are so pervasive in everyday life), but we can lose a certain sensitivity. People do become morally insensitive, relatively speaking—missing opportunities they once would have noticed, although perhaps when confronted with a failure they might recognize that they had failed, showing at least that they hadn't literally 'forgotten the difference between right and wrong'. If the moral virtues are acquired habits rather than innate gifts, it is always possible that one can lose relative proficiency in these habits. Also, just as one's interests and skills sometimes change over the course of a life as new perceptions and influences take hold, it seems too that aspects of our moral characters can likewise alter. (Consider religious conversion experiences.) Once we grant the possibility of such changes in moral character, the need for a more 'character-free' way of assessing action becomes evident. Character is not a permanent fixture, but rather plastic. A more reliable yardstick is sometimes needed.[13]

e. Moral Backsliding. Finally, the focus on good and bad agents rather than on right and wrong actions may lead to a peculiar sort of moral backsliding. Because the emphasis in agent ethics is on long-term, characteristic patterns of behaviour, its advocates run the risk of overlooking occasional lies or acts of selfishness on the ground that such performances are mere temporary aberrations—acts out of character. Even the just man may on occasion act unjustly, so why haggle over specifics? It is unbecoming to a virtue theorist to engage in such pharisaic calculations. But once he commits himself to the view that assessments of moral worth are not simply a matter of whether we have done the right thing, backsliding may result: 'No matter how many successes some people have, they still feel they "are" fundamentally honest,'[14] At some point, such backsliding is bound to lead to self-deception.

I have argued that there is a common source behind each of these vices.

[13] One possibility here might be to isolate specific traits and then add that the virtuous agent ought to *retain* such traits throughout any character changes. (E.g.: 'The good man will not do what is base, regardless of whether he be Christian, Jew, or atheist.') However, it is my view that very few if any moral traits have such a 'transcharacter' status. The very notion of what counts as a virtue or vice itself changes radically when one looks at different traditions. (Compare Aristotle's praise for *megalopsuchia* or pride as the 'crown of the virtues' with the New Testament emphasis on humility.) Also, one would expect basic notions about what is base or noble to themselves undergo shifts of meaning as they move across traditions.

[14] Becker, 'The Neglect of Virtue', 112.

The virtue theorist is committed to the claim that the primary object of moral evaluation is not the act or its consequences but rather the agent—specifically, those character traits of the agent which are judged morally relevant. This is not to say that virtue ethics does not ever address the issue of right and wrong actions, but rather that it can only do so in a derivative manner. Sometimes, however, it is clearly acts rather than agents which ought to be the primary focus of moral evaluation.

WHO IS VIRTUOUS?

There is also an epistemological issue which becomes troublesome when one focuses on qualities of persons rather than on qualities of acts. Baldly put, the difficulty is that we do not seem to be able to know with any degree of certainty who really is virtuous and who vicious. For how is one to go about establishing an agent's true moral character? The standard strategy is what might be called the 'externalist' one: we try to infer character by observing conduct. While not denying the existence of some connection between character and conduct, I believe that the connection between the two is not nearly as tight as externalists have assumed. The relationship is not a necessary one, but merely contingent. Virtue theorists themselves are committed to this claim, though they have not always realized it. For one central issue behind the 'Being vs. Doing' debate is the virtue theorist's contention that the moral value of Being is not reducible to or dependent on Doing; that the measure of an agent's character is not exhausted by or even dependent on the values of the actions which he may perform. On this view, the most important moral traits are what may be called 'spiritual' rather than 'actional'.[15]

Perhaps the most famous example of a spiritual virtue would be Plato's definition of justice (*dikaiosunē*). Plato, it will be remembered, argued that attempts to characterize *dikaiosunē* in terms of an agent's conduct are misguided and place the emphasis in the wrong place. *Dikaiosunē* for Plato is rather a matter of the correct harmonious relationship between the three parts of the soul: 'It does not lie in a man's external actions, but in the way he acts within himself (*tēn entos*), really concerned with himself and his inner parts (*peri eauton kai ta eautou*)' (*Republic* 443d). Other spiritual virtues would include such attitudes as self-respect and integrity. These

[15] I have borrowed this terminology from G. W. Trianosky-Stillwell, 'Should We Be Good? The Place of Virtue in Our Morality' (doctoral dissertation, University of Michigan, 1980).

are traits which do have a significant impact on what we do, but whose moral value is not wholly derivable from the actions to which they may give rise.

If there are such spiritual virtues, and if they rank among the most important of moral virtues, then the externalist strategy is in trouble. For those who accept spiritual virtues, the Inner is not reducible to or dependent on the Outer. We cannot always know the moral value of a person's character by assessing his or her actions.

But suppose we reject the externalist approach and take instead the allegedly direct internalist route. Suppose, that is, that we could literally 'see inside' agents and somehow observe their character traits first hand. (The easiest way to envision this is to assume that some sort of identity thesis with respect to moral psychology and neurophysiology is in principle correct. Lest the reader object that this is only a modern materialist's silly pipe dream, I might add that at least one commentator has argued that Aristotle's considered view was that the presence of the virtues and vices depends on modifications of the brain and nervous system; and that the relevant mental processes in ethics have accompanying bodily states.[16]) Here the goal will be to match specific virtues with specific chemicals, much in the manner that identity theorists have sought to match other types of mental events with other specific neurophysiological events. However, even on this materialistic reading of the internalist strategy, nothing could be settled about virtues by analysing chemicals without first deciding who has what virtue. For we would first need to know who possessed and exhibited which virtue, and then look for specific physical traces in him that were missing in other agents. But as indicated earlier in my discussion of the externalist strategy, this is precisely what we don't know. An analogy might be the attempt to determine which objects have which colours. Regardless of how much we know about the physical make-up of the objects in question, we must first make colour judgements. However, at this point the analogy breaks down, for the epistemological problems involved in making colour judgements are not nearly as troublesome as are those involved in making virtue judgements.[17]

To raise doubts about our ability to know who is virtuous is to bring scepticism into the centre of virtue ethics, for it is to call into question our ability to identify the very object of our enquiry. This is not the same scepticism which has concerned recent writers such as Bernard Williams

[16] W. F. R. Hardie, *Aristotle's Ethical Theory* (2nd edn., Oxford, 1980), ch. VI, esp. pp. 111–13.

[17] I am indebted to Bill Robinson for help on this criticism of the internalist strategy.

and Thomas Nagel, when they reflect on the fact that 'the natural objects of moral assessment are disturbingly subject to luck'.[18] Theirs is more a scepticism *about* morality, while mine is a scepticism *within* morality. The sort of scepticism to which I am drawing attention occurs after one has convinced oneself that there are genuine moral agents who really do things rather than have things happen to them. As such, my scepticism is narrower but also more morality-specific: it concerns not so much queries about causality and free will as doubts about our ability to know the motives of our own behaviour. As Kant wrote, 'the real morality of actions, their merit or guilt, even that of our own conduct . . . remains entirely hidden from us'.[19] Aquinas too subscribed to a similar scepticism: 'Man is not competent to judge of interior movements, that are hidden, but only of exterior acts which are observable; and yet for the perfection of virtue it is necessary for man to conduct himself rightly in both kinds of acts.'[20]

Now it may be objected here that I am making too much of this epistemological error, that no one actually 'lives it' or contests the fact that it is an error. But I think not. To advocate an ethics of virtue is, among other things, to presuppose that we can clearly differentiate the virtuous from the vicious. Otherwise, the project lacks applicability.

Consider for a moment the Aristotelian notion of the *spoudaios* (good man) or *phronimos* (man of practical wisdom)—two essentially synonymous terms which together have often been called the touchstone of Aristotle's ethics. Again and again in the *Nicomachean Ethics* the *spoudaios/phronimos* is pointed to as the solution to a number of unanswered problems in Aristotle's ethical theory. For instance, we are told to turn to the *spoudaios* in order to learn what really is pleasurable (1113^{a}26–8). And we must turn to an actual *phronimos* in order to find out what the abstract and mysterious *orthos logos* really is (right reason or rational principle—a notion which plays a key role in the definition of virtue) (1107^{a}2, 1144^{b}24). Even in discussing the intellectual virtue of *phronēsis* or practical wisdom, Aristotle begins by announcing that 'we shall get at the truth by considering who are the persons we credit with it' (1140^{a}24). But who are the *phronimoi*, and how do we know one when we see one? Aristotle does say that Pericles 'and men like him' are *phronimoi*, 'because they can see what is good for themselves and what is good for men in general' (1140^{b}8–10). However, beyond this rather casual remark

[18] Thomas Nagel, 'Moral Luck', in *Mortal Questions* (Cambridge, 1979), 28. See also Bernard Williams, 'Moral Luck', in *Moral Luck* (Cambridge, 1981).

[19] Kant, *Critique of Pure Reason*, A552 = B580 , n. 1.

[20] Thomas Aquinas, Saint. *Summa Theologica*, I–II Q. 91, a. 4.

he does not give the reader any hints on how to track down a *phronimos*. Indeed, he does not even see it as a problem worth discussing.

The reasons for this strange lacuna, I suggest, are two. First, Aristotle is dealing with a small face-to-face community, where the pool of potential *phronimoi* generally come from certain well established families who are well known throughout the *polis*. Within a small face-to-face community of this sort, one would naturally expect to find wide agreement about judgements of character. Second, Aristotle's own methodology is itself designed to fit this sort of moral community. He is not advocating a Platonic ethics of universal categories.

Within the context of a *polis* and an ethical theory intended to accompany it, the strategy of pointing to a *phronimos* makes a certain sense. However, to divorce this strategy from its social and economic roots and then to apply it to a very different sort of community—one where people really do not know each other all that well, and where there is wide disagreement on values—does not. And this, I fear, is what contemporary virtue ethicists have tried to do.[21]

STYLE OVER SUBSTANCE

In emphasizing Being over Doing, the Inner over the Outer, virtue theorists also lay themselves open to the charge that they are more concerned with style than with substance. For as I argued earlier, virtue theorists are committed to the view that the moral value of certain key character traits is not exhausted by or even dependent on the value of the actions to which they may give rise. When this gulf between character and conduct is asserted, and joined with the claim that it is agents rather than actions which count morally, the conclusion is that it is not the substance of an agent's actions which is the focus of moral appraisal. The implication here seems to be that if you have style, i.e., the style of the virtuous person, as defined in the context of a concrete moral tradition, it doesn't so much matter what the results are. ('It's not whether you win or lose, but how you play the game that counts.') As Frankena remarks, in a passage which underscores an alleged basic difference between ancient and contemporary virtue ethics:

> The Greeks held . . . that being virtuous entails not just having good motives or intentions but also doing the right thing. Modern views typically differ from Greek views here; perhaps because of the changed ways of thinking introduced by the

[21] I would like to thank Arthur Adkins for discussion on these points.

Judeo-Christian tradition, we tend to believe that being morally good does not entail doing what is actually right . . . even if we believe (as I do) that doing what is actually right involves more than only having a good motive or intention. Today many people go so far as to think that in morality it does not matter much *what* you do; all that matters, they say, is *how* you do it. To parody a late cigarette advertisement; for them it's not how wrong you make it, it's how you make it wrong.[22]

But it is sophistry to claim that the consequences of the lies of gentlemen or Aristotelian *kaloikagathoi* aren't very important, or that the implications of their rudeness are somehow tempered by the fact that they are who they are. This line of thought flies in the face of our basic conviction that moral assessment must strive towards impartiality and the bracketing of morally irrelevant social and economic data.

It seems to me that this particular vice of virtue ethics is analogous to the Hegelian 'duty for duty's sake' critique of formalist deontologies. Virtue-based and duty-based theories are both subject to the 'style over substance' charge because their notion of ends is too weak. Both types of theory speak of ends only in a derivative sense. For the duty-based theorist, the good is an inherent feature of dutiful action, so that the only proclaimed end is right action itself. For the virtue-based theorist, the good is defined in terms of the virtuous agent. ('Virtue is its own reward.') Aristotle, as noted earlier, in distinguishing the true from the apparent good, remarks that 'that which is in truth an object of wish is an object of wish to the good man (*spoudaios*), while any chance thing may be so to the bad man' (*En* 1113^{a}26–28).

While no one (except the most obstinate utilitarian) would deny these two respective ends their place in a list of moral goods, it appears that there is another important type of end which is left completely unaccounted for. This second type of end is what may be called a *product-end*, a result or outcome of action which is distinct from the activity that produces it. (An example would be a catastrophe or its opposite.) Virtue-based and duty-based theories, on the other hand, can account only for *activity-ends*, ends which are inherent features of (virtuous or dutiful) action. Virtue-based theories then, like their duty-based competitors, reveal a structural defect in their lack of attention to product-ends.[23]

Now it might be said that the 'style-over-substance' charge is more

[22] William K. Frankena, *Thinking About Morality* (Ann Arbor, 1980), 52–3.

[23] My own position on this topic is contra that of utilitarianism. I believe that activity-ends are clearly the more important of the two, and that most product-ends ultimately derive their moral value from more fundamental activity-ends. (The importance of saving lives, for instance, borrows its value from the quality of life it makes possible. 'Life at any price' is nonsense.) But I also believe, contra deontology and virtue ethics, that any adequate moral theory must find room for both types of ends.

appropriately directed at those who emphasize Doing over Being, since one can do the right things just to conform or for praise. One can cultivate the externalities, but be inwardly wretched or shallow. I grant that this is a problem for act theorists, but it is a slightly different criticism from mine, using different senses of the words 'style' and 'substance'. 'Style', as used in my criticism, means roughly: 'morally irrelevant mannerisms and behaviour', while 'substance', as I used it, means something like: 'morally relevant results of action'. The 'substance' in this new criticism refers to good moral character and the acts which flow from it, while 'style' here means more 'doing the right thing, but without the proper fixed trait behind it'. However, granted that both 'style over substance' criticisms have some validity, I would also argue that mine points to a greater vice. It is one thing to do what is right without the best disposition, it is another not to do what is right at all.

UTOPIANISM

The last vice I shall mention has a more socio-historical character. It seems to me that there is a bit of utopianism behind the virtue theorist's complaints about the ethics of rules. Surely, one reason there is more emphasis on rules and regulations in modern society is that things have become more complex. Our moral community (in so far as it makes sense to speak of 'community' in these narcissistic times) contains more ethnic, religious, and class groups than did the moral community which Aristotle theorized about. Unfortunately, each segment of society has not only its own interests but its own set of virtues as well. There is no general agreed upon and significant expression of desirable moral character in such a world. Indeed, our pluralist culture prides itself on and defines itself in terms of its alleged value neutrality and its lack of allegiance to any one moral tradition. This absence of agreement regarding human purposes and moral ideals seems to drive us (partly out of lack of alternatives) to a more legalistic form of morality. To suppose that academic theorists can alter the situation simply by re-emphasizing certain concepts is illusory. Our world lacks the sort of moral cohesiveness and value unity which traditional virtue theorists saw as prerequisites of a viable moral community.[24]

The table of vices sketched above is not intended to be exhaustive, but even in its incomplete state I believe it spells trouble for virtue-based moral theories. For the shortcomings described are not esoteric—they

[24] For similar criticism, see Mayo, *Ethics and the Moral Life*, 217; and MacIntyre, *After Virtue*.

concern mundane features of moral experience which any minimally adequate moral theory should be expected to account for. While I do think that contemporary virtue theorists are correct in asserting that any adequate moral theory must account for the fact of character, and that no ethics of rules, pure and unsupplemented, is up to this job, the above analysis also suggests that no ethics of virtue, pure and unsupplemented, can be satisfactory.

My own view (which can only be stated summarily here) is that we need to begin efforts to coordinate irreducible or strong notions of virtue along with irreducible or strong conceptions of the various act notions into our conceptual scheme of morality. This appeal for coordination will not satisfy those theorists who continue to think in the single-element or mononomic tradition (a tradition which contemporary virtue-based theorists have inherited from their duty-based and goal-based ancestors), but I do believe that it will result in a more realistic account of our moral experience. The moral field is not unitary, and the values we employ in making moral judgements sometimes have fundamentally different sources. No single reductive method can offer a realistic means of prioritizing these different values. There exists no single scale by means of which disparate moral considerations can always be measured, added, and balanced.[25] The theoretician's quest for conceptual economy and elegance has been won at too great a price, for the resulting reductionist definitions of the moral concepts are not true to the facts of moral experience. It is important now to see the ethics of virtue and the ethics of rules as adding up, rather than as cancelling each other out.

[25] See Thomas Nagel, 'The Fragmentation of Value', in *Mortal Questions*, 131–2, 135. A similar position is defended by Charles Taylor in his recent essay, 'The Diversity of Goods', in A. Sen and B. Williams (eds.), *Utilitarianism and Beyond* (Cambridge, 1982).

Earlier versions of this essay were read at the 1982 American Philosophical Association Pacific Division Meetings, and at the 1981 Iowa Philosophical Society Meeting at Grinnell College. I am very grateful for useful criticisms and suggestions offered on these occasions. I would also like to thank Marcia Baron, Lawrence Becker, James Gustafson, W. D. Hamlyn, Bob Hollinger, Joe Kupfer, and Warner Wick for criticisms of earlier drafts. Portions of the present version are taken from my doctoral dissertation, 'The Elements of Ethics: Toward a Topography of the Moral Field' (University of Chicago, 1981).

11

VIRTUE THEORY AND ABORTION

ROSALIND HURSTHOUSE

The sort of ethical theory derived from Aristotle, variously described as virtue ethics, virtue-based ethics, or neo-Aristotelianism, is becoming better known, and is now quite widely recognized as at least a possible rival to deontological and utilitarian theories. With recognition has come criticism, of varying quality. In this article I shall discuss nine separate criticisms that I have frequently encountered, most of which seem to me to betray an inadequate grasp either of the structure of virtue theory or of what would be involved in thinking about a real moral issue in its terms. In the first half I aim particularly to secure an understanding which will reveal that many of these criticisms are simply misplaced, and to articulate what I take to be the major criticism of virtue theory. I reject this criticism, but do not claim that it is necessarily misplaced. In the second half I aim to deepen that understanding and highlight the issues raised by the criticisms by illustrating what the theory looks like when it is applied to a particular issue, in this case, abortion.

VIRTUE THEORY

Virtue theory can be laid out in a framework that reveals clearly some of the essential similarities and differences between it and some versions of deontological and utilitarian theories. I begin with a rough sketch of familiar versions of the latter two sorts of theory, not, of course, with the intention of suggesting that they exhaust the field, but on the assumption that their very familiarity will provide a helpful contrast with virtue theory. Suppose a deontological theory has basically the following framework. We begin with a premiss providing a specification of right action:

P.1. An action is right iff it is in accordance with a moral rule or principle.

This is a purely formal specification, forging a link between the concepts of *right action* and *moral rule*, and gives one no guidance until one knows what a moral rule is. So the next thing the theory needs is a premiss about that:

P.2. A moral rule is one that . . .

Historically, an acceptable completion of P.2 would have been

(i) is laid on us by God

or

(ii) is required by natural law.

In secular versions (not, of course, unconnected to God's being pure reason, and the universality of natural law) we get such completions as

(iii) is laid on us by reason

or

(iv) is required by rationality

or

(v) would command universal rational acceptance

or

(vi) would be the object of choice of all rational beings

and so on. Such a specification forges a second conceptual link, between the concepts of *moral rule* and *rationality*.

We have here the skeleton of a familiar version of a deontological theory, a skeleton which reveals that what is essential to any such version is the links between *right action*, *moral rule*, and *rationality*. That these form the basic structure can be seen particularly vividly if we lay out the familiar act-utilitarianism in such a way as to bring out the contrasts.

Act-utilitarianism begins with a premiss that provides a specification of right action:

P.1. An action is right iff it promotes the best consequences.

It thereby forges the link between the concepts of *right action* and *consequences*. It goes on to specify what the best consequences are in its second premiss:

P.2. The best consequences are those in which happiness is maximized.

It thereby forges the link between *consequences* and *happiness*.

Now let us consider what a skeletal virtue theory looks like. It begins with a specification of right action:

P.1. An action is right iff it is what a virtuous agent would do in the circumstances.[1]

This, like the first premisses of the other two sorts of theory, is a purely formal principle, giving one no guidance as to what to do, which forges the conceptual link between *right action* and *virtuous agent*. Like the other theories, it must, of course, go on to specify what the latter is. The first step towards this may appear quite trivial, but is needed to correct a prevailing tendency among many critics to define the virtuous agent as one who is disposed to act in accordance with a deontologist's moral rules.

P.1*a*. A virtuous agent is one who acts virtuously, that is, one who has and exercises the virtues.

This subsidiary premiss lays bare the fact that virtue theory aims to provide a non-trivial specification of the virtuous agent *via* a non-trivial specification of the virtues, which is given in its second premiss:

P.2. A virtue is a character trait a human being needs to flourish or live well.

This premiss forges a conceptual link between *virtue* and *flourishing* (or *living well* or *eudaimonia*). And, just as deontology, in theory, then goes on to argue that each favoured rule meets its specification, so virtue ethics, in theory, goes on to argue that each favoured character trait meets its.

There are the bare bones of virtue theory: here follow five brief comments directed to some misconceived criticisms which should be cleared out of the way.

First, the theory does not have a peculiar weakness or problem in virtue of the fact that it involves the concept of *eudaimonia* (a standard criticism

[1] It should be noted that this premiss intentionally allows for the possibility that two virtuous agents, faced with the same choice in the same circumstances, may act differently. For example, one might opt for taking her father off the life-support machine and the other for leaving her father on it. The theory requires that neither agent thinks that what the other does is wrong (see n. 4 below), but it explicitly allows that no action is uniquely right in such a case—both are right. It also intentionally allows for the possibility that in some circumstances—those into which no virtuous agent could have got herself—no action is right. I explore this premiss at greater length in 'Applying Virtue Ethics', in *Virtues and Reasons*, ed. Rosalind Hursthouse, Gavin Lawrence, and Warren Quinn (Oxford, 1995).

being that this concept is hopelessly obscure). Now no virtue theorist will pretend that the concept of human flourishing is an easy one to grasp. I will not even claim here (though I would elsewhere) that it is no more obscure than the concepts of *rationality* and *happiness*, since, if our vocabulary were more limited, we might, *faute de mieux*, call it (human) *rational happiness*, and thereby reveal that it has at least some of the difficulties of both. But virtue theory has never, so far as I know, been dismissed on the grounds of the *comparative* obscurity of this central concept; rather, the popular view is that it has a problem with this which deontology and utilitarianism in no way share. This, I think, is clearly false. Both *rationality* and *happiness*, as they figure in their respective theories, are rich and difficult concepts—hence all the disputes about the various tests for a rule's being an object of rational choice, and the disputes, dating back to Mill's introduction of the higher and lower pleasures, about what constitutes happiness.

Secondly, the theory is not trivially circular; it does not specify right action in terms of the virtuous agent and then immediately specify the virtuous agent in terms of right action. Rather, it specifies her in terms of the virtues, and then specifies these, not merely as dispositions to right action, but as the character traits (which are dispositions to feel and react as well as act in certain ways) required for *eudaimonia*.[2]

Thirdly, it does answer the question 'What should I do?' as well as the question 'What sort of person should I be?' (That is, it is not, as one of the catchphrases has it, concerned only with Being and not with Doing.)

Fourthly, the theory does, to a certain extent, answer this question by coming up with rules or principles (contrary to the common claim that it does not come up with any rules or principles). Every virtue generates a positive instruction (act justly, kindly, courageously, honestly, etc.) and every vice a prohibition (do not act unjustly, cruelly, like a coward, dishonestly, etc.). So trying to decide what to do within the framework of virtue theory is not, as some people seem to imagine, necessarily a matter of taking one's favoured candidate for a virtuous person and asking oneself,

[2] There is, of course, the further question of whether the theory eventually describes a larger circle and winds up relying on the concept of right action in its interpretation of *eudaimonia*. In denying that the theory is trivially circular, I do not pretend to answer this intricate question. It is certainly true that virtue theory does not claim that the correct conception of *eudaimonia* can be got from 'an independent "value-free" investigation of human nature' (John McDowell, 'The Role of *Eudaimonia* in Aristotle's Ethics', Amélie O. Rorty (ed.), *Essays on Aristotle's Ethics* (Berkeley and Los Angeles, 1980)). The sort of training that is required for acquiring the correct conception no doubt involves being taught from early on such things as 'Decent people do this sort of thing, not that' and 'To do such and such is the mark of a depraved character' (cf. *Nicomachean Ethics* 1110^{a}22). But whether this counts as relying on the concept of right (or wrong) action seems to me very unclear and requiring much discussion.

'What would they do in these circumstances?' (as if the raped 15-year-old girl might be supposed to say to herself, 'Now would Socrates have an abortion if he were in my circumstances?' and as if someone who had never known or heard of anyone very virtuous were going to be left, according to the theory, with no way to decide what to do at all). The agent may instead ask herself, 'If I were to do such and such now, would I be acting justly or unjustly (or neither), kindly or unkindly [and so on]?' I shall consider below the problem created by cases in which such a question apparently does not yield an answer to 'What should I do?' (because, say, the alternatives are being unkind or being unjust); here my claim is only that it sometimes does—the agent may employ her concepts of the virtues and vices directly, rather than imagining what some hypothetical exemplar would do.

Fifthly, (a point that is implicit but should be made explicit), virtue theory is not committed to any sort of reductionism which involves defining all our moral concepts in terms of the virtuous agent. On the contrary, it relies on a lot of very significant moral concepts. Charity or benevolence, for instance, is the virtue whose concern is the *good* of others; that concept of *good* is related to the concept of *evil* or *harm*, and they are both related to the concepts of the *worthwhile*, the *advantageous*, and the *pleasant*. If I have the wrong conception of what is worthwhile and advantageous and pleasant, then I shall have the wrong conception of what is good for, and harmful to, myself and others, and, even with the best will in the world, will lack the virtue of charity, which involves getting all this right. (This point will be illustrated at some length in the second half of this article; I mention it here only in support of the fact that no virtue theorist who takes her inspiration from Aristotle would even contemplate aiming at reductionism.[3])

Let me now, with equal brevity, run through two more standard criticisms of virtue theory (the sixth and seventh of my nine) to show that, though not entirely misplaced, they do not highlight problems peculiar to that theory but, rather, problems that are shared by familiar versions of deontology.

One common criticism is that we do not know which character traits are the virtues, or that this is open to much dispute, or particularly subject to the threat of moral scepticism or 'pluralism'[4] or cultural relativism. But the

[3] Cf. Bernard Williams's point in *Ethics and the Limits of Philosophy* (London, 1985) that we need an enriched ethical vocabulary, not a cut-down one.

[4] I put *pluralism* in scare quotes to serve as a warning that virtue theory is not incompatible with all forms of it. It allows for 'competing conceptions' of *eudaimonia* and the worthwhile, for instance, in the sense that it allows for a plurality of flourishing lives—the theory need not follow Aristotle in specifying the life of contemplation as the only one that truly constitutes *eudaimonia*

parallel roles played by the second premisses of both deontological and virtue theories reveal the way in which both sorts of theory share this problem. It is at the stage at which one tries to get the right conclusions to drop out of the bottom of one's theory that, *theoretically*, all the work has to be done. Rule deontologists know that they want to get 'don't kill', 'keep promises', 'cherish your children', and so on as the rules that meet their specification, whatever it may be. They also know that any of these can be disputed, that some philosopher may claim, of any one of them, that it is reasonable to reject it, and that at least people claim that there has been, for each rule, some culture which rejected it. Similarly, the virtue theorists know that they want to get justice, charity, fidelity, courage, and so on as the character traits needed for *eudaimonia*; and they also know that any of these can be disputed, that some philosopher will say of any one of them that it is reasonable to reject it as a virtue, and that there is said to be, for each character trait, some culture that has thus rejected it.

This is a problem for both theories, and the virtue theorist certainly does not find it any harder to argue against moral scepticism, 'pluralism', or cultural relativism than the deontologist. Each theory has to stick out its neck and say, in some cases, 'This person/these people/other cultures are (or would be) in error,' and find some grounds for saying this.

Another criticism (the seventh) often made is that virtue ethics has unresolvable conflict built into it. 'It is common knowledge', it is said, 'that the requirements of the virtues can conflict; charity may prompt me to end the frightful suffering of the person in my care by killing him, but justice bids me to stay my hand. To tell my brother that his wife is being unfaithful to him would be honest and loyal, but it would be kinder to keep quiet about it. So which should I do? In such cases, virtue ethics has nothing helpful to say.' (This is one version of the problem, mentioned above, that considering whether a proposed action falls under a virtue or vice term does not always yield an answer to 'What should I do?')

The obvious reply to this criticism is that rule deontology notoriously suffers from the same problem, arising not only from the fact that its rules can apparently conflict, but also from the fact that, at first blush, it appears

(if he does). But the conceptions 'compete' only in the sense that, within a single flourishing life, not everything worthwhile can be fitted in; the theory does not allow that two people with a correct conception of *eudaimonia* can disagree over whether the way the other is living constitutes flourishing. Moreover, the theory is committed to the strong thesis that the same set of character traits is needed for *any* flourishing life; it will not allow that, for instance, soldiers need courage but wives and mothers do not, or that judges need justice but can live well despite lacking kindness. (This obviously is related to the point made in n. 1 above.) For an interesting discussion of pluralism (different interpretations thereof) and virtue theory, see Douglas B. Rasmussen, 'Liberalism and Natural End Ethics', *American Philosophical Quarterly*, 27 (1990), 153–61.

that one and the same rule (e.g., preserve life) can yield contrary instructions in a particular case.[5] As before, I agree that this is a problem for virtue theory, but deny that it is a problem peculiar to it.

Finally, I want to articulate, and reject, what I take to be the major criticism of virtue theory. Perhaps because it is *the* major criticism, the reflection of a very general sort of disquiet about the theory, it is hard to state clearly—especially for someone who does not accept it—but it goes something like this.[6] My interlocutor says:

> Virtue theory can't *get* us anywhere in real moral issues because it's bound to be all assertion and no argument. You admit that the best it can come up with in the way of action-guiding rules are the ones that rely on the virtue and vice concepts, such as 'act charitably', 'don't act cruelly', and so on; and, as if that weren't bad enough, you admit that these virtue concepts, such as charity, presuppose concepts such as the *good*, and the *worthwhile*, and so on. But that means that any virtue theorist who writes about real moral issues must rely on her audience's agreeing with her application of all these concepts, and hence accepting all the premisses in which those applications are enshrined. But some other virtue theorist might take different premisses about these matters, and come up with very different conclusions, and, within the terms of the theory, there is no way to distinguish between the two. While there is agreement, virtue theory can repeat conventional wisdom, preserve the status quo, but it can't get us anywhere in the way that a normative ethical theory is supposed to, namely, by providing rational grounds for acceptance of its practical conclusions.

My strategy will be to split this criticism into two: one (the eighth) addressed to the virtue theorist's employment of the virtue and vice concepts enshrined in her rules—act charitably, honestly, and so on—and the other (the ninth) addressed to her employment of concepts such as that of the *worthwhile*. Each objection, I shall maintain, implicitly appeals to a certain *condition of adequacy* on a normative moral theory, and in each case, I shall claim, the condition of adequacy, once made explicit, is utterly implausible.

Yes, it is true that when she discusses real moral issues, the virtue theorist has to assert that certain actions are honest, dishonest, or neither; charitable, uncharitable, or neither. And it is true that this is often a very difficult matter to decide; her rules are not always easy to apply. But this counts as a criticism of the theory only if we assume, as a condition of adequacy, that any adequate action-guiding theory must make the difficult

[5] e.g., in Williams's Jim and Pedro case in J. J. C. Smart and Bernard Williams, *Utilitarianism: For and Against* (London, 1973).

[6] Intimations of this criticism constantly come up in discussion; the clearest statement of it I have found is by Onora O'Neill, in her review of Stephen Clark's *The Moral Status of Animals*, in *Journal of Philosophy*, 77 (1980), 440–6. For a response I am much in sympathy with, see Cora Diamond, 'Anything But Argument?', *Philosophical Investigations*, 5 (1982), 23–41.

business of knowing what to do if one is to act well easy, that it must provide clear guidance about what ought not to be done which any reasonably clever adolescent could follow if she chose. But such a condition of adequacy is implausible. Acting rightly *is* difficult, and *does* call for much moral wisdom, and the relevant condition of adequacy, which virtue theory meets, is that it should have built into it an explanation of a truth expressed by Aristotle,[7] namely, that moral knowledge—unlike mathematical knowledge—cannot be acquired merely by attending lectures and is not characteristically to be found in people too young to have had much experience of life. There are youthful mathematical geniuses, but rarely, if ever, youthful moral geniuses, and this shows us something significant about the sort of knowledge that moral knowledge is. Virtue ethics builds this in straight off precisely by couching its rules in terms whose application may indeed call for the most delicate and sensitive judgement.

Here we may discern a slightly different version of the problem that there are cases in which applying the virtue and vice terms does not yield an answer to 'What should I do?' Suppose someone 'youthful in character', as Aristotle puts it, having applied the relevant terms, finds herself landed with what is, unbeknownst to her, a case not of real but of apparent conflict, arising from a misapplication of those terms. Then she will not be able to decide what to do unless she knows of a virtuous agent to look to for guidance. But her quandary is (*ex hypothesi*) the result of her lack of wisdom, and just what virtue theory expects. Someone hesitating over whether to reveal a hurtful truth, for example, thinking it would be kind but dishonest or unjust to lie, may need to realize, with respect to these particular circumstances, not that kindness is more (or less) important than honesty or justice, and not that honesty or justice sometimes requires one to act unkindly or cruelly, but that one does people no kindness by concealing this sort of truth from them, hurtful as it may be. This is the *type* of thing (I use it only as an example) that people with moral wisdom know about, involving the correct application of *kind*, and that people without such wisdom find difficult.

What about the virtue theorist's reliance on concepts such as that of the *worthwhile*? If such reliance is to count as a fault in the theory, what condition of adequacy is implicitly in play? It must be that any good normative theory should provide answers to questions about real moral issues whose truth is in no way determined by truths about what is worthwhile, or what really matters in human life. Now although people are initially inclined to reject out of hand the claim that the practical conclu-

[7] Aristotle, *Nicomachean Ethics* 1142ª12–16.

sions of a normative moral theory have to be based on premisses about what is truly worthwhile, the alternative, once it is made explicit, may look even more unacceptable. Consider what the condition of adequacy entails. If truths about what is worthwhile (or truly good, or serious, or about what matters in human life) do *not* have to be appealed to in order to answer questions about real moral issues, then I might sensibly seek guidance about what I ought to do from someone who had declared in advance that she knew nothing about such matters, or from someone who said that, although she had opinions about them, these were quite likely to be wrong but that this did not matter, because they would play no determining role in the advice she gave me.

I should emphasize that we are talking about real moral issues and real guidance; I want to know whether I should have an abortion, take my mother off the life-support machine, leave academic life and become a doctor in the Third World, give up my job with the firm that is using animals in its experiments, tell my father he has cancer. Would I go to someone who says she has *no* views about what is worthwhile in life? Or to someone who says that, as a matter of fact, she tends to think that the only thing that matters is having a good time, but has a normative theory that is consistent both with this view and with my own rather more puritanical one, which will yield the guidance I need?

I take it as a premiss that this is absurd. The relevant condition of adequacy should be that the practical conclusions of a good normative theory *must* be in part determined by premisses about what is worthwhile, important, and so on. Thus I reject this 'major criticism' of virtue theory, that it cannot get us anywhere in the way that a normative moral theory is supposed to. According to my response, a normative theory which any clever adolescent can apply, or which reaches practical conclusions that are in no way determined by premisses about what is truly worthwhile, serious, and so on, is guaranteed to be an inadequate theory.

Although I reject this criticism, I have not argued that it is misplaced and that it necessarily manifests a failure to understand what virtue theory is. My rejection is based on premisses about what an adequate normative theory must be like—what sorts of concepts it must contain, and what sort of account it must give of moral knowledge—and thereby claims, implicitly, that the 'major criticism' manifests a failure to understand what an *adequate normative theory* is. But, as a matter of fact, I think the criticism is often made by people who have no idea of what virtue theory looks like when applied to a real moral issue; they drastically underestimate the variety of ways in which the virtue and vice concepts, and the others, such as that of the *worthwhile*, figure in such discussion.

As promised, I now turn to an illustration of such discussion, applying virtue theory to abortion. Before I embark on this tendentious business, I should remind the reader of the aim of this discussion. I am not, in this article, trying to solve the problem of abortion; I am illustrating how virtue theory directs one to think about it. It might indeed be said that thinking about the problem in this way 'solves' it by *dis*solving it, in so far as it leads one to the conclusion that there is no single right answer, but a variety of particular answers, and in what follows I am certainly trying to make that conclusion seem plausible. But, that granted, it should still be said that I am not trying to 'solve the problem*s*' in the practical sense of telling people that they should, or should not, do this or that if they are pregnant and contemplating abortion in these or those particular circumstances.

I do not assume, or expect, that all of my readers will agree with everything I am about to say. On the contrary, given the plausible assumption that some are morally wiser than I am, and some less so, the theory has built into it that we are bound to disagree on some points. For instance, we may well disagree about the particular application of some of the virtue and vice terms; and we may disagree about what is worthwhile or serious, worthless or trivial. But my aim is to make clear how these concepts figure in a discussion conducted in terms of virtue theory. What is at issue is whether these concepts are indeed the ones that should come in, that is, whether virtue theory should be criticized for employing them. The problem of abortion highlights this issue dramatically, since virtue theory quite transforms the discussion of it.

ABORTION

As everyone knows, the morality of abortion is commonly discussed in relation to just two considerations: first, and predominantly, the status of the foetus and whether or not it is the sort of thing that may or may not be innocuously or justifiably killed; secondly, and less predominantly (when, that is, the discussion concerns the *morality* of abortion rather than the question of permissible legislation in a just society), women's rights. If one thinks within this familiar framework, one may well be puzzled about what virtue theory, as such, could contribute. Some people assume the discussion will be conducted solely in terms of what the virtuous agent would or would not do (cf. the third, fourth, and fifth criticisms above). Others assume that only justice, or at most justice and charity,[8] will be

[8] It seems likely that some people have been misled by Foot's discussion of euthanasia (through no fault of hers) into thinking that a virtue theorist's discussion of terminating human

applied to the issue, generating a discussion very similar to Judith Jarvis Thomson's.[9]

Now if this is the way the virtue theorist's discussion of abortion is imagined to be, no wonder people think little of it. It seems obvious in advance that in any such discussion there must be either a great deal of extremely tendentious application of the virtue terms *just*, *charitable*, and so on or a lot of rhetorical appeal to 'this is what only the virtuous agent knows'. But these are caricatures; they fail to appreciate the way in which virtue theory quite transforms the discussion of abortion by dismissing the two familiar dominating considerations as, in a way, fundamentally irrelevant. In what way or ways, I hope to make both clear and plausible.

Let us first consider women's rights. Let me emphasize again that we are discussing the *morality* of abortion, not the rights and wrongs of laws prohibiting or permitting it. If we suppose that women do have a moral right to do as they choose with their own bodies, or, more particularly, to terminate their pregnancies, then it may well follow that a *law* forbidding abortion would be unjust. Indeed, even if they have no such right, such a law might be, as things stand at the moment, unjust, or impractical, or inhumane: on this issue I have nothing to say in this article. But, putting all questions about the justice or injustice of laws to one side, and supposing only that women have such a moral right, *nothing* follows from this supposition about the morality of abortion, according to virtue theory, once it is noted (quite generally, not with particular reference to abortion) that in exercising a moral right I can do something cruel, or callous, or selfish, light-minded, self-righteous, stupid, inconsiderate, disloyal, dishonest—that is, act viciously.[10] Love and friendship do not survive their parties' constantly insisting on their rights, nor do people live well when they think that getting what they have a right to is of pre-eminent importance; they harm others, and they harm themselves. So whether women have a moral right to terminate their pregnancies is irrelevant within virtue theory, for it

life will be conducted exclusively in terms of justice and charity (and the corresponding vice terms) (Philippa Foot, 'Euthanasia', *Philosophy and Public Affairs*, 6/2 (Winter 1977), 85–112). But the act-category *euthanasia* is a very special one, at least as defined in her article, since such an act must be done 'for the sake of the one who is to die'. Building a virtuous motivation into the specification of the act in this way immediately rules out the application of many other vice terms.

[9] Judith Jarvis Thomson, 'A Defense of Abortion', *Philosophy and Public Affairs*, 1/1 (Fall 1971), 47–66. One could indeed regard this article as proto-virtue theory (no doubt to the surprise of the author) if the concepts of callousness and kindness were allowed more weight.

[10] One possible qualification: if one ties the concept of justice very closely to rights, then if women do have a moral right to terminate their pregnancies it *may* follow that in doing so they do not act unjustly. (Cf. Thomson, 'A Defense of Abortion'.) But it is debatable whether even that much follows.

is irrelevant to the question 'In having an abortion in these circumstances, would the agent be acting virtuously or viciously or neither?'

What about the consideration of the status of the foetus—what can virtue theory say about that? One might say that this issue is not in the province of *any* moral theory; it is a metaphysical question, and an extremely difficult one at that. Must virtue theory then wait upon metaphysics to come up with the answer?

At first sight it might seem so. For virtue is said to involve knowledge, and part of this knowledge consists in having the *right* attitude to things. 'Right' here does not just mean 'morally right' or 'proper' or 'nice' in the modern sense; it means 'accurate, true'. One cannot have the right or correct attitude to something if the attitude is based on or involves false beliefs. And this suggests that if the status of the foetus is relevant to the rightness or wrongness of abortion, its status must be known, as a truth, to the fully wise and virtuous person.

But the sort of wisdom that the fully virtuous person has is not supposed to be recondite; it does not call for fancy philosophical sophistication, and it does not depend upon, let alone wait upon, the discoveries of academic philosophers.[11] And this entails the following, rather startling, conclusion: that the status of the foetus—that issue over which so much ink has been spilt—is, according to virtue theory, simply not relevant to the rightness or wrongness of abortion (within, that is, a secular morality).

Or rather, since that is clearly too radical a conclusion, it is in a sense relevant, but only in the sense that the familiar biological facts are relevant. By 'the familiar biological facts' I mean the facts that most human societies are and have been familiar with—that, standardly (but not invariably), pregnancy occurs as the result of sexual intercourse, that it lasts about nine months, during which time the foetus grows and develops, that standardly it terminates in the birth of a living baby, and that this is how we all come to be.

It might be thought that this distinction—between the familiar biological facts and the status of the foetus—is a distinction without a difference. But this is not so. To attach relevance to the status of the foetus, in the sense in which virtue theory claims it is not relevant, is to be gripped by the conviction that we must go beyond the familiar biological facts, deriving

[11] This is an assumption of virtue theory, and I do not attempt to defend it here. An adequate discussion of it would require a separate article, since, although most moral philosophers would be chary of claiming that intellectual sophistication is a necessary condition of moral wisdom or virtue, most of us, from Plato onwards, tend to write as if this were so. Sorting out which claims about moral knowledge are committed to this kind of élitism and which can, albeit with difficulty, be reconciled with the idea that moral knowledge can be acquired by anyone who really wants it would be a major task.

some sort of conclusion from them, such as that the foetus has rights, or is not a person, or something similar. It is also to believe that this exhausts the relevance of the familiar biological facts, that all they are relevant to is the status of the foetus and whether or not it is the sort of thing that may or may not be killed.

These convictions, I suspect, are rooted in the desire to solve the problem of abortion by getting it to fall under some general rule such as 'You ought not to kill anything with the right to life but may kill anything else.' But they have resulted in what should surely strike any non-philosopher as a most bizarre aspect of nearly all the current philosophical literature on abortion, namely, that, far from treating abortion as a unique moral problem, markedly unlike any other, nearly everything written on the status of the foetus and its bearing on the abortion issue would be consistent with the facts of human reproduction (to say nothing of family life) being totally different from what they are. Imagine that you are an alien extraterrestrial anthropologist who does not know that the human race is roughly 50 per cent female and 50 per cent male, or that our only (natural) form of reproduction involves heterosexual intercourse, viviparous birth, and the female's (and only the female's) being pregnant for nine months, or that females are capable of childbearing from late childhood to late middle age, or that childbearing is painful, dangerous, and emotionally involving—do you think you would pick up these facts from the hundreds of articles written on the status of the foetus? I am quite sure you would not. And that, I think, shows that the current philosophical literature on abortion has got badly out of touch with reality.

Now if we are using virtue theory, our first question is not 'What do the familiar biological facts show—what can be derived from them about the status of the foetus?' but 'How do these facts figure in the practical reasoning, actions and passions, thoughts and reactions, of the virtuous and the non-virtuous? What is the mark of having the right attitude to these facts and what manifests having the wrong attitude to them?' This immediately makes essentially relevant not only all the facts about human reproduction I mentioned above, but a whole range of facts about our emotions in relation to them as well. I mean such facts as that human parents, both male and female, tend to care passionately about their offspring, and that family relationships are among the deepest and strongest in our lives—and, significantly, among the longest-lasting.

These facts make it obvious that pregnancy is not just one among many other physical conditions; and hence that anyone who genuinely believes that an abortion is comparable to a haircut or an appendectomy is mistaken.[12] The fact that the premature termination of a pregnancy is, in some sense, the cutting-off of a new human life, and thereby, like the procreation of a new human life, connects with all our thoughts about human life and death, parenthood, and family relationships, must make it a serious matter. To disregard this fact about it, to think of abortion as nothing but the killing of something that does not matter, or as nothing but the exercise of some right or rights one has, or as the incidental means to some desirable state of affairs, is to do something callous and light-minded, the sort of thing that no virtuous and wise person would do. It is to have the wrong attitude not only to foetuses, but more generally to human life and death, parenthood, and family relationships.

Although I say that the facts make this obvious, I know that this is one of my tendentious points. In partial support of it I note that even the most dedicated proponents of the view that deliberate abortion is just like an appendectomy or haircut rarely hold the same view of spontaneous abortion, that is, miscarriage. It is not so tendentious of me to claim that to react to people's grief over miscarriage by saying, or even thinking, 'What a fuss about nothing!' would be callous and light-minded, whereas to try to laugh someone out of grief over an appendectomy scar or a botched haircut would not be. It is hard to give this point due prominence within act-centred theories, for the inconsistency is an inconsistency in attitude about the seriousness of loss of life, not in beliefs about which acts are right or wrong. Moreover, an act-centred theorist may say, 'Well, there is nothing wrong with *thinking* "What a fuss about nothing!" as long as you do not say it and hurt the person who is grieving. And besides, we cannot be held responsible for our thoughts, only for the intentional actions they give rise to.' But the character traits that virtue theory emphasizes are not simply dispositions to intentional actions, but a seamless disposition to certain actions and passions, thoughts and reactions.

To say that the cutting-off of a human life is always a matter of some

[12] Mary Anne Warren, in 'On the Moral and Legal Status of Abortion', *Monist*, 57 (1973), sect. 1, says of the opponents of restrictive laws governing abortion that 'their conviction (for the most part) is that abortion is not a *morally* serious and extremely unfortunate, even though sometimes justified, act, comparable to killing in self-defense or to letting the violinist die, but rather is closer to being a *morally neutral* act, like cutting one's hair' (emphasis added). I would like to think that no one *genuinely* believes this. But certainly in discussion, particularly when arguing against restrictive laws or the suggestion that remorse over abortion might be appropriate, I have found that some people *say* they believe it (and often cite Warren's article, albeit inaccurately, despite its age). Those who allow that it is morally serious, and far from morally neutral, have to argue against restrictive laws, or the appropriateness of remorse, on a very different ground from that laid down by the premiss 'The foetus is just part of the woman's body (and she has a right to determine what happens to her body and should not feel guilt about anything she does to it).'

seriousness, at any stage, is not to deny the relevance of gradual foetal development. Notwithstanding the well-worn point that clear boundary lines cannot be drawn, our emotions and attitudes regarding the foetus do change as it develops, and again when it is born, and indeed further as the baby grows. Abortion for shallow reasons in the later stages is much more shocking than abortion for the same reasons in the early stages in a way that matches the fact that deep grief over miscarriage in the later stages is more appropriate than it is over miscarriage in the earlier stages (when, that is, the grief is solely about the loss of *this* child, not about as might be the case, the loss of one's only hope of having a child or of having one's husband's child). Imagine (or recall) a woman who already has children; she has not intended to have more, but finds herself unexpectedly pregnant. Though contrary to her plans, the pregnancy, once established as a fact, is welcomed—and then she loses the embryo almost immediately. If this were bemoaned as a tragedy, it would, I think, be a misapplication of the concept of what is tragic. But it may still properly be mourned as a loss. The grief is expressed in such terms as 'I shall always wonder how she or he would have turned out' or 'When I look at the others, I shall think, "How different their lives would have been if this other one had been part of them."' It would, I take it, be callous and light-minded to say, or think, 'Well, she has already *got* four children; what's the problem?'; it would be neither, nor arrogantly intrusive in the case of a close friend, to try to correct prolonged mourning by saying, 'I know it's sad, but it's not a tragedy; rejoice in the ones you have.' The application of *tragic* becomes more appropriate as the foetus grows, for the mere fact that one has lived with it for longer, conscious of its existence, makes a difference. To shrug off an early abortion is understandable just because it is very hard to be fully conscious of the foetus's existence in the early stages and hence hard to appreciate that an early abortion is the destruction of life. It is particularly hard for the young and inexperienced to appreciate this, because appreciation of it usually comes only with experience.

I do not mean 'with the experience of having an abortion' (though that may be part of it) but, quite generally, 'with the experience of life'. Many women who have borne children contrast their later pregnancies with their first successful one, saying that in the later ones they were conscious of a new life growing in them from very early on. And, more generally, as one reaches the age at which the next generation is coming up close behind one, the counterfactuals 'If I, or she, had had an abortion, Alice, or Bob, would not have been born' acquire a significant application, which casts a new light on the conditionals 'If I or Alice have an abortion then some Caroline or Bill will not be born.'

The fact that pregnancy is not just one among many physical conditions does not mean that one can never regard it in that light without manifesting a vice. When women are in very poor physical health, or worn out from childbearing, or forced to do very physically demanding jobs, then they cannot be described as self-indulgent, callous, irresponsible, or light-minded if they seek abortions mainly with a view to avoiding pregnancy as the physical condition that it is. To go through with a pregnancy when one is utterly exhausted, or when one's job consists of crawling along tunnels hauling coal, as many women in the nineteenth century were obliged to do, is perhaps heroic, but people who do not achieve heroism are not necessarily vicious. That they can view the pregnancy only as eight months of misery, followed by hours if not days of agony and exhaustion, and abortion only as the blessed escape from this prospect, is entirely understandable and does not manifest any lack of serious respect for human life or a shallow attitude to motherhood. What it does show is that something is terribly amiss in the conditions of their lives, which makes it so hard to recognize pregnancy and childbearing as the good that they can be.

In relation to this last point I should draw attention to the way in which virtue theory has a sort of built-in indexicality. Philosophers arguing against anything remotely resembling a belief in the sanctity of life (which the above claims clearly embody) frequently appeal to the existence of other communities in which abortion and infanticide are practised. We should not automatically assume that it is impossible that some other communities could be morally inferior to our own; maybe some are, or have been, precisely in so far as their members are, typically, callous or light-minded or unjust. But in communities in which life is a great deal tougher for everyone than it is in ours, having the right attitude to human life and death, parenthood, and family relationships might well manifest itself in ways that are unlike ours. When it is essential to survival that most members of the community fend for themselves at a very young age or work during most of their waking hours, selective abortion or infanticide might be practised either as a form of genuine euthanasia or for the sake of the community and not, I think, be thought callous or light-minded. But this does not make everything all right; as before, it shows that there is something amiss with the conditions of their lives, which are making it impossible for them to live really well.[13]

The foregoing discussion, in so far as it emphasizes the right attitude to human life and death, parallels to a certain extent those standard discus-

[13] For another example of the way in which 'tough conditions' can make a difference to what is involved in having the right attitude to human life and death and family relationships, see the concluding sentences of Foot, 'Euthanasia'.

sions of abortion that concentrate on it solely as an issue of killing. But it does not, as those discussions do, gloss over the fact, emphasized by those who discuss the morality of abortion in terms of women's rights, that abortion, wildly unlike any other form of killing, is the termination of a pregnancy, which is a condition of a woman's body and results in *her* having a child if it is not aborted. This fact is given due recognition not by appeal to women's rights but by emphasizing the relevance of the familiar biological and psychological facts and their connection with having the right attitude to parenthood and family relationships. But it may well be thought that failing to bring in women's rights still leaves some important aspects of the problem of abortion untouched.

Speaking in terms of women's rights, people sometimes say things like, 'Well, it's her life you're talking about too, you know; she's got a right to her own life, her own happiness.' And the discussion stops there. But in the context of virtue theory, given that we are particularly concerned with what constitutes a good human life, with what true happiness or *eudaimonia* is, this is no place to stop. We go on to ask, 'And is this life of hers a good one? Is she living well?'

If we are to go on to talk about good human lives, in the context of abortion, we have to bring in our thoughts about the value of love and family life, and our proper emotional development through a natural life cycle. The familiar facts support the view that parenthood in general, and motherhood and childbearing in particular, are intrinsically worthwhile, are among the things that can be correctly thought to be partially constitutive of a flourishing human life.[14] If this is right, then a woman who opts for not being a mother (at all, or again, or now) by opting for abortion may thereby be manifesting a flawed grasp of what her life should be, and be about—a grasp that is childish, or grossly materialistic, or shortsighted, or shallow.

I said '*may* thereby': this *need* not be so. Consider, for instance, a woman who has already had several children and fears that to have another will seriously affect her capacity to be a good mother to the ones she has—she does not show a lack of appreciation of the intrinsic value of being a parent by opting for abortion. Nor does a woman who has been a good mother and is approaching the age at which she may be looking forward to being a good grandmother. Nor does a woman who discovers that her pregnancy may well kill her, and opts for abortion and adoption. Nor, necessarily,

[14] I take this as a premiss here, but argue for it in some detail in my *Beginning Lives* (Oxford, 1987). In this connection I also discuss adoption and the sense in which it may be regarded as 'second best', and the difficult question of whether the good of parenthood may properly be sought, or indeed bought, by surrogacy.

does a woman who has decided to lead a life centred around some other worthwhile activity or activities with which motherhood would compete.

People who are childless by choice are sometimes described as 'irresponsible', or 'selfish', or 'refusing to grow up', or 'not knowing what life is about.' But one can hold that having children is intrinsically worthwhile without endorsing this, for we are, after all, in the happy position of there being more worthwhile things to do than can be fitted into one lifetime. Parenthood, and motherhood in particular, even if granted to be intrinsically worthwhile, undoubtedly take up a lot of one's adult life, leaving no room for some other worthwhile pursuits. But some women who choose abortion rather than having their first child, and some men who encourage their partners to choose abortion, are not avoiding parenthood for the sake of other worthwhile pursuits, but for the worthless one of 'having a good time', or for the pursuit of some false vision of the ideals of freedom or self-realization. And some others who say 'I am not ready for parenthood yet' are making a mistake about the extent to which one can manipulate the circumstances of one's life so as to make it fulfil some dream that one has. Perhaps one's dream is of having two perfect children, a girl and a boy, within a perfect marriage, in financially secure circumstances, with an interesting job of one's own. But to care too much about that dream, to demand of life that it give it to one and to act accordingly, may be both greedy and foolish, and is to run the risk of missing out on happiness entirely. Not only may fate make the dream impossible, or destroy it, but one's own attachment to it may make it impossible. Good marriages, and the most promising children, can be destroyed by just one adult's excessive demand for perfection.

Once again, this is not to deny that girls may quite properly say 'I am not ready for motherhood yet', especially in our society, and, far from manifesting irresponsibility or light-mindedness, show an appropriate modesty or humility, or a fearfulness that does not amount to cowardice. However, even when the decision to have an abortion is the right decision—one that does not itself fall under a vice-related term and thereby one that the perfectly virtuous could recommend—it does not follow that there is no sense in which having the abortion is wrong, or guilt appropriate. For, by virtue of the fact that a human life has been cut short, some evil has probably been brought about,[15] and that circumstances make the decision

[15] I say 'some evil has probably been brought about' on the ground that (human) life is (usually) a good and hence (human) death usually an evil. The exceptions would be (*a*) where death is actually a good or a benefit, because the baby that would come to be if the life were not cut short would be better off dead than alive, and (*b*) where death, though not a good, is not an

to bring about some evil the right decision will be a ground for guilt if getting into those circumstances in the first place itself manifested a flaw in character.

What 'gets one into those circumstances' in the case of abortion is, except in the case of rape, one's sexual activity and one's choices, or the lack of them, about one's sexual partner and about contraception. The virtuous woman (which here of course does not mean simply 'chaste woman' but 'woman with the virtues') has such character traits as strength, independence, resoluteness, decisiveness, self-confidence, responsibility, serious-mindedness, and self-determination—and no one, I think, could deny that many women become pregnant in circumstances in which they cannot welcome or cannot face the thought of having *this* child precisely because they lack one or some of these character traits. So even in the cases where the decision to have an abortion is the right one, it can still be the reflection of a moral failing—not because the decision itself is weak or cowardly or irresolute or irresponsible or light-minded, but because lack of the requisite opposite of these failings landed one in the circumstances in the first place. Hence the common universalized claim that guilt and remorse are never appropriate emotions about an abortion is denied. They may be appropriate, and appropriately inculcated, even when the decision was the right one.

Another motivation for bringing women's rights into the discussion may be to attempt to correct the implication, carried by the killing-centred approach, that in so far as abortion is wrong, it is a wrong that only women do, or at least (given the preponderance of male doctors) that only women instigate. I do not myself believe that we can thus escape the fact that nature bears harder on women than it does on men,[16] but virtue theory can certainly correct many of the injustices that the emphasis on women's rights is rightly concerned about. With very little amendment, everything that has been said above applies to boys and men too. Although the abortion decision is, in a natural sense, the woman's decision, proper to her, boys and men are often party to it, for well or ill, and even when they are not, they are bound to have been party to the circumstances that brought it up. No less than girls and women, boys and men can, in their actions, manifest self-centredness, callousness, and light-mindedness about life and parenthood in relation to abortion. They can be self-centred or courageous about the possibility of disability in their offspring; they

evil either, because the life that would be led (e.g., in a state of permanent coma) would not be a good. (See Foot, 'Euthanasia'.)

[16] I discuss this point at greater length in *Beginning Lives*.

need to reflect on their sexual activity and their choices, or the lack of them, about their sexual partner and contraception; they need to grow up and take responsibility for their own actions and life in relation to fatherhood. If it is true, as I maintain, that in so far as motherhood is intrinsically worthwhile, being a mother is an important purpose in women's lives, being a father (rather than a mere generator) is an important purpose in men's lives too, and it is adolescent of men to turn a blind eye to this and pretend that they have many more important things to do.

CONCLUSION

Much more might be said, but I shall end the actual discussion of the problem of abortion here, and conclude by highlighting what I take to be its significant features. These hark back to many of the criticisms of virtue theory discussed earlier.

The discussion does not proceed simply by our trying to answer the question 'Would a perfectly virtuous agent ever have an abortion and, if so, when?'; virtue theory is not limited to considering 'Would Socrates have had an abortion if he were a raped, pregnant 15-year-old?' nor automatically stumped when we are considering circumstances into which no virtuous agent would have got herself. Instead, much of the discussion proceeds in the virtue- and vice-related terms whose application, in several cases, yields practical conclusions (cf. the third and fourth criticisms above). These terms are difficult to apply correctly, and anyone might challenge my application of any one of them. So, for example, I have claimed that some abortions, done for certain reasons, would be callous or light-minded; that others might indicate an appropriate modesty or humility; that others would reflect a greedy and foolish attitude to what one could expect out of life. Any of these examples may be disputed, but what is at issue is, should these difficult terms be there, or should the discussion be couched in terms that all clever adolescents can apply correctly? (Cf. the first half of the 'major objection' above.)

Proceeding as it does in the virtue- and vice-related terms, the discussion thereby, inevitably, also contains claims about what is worthwhile, serious and important, good and evil, in our lives. So, for example, I claimed that parenthood is intrinsically worthwhile, and that having a good time was a worthless end (in life, not on individual occasions); that losing a foetus is always a serious matter (albeit not a tragedy in itself in the first trimester) whereas acquiring an appendectomy scar is a trivial one; that (human) death is an evil. Once again, these are difficult matters, and anyone might challenge any one of my claims. But what is at issue is, as before, should those difficult claims be there or can one reach practical conclusions about real moral issues that are in no way determined by premisses about such matters? (Cf. the fifth criticism, and the second half of the 'major criticism'.)

The discussion also thereby, inevitably, contains claims about what life is like (e.g., my claim that love and friendship do not survive their parties' constantly insisting on their rights; or the claim that to demand perfection of life is to run the risk of missing out on happiness entirely). What is at issue is, should those disputable claims be there, or is our knowledge (or are our false opinions) about what life is like irrelevant to our understanding of real moral issues? (Cf. both halves of the 'major criticism'.)

Naturally, my own view is that all these concepts should be there in any discussion of real moral issues, and that virtue theory, which uses all of them, is the right theory to apply to them. I do not pretend to have shown this. I realize that proponents of rival theories may say that, now that they have understood how virtue theory uses the range of concepts it draws on, they are more convinced than ever that such concepts should not figure in an adequate normative theory, because they are sectarian, or vague, or too particular, or improperly anthropocentric, and reinstate what I called the 'major criticism'. Or, finding many of the details of the discussion appropriate, they may agree that many, perhaps even all, of the concepts should figure, but argue that virtue theory gives an inaccurate account of the way the concepts fit together (and indeed of the concepts themselves) and that another theory provides a better account; that would be interesting to see. Moreover, I admitted that there were at least two problems for virtue theory: that it has to argue against moral scepticism, 'pluralism', and cultural relativism, and that it has to find something to say about conflicting requirements of different virtues. Proponents of rival theories might argue that their favoured theory provides better solutions to these problems than virtue theory can. Indeed, they might criticize virtue theory for finding problems here at all. Anyone who argued for at least one of moral scepticism, 'pluralism', or cultural relativism could presumably do so (provided their favoured theory does not find a similar problem); and a utilitarian might say that benevolence is the only virtue and hence that virtue theory errs when it discusses even apparent conflicts between the requirements of benevolence and some other character trait such as honesty.

Defending virtue theory against all possible, or even likely, criticisms of it would be a lifelong task. As I said at the outset, in this article I aimed to defend the theory against some criticisms which I thought arose from an inadequate understanding of it, and to improve that understanding. If I have succeeded, we may hope for more comprehending criticisms of virtue theory than have appeared hitherto.[17]

[17] Versions of this article have been read to philosophy societies at University College, London, Rutgers University, and the Universities of Dundee, Edinburgh, Oxford, Swansea, and California–San Diego; at a conference of the Polish and British Academies in Cracow in 1988 on 'Life, Death and the Law', and as a symposium paper at the Pacific Division of the American Philosophical Association in 1989. I am grateful to the many people who contributed to the discussions of it on these occasions, and particularly to Philippa Foot and Anne Jaap Jacobson for private discussion.

12

AGENT-BASED VIRTUE ETHICS

MICHAEL SLOTE

A tremendous revival of interest in virtue ethics has recently been taking place, but in this paper I would like to discuss some important virtue-ethical possibilities that have yet to be substantially explored. Till now Aristotle has been the principal focus of new interest in virtue ethics, but it is possible to pursue virtue ethics in a more *agent-based* fashion than what we (or some of us) find in Aristotle, and I am going to explore that possibility here and attempt to explain why such a more radical approach is not as outré, misconceived, inappropriate, or obviously unpromising as it is sometimes held to be.[1]

AGENT-BASED VS. AGENT-FOCUSED VIRTUE ETHICS

An agent-based approach to virtue ethics treats the moral or ethical status of acts as entirely derivative from independent and fundamental aretaic (as opposed to deontic) ethical characterizations of motives, character traits, or individuals, and such agent-basing is arguably not to be found in Aristotle, at least on one kind of standard interpretation. Certainly, Aristotle seems to put a greater emphasis on the evaluation of agents and character traits than he does on the evaluation of actions. Moreover, for Aristotle an act is noble or fine if it is one that a noble or virtuous individual would perform, and he does say that the virtuous individual is the measure of virtue in action. But Aristotle also allows that properly guided or momentarily inspired individuals can perform fine or good or virtuous acts even if

Michael Slote, 'Agent-Based Virtue Ethics', *Midwest Studies in Philosophy*, 20 (1995), 83–101. Reprinted by permission of the Editor of *Midwest Studies in Philosophy*.

[1] For discussion of what it is for an ethical view to count as a form of virtue ethics, see my *From Morality to Virtue* (Oxford, 1992), ch. 5, and Marcia Baron, 'Varieties of Ethics of Virtue', *American Philosophical Quarterly*, 22 (1985), 52 n. I shall not much stress the fact that virtue theories are supposed to prefer aretaic characterizations in terms of excellence, moral goodness, or admirability to deontic evaluations making use of notions like 'ought', 'wrong', and 'obligation'.

the individuals are not themselves good or virtuous, and, in addition, he characterizes the virtuous individual as someone who *sees* or *perceives* what is good or fine or right to do in any given situation.

Such language clearly implies that the virtuous individual does what is noble or virtuous because it is the noble—e.g. courageous—thing to do, rather than its being the case that what is noble—or courageous—to do has this status simply because the virtuous individual will choose or has chosen it. Even if right or fine actions cannot be defined in terms of rules, what makes them right or fine, for Aristotle, is not that they have been chosen in a certain way by a certain sort of individual. So their status as right or fine or noble is treated as in some measure independent of agent-evaluations, and that is incompatible with agent-basing as we defined it just above. (If the virtuous individual is the measure of what is fine or right, that may simply mean that she is in the *best possible position to know/perceive* what is fine or right.)

Thus we must distinguish a virtue-ethical theory like Aristotle's (as commonly interpreted), which focuses more on virtuous individuals and individual traits than on actions and is thus in some sense *agent-focused*, from agent-based views which, unlike Aristotle,[2] treat the moral or ethical status of actions as entirely derivative from independent and fundamental ethical/aretaic facts (or claims) about the motives, dispositions, or inner life of the individuals who perform them. Views of the latter kind clearly represent an extreme or radical form of virtue ethics, and indeed it is somewhat difficult to find clear-cut historical examples of such agent-basing. In fact, the only absolutely clear-cut example of agent-basing I have found is that of the nineteenth-century British ethicist James Martineau. Other potential historical examples of agent-basing—notably, Hume, Leslie Stephen, Nietzsche, Abelard, Augustine, and Kant—offer different forms of resistance to such interpretation, and even Plato, who insists that we evaluate actions by reference to the health and virtue of the individual soul, seems to think that (appreciation of) the Form of the Good represents a level of evaluation prior to the evaluation of souls, with souls

[2] In 'Virtue Theory and Abortion' (Chapter 11 in this volume), Rosalind Hursthouse interprets Aristotle as deriving all evaluations of actions from independent judgements about what counts as a virtue, but basing the latter, in turn, in judgements about, a conception of, *eudaimonia*. But, if Aristotle regards virtuous living as a/the primary component of *eudaimonia*, it becomes difficult to see how Aristotelianism can be grounded in the way indicated by Hursthouse, and in any event such an interpretation does not treat Aristotelian ethics as agent-based: act-evaluations may be derivative from independent aretaic character evaluations, but the latter are not fundamental and are supposed to be grounded in a theory or view of *eudaimonia*. (I assume here that *eudaimonia* and the ideas of well-being and a good life are not themselves aretaic, even though some ethical views treat them as closely connected to or based in aretaic notions. On this point see my *From Morality to Virtue*, ch. 13.)

counting as virtuous when properly appreciating and being guided by the value inherent in the Form of the Good. To that extent, Plato's view is not agent-*based*, but I believe there is a way of freeing the Platonic approach from dependence on the Forms, and the first form of agent-basing I shall be describing has its ultimate inspiration in Plato. The other ways of agent-basing I shall go on to describe can be seen as more plausible simplifying variants on Martineau's moral theory. But before I say more about particular ways of developing agent-based virtue theories, there are some very worrying objections to the whole idea of agent-basing that must first be addressed.[3]

OBJECTIONS TO AGENT-BASING

One thing that seems wrong in principle with any agent-based approach to moral evaluation is that it appears to obliterate the common distinction between doing the right thing and doing the right thing for the right reasons. Sidgwick's well-known example of the prosecutor who does his duty by trying to convict a defendant, but who is motivated by malice rather than by a sense of duty, seems to illustrate the distinction in question, and it may well seem that agent-based virtue eithics would have difficulty here because of the way it understands rightness in terms of good motivations and wrongness in terms of the having of bad motives. If actions are wrong when they result from morally bad motives, will that not mean that the prosecutor does the wrong thing in prosecuting someone out of malice (assuming that malice is morally criticizable in general or in this particular case)? And is that not a rather unfortunate consequence of the agent-based approach?

I am not sure. Sidgwick himself seems to grant a certain plausibility to the idea that the prosecutor acts wrongly if he prosecutes from malice.[4]

[3] Ideal observer theories (and response dependence views) are not necessarily agent-based, for even if they define rightness in terms of the attitudes of an observer defined as having what are ordinarily considered to be virtues, e.g. disinterestedness, objectivity, lack of bias, or what have you, the theory does not (need not) *say* that these inner traits are virtues nor attempt to spell out what all the virtues are independently of its specification of the right. Indeed, on standard formulations, ideal observer theories leave it open that an ideal observer should condemn her own disinterestedness or lack of bias, and so such theories clearly do not commit themselves to any account of good inner traits or motives as the basis for their accounts of right action.

[4] Henry Sidgwick *The Methods of Ethics* (7th edn., London, 1907), 202. In what follows I have simplified matters by assuming that the malicious prosecutor must either prosecute or let the potential defendant go free; but in any realistic scenario, he would be able to recuse himself and let someone else decide about the prosecution. Doing so would fail to exhibit either malice or

What *is* implausible is merely the claim that the prosecutor has no obligation to prosecute. And that does not follow from the agent-based assumption that he acts wrongly if he prosecutes from malice. Sidgwick of course points out that, if he is sufficiently motivated by malice, the prosecutor may be unable to do his duty entirely or even substantially for the right kind of reason. But this merely entails that there is no way the prosecutor who is motivated thus can avoid acting wrongly if he prosecutes. It does not mean it is morally all right for him *not* to prosecute, or thus that he has no duty or obligation to prosecute.

But how can such a duty be understood in agent-based terms? Well, consider the possibility that *if he does not prosecute*, the prosecutor's motivation will *also* be bad. Those who talk about the malicious prosecutor case often fail to mention the motives that might lead him *not* to prosecute. With malice present or even in the absence of malice, if the prosecutor does not prosecute, one very likely explanation will be that he lacks real or strong concern for doing his job and playing the contributing social role that involves. Imagine, for example, that horrified by his own malice he decides not to prosecute. This too will be motivated by a bad motive, insufficient concern for the public (or general human) good or for making his contribution to society—motives I shall have a good deal more to say about in discussing positive versions of agent-based views.

So the idea that motives are the basis for evaluating actions that they cause or that express them does not have particularly untoward results. And it allows us something like the distinction between doing the right thing and doing the right thing for the right reason. In particular, it allows us to say that the prosecutor has a duty to prosecute, because if he does not, we shall in the normal course (barring a heart attack, nervous breakdown, religious conversion, and such like) be able to attribute to him motivation, or deficient or defective motivation, of a kind that makes his act wrong. Yet we can also say that, if he prosecutes, he acts (will act) wrongly, even if another person, with different motivation, would have acted rightly in doing so. This allows us then to distinguish between doing one's duty for the right reasons and thus acting rightly, on the one hand, and doing one's duty for the wrong reasons and thus acting wrongly. This is very close to the distinction between right action and acting rightly for the right reasons, except for the fact it supposes that, when the reasons are not right, the action itself is actually *wrong*. But we have already seen that this idea is not in itself particularly implausible. And what we now see is

unconcern for the public good, and would count as morally right and permissible according to an agent-based view.

that the above-mentioned complaint against agent-basing boils down to a faulty assumption about the inability of such views to make fine-grained distinctions of the sort we have just succeeded in making.

However, there is another objection to the whole idea of agent-basing that may more fundamentally represent what seems objectionable and even bizarre about any such approach to morality/ethics. If the evaluation of actions ultimately derives from that of (the inner states of) agents, then it would appear to follow that if one is the right sort of person or possesses the right sort of inner states, it cannot morally matter what one actually *does*, so that the person, or at least her actions, are subject to no genuine moral requirements or constraints. In this light, agent-basing seems a highly autistic and antinomian approach to ethics, an approach that seems to undermine the familiar, intuitive notion that the moral or ethical life involves—among other things—*living up to* certain *standards* of behaviour or action. Such an implication would seem to be totally unacceptable from the standpoint of anyone who takes ethics and the moral life seriously, and indeed this train of reasoning once caused me to abandon the whole idea of agent-based morality, before I saw, as I believe I now do, that the implications drawn just now do not in fact follow in any way from agent-basing.[5] A view can be agent-based and still not treat actions as right or admirable simply because they are done by a virtuous individual or by someone with an admirable or good inner state. Nor does an agent-based theory have to say, with respect to each and every action a virtuous agent is capable of performing, that, if she were to perform that action, it would automatically count as a good or admirable thing for her to have done.

Thus consider a very simple view according to which (roughly) benevolence is the only good motive and acts are right, admirable, or good to the extent they exhibit or express benevolent motivation. (We can also assume actions are wrong or bad if they exhibit the opposite of benevolence or are somehow deficient in benevolence.) To the extent this view treats benevolence as fundamentally and inherently admirable or morally good, it is agent-based; but such a view does not entail that the virtuous individual with admirable inner states can simply choose any actions she pleases (among those lying within her power) without the admirability or goodness of her behaviour or actions being in any way compromised or diminished. For, assuming only some reasonable form of free-will compatibilism, a benevolent agent is typically *capable* of choosing many actions that *fail to*

[5] Similar worries could also occur about views (like Aristotle as interpreted by Hursthouse) that treat act-evaluations as derivative from aretaic agent-characterizations but base the latter in some other type of ethical consideration. The worries are misplaced for exactly the same reasons described in the main text in connection with agent-basing.

express or exhibit her benevolence. And, if one is not *entirely* or *perfectly* benevolent, then one may well be capable of choosing actions that exhibit the opposite of or a deficiency in this motive. Thus, if one is benevolent and sees an individual who needs one's help, one may help and, in doing so, exhibit one's benevolence. But it is also presumably within one's power to refuse to help, and if one does, then one's actions will not exhibit benevolence and will presumably be less admirable than they could or would have been otherwise. Of course, the really or perfectly benevolent person will not refuse to help, but the point is that she could, and such refusal and the actions it would give rise to do not count as admirable according to the simplified agent-based view that makes benevolence the touchstone of all moral evaluation.

So it is not true to say that agent-basing entails that what one does cannot matter morally or that it cannot matter if one has good enough motivation. The person who expresses and exhibits benevolence in her actions performs actions that, in agent-based terms, may count as ethically superior to other actions she might or could have performed, namely, actions (perhaps including refrainings) that would *not* have expressed or exhibited benevolence. Acts therefore do not count as admirable or virtuous for an agent-based theory of the sort just roughly introduced merely because they are or would be done by someone who in fact is admirable or possesses admirable motivation—they have to exhibit, express, or further such motivation or be such that they *would* exhibit, etc., such motivation if they occurred, in order to qualify as admirable or virtuous.

By the same token, actions will count as wrong or contrary to obligation only if they exhibit bad or deficient motivation, and this means for one thing that agent-basing is entirely consistent with '"ought" implies "can".' Given compatibilism, even a malicious person will have the power to refrain from any particular act of harming others, and since refraining would in no way *exhibit* or *come from* his maliciousness, it would be morally permissible. But since agent-basing says that actions *are* wrong if they exhibit or proceed from *bad* motives, it is once again simply not true that agent-based theories inevitably treat human actions as subject to no moral standards or requirements. Rather, those requirements and standards operate and bind, as it were, *from within*.

But even this metaphor must be taken with caution, because it seems to imply that for agent-based views the direction of fit between world and moral agent is all one way: from agent to world, and this too suggests a kind of autism or isolation from the world that makes one wonder how any such form of ethics can possibly be plausible or adequate. However, agent-basing does not in fact entail isolation from or the irrelevance of facts about the world, and one sees this if one considers how the kinds of motivation such theories specify as fundamentally admirable invariably wish and need to take the world into account. If one is really benevolent, for example, one does not just throw good things around or give them to the first person one sees. Benevolence is not really benevolence in the fullest sense unless one cares about who exactly is needy and to what extent they are needy, and such care, in turn, criterially involves wanting and making efforts to know relevant facts, so that one's benevolence can be really useful. Thus, even if universal benevolence is a ground-floor moral value, someone who acts from such a motive must be open to, seek contact with, and be influenced by the world around her—her decisions will not be made in splendid causal/epistemic isolation from what most of us would take to be the morally relevant realities, so the worries mentioned just above really have no foundation.[6]

Having quelled the charges of autism and antinomianism that it is initially so tempting to launch against agent-basing, I would like now to consider—too briefly, I am afraid—how agent-based approaches might best be developed in the current climate of ethics. Looking back at the somewhat sparse history of agent-based approaches, it strikes me that there are basically two possible ways in which one may naturally develop the idea of agent-basing: one of them I call 'cool', the other 'warm'. I mentioned earlier that Plato relates the morality of individual actions to the health and virtue of the soul, but in the *Republic* (book IV) Plato also uses the images of a strong and of a beautiful soul to convey what he takes to be the inner touchstone of all good human action. And I believe that ideas about health and, especially, strength can serve as the aretaic foundations for one kind of agent-based virtue ethics. Since, in addition, it is natural to wonder how any sort of *humane concern for other people* can be derived from notions like health and strength, agent-based approaches of this first kind can be conveniently classified as 'cool'.

By contrast, James Martineau's agent-based conception of morality treats compassion as the highest of secular motives, and some of the philosophers who have come closest to presenting agent-based views (Hume, Hutcheson, and nowadays Jorge Garcia) have placed a special emphasis on compassion or, to use a somewhat more general term,

[6] Of course, if someone makes every effort to learn about things and is foiled by reality or his own innate lack of intelligence, his benevolence will not have its intended effect and may actually cause a great deal of harm. But the personal defect here, if any, is presumably cognitive, not moral. So when such an agent brings about bad results, an agent-based view may still plausibly say that the agent did not act morally wrongly. (Even then we might say that the agent did not 'do the right thing'; but that is a more objective use of 'right' and is not the act-characterizing moral notion agent-based virtue ethics *primarily* wishes to capture.)

benevolence as a motive. I believe the latter notion can provide the focus for a second kind of agent-based view (actually, as it turns out, a pair of views) that deserves our attention, and since this second kind of view builds humane concern explicitly into its aretaic foundations, it is natural to think of it as 'warm'.

Since Plato's discussion of health and strength is older than any discussion of benevolence I know of, I would like first to consider agent-basing as anchored in the cool idea of strength. But metaphors/images of health and strength also play an important role in Stoicism, in Spinoza, and in Nietzsche, though none of the latter offers a perfectly clear-cut example of an agent-based account of ethics. Still, these views cluster around the same notions that fascinate and influence Plato, and I believe they can naturally by extrapolated to a modern-day version of Plato's virtue-ethical approach and, in particular, to a genuinely agent-based theory that regards inner strength, in various of its forms, as the sole foundation for an understanding of the morality of human action.

MORALITY AS INNER STRENGTH

For Plato, good action is to be understood in terms of the seemingly consequentialistic idea of creating and/or sustaining the strength (or health, etc.) of the soul,[7] but to me it seems more promising to explore the idea of actions that *express* or *exhibit* inner strength, and so *morality as inner strength*, as it seems natural to call it, will proceed (without making any appeal to the supposed value of the Forms) on that basis.

Now the idea that there is something intuitively admirable about being strong inside, something requiring no appeal to or defence from *other ideas*, can perhaps be made more plausible by being more specific about the kinds of inner disposition and motivation I have in mind in speaking of inner strength. What *does not* seem plausible, however, is the idea that any contemporaneously relevant and inclusive morality of human action could be based *solely* in ideas about inner strength. What does inner strength have to do with being kind to people, with not deceiving them, with not harming them? And if it does not relate to these sorts of things, it clearly cannot function as a general groundwork for morality.

The same problem, the same question, comes up in connection with Plato's defence of morality in the *Republic*. The *Republic* begins with the problem of explaining why anyone should be moral or just in the conven-

[7] *Republic* bk. IV, S. 443–4.

tional sense of not deceiving, stealing, and the like, but Plato ends up defining justice in terms of the health or strength of the soul and never adequately explains why such a soul would refrain from what are ordinarily regarded as unjust or immoral actions. Even the appeal to the Form of the Good seems just a form of handwaving in connection with these difficulties, because even though Plato holds that a healthy soul must be guided by the Good, we are not told enough about the Good to know why it would direct us away from lying, stealing, and the like. Does not a similar problem arise for any cool agent-based theory appealing fundamentally to the notion of inner strength? It certain appears to, but perhaps the appearance can be dispelled by *pointing out connections between certain kinds of strength and other-regarding morality that have largely gone unnoticed*. Let us begin by considering how strength in the form of *self-reliance* gives rise to a concern for the well-being of others.

Most children envy the self-reliance of their parents and want to be like them, rather than continuing to depend on them or others to do things for them. Moreover, the efforts to learn to do things for oneself and eventually make one's own way in the world expresses a kind of inner self-sufficiency that we think well of. The contrary desire, which we would call parasitism, is, most of us think, inherently deplorable; and someone who willingly remains dependent on others rather than in any substantial degree striking out on her own seems to us pathetic and *weak*. Notice here too that the accusation of weak dependency depends more on the motivation than on the abilities of the accused. A person who is *capable* of leaving the family nest but *unwilling* to do so is considered dependent and weak and a parasite *because of his motivation*. The accusation of parasitism does not apply to a handicapped person who strives but fails to be entirely self-supporting or to a welfare mother in a similar position. So a morality that bases everything on *inner* strength can say that motivational (as opposed to achieved) self-reliance demonstrates inner strength and self-sufficiency and is thus inherently admirable, whereas motivational parasitism is a form of dependency and inherently weak and deplorable. It can then go on to say that acts that exhibit the one motive are right and even good, whereas those exhibiting the latter are wrong. And having appealed to our aretaic intuitions about strength and self-sufficiency in this way and without recourse to *any further arguments*, morality as strength is thus far at least an example of agent-basing. The admirability of wanting to be independent and not a parasite is not a function of its consequences for anyone's happiness, but, according to the present view, is and can be recognized to be admirable apart from any consequences, and I think this idea strikes a resonant note in many of us. Certainly, we think it will have good results if people want to be and succeed in being self-reliant in their lives—they will help themselves and, as we shall shortly see, they will tend to help others too. (I am not assuming that attempts at *total, godlike* self-reliance make any sense for beings with our social and personal needs.) But our low opinion of dependent weakness is not based, or solely based, on assumptions about results.

Consider, for example, the courage it takes to face unpleasant facts about oneself or the universe. Self-deception about whether one has cancer may make the end of one's life less miserable and even make things easier for those taking care of one; but still it seems far more admirable to face such facts. And intuitively such courage is not admired for the good it does people, but rather because we find courage, and the inner or personal strength it demonstrates, inherently admirable and in need of no further defence or justification. All arguments, all theories, need to start somewhere in intuitive or convincing assumptions, and in this case, therefore, it would appear that the admirability of inner strength is a ground-floor or fundamental aretaic assumption of the sort appropriate to agent-basing.

By the same token, the desire to be useful and not totally dependent on others—what we can call motivational (as opposed to achieved) self-reliance and self-sufficiency—seems admirable to us independently of any (further) argument or justification. We admire, for example, a handicapped person who makes persistent but largely unsuccessful efforts to do things for himself and earn his own money, but in such a case those efforts may frustrate and annoy the handicapped individual, and he may be less happy and contented than if he had simply allowed things to be done for him. For all we know, his motivational self-reliance might also do nothing to lift the burden of caring for him from others, and our admiration for such a person as compared with someone with no qualms about taking everything from others is thus not reasonably thought to be based on consequentialistic considerations. Rather, we seem to think of this form of strength and self-sufficiency in the same way we regard the strength to face facts, as something inherently and fundamentally admirable; and so the question now before us is just *how much* of our ordinary other-regarding morality can be based in considerations of inner strength.

Our admiration for self-reliance as opposed to parasitism can be used, in the first instance, to undergird and justify a good deal of activity devoted to the well-being of other people. To depend passively on society or others in the way a child depends on his parents counts as an instance of parasitism and is wrong and deplorable as such, whether we are talking about welfare chiselling, on the one hand, or, on the other, the leisured existence of the wealthy; and a person who is opposed to parasitism will presumably want to *be* useful and *make* a contribution to society, so as to counterbalance all that has been done for him by others.

Notice, furthermore, that this desire is not egoistic or self-interested, even if it presupposes one's self-interest has been served by others. For one's motive here is not the instrumental one of making a contribution in order that others may be more likely to help one in the future, but looks back to help one has already received and seeks *with no ulterior motive to counterbalance or repay that help*.

The appeal to a desire to repay and make a positive contribution to society and particular others allows us to criticize both the harming of others and failures to contribute to others' well-being. But the imperative of self-reliance or non-parasitism also connects with the 'deontological' side of our ordinary moral thinking, with our obligations to keep promises, not to be deceptive, to tell the truth, etc. For those who rely on others to believe their promises and who have benefited from others' keeping promises to *them* would count as parasites upon the social practice of promising if they refused to keep their promises. More needs to be said here, but, given space constraints, we ought to move on to consider some forms of inner strength we have not yet mentioned.

We have spoken of self-sufficiency understood in the sense of self-reliance, but such self-sufficiency and strength *vis-à-vis* other *people* is different from a kind of self-sufficiency in regard to *things* that we also think well of—namely, the self-sufficiency shown by those who are moderate in their needs or desires. Those who do not desire, or so strongly desire, many things that most of us desire, those who are contented with what would not be enough to satisfy most people, seem less needy, less greedy, less dependent on things than those others, and since neediness and dependency seem to be ways of being weak (inside), a certain independence from and self-sufficiency in regard to things that people can crave represents another form of inner strength that is admirable in itself.

Interestingly, this new form of self-sufficient strength can help us to justify some further kinds of altruistic behaviour, and, ironically enough, it is Nietzsche, the self-avowed egoist, who shows us how to do this. The kind of moderation of desire that can be justified in terms of an ideal of self-sufficiency is not particularly directed to the good of others, but, as Nietzsche points out in *Beyond Good and Evil* (section 260), *Joyful Wisdom* (section 55), and many other places, one can also be moved to give things to other people out of a self-sufficient sense of having more than enough, a superabundance, of things. Nietzsche thinks this kind of 'noble' giving is ethically superior to giving based in pity or a sense of obligation, but, quite apart from this further judgement, it seems clear that Nietzsche has pointed out a further way in which benefiting others can be justified in terms of our ideal of inner strength. For the person who begrudges things to others no matter how much he has seems needy, pathetic, too dependent on the things he keeps for himself, and can be criticized as lacking self-sufficiency in regard to the good things of this world.

Notice that, although generosity based on this kind of self-sufficiency presupposes that the giver is genuinely satisfied with the good things she has, it is not egoistic. One generously gives to others out of a sense of one's own well-being but not in order to *promote* that well-being or (necessarily) in order to *repay* people for previous help, and this therefore counts as a form of altruism additional to the kind that develops out of self-reliance. Such self-sufficient generosity can serve rather widely as a touchstone for social and individual moral criticism, but, once again, there is no space here to go into the details.[8] What is important at this point is that the cool notion of inner strength has sides to it that allow a defence of various forms of altruism and of the honouring of commitments.

In fact, I believe there are four basic facets to the idea of inner strength, all with a role to play in morality as inner strength. We have mentioned three: courage to face facts and, let me add, to face danger; self-sufficient self-reliance; and self-sufficient moderation and generosity. Now let me mention a fourth kind of inner strength: strength of purpose as involving both keeping to purposes and intentions over time and following one's better judgement (not being weak-willed) at the time one is supposed to act on some intention. I do not propose at this point to go any further, though, into the details of morality as strength. Clearly, if we have four different kinds of inner strength, we need to say something about their relative importance and about how they interact to yield an intuitive and thoroughgoing account of ethical phenomena. But I want at this point to indicate a general problem with this whole approach that has led me to think there are probably more promising ways to develop an agent-based virtue ethics.

The problem, in a nutshell, is that morality as strength treats benevolence, compassion, kindness, and the like as only *derivatively* admirable and morally good. And this seems highly implausible to the modern moral consciousness. Certainly, compassion cannot always have its way; it sometimes must yield to considerations of justice, and a compassion or generosity that never pays any heed to the agent's own needs seems lacking in self-respect, masochistic, ethically unattractive. But still, even if compas-

[8] For more on how the motive of self-sufficient generosity tends to limit individual acquisitiveness and to lead towards social egalitarianism, see my 'Virtue Ethics and Democratic Values', *Journal of Social Philosophy*, 24 (1993), 5–37.

sion has to be limited or qualified by other values, it counts with us as a *very important basic moral value.* And it seems to distort the aretaic value we place on (warm) compassion, benevolence, and kindness to regard them as needing justification in terms of the (cool) ideal of inner strength or any other different value. (Such a criticism clearly also touches the Kantian account of benevolence.) So I would propose at this point to introduce and discuss certain warm forms of agent-based virtue ethics that are immune to this problem precisely because they base all morality on the aretaic value, the moral admirability, of one or another kind of benevolence. Moreover, as I mentioned earlier, Martineau's *Types of Ethical Theory* is the clearest example of agent-basing one can find in the entire history of ethics, and I believe that the advantages of virtue ethics based on compassion or benevolence can best be brought to light by first considering the structure of Martineau's theory and the criticisms that Henry Sidgwick made of that theory.

MORALITY AS UNIVERSAL BENEVOLENCE

Martineau gives a ranking of human motives from lowest to highest and, assuming as he does that all moral decisions involve a conflict between two such motives, holds that right action is action from the higher of the two motives, wrong action action from the lower of the two.[9] Martineau's hierarchy of motives ascends (roughly) as follows: vindictiveness; love of sensual pleasure; love of gain; resentment/fear/antipathy; ambition/love of power; compassion; and, at the apex, reverence for the Deity.

Sidgwick objects to the rigidity of this hierarchy, pointing out that circumstances and consequences may affect the preferability of acting from one or another of the motives Martineau has ranked.[10] Thus contrary to Martineau there are times when it is better for reasons of justice to act from resentment rather than compassion, and the love of sensual pleasure might sometimes prevail over a love or power or gain (especially if the latter were already being given ample play). Sidgwick concludes that conflicts between lower motives can only be resolved by appeal to the highest ranked motive or, alternatively, to some supremely regulative general motive like justice, prudence, or universal benevolence—none of which is contained among the more particular motives of Martineau's hierarchy. That is, all conflicts of Martineau's lower motives should be settled by

[9] See James Martineau, *Types of Ethical Theory* (2 vols.; Oxford, 1885).
[10] See Sidgwick, *Methods of Ethics*, bk. III, ch. xii.

reference to reverence for the Deity or by reference to some regulative or 'master' motive like benevolence. (This would not be necessary if we could devise a more plausible and less priggish hierarchy than Martineau's, but no one has yet suggested a way of doing that.)

Sidgwick then goes on to make one further (mistaken) assumption. He assumes that for a motive to be regulative, it must be regulative in relation to the ultimate *ends* or *goals* of that motive. And this entails that, if we confine ourselves to secular motives, take seriously the fact that compassion is the highest secular motive in Martineau's ranking, and as a result choose universal benevolence as supremely regulative, then actions and motives will be judged in terms of the goal of universal benevolence—namely, human or sentient happiness. Somehow, we have ended up not with a more orderly or unified form of agent-based view, but with *act-utilitarianism.* And this has happened because Sidgwick ignores the possibility of an agent-based view that judges actions from either of two conflicting motives in terms of how well the two motives exemplify or approximate to the motive of universal benevolence *rather than* in terms of whether those actions achieve or are likely to achieve certain goals that universal benevolence aims at.

Thus suppose someone knows that he can help a friend in need, but that he could instead have fun swimming. The good he can do for himself by swimming is a great deal less than what he can do for his friend, but he also knows that if he swims, certain strangers will somehow indirectly benefit and the benefit will be greater than anything he can provide for his needy friend. However, the man does not at all care about the strangers, and, though he does care about his friend, he ends up taking a swim. In that case, both actualist and expectabilist versions of act-utilitarianism will regard his action as the morally best available to him in the circumstances. It has better consequences for human happiness than any alternative, and its expectable utility is greater than the alternative of helping his friend, since the man *knows* he will do more good, directly and indirectly, by swimming. But there is a difference between *expecting* or *knowing* that an act will have good consequences and being *motivated* to produce those consequences, and if we judge actions in agent-based fashion by how closely their motives exemplify or approximate to universal benevolence, then it is morally *less* good for him to go swimming for the selfish reason he does than to have sought to help his needy friend, and this is precisely the opposite of what standard forms of act-utilitarianism have to say about this situation.

Thus, in order to rule out agent-based views using the notion of compassion or benevolence, it is not enough to undermine complicated views like Martineau's, for we have seen that there can be an agent-based *analogue* of utilitarianism that morally judges everything, in unified or monistic fashion, by reference to universal benevolence as a *motive that seeks* certain ends rather than, in the utilitarian manner, by reference to the actual or probable *occurrence* of those ends. And this distinctive *morality as universal benevolence*—which as it were turns utilitarianism *outside in*—contrasts with utilitarianism in some striking further ways we have not yet mentioned.

Utilitarians and consequentialists evaluate motives and intentions in the same way as actions—namely, in terms of their consequences. (I shall here ignore rule-utilitarianism because of what I take to be its inherent difficulties.) Thus consider someone whose motives would ordinarily be thought not to be morally good, a person who gives money for the building of a hospital, but who is motivated only by a desire to see her name on a building or a desire to get a reputation for generosity as a means to launching a political career. Utilitarians and consequentialists will typically say that her particular motivation, her motivation in those circumstances, is morally good, whereas morality as universal benevolence, because it evaluates motives in terms of how well they approximate to universal benevolence, will be able, more intuitively, to treat such motivation as less than morally good (even if not very *bad* either). Of course, when we learn of what such a person is doing and, let us assume, of her selfish motivation, we may well be happy and think it a good thing that she has the egotistical motives she has on the occasion in question, given their good consequences (and our own benevolence). But we ordinarily *distinguish* between motives that, relative to circumstances, we are glad to see and it is good to have occur and motives we genuinely admire as morally good, and consequentialism standardly leads to a denial and collapse of this plausible distinction by morally evaluating motives solely in terms of their consequences. By contrast, morality as universal benevolence, precisely because it insists that the *moral* evaluation of motives depends on their inherent character as motives rather than on their consequences, allows for the distinction and comes much closer to an intuitive conception of what makes motives morally better or worse.

As an agent-based analogue of utilitarianism, morality as universal benevolence is, however, open to many of the criticisms that have recently been directed at utilitarianism—among them, the claim that such views demand too much self-sacrifice. But this last problem can perhaps be dealt with on analogy with the way utilitarianism and consequentialism have attempted to deal with the criticism of overdemandingness—namely, either by arguing against it outright or by accommodating it through an adjustment of their principle(s) of right action. A satisficing version of (utilitarian) consequentialism can say that right action requires only that one do enough good, and it can then offer some agent-neutral conception of what it is, in various situations, to do enough good for humankind considered as a whole. And a satisficing version of morality as universal benevolence can (in a manner already indicated in the way we stated that view earlier) say that acts are right if they come from a motive (together with underlying moral dispositions) that is *close enough* to universal benevolence—rather than insisting that only acts exemplifying the highest motive, universal benevolence, can count as morally acceptable. Someone who devoted most of her time, say, to the rights of consumers or to peace in Northern Ireland might then count as acting and living rightly, even if she were not universally concerned with human welfare and sometimes preferred simply to enjoy herself. So there are versions of morality as universal benevolence that allow us to meet the criticism of overdemandingness, even if we think that criticism does have force against versions of the view that require us always to have the morally best motives or moral dispositions, when we act.

Some forms of utilitarianism are also, however, criticized for having an overly narrow conception of human well-being and in particular for treating all well-being as a matter of the balance of pleasure over pain. This criticism does not hold for (certain) pluralistic forms of consequentialism, and neither, interestingly enough, does it apply to morality as universal benevolence. The latter is not committed to any particular conception of human well-being and is quite happy to allow us to admire a person's concern and compassion for human beings without attributing to that person or ourselves having a settled view of what human well-being consists in.

Finally, utilitarianism has been criticized for its inability to account for certain aspects of deontology, and these criticisms would undoubtedly also extend to morality as universal benevolence. Strict deontology tells us we would be wrong to kill one person in a group in order to prevent everyone in the group, including the person in question, from being killed by some menacing third party. But although Kantian ethics indeed seems to demand that we refrain from killing the one person, it is not clear that our ordinary thinking actually insists on such a requirement. Bernard Williams, for example, says that the question whether to kill one to save the rest is more difficult than utilitarianism can allow, but he also grants that utilitarianism probably gives the right answer about what to do in such a case.[11] Moreover, since benevolence involves not only the desire to do what is good or best overall for the people one is concerned about, *but also the desire that no one of those people should be hurt or suffer*, morality as universal benevolence can explain why we might be horrified at killing one to save many, even if in the end it holds that that is what we morally ought to do. I conclude, then, that, although both consequentialism and morality as universal benevolence are open to a good many familiar criticisms, they have ways of responding to the criticisms. Moreover, they have systematic advantages over many other approaches to morality because of their relative systematicity or unified structure. But, as I suggested earlier, morality as universal benevolence seems to have intuitive advantages over its more familiar utilitarian/consequentialist analogues. Though it is a view that to the best of my knowledge has not previously been explicitly stated or defended, it is in many ways more commonsensical and plausible than utilitarianism and consequentialism, and at the same time its reliance on the ideas of benevolence and universality ought to render it attractive to defenders of the latter views and make them ask themselves whether it would not be better to accept an agent-based 'interiorized' version of their own doctrines. If consequentialism and utilitarianism have present-day viability and appeal, agent-based morality as universal benevolence does too.[12]

MORALITY AS CARING

However, we have not yet exhausted the promising possibilities of agent-basing, and at this point I would like us to consider one final way of utilizing the idea of benevolence within an agent-based virtue ethics. Some educationists and philosophers have recently been exploring and developing the idea of an ethic or morality of *caring*, and I would like now to push or disambiguate this idea in the direction of a new kind of warm agent-based view.

It is possible to ground an agent-based ethical theory in an ideal of *partial or particularistic benevolence*, of caring *more* for some than for

[11] See Bernard Williams, 'A Critique of Utilitarianism', in J. Smart and B. Williams, *Utilitarianism: For and Against* (Cambridge, 1985), esp. p. 117.

[12] In his *Inquiry into the Original of Our Ideas of Beauty and Virtue* (London, 1725), Francis Hutcheson takes universal benevolence to be inherently the morally best or highest motive, but evaluates actions in terms of how well they further the goal(s) of such benevolence. Such a view lies midway between morality as universal benevolence and utilitarianism, morally assessing motives in the manner of the former, but actions in the manner of the latter. As a result it is open to the usual objections that are made of hybrid moral views (like rule-utilitarianism).

others. We find at least the potential for such a view in St Augustine's claim that all virtue is based in love for God (though Augustine at various points appears to import non-agent-based elements into his arguments).[13] But it is also possible to develop a purely secular agent-based view that puts a premium on caring for or benevolence towards some people more than others, and it is this possibility that I want to consider in what follows.

In her ground-breaking *In a Different Voice*, Carol Gilligan argued that men tend to conceive morality in terms of rights, justice, and autonomy, whereas women more frequently think of the moral in terms of caring, responsibility, and interrelation with others. And at about the same time Nel Noddings, in *Caring: A Feminine Approach to Ethics and Moral Education*, sought to articulate and defend in its own right a 'feminine' morality centred specifically around the idea of caring.[14] But when one reads Noddings, one is left unclear as to whether she intends her ethics of caring to be agent-based. The notion of agent-basing has only recently become a tool of ethical theory, and there is no reason to expect Noddings, writing some years back, to have related her work to that notion. But given recent developments, especially in virtue ethics, it is perhaps interesting to consider whether the morality of caring cannot be seen as agent-based and thereby given a firmer or more definite theoretical grounding.

In her book, Noddings seems to want to relate everything in morality to particularistic caring, rather than bringing in independent principles of justice or truth-telling or what-have-you, but there is still a potential obstacle to seeing her ethics as agent-based. For, although she emphasizes the moral goodness of acting from care, she also says that we should try to *promote* caring in the world, and this sounds like a consequentialistic and indeed perfectionistic element in her views. (Perfectionism is a form of consequentialism that tells us, roughly, to focus ultimately on whether our acts produce virtue and excellence, not on their results for happiness.) If she believes in a fundamental imperative to produce or promote caring in the world, then Noddings's view is clearly not agent-based, but I do not think what we know of Noddings's views settles the issue of whether her views are implicitly agent-based, because she never says that the promotion of caring is a fundamental moral value, and if it is not, then there is in fact a way of *deriving* it from an agent-based partialistic ethic of caring.

[13] Augustine, *De Moribus Ecclesiae Catholicae* 15.25.

[14] See Carol Gilligan, *In a Different Voice: Psychological Theory and Women's Development* (Cambridge, Mass.: 1982; and Nel Noddings, *Caring: A Feminine Approach to Ethics and Moral Education* (Berkeley and Los Angeles, 1984).

Consider the reasons one might have for trying to get (certain) people to care more about (certain other) people. Could not one's reason be that, by getting them to care more, one could eventually bring about more good for humanity generally or for the people one cares about? If one really wants to help (certain) people, working to get them to care for one another's welfare might have a multiplier effect, allowing one at least indirectly to help more people overall than if one always simply promoted welfare directly. A caring person might thus see the promotion of caring as the best way to promote what she as a caring person is concerned about, and in that measure, the concern for and promotion of virtuous caring on the part of others would be an instance of caring itself conceived as a fundamental form of moral excellence and would thus be accommodatable within an agent-based theory of the moral value of caring. Perfectionism and good results as such would not have to come into the matter. But, as I say, I am not sure Noddings is best interpreted in this way and only suggest it because the agent-based theory we have just arrived at is at the very least interesting and promising in its own right.

An agent-based moral theory that puts a moral premium on particularistic caring presumably needs to say more than Noddings herself says about self-concern and about appropriate attitudes and actions towards strangers. No reasonable ethics should decry or begrudge self-concern and a degree of self-assertiveness in moral agents, and, as feminists and others have recently noted, it would be ironic and morally counter-productive for any new ethics to focus exclusively on aspects of feminine moral thought and activity that have typically restricted and been used to restrict the freedom and self-fulfilment of women. An ethic of care or concern exclusively or even primarily for favoured *others* seems, then, to be morally retrograde, but there is no reason why a feminine or feminist ethic of caring, developed specifically in an agent-based fashion, should not say that it is best and most admirable to be motivated by concern for others *in balance with* self-concern and that all and only actions and activities that are consonant with and display such balance are morally acceptable.[15]

There is also the problem of appropriate concern for and treatment of strangers. But a partialistic morality that advocated greater concern for near and dear might still deplore *indifference* to strangers, and, if the moral floor of non-indifference, of humane caring, is not set too low, an agent-

[15] On the idea that we should balance self-concern with concern for other people (considered as a class), see my *From Morality to Virtue*, ch. 6. However, I am not denying that it is often difficult to disentangle self-interest from altruism, as, for example, when the help one has given one's own children or a friend represents a happy achievement of one's own life.

based morality as caring will be able to treat the usual questions of justice and human rights in a plausible, but highly distinctive way.[16]

Defenders of universality and impartiality may object at this point that the ethic of caring does not provide *enough* assurance that strangers will be properly treated and so argue for the theoretical preferability of morality as universal benevolence among agent-based doctrines. But partialists can reply that devotion to particular individuals seems morally preferable to and more admirable than any sort of impartial benevolence, and it is not clear who has the better case here. Note, however, that some partialists claim that particularistic caring is obligatory and admirable because *necessary to important human goods* that are realizable only in close relationships. Such an explanation takes us away from agent-basing, but I wonder how cogent it is. If parental love is obligatory and admirable *because* essential to the good(s) of family life, why is a child not just as obligated to take things from her parents and accounted admirable for doing so? The difference here seems to depend on a *fundamental difference in admirability* between caring for and being cared for, and that sits well with an agent-based morality that deems caring admirable as such and apart from its helping to realize certain goods. Similarly, the devotion of a tutor to a retarded child can be very admirable, even if it might be *better* if their relationship were not needed. The admirability of such caring seems not to be grounded in the desirability of a relationship, but, again, to stand in no need of further justification, so a morality of caring should have no qualms, I think, about conceiving itself as agent-based.

APPLYING AGENT-BASED VIEWS

However, our two favoured forms of agent-based virtue ethics—morality as universal benevolence and morality as caring—face a further difficulty that must now be mentioned. If someone is faced with a perplexing moral problem, it somehow seems irrelevant and even objectionable for her to examine *her own motives rather than facts about people and the world* in

[16] In a 1988 talk to the Society for Women in Philosophy, Noddings said that our obligations to strangers cannot be accommodated through the notion of caring, because caring requires an on-going relationship. But rather than in this way give up on the idea of a total morality of caring, I think we should try to make sense of the idea of a morally requisite minimum level of care/concern for distant strangers (who after all do share the planet and many other things with us). Virginia Held (in *Feminist Morality* (Chicago, 1993), 223) makes some suggestive remarks in this direction, and I believe that, if we develop a morality of caring in this way, we will end up with a kind of 'inverse-care law' that requires less—but still substantial—concern for people the further they are from one in sociological and/or personal terms.

order to solve it. Yet is not this what agent-basing allows for and even prescribes? For example, does not morality as (universal or partialistic) benevolence tell us that whether it is morally good, right, or acceptable, say, to oppose the taking of heroic measures to keep an aged dying parent alive depends on the motives of the person in question, and is this at all helpful for someone who *does not know* whether to advocate or oppose heroic measures for a dying or suffering parent? Looking inward at or for motives presumably will not help to solve that person's problem, and so, where we most need moral guidance, it would seem that agent-basing not only is irrelevant but makes it impossible to find a solution to one's moral difficulties.

Some defenders of virtue ethics are willing to grant that virtue ethics—whether agent-based or otherwise—cannot be applied to practical moral issues, but would claim none the less that virtue ethics can give us the correct theory or view of morality.[17] However, it would be better for virtue ethics if we could show that (agent-based) virtue ethics *can* be applied, and I believe we can accomplish this by making further use of what was said earlier about the way that an internal state like benevolence focuses on, and concerns itself with gathering facts about, the world. If one morally judges a certain course of action or decision by reference to, say, the benevolence of the motives of its agent, one is judging in relation to an inner factor that itself makes reference to and takes account of facts about people in the world. One's inward gaze effectively 'doubles back' on the world and allows one, as we shall see in more detail in a moment, to take facts about the world into account in one's attempt to determine what is morally acceptable or best to do. But neither, on the other hand, is this doubling-back unnecessarily duplicative or wasteful of moral effort, if we assume that motive is fundamentally at least relevant to the *moral* character of any action. For if we judge the actions or ourselves or others simply by their effects in the world, we end up unable to distinguish accidentally or ironically useful actions (or slips on banana peels) from actions that we actually morally admire and that are morally good and praiseworthy.

Consider, then, someone who hears that her aged mother has suddenly been taken to the hospital and who flies from a distant city to be with her. Given morality as benevolence in some form or other and assuming she is her mother's sole living relative, how should she resolve the issue of what morally she ought to do with or for her parent when she gets to the hospital? Should she or should she not, for example, advocate heroic measures to save her mother? Surely morality as (one or another form of)

[17] See e.g. Edmund Pincoffs, *Quandaries and Virtues* (Lawrence, Kan., 1986).

benevolence does not give her an answer to this question, but what is worth noting is that, given the woman's ignorance, as we are assuming, of her mother's particular condition and prospects, there is no reason for most moral theories to offer an answer to that question at this point. But morality as benevolence *does* offer her an answer to the question what morally she should do when she gets to the hospital. It tells her she morally ought (would be wrong not) to find out more about her mother's condition and prospects, as regards quality and duration of life and certainly as regards future suffering and incapacity. And it can tell her this by reference to her actual motives, because if she does not find out more and decides what to do or to advocate about her mother solely on the basis of present relative ignorance, she will demonstrate a callousness (towards her mother) that is very far from benevolent. To decide to pull the plug or not allow heroic measures without finding out more about her mother would demonstrate indifference or callousness towards her and on that basis morality as benevolence can make the moral judgement that she ought to find out more before making any decision. (Morality as inner strength could be shown to yield a similar conclusion.)

Then, once the facts have emerged and assuming they are fairly clear-cut and point to horrendously painful and debilitating prospects for her mother, the woman's decision is once again plausibly derivable from morality as benevolence. At that point, it would be callous of her to insist on heroic measures and benevolent not to do so and the proper moral decision can thus be reached by agent-based considerations.

But surely, someone might say, the woman herself does not think in such terms. She is worried about whether her mother would have a painful or pleasant future existence, for example, not about whether she herself would be acting callously if she sought to prolong the mother's existence. Are you sure? Could she not morally justify her decision not to allow heroic measures *either* by reference simply to likely future sufferings if the mother were kept alive or by saying, more complexly and richly: it would be (have been) callous of me to try to keep her alive, given her prospects? Surely, there is nothing unusual or untoward about the latter as an expression of moral problem-solving.[18]

Think, for example, about the arguments that, as a matter of historic

[18] If the woman thinks 'I mustn't keep her alive, because if I do, I won't deserve to be considered—or be able to regard myself as—a kind person,' she is self-absorbed and shows herself less than ideally benevolent or kind. But the mere thought that it would be unkind or callous if one were to keep one's mother alive, given her prospects, seems compatible with the highest kindness. The reference to one's own motives required for the practical application of an agent-based morality as benevolence need in no way undercut the benevolence that such a view prizes.

fact, were made in advocacy of the North American Free Trade Agreement (NAFTA). Both Vice-President Gore and House Minority Leader Robert Michel defended the agreement on the grounds that to reject it would be to adopt a cringing, fearful, or despairing attitude to the world and/or America's future. They could have spoken more directly about consequences, but there is nothing unreasonable about the way they addressed the issue, and so I want to conclude that, given the outward-looking character of inner motives, agent-based views have resources for the resolution of moral issues that parallel those available to such practically applicable moral theories as utilitarianism and consequentialism more generally.

Our ordinary thinking in response to difficult or not-so-difficult practical moral issues can invoke either motives or consequences or both. Consequentialism, however, solves such issues by appealing ultimately to consequences and only indirectly and as a method of useful approximation to considerations of motives like impartial benevolence. Agent-based morality as benevolence solves the problem in the opposite fashion by appealing ultimately to motives, but taking in consequences indirectly, to the extent they are considered by (people with) such motives and investigated in response to such motives. Each approach allows for the case-by-case solution of many moral difficulties or problems, and so, with regard to the whole question of applied ethics, neither approach seems to have the advantage, and there is no reason to criticize agent-basing for being irrelevant to practical moral problems or making their solution impossible to achieve.[19]

Certainly, there will be times when morality as benevolence will not be able to solve our moral difficulties. For example, if the facts about her mother's prospects cannot be learned or turn out to be highly complicated, morality as benevolence will be stymied. But any consequentialism worthy of the name will also come up empty in such a case, and it is a strength of such views, but no less of agent-based morality as benevolence, whether in partialistic or universalistic form, that such views do not presume to know the answers to difficult moral questions in cases that *outrun our human knowledge or reasoning powers*. Any ethical theory that makes it too easy

[19] I am not assuming that someone who is benevolent or accepts a theory like morality as (universal or partial) benevolence has to think explicitly in moral terms to find the answer to a practical moral question. If she just wants to know what would be the (most) benevolent thing to do, finds out, and then acts accordingly, we may well want to regard her as thereby having answered the practical moral question others might pose using explicitly moral language. But that is not to say that such a person *cannot* deal with moral difficulties in explicitly moral terms. A benevolent person can easily be concerned to do what is right *given her own view that benevolence defines or determines rightness*.

always to know what to do or feel will seem to that extent flawed or even useless because untrue to our soberer sense of the wrenching complexity of moral phenomena.

Since the revival of virtue ethics, those interested in the subject have focused mainly on Aristotle and on neo-Aristotelian ideas. I have myself defended neo-Aristotelian ideas in *From Morality to Virtue*, but we have seen here that certain forms of agent-based virtue ethics also have real promise and possibilities. In a period when virtue ethics is flexing its muscles, it needs a more varied diet than Aristotle or Aristotelianism alone can provide.[20]

[20] I am indebted to Gerald Barnes, Jeanette Emt, Brad Hooker, Rosalind Hursthouse, Jonas Josefsson, Georges Rey, and, especially, Christine Swanton for helpful criticisms and suggestions.

13

WHAT DO WOMEN WANT IN A MORAL THEORY?

ANNETTE BAIER

When I finished reading Carol Gilligan's *In a Different Voice*,[1] I asked myself the obvious question for a philosopher reader: what differences should one expect in the moral philosophy done by women, supposing Gilligan's sample of women to be representative and supposing her analysis of their moral attitudes and moral development to be correct? Should one expect women to want to produce moral theories, and if so, what sort of moral theories? How will any moral theories they produce differ from those produced by men?

Obviously one does not have to make this an entirely a priori and hypothetical question. One can look and see what sort of contributions women have made to moral philosophy. Such a look confirms, I think, Gilligan's findings. What one finds *is* a bit different in tone and approach from the standard sort of the moral philosophy as done by men following in the footsteps of the great moral philosophers (all men). Generalizations are extremely rash, but when I think of Philippa Foot's work on the moral virtues, Elizabeth Anscombe's work on intention and on modern moral philosophy, Iris Murdoch's philosophical writings, Ruth Barcan Marcus's work on moral dilemmas, the work of the radical feminist moral philosophers who are not content with orthodox Marxist lines of thought, Jenny Teichman's book on illegitimacy, Susan Wolf's articles, Claudia Card's essay on mercy, Sabina Lovibond's writings, Gabriele Taylor's work on pride, love, and on integrity, Cora Diamond's and Mary Midgley's work on our attitude towards animals, Sissela Bok's work on lying and on secrecy, Virginia Held's work, the work of Alison Jaggar, Marilyn Frye, and many others, I seem to hear a different voice from the standard moral philosophers' voice. I hear the voice Gilligan heard, made reflective and

From Annette Baier, *Moral Prejudices* (Cambridge, Mass.: Harvard University Press, 1994), 1–17. Reprinted by permission.

[1] Carol Gilligan, *In a Different Voice: Psychological Theory and Women's Development* (Cambridge, Mass., 1982).

philosophical. What women want in moral philosophy is what they are providing. And what they are providing seems to me to confirm Gilligan's theses about women. One has to be careful here, of course, for not all important contributions to moral philosophy by women fall easily into the Gilligan stereotype or its philosophical extension. Nor has it been only women who have been proclaiming discontent with the standard approach in moral philosophy and trying new approaches. Michael Stocker, Alasdair MacIntyre, and Ian Hacking when he assesses the game-theoretic approach to morality,[2] all should be given the status of honorary women, if we accept the hypothesis that there are some moral insights for whatever reason women seem to attain more easily or more reliably than men do. Still, exceptions confirm the rule, so I shall proceed undaunted by these important exceptions to my generalizations.

If Hacking is right, preoccupation with prisoner's and prisoners' dilemmas is a big boys' game, and a pretty silly one too. It is, I think, significant that women have not rushed into the field of game-theoretic moral philosophy, and that those who have dared enter that male locker room have said distinctive things there. Edna Ullmann Margalit's book *The Emergence of Norms* put prisoner's dilemma in its limited moral place. Supposing that at least part of the explanation for the relatively few women in this field is disinclination rather than disability, one might ask if this disinclination also extends to the construction of moral theories. For although we find out what sort of moral philosophy women want by looking to see what they have provided, if we do that for moral theory, the answer we get seems to be 'none'. None of the contributions to moral philosophy by women really counts as a moral theory, nor is seen as such by its author.

Is it that reflective women, when they become philosophers, want to do without moral theory, want no part in the construction of such theories? To conclude this at this early stage, when we have only a few generations of women moral philosophers to judge from, would be rash indeed. The term 'theory' can be used in wider and narrower ways, and in its widest sense a moral theory is simply an internally consistent fairly comprehensive account of what morality is and when and why it merits our acceptance and support. In that wide sense, a moral theory is something it would take a sceptic, or one who believes that our intellectual vision is necessarily blurred or distorted when we let it try to take in too much, to be an antitheorist. Even if there were some truth in the latter claim, one might

[2] Ian Hacking, 'Winner Take Less', a review of *The Evolution of Cooperation* by Robert Axelrod, *New York Review of Books*, 31 (28 June 1984).

compatibly with it still hope to build up a coherent total account by a mosaic method, assembling a lot of smaller-scale works until one had built up a complete account—say, taking the virtues or purported virtues one by one until one had a more or less complete account. But would that sort of comprehensiveness in one's moral philosophy entitle one to call the finished work a moral theory? If it would, then many women moral philosophers today can be seen as engaged in moral theory construction. In the weakest sense of 'theory', as a coherent near-comprehensive account, there are plenty of incomplete theories to be found in the works of women moral philosophers. And in *that* sense of theory, most of what are recognized as the current moral theories are also incomplete, because they do not yet purport to be really comprehensive. Wrongs to animals and wrongful destruction of our physical environment are put to one side by John Rawls, and in most 'liberal' theories there are only hand waves concerning our proper attitude towards our children, towards the ill, towards our relatives, friends, and lovers.

Is comprehensiveness too much to ask of a moral theory? The paradigm examples of moral theories—those that are called by their authors 'moral theories'—are distinguished not by the comprehensiveness of their internally coherent account but by the *sort* of coherence which is aimed at over a fairly broad area. Their method is not the mosaic method but the broad brushstroke method. Moral theories, as we know them, are, to change the art form, vaults rather than walls—they are not built by assembling painstakingly made brick after brick. In *this* sense of theory—a fairly tightly systematic account of a large area of morality, with a keystone supporting all the rest—women moral philosophers have not yet, to my knowledge, produced moral theories or claimed that they have.

Leaving to one side the question of what purpose (other than good clean intellectual fun) is served by such moral theories, and supposing for the sake of argument that women can, if they wish, systematize as well as the next man and, if need be, systematize in a mathematical fashion as well as the next mathematically minded moral philosopher, then what key concept or guiding motif might hold together the structure of a moral theory hypothetically produced by a reflective woman, Gilligan-style, who has taken up moral theorizing as a calling? What would be a suitable central question, principle, or concept to structure a moral theory which might accommodate those moral insights which women tend to have more readily than men, and to answer those moral questions which, it seems, worry women more than men? I hypothesized that the women's theory, expressive mainly of women's insights and concerns, would be an ethics of love, and this hypothesis seems to be Gilligan's too, since she has gone on from *In a Different Voice* to write about the limitations of Freud's understanding of love as women know it.[3] But presumably women theorists will be like enough to men to want their moral theory to be acceptable to all, so acceptable both to reflective women and to reflective men. Like any good theory, it will need not to ignore the partial truth of previous theories. It must therefore accommodate both the insights men have more easily than women and those women have more easily than men. It should swallow up its predecessor theories. Women moral theorists, if any, will have this very great advantage over the men whose theories theirs supplant, that they can stand on the shoulders of male moral theorists, as no man has yet been able to stand on the shoulders of any female moral theorist. There can be advantages as well as handicaps in being latecomers. So women theorists will need to connect their ethics of love with what has been the men theorists' preoccupation, namely, obligation.

The great and influential moral theorists have in the modern era taken *obligation* as the key and the problematic concept, and have asked what justifies treating a person as morally bound or obliged to do a particular thing. Since to be bound is to be unfree, by making obligation central one at the same time makes central the question of the justification of coercion, of forcing or trying to force someone to act in a particular way. The concept of obligation as justified limitation of freedom does just what one wants a good theoretical concept to do—to divide up the field (as one looks at different ways one's freedom may be limited, freedom in different spheres, different sorts and versions and levels of justification) and at the same time to hold the subfields together. There must in a theory be some generalization and some speciation or diversification, and a good rich key concept guides one both in recognizing the diversity and in recognizing the unity in it. The concept of obligation has served this function very well for the area of morality it covers, and so we have some fine theories about that area. But as Aristotelians and Christians, as well as women, know, there is a lot of morality *not* covered by that concept, a lot of very great importance even for the area where there are obligations.

This is fairly easy to see if we look at what lies behind the perceived obligation to keep promises. Unless there is some good moral reason why someone should assume the responsibility of rearing a child to be *capable* of taking promises seriously, once she understands what a promise is, the obligation to obey promises will not effectively tie her, and any force applied to punish her when she breaks promises or makes fraudulent ones

[3] Carol Gilligan, 'The Conquistador and the Dark Continent: Reflections on the Psychology of Love', *Daedalus*, 113 (Summer 1984), 75–95.

will be of questionable justice. Is there an *obligation* on someone to make the child into a morally competent promisor? If so, on whom? Who has failed in his or her obligations when, say, war orphans who grew up without parental love or any other love arrive at legal adulthood very willing to be untrue to their word? Who failed in what obligation in all those less extreme cases of attempted but unsuccessful moral education? The parents who didn't produce promise-keeping offspring? Those who failed to educate the parents in how to educate their children (whoever it might be who could plausibly be thought to have the responsibility for training parents to fulfil their obligations)? The liberal version of our basic moral obligations tends to be fairly silent on who has what obligations to new members of the moral community, and it would throw most theories of the justification of obligations into some confusion if the obligation to rear one's children lovingly were added to the list of obligations. Such evidence as we have about the conditions in which children do successfully 'learn' the morality of the community of which they are members suggests that we cannot substitute 'conscientiously' for 'lovingly' in this hypothetical extra needed obligation. But an obligation to love, in the strong sense needed, would be an embarrassment to the theorist, given most accepted versions of 'ought implies can'.

It is hard to make fair generalizations here, so I shall content myself with indicating how this charge I am making against the current men's moral theories, that their version of the justified list of obligations does not ensure the proper care of the young and so does nothing to ensure the stability of the morality in question over several generations, can be made against what I regard as the best of the men's recent theories, Rawls's theory of justice. One of the great strengths of Rawls's theory is the careful attention given to the question of how just institutions produce the conditions for their continued support, across generations, and in particular of how the sense of justice will arise in children, once there are minimally just institutions structuring the social world into which they are born. Rawls, more than most moral theorists, has attended to the question of the stability of his just society, given what we know about child development. But Rawls's sensitive account of the conditions for the development of that sense of justice needed for the maintenance of his version of a just society takes it for granted that there will be loving parents rearing the children in whom the sense of justice is to develop. 'The parents, we may suppose, love the child, and in time the child comes to love and trust the parents.' Why may we suppose this? Not because compliance with Rawls's version of our obligations and duties will ensure it. Rawls's theory, like so many other theories of obligation, in the end must take out a loan not only on the natural duty of parents to care for children (which he will have no trouble including) but on the natural *virtue* of parental love (or even a loan on the maternal instinct?). The virtue of being a *loving* parent must supplement the natural duties and the obligations of justice, if the just society is to last beyond the first generation. And as Nancy Chodorow's work indicates, the loving parents must also accept a certain division of child-care responsibility if their version of the obligations and virtues of men and of women is, along with their version of the division of labour accompanying that allocation of virtues, to be passed on.

Reliance on a recognized obligation to turn oneself into a good parent or else to avoid becoming a parent would be a problematic solution. Good parents tend to be the children of good parents, so this obligation would collapse into the obligation to avoid parenthood unless one expected to be a good parent. That, given available methods of contraception, may itself convert into the obligation, should one expect not to be a good parent, to sexual abstinence, or sterilization, or resolute resort to abortion when contraception fails. The conditional obligation to abort, and in effect also the conditional obligation to sterilization, falls on the women. There may be conditions in which the rational moral choice is between obligatory sexual abstinence and obligatory sterilization, but obligatory abortion, such as women in China now face, seems to me a moral monster. I do not believe that liberal moral theorists will be able to persuade reflective women that a morality that in any conditions makes abortion obligatory, as distinct from permitted or advisable or, on occasion, best, is in their own as well as their male fellows' long-term self-interest. It would be tragic if such moral questions in the end came to the question of whose best interests to sacrifice, men's or women's. I do not believe they *do* come to this, but should they, then justice would require that, given the long history of the subordination of women's to men's interests, men's interests be sacrificed. Justice, of course, never decides these issues unless power reinforces justice, so I am not predicting any victory for women, should it ever come to a fight over obligatory abortion or over who is to face obligatory sterilization.

No liberal moral theorist, as far as I know, is advocating obligatory abortion or obligatory sterilization when necessary to prevent the conception of children whose parents do not expect to love them. My point rather is that they escape this conclusion only by avoiding the issue of what is to ensure that new members of the moral community do get the loving care they need to become morally competent persons. Liberal moral theories assume that women either will provide loving maternal care, or will persuade their mates to provide loving paternal care, or when pregnant will decide for abortion, encouraged by their freedom-loving men. These theories, in other words, exploit the culturally encouraged maternal instinct and/or the culturally encouraged docility of women. The liberal system would receive a nasty spanner in its works should women use their freedom of choice as regards abortion to choose *not* to abort, and then leave their newborn children on their fathers' doorsteps. That would test liberal morality's ability to provide for its own survival.

At this point it may be objected that every moral theory must make some assumptions about the natural psychology of those on whom obligations are imposed. Why shouldn't the liberal theory count on a continuing sufficient supply of good loving mothers, as it counts on continuing self-interest and, perhaps, on a continuing supply of pugnacious men who are able and willing to become good soldiers, without turning any of these into moral *obligations*? Why waste moral resources recognizing as obligatory or as virtuous what one can count on getting without moral pressure? If, in the moral economy, one can get enough good mothers and good warriors 'for free', why not gladly exploit what nature and cultural history offer? I cannot answer this question fully here, but my argument does depend upon the assumption that a decent morality will *not* depend for its stability on forces to which it gives no moral recognition. Its account books should be open to scrutiny, and there should be no unpaid debts, no loans with no prospect of repayment. I also assume that once we are clear about these matters and about the interdependencies involved, our principles of justice will not allow us to recognize either a special obligation on every woman to initiate the killing of the foetus she has conceived, should she and her mate be, or think they will be, deficient in parental love, or a special obligation on every young man to kill those his elders have labelled enemies of his country. Both such 'obligations' are prima facie suspect, and difficult to make consistent with any of the principles supposedly generating obligations in modern moral theories. I also assume that, on reflection, we will not want to recognize as *virtues* the character traits of women and men which lead them to supply such life and death services 'for free'. Neither maternal servitude, nor the resoluteness needed to kill off one's children to prevent their growing up unloved, nor the easy willingness to go out and kill when ordered to do so by authorities seems to me to be a character trait a decent morality will encourage by labelling it a virtue. But the liberals' morality must somehow encourage such traits if its stability depends on enough people showing them. There is, then, understandable motive for liberals' avoidance of the question of whether such qualities are or are not morally approved of, and of whether or not there is any obligation to act as one with such character traits would act.

It is symptomatic of the bad faith of liberal morality as understood by many of those who defend it that issues such as whether to fight or not to fight, to have or not to have an abortion, or to be or not to be an unpaid maternal drudge are left to individual conscience. Since there is no coherent guidance liberal morality can give on these issues, which clearly are *not* matters of moral indifference, liberal morality tells each of us, 'the choice is yours', hoping that enough will choose to be self-sacrificial life providers and self-sacrificial death dealers to suit the purposes of the rest.

Rawls's theory does explicitly face the question of the moral justification of refusal to bear arms, and of how a just society justly provides for its own defence. The hardships imposed on conscripted soldiers are, he says, a necessary evil, and the most that just institutions can do is to 'make sure that the risks of suffering from those misfortunes are more or less evenly shared by all members of society over the course of their life, and that there is no avoidable class bias in selecting those who are called for duty'. What of sex/gender bias? Or is that assumed to be unavoidable? Rawls's principles seem to me to imply that women should be conscripted, if anyone is (and I think that is right), but since he avoids the questions of justice between men and women one does not know whether he intended this implication. His suggestion that one argument in favour of a conscripted army is that it is less likely to be an instrument of unjustified foreign adventures will become even stronger, I believe, if half the conscripts are women. Like most male moral theorists, Rawls does not discuss the morality of having children, refusing to have them, refusing to care for them, nor does he discuss how just institutions might equalize the responsibilities involved in ensuring that there be new members of society and that they become morally competent members of it, so one does not know whether he accepts a gender-based division of social service here, leaving it to the men to do the dangerous defensive destruction of life and cities while the support of new life, and any costs going or contrived to go with that, are left to the women. I hope that is not what he meant.

I do not wish, by having myself spoken of these two traditionally gender-based allocations of responsibility (producing and caring for new human life and the destruction of the lives of those officially labelled enemies) together, to leave the impression that I see any parallel between them except that they have both been treated as gender based and that both present embarrassments for liberal moral theory. Not all allocations of responsibility are allocations of burdens, and parenthood, unlike unchosen military life, need not be seen as essentially burden bearing. Good mothers and good soldiers make contributions of very different sorts and sort of importance to the ongoing life of a moral community, and they should not be seen, as they sometimes are, as fair mutual substitutes, as forms of social service. Good mothers will always be needed by a moral community, in the best conditions as well as the worst; the need for good military men, though foreseeably permanent, is a sign of some failure of our morality, a failure of our effectively acted upon moral laws to be valid theorems for the conservation of men in multitudes. Nor do the burdens of soldiering have any real analogue in the case of motherhood, which today *need* not impose real costs on the mother. If there are significant costs—loss of career opportunity, improperly recompensed drudgery in the home, or health risks—this is due to bad but largely remediable social arrangements, as the failure of parents to experience any especially parental satisfactions may be also due to bad but remediable socially produced attitudes toward parental responsibility. We do not, I think, want our military men to enjoy killing the enemy and destroying their cities, and any changes we made in social customs and institutions to make such pleasures more likely would be deplorable ones. Military life in wartime should always be seen as a sacrifice, while motherhood should never need to be seen as self-sacrificial service. If it is an honour and a privilege to bear arms for one's country, as we understandably tell our military conscripts and volunteers, part of the honour is being trusted with activities that are a necessary evil, being trusted not to enjoy their evil aspects, and being trusted to see the evil as well as the necessity. Only if we contrive to make the bringing into the world of new persons as nasty a business as killing already present persons will there be any just reason to exclude young women from conscripted armies or to exclude men from equal parental responsibility.

Granted that the men's theories of obligation need supplementation, to have much chance of integrity and coherence, and that the women's hypothetical theories will want to cover obligation as well as love, then what concept brings them together? My tentative answer is—the concept of appropriate trust, oddly neglected in moral theory. This concept also nicely mediates between reason and feeling, those tired old candidates for moral authority, since to trust is neither quite to believe something about the trusted nor necessarily to feel any emotion towards them—but to have a belief-informed and action-influencing attitude. To make it plausible that the neglected concept of appropriate trust is a good one for the enlightened moral theorist to make central, I need to show, or begin to show, how it could include obligation, indeed shed light on obligations and their justification, as well as include love, the other moral concerns of Gilligan's women, and many of the topics women moral philosophers have chosen to address, mosaic fashion. I would also need to show that it could connect all of these in a way which holds out promise both of synthesis and of comprehensive moral coverage. A moral theory which looked at the conditions for proper trust of all the various sorts we show, and at what sorts of reasons justify inviting such trust, giving it, and meeting it, would, I believe, not have to avoid turning its gaze on the conditions for the survival of the practices it endorses, so it could avoid that unpleasant choice many current liberal theories seem to have—between incoherence and bad faith. I do not pretend that we will easily agree once we raise the questions I think we should raise, but at least we may have a language adequate to the expression of both men's and women's moral viewpoints.

My trust in the concept of trust is based in part on my own attempts to restate and consider what is right and what wrong with men's theories, especially Hume's, which I consider the best of the lot. I have found myself reconstructing his account of the artifices of justice as an account of the progressive enlargement of a climate of trust, and have found that a helpful way to see it. It has some textual basis, but is nevertheless a reconstruction, and one I have found, immodestly, an improvement. So it is because I have tried the concept and explored its dimensions a bit—the variety of goods we may trust others not to take from us, the sort of security or insurance we have when we do, the sorts of defences or potential defences we lay down when we trust, the various conditions for reasonable trust of various types—that I am hopeful about its power as a theoretical, and not just an exegetical, tool. I also found myself needing to use it when I made a brief rash attempt at that women's topic, caring (invited in by a male philosopher,[4] I should say). I am reasonably sure that trust does generalize some central moral features of the recognition of binding obligations and moral virtues and of loving, as well as of other important relations between persons, such as teacher–pupil, confider–confidante, worker to co-worker in the same cause, and professional to client. Indeed it is fairly obvious that love, the main moral phenomenon women want attended to, involves trust, so I anticipate little quarrel when I claim that, if we had a moral theory spelling out the conditions for appropriate trust and distrust, that would include a morality of love in all its variants—parental love, love of children for their parents, love of family members, love of friends, of lovers in the strict sense, of co-workers, of one's country and its figureheads, of exemplary heroines and heroes, of goddesses and gods.

Love and loyalty demand maximal trust of one sort, and maximal trustworthiness, and in investigating the conditions for maximal trust and maximal risk we must think about the ethics of love. More controversial may be

[4] 'Caring about Caring', a response to Harry Frankfurt's 'What We Care About', both in 'Matters of the Mind', *Synthèse*, 53 (Nov. 1982): 257–90. My paper is also included in my *Postures of the Mind: Essays on Mind and Morals* (Minneapolis, Minn., 1985).

my claim that the ethics of obligation will also be covered. I see it as covered because to recognize a set of obligations is to trust some group of persons to instil them, to demand that they be met, possibly to levy sanctions if they are not, and this is to trust persons with very significant coercive power over others. Less coercive but still significant power is possessed by those shaping our conception of the virtues and expecting us to display them, approving when we do, disapproving and perhaps shunning us when we do not. Such coercive and manipulative power over others requires justification, and is justified only if we have reason to trust those who have it to use it properly and to use the discretion which is always given when trust is given in a way which serves the purpose of the whole system of moral control, and not merely self-serving or morally improper purposes. Since the question of the justification of coercion becomes, at least in part, the question of the wisdom of trusting the coercers to do their job properly, the morality of obligation, in as far as it reduces to the morality of coercion, is covered by the morality of proper trust. Other forms of trust may also be involved, but trusting enforcers with the use of force is the most problematic form of trust involved.

The coercers and manipulators are, to some extent, all of us, so to ask what our obligations are and what virtues we should exhibit is to ask what it is reasonable to trust us to demand, expect, and contrive to get from one another. It becomes, in part, a question of what powers we can in reason trust ourselves to exercise properly. But self-trust is a dubious or limit case of trust, so I prefer to postpone the examination of the concept of proper self-trust at least until proper trust of others is more clearly understood. Nor do we distort matters too much if we concentrate on those cases where moral sanctions and moral pressure and moral manipulation are not self-applied but applied to others, particularly by older persons to younger persons. Most moral pressuring that has any effect goes on in childhood and early youth. Moral sanctions may continue to be applied, formally and informally, to adults, but unless the criminal courts apply them it is easy enough for adults to ignore them, to brush them aside. It is not difficult to become a sensible knave, and to harden one's heart so that one is insensible to the moral condemnation of one's victims and those who sympathize with them. Only if the pressures applied in the morally formative stage have given one a heart that rebels against the thought of such ruthless independence of what others think will one see any reason *not* to ignore moral condemnation, not to treat it as mere powerless words and breath. Condemning sensible knaves is as much a waste of breath as arguing with them—all we can sensibly do is to try to protect children against their influence, and ourselves against their knavery. Adding to the criminal law will not be the way to do the latter, since such moves will merely challenge sensible knaves to find new knavish exceptions and loopholes, not protect us from sensible knavery. Sensible knaves are precisely those who exploit us without breaking the law. So the whole question of when moral pressure of various sorts, formative, reformative, and punitive, ought to be brought to bear by whom is subsumed under the question of whom to trust when and with what, and for what good reasons.

In concentrating on obligations, rather than virtues, modern moral theorists have chosen to look at the cases where more trust is placed in enforcers of obligations than is placed in ordinary moral agents, the bearers of the obligations. In taking, as contractarians do, contractual obligations as the model of obligations, they concentrate on a case where the very minimal trust is put in the obligated person, and considerable punitive power entrusted to the one to whom the obligation is owed (I assume here that Hume is right in saying that when we promise or contract, we formally subject ourselves to the penalty, in case of failure, of never being trusted as a promisor again). This is an interesting case of the allocation of trust of various sorts, but it surely distorts our moral vision to suppose that *all* obligations, let alone all morally pressured expectations we impose on others, conform to that abnormally coercive model. It takes very special conditions for it to be safe to trust persons to inflict penalties on other persons, conditions in which either we can trust the penalizers to have the virtues necessary to penalize wisely and fairly, or else we can rely on effective threats to keep unvirtuous penalizers from abusing their power—that is to say, rely on others to coerce the first coercers into proper behaviour. But that reliance too will either be trust or will have to rely on threats from coercers of the coercers of coercers, and so on. Morality on this model becomes a nasty, if intellectually intriguing, game of mutual mutually corrective threats. The central question of who should deprive whom of what freedom soon becomes the question of whose anger should be dreaded by whom (the theory of obligation), supplemented perhaps by an afterthought on whose favour should be courted by whom (the theory of the virtues).

Undoubtedly some important part of morality does depend in part on a system of threats and bribes, at least for its survival in difficult conditions when normal goodwill and normally virtuous dispositions may be insufficient to motivate the conduct required for the preservation and justice of the moral network of relationships. But equally undoubtedly life will be nasty, emotionally poor, and worse than brutish (even if longer), if that is all morality is, or even if that coercive structure of morality is regarded as the backbone, rather than as an available crutch, should the main support fail. For the main support has to come from those we entrust with the job of rearing and training persons so that they can be trusted in various ways, some trusted with extraordinary coercive powers, some with public decision-making powers, all trusted as parties to promise, most trusted by some who love them and by one or more willing to become co-parents with them, most trusted by dependent children, dependent elderly relatives, sick friends, and so on. A very complex network of a great variety of sorts of trust structures our moral relationships with our fellows, and if there is a *main* support to this network it is the trust we place in those who respond to the trust of new members of the moral community, namely, children, and prepare them for new forms of trust.

A theory which took as its central question 'Who should trust whom with what, and why?' would not have to forgo the intellectual fun and games previous theorists have had with the various paradoxes of morality—curbing freedom to increase freedom, curbing self-interest the better to satisfy self-interest, not aiming at happiness in order to become happier. For it is easy enough to get a paradox of trust to accompany or, if I am right, to generalize the paradoxes of freedom, self-interest, and hedonism. To trust is to make oneself or to let oneself be more vulnerable than one might have been to harm from others—to give them an opportunity to harm one, in the confidence that they will not take it, because they have no good reason to. Why would one take such a risk? For risk it always is, given the partial opaqueness to us of the reasoning and motivation of those we trust and with whom we cooperate. Our confidence may be, and quite often is, misplaced. That is what we risk when we trust. If the best reason to take such a risk is the expected gain in security which comes from a climate of trust, then in trusting we are always giving up security to get greater security, exposing our throats so that others become accustomed to not biting. A moral theory which made proper trust its central concern could have its own categorical imperative, could replace obedience to self-made laws and freely chosen restraint on freedom with security-increasing sacrifice of security, distrust in the promoters of a climate of distrust, and so on.

Such reflexive use of one's central concept, negative or affirmative, is an intellectually satisfying activity which is bound to have appeal to those system lovers who want to construct moral theories, and it may help them design their theory in an intellectually pleasing manner. But we should beware of becoming hypnotized by our slogans or of sacrificing truth to intellectual elegance. Any theory of proper trust should not *prejudge* the question of when distrust is proper. We might find more objects of proper distrust than just the contributors to a climate of reasonable distrust, just as freedom should be restricted not just to increase human freedom but to protect human life from poisoners and other killers. I suspect, however, that all the objects of reasonable distrust are more reasonably seen as falling into the category of ones who contribute to a decrease in the scope of proper trust than can all who are reasonably coerced be seen as themselves guilty of wrongful coercion. Still, even if all proper trust turns out to be for such persons and on such matters as will increase the scope or stability of a climate of reasonable trust, and all proper distrust for such persons and on such matters as increase the scope of reasonable distrust, overreliance on such nice reflexive formulae can distract us from asking all the questions about trust which need to be asked if an adequate moral theory is to be constructed around that concept. These questions should include when to *respond* to trust with *un*trustworthiness, when and when not to invite trust, as well as when to give and refuse trust. We should not assume that promiscuous trustworthiness is any more a virtue than is undiscriminating distrust. It is appropriate trustworthiness, appropriate trustingness, appropriate encouragement to trust which will be virtues, as will be judicious untrustworthiness, selective refusal to trust, discriminating discouragement of trust.

Women are particularly well placed to appreciate these last virtues, since they have sometimes needed them to get into a position even to consider becoming moral theorizers. The long exploitation and domination of women by men depended on men's trust in women and women's trustworthiness to play their allotted role and so to perpetuate their own and their daughters' servitude. However keen women now are to end the lovelessness of modern moral philosophy, they are unlikely to lose sight of the cautious virtue of appropriate distrust or of the tough virtue of principled betrayal of the exploiters' trust.

Gilligan's girls and women saw morality as a matter of preserving valued ties to others, of preserving the conditions for that care and mutual care without which human life becomes bleak, lonely, and after a while, as the mature men in her study found, not self-affirming, however successful in achieving the egoistic goals which had been set. The boys and men saw morality as a matter of finding workable traffic rules for self-assertors, so that they might not needlessly frustrate one another and so that they could, should they so choose, cooperate in more positive ways to mutual advantage. Both for the women's sometimes unchosen and valued ties with others and for the men's mutual respect as sovereigns and subjects of the same minimal moral traffic rules (and for their more voluntary and more selective associations of profiteers), trust is important. Both men and women are concerned with cooperation, and the dimensions of trust-distrust structure the different cooperative relations each emphasize. The various considerations which arise when we try to defend an answer to any question about the appropriateness of a particular form of cooperation with its distinctive form of trust or distrust, that is, when we look into the terms of all sorts of cooperation, at the terms of trust in different cases of trust, at what are fair terms and what are trust-enhancing and trust-preserving terms, are suitably many and richly interconnected. A moral theory (or family of theories) that made trust its central problem could do better justice to men's and women's moral intuitions than do the going men's theories. Even if we don't easily agree on the answer to the question of who should trust whom with what, who should accept and who should meet various sorts of trust, and why, these questions might enable us better to reason morally together than we can when the central moral questions are reduced to those of whose favour one must court and whose anger one must dread. But such programmatic claims as I am making will be tested only when women standing on the shoulders of men, or men on the shoulders of women, or some theorizing Tiresias actually works out such a theory. I am no Tiresias, and have not foresuffered all the labour pains of such a theory. I aim here only to fertilize.

POSTSCRIPT

This essay was written before Carol Gilligan had withdrawn the suggestion in *A Different Voice* that there is some intrinsic connection between being female and taking up the care perspective. This essay refers to the early, and not to the revised, Gilligan views.

Some clarification may be in order to explain why I conferred on Alasdair MacIntyre the title of honorary woman, when to feminists such as Susan Moller Okin[5] he represents a particularly extreme version of patriarchal thinking. It was MacIntyre's anti-Kantian writings that made me regard him as an ally, and also his nostalgia for a virtues-centred variant of ethics. But I agree with Okin that his increasingly explicit defence of a patriarchal religious tradition does make the honour that I did him look undeserved.

[5] Susan Moller Okin, *Justice, Gender, and the Family* (New York, 1989), esp. ch. 3.

NOTES ON THE CONTRIBUTORS

G. E. M. Anscombe was Professor of Philosophy at the University of Cambridge and is the author of *Intention*, *An Introduction to Wittgenstein's Tractatus*, and (with P. T. Geach) *Three Philosophers*. Her collected papers were published in three volumes in 1981.

Annette Baier was Distinguished Service Professor at the University of Pittsburgh. She has published many articles in the philosophy of mind, ethics, and the history of philosophy, some of which are collected in *Postures of the Mind* (1985). More recently, she has published *A Progress of Sentiments: Reflections on Hume's Treatise* and *Moral Prejudices: Essays on Ethics*. Her current work in ethics is on trust, and she is working on a commentary on Descartes's *Meditations*.

Roger Crisp is Fellow and Tutor in Philosophy at St Anne's College, Oxford. He edited *How Should One Live? Essays on the Virtues* for Oxford University Press, is editor of *Utilitas*, and author of the Routledge Philosophy Guidebook to J. S. Mill's *Utilitarianism*.

Philippa Foot, who lives in Oxford, is Griffin Professor Emeritus at the University of California at Los Angeles and Honorary Fellow of Somerville College, Oxford. She published a collection *Virtues and Vices* in 1978 and is currently writing a book entitled *The Grammar of Goodness* for Oxford University Press.

Rosalind Hursthouse is Head of the Philosophy Dept at the Open University. She is the author of *Beginning Lives* and is currently turning a dozen previously published articles on virtue ethics and Aristotle into a book. She has recently co-edited *Virtues and Reasons*, a *Festschrift* for Philippa Foot.

Robert B. Louden is Professor of Philosophy at the University of Southern Maine. He is the author of *Morality and Moral Theory: A Reappraisal and Reaffirmation* (1992), is co-editor of *The Greeks and Us* (1996), and has translated Kant's writings on education for the Cambridge edition of the *Works of Immanuel Kant*. He is currently writing a book on *Kant's Impure Ethics*.

John McDowell taught at University College Oxford, before moving to the University of Pittsburgh, where he is at present a University Professor. He is a Fellow of the British Academy and a Fellow of the American Academy of Arts and Sciences. His work includes *Mind and World* (1994) and a number of articles in various areas of philosophy.

Alasdair MacIntyre teaches philosophy at Duke University. He is the author of *A Short History of Ethics* and most recently of *Three Rival Versions of Moral Enquiry*.

Iris Murdoch has been a Fellow of St Anne's College, Oxford, since 1948. She made her début as a writer in 1954 with *Under the Net*. Besides many novels and plays, she is the author of *Sartre, Romantic Rationalist*, *The Fire and the Sun: Why Plato Banished the Artists*, *Acastos: Two Platonic Dialogues*, and *Metaphysics as a Guide to Morals*.

J. B. Schneewind teaches philosophy at the Johns Hopkins University. Since publishing *Sidgwick's Ethics and Victorian Moral Philosophy* in 1977, he has been studying the historical background to Kant's moral philosophy.

Michael Slote is Professor of Philosophy at the University of Maryland. He is the author of *From Morality to Virtue*, and is currently collaborating with Marcia Baron and Philip Pettit on a book debating the merits of Kantian ethics, consequentialism, and virtue ethics.

Michael Stocker is Guttag Professor of Ethics and Political Philosophy at Syracuse University. He is the author of *Plural and Conflicting Values* and *Valuing Emotions*.

Bernard Williams has been since 1988 Deutsch Professor of Philosophy at the University of California, Berkeley. From 1979 to 1987 he was Provost of King's College, Cambridge, and from 1990 to 1996, White's Professor of Moral Philosophy at Oxford. He is a Fellow of the British Academy.

Susan Wolf is Professor of Philosophy at the Johns Hopkins University in Baltimore, Maryland. She is the author of *Freedom Within Reason* (1990), on free will and moral responsibility, and has written numerous articles on ethics and the philosophy of mind. Her current research focuses on the relations between happiness, morality, and meaningfulness in life.

BIBLIOGRAPHY

I. ANTHOLOGIES

CARD, C., and HUNT, L. (eds.), *Character: Essays in Moral Psychology* (Ithaca, NY, 1990).

CRISP, R. (ed.), *How Should One Live? Essays on the Virtues* (Oxford, 1996).

FLANAGAN, O., and RORTY, A. (eds.), *Identity, Character, and Morality: Essays in Moral Psychology* (Cambridge, Mass., 1990).

FRENCH, P., UEHLING, T., Jr., and WETTSTEIN, H. (eds.), *Ethical Theory: Character and Virtue*, *Midwest Studies in Philosophy*, 13 (Notre Dame, 1988).

KRUSCHWITZ, R., and ROBERTS, R. (eds.), *The Virtues: Contemporary Essays on Moral Character* (Belmont, Cal., 1987).

Philosophia, 20 (1990): *On Virtue*.

II. CLASSICAL TEXTS

ARISTOTLE, *Nicomachean Ethics*.

HUME, D., *An Enquiry Concerning the Principles of Morals*.

KANT, I., *The Metaphysics of Morals*.

MACHIAVELLI, N., *The Prince*.

MARTINEAU, J., *Types of Ethical Theory* (Oxford, 1885).

PLATO, *The Republic*.

SCHOPENHAUER, A., *On the Basis of Morality*, trans. E. Payne (Indianapolis, 1965).

III. CENTRAL MODERN TEXTS

ALDERMAN, H., 'By Virtue of a Virtue', *Review of Metaphysics*, 36 (1982).

ANNAS, J., *The Morality of Happiness* (Oxford, 1993).

BAIER, A., *Moral Prejudices* (Cambridge, Mass., 1994).

FOOT, P., *Virtues and Vices* (Oxford, 1978).

FRANKENA, W. 'Prichard and the Ethics of Virtue: Notes on a Footnote', *Monist*, 54 (1970).

GEACH, P., *The Virtues* (Cambridge, 1977).

HAMPSHIRE, S., *Morality and Conflict* (Oxford, 1983).

LAIRD, J., 'Act-Ethics and Agent-Ethics', *Mind*, 55 (1946).

MACINTYRE, A., *After Virtue* (London, 1981).

PEARS, D., 'Courage as a Mean', in A. Rorty (ed.), *Essays on Aristotle's Ethics* (Berkeley and Los Angeles, 1980).

PINCOFFS, E., *Quandaries and Virtues* (Lawrence, Kan., 1986).

SLOTE, M., *From Morality to Virtue* (Oxford, 1995).

SWANTON, C., 'Profiles of the Virtues', *Pacific Philosophical Quarterly*, 76 (1995).

TRIANOSKY, G., 'What is Virtue Ethics all about?', *American Philosophical Quarterly*, 27 (1990).

VON WRIGHT, G. H., *The Varieties of Goodness* (London, 1963), chapter 7.
WALLACE, J., *Virtues and Vices* (Ithaca, NY, 1978).
WIGGINS, D., 'Categorical Requirements: Kant and Hume on the Idea of Duty', *Monist*, 74 (1991).
WILLIAMS, B., *Ethics and the Limits of Philosophy* (London, 1985).

IV. VIRTUE, CHARACTER AND THE EMOTIONS

BENNETT, J., 'The Conscience of Huckleberry Finn', *Philosophy*, 49 (1974).
BLUM, L., *Friendship, Altruism, and Morality* (London, 1980).
DENT, N., *The Moral Psychology of the Virtues* (Cambridge, 1984).
HUDSON, S., *Human Character and Morality* (London, 1986).
KEKES, J., 'Moral Sensitivity', *Philosophy*, 59 (1984).
SOLOMON R., 'Emotions and Choice', in A. Rorty (ed.), *Explaining Emotions* (Berkeley and Los Angeles, 1973).
STOCKER, M., 'Desiring the Bad: An Essay in Moral Psychology', *Journal of Philosophy*, 76 (1979).
WILLIAMS, B., 'Persons, Character, and Morality', in A. Rorty (ed.), *The Identities of Persons* (Berkeley and Los Angeles, 1976); repr. in B. Williams, *Moral Luck* (Cambridge, 1981).

V. VIRTUE AND GENDER

BLUM, L., 'Gilligan and Kohlberg: Implications for Moral Theory', *Ethics*, 98 (1988).
FLANAGAN, O., 'Virtue, Sex, and Gender: Some Philosophical Reflections on the Moral Psychology Debate', *Ethics*, 92 (1982).
GILLIGAN, C., *In a Different Voice* (Cambridge, Mass., 1982).
NODDINGS, N., *Caring: A Feminine Approach to Ethics and Moral Education* (Berkeley and Los Angeles, 1984).
OKIN, S., 'Justice and Gender', *Philosophy and Public Affairs*, 16 (1989).

VI. UTILITARIANISM AND VIRTUE

ADAMS, R., 'Motive Utilitarianism', *Journal of Philosophy*, 73 (1976).
CRISP, R., 'Utilitarianism and the Life of Virtue', *Philosophical Quarterly*, 42 (1992).
FOOT, P., 'Utilitarianism and the Virtues', *Mind*, 94 (1985).
HARE, R., *Moral Thinking: Its Levels, Methods, and Point* (Oxford, 1981).
RAILTON, P., 'Alienation, Consequentialism, and the Demands of Morality', *Philosophy and Public Affairs*, 13 (1984).

VII. KANTIANISM, IMPARTIALITY, AND VIRTUE

BARON, M., 'The Alleged Moral Repugnance of Acting from Duty', *Journal of Philosophy*, 81 (1984).

COTTINGHAM, J., 'The Ethics of Self-Concern', *Ethics*, 101 (1991).
DENT, N., 'Duty and Inclination', *Mind*, 83 (1974).
HERMAN, B., 'On the Value of Acting from the Motive of Duty', *Philosophical Review*, 90 (1981).
OLDENQUIST, A., 'Loyalties', *Journal of Philosophy*, 79 (1982).
O'NEILL, O., 'Duties and Virtues', *Philosophy*, 35, suppl. (1993).

VIII. VIRTUE AND PRACTICAL ETHICS

BOGEN, J., 'Suicide and Virtue', in D. Mayo (ed.), *Suicide: The Philosophical Issues* (New York, 1980).
GARCIA, J., 'The Heart of Racism', *Journal of Social Philosophy*, 26 (1996).
HILL, T., 'Ideals of Human Excellence and Preserving Natural Environments', *Environmental Ethics*, 5 (1983).
PINCOFFS, E., 'Virtue, the Quality of Life, and Punishment', *Monist*, 63 (1980).
PUTMAN, D., 'Virtue and the Practice of Modern Medicine', *Journal of Medicine and Philosophy*, 13 (1988).
SOLOMON, R., *Ethics and Excellence: Co-operation and Integrity in Business* (New York, 1994).

IX. VIRTUE AND POLITICS

ARISTOTLE, *The Politics*.
BERGER, P., 'On the Obsolescence of the Concept of Honour', *European Journal of Sociology*, 11 (1970).
GALSTON, W., *Liberal Purposes: Goods, Virtues, and Diversity in the Liberal State* (New York, 1991).
HURSTHOUSE, R., 'After Hume's Justice', *Proceedings of the Aristotelian Society*, 91 (1990–1).
MACEDO, S., *Liberal Virtues* (Oxford, 1990).
NUSSBAUM, M., 'Aristotelian Social Democracy', in R. Douglass, G. Mara, and H. Richardson (eds.), *Liberalism and the Good* (London, 1990).
TAYLOR, C., *Sources of the Self* (Cambridge, 1989).

INDEX OF NAMES